Making Capitalism
Without Capitalists

Making Capitalism Without Capitalists

Class Formation and Elite Struggles in
Post-Communist Central Europe

GIL EYAL, IVÁN SZELÉNYI,
AND ELEANOR TOWNSLEY

VERSO

London • New York

First published by Verso 1998

© Gil Eyal, Iván Szelényi and Eleanor Townsley 1998

All rights reserved

Verso

UK: 6 Meard Street, London W1V 3HR

USA: 180 Varick Street, New York NY 10014–4606

Verso is the imprint of New Left Books

ISBN 1–85984–819–2

ISBN 1–85984–221–6 (pbk)

British Library Cataloguing in Publication Data

A catalogue record for this book is available from the British Library

Library of Congress Cataloging-in-Publication Data

Eyal, Gil.

Making capitalism without capitalists: class formation and elite
stuggles in post-communist Central Europe/Gil Eyal,
Iván Szelényi, and Eleanor Townsley.

p.   cm.

ISBN 1–85984–819–2

1. Capitalism—Europe, Eastern. 2. Social stucture—Europe, Eastern.
3. Post-communism—Europe, Eastern. I. Szelényi, Iván.
II. Townsley, Eleanor R., 1967– . III. Title.

HC244.E97 1998   98–30214

305.5′0947—dc21   CIP

Typeset by M Rules

Printed by Biddles Ltd, Guildford and King's Lynn

Contents

Acknowledgements

We would like to thank several people for their constructive criticism, their insightful comments and their valuable suggestions.

Our thanks go to Szonja Szelényi and Donald Treiman, co-principal investigators of the 'Social Stratification in Eastern Europe after 1989' Project.

We are also very grateful to the members of the national teams in the three countries: Jozsef Böröcz, Tamás Kolosi, Imre Kovack, Janos Ladanyi, Petr Mateju, Ákos Rona-Tas, Jacek Wasiliewski, Edmund Wnuk-Lipinski, and the late Rudolf Andorka. Thank you too to members of the UCLA team: Éva Fodor, Eric Hanley, Larry King, Eric Kostello, and Matthew McKeever.

At Verso, we would like to thank Jane Hindle and Gillian Beaumont for editorial support, and particularly Perry Anderson, who read the manuscript and gave us a detailed assessment. Thanks also to Caleb Southworth and Rebecca Emigh for early constructive readings.

Finally, we would like to acknowledge institutional support for the research from the National Science Foundation, the National Council for Soviet and East European Research, the Joint Council for East European Studies of the American Council of Learned Societies and the Social Science Research Council, the Institute for Global Conflict and Co-operation, the University of California, Los Angeles, the Center for German and European Studies, the University of California, Berkeley, and the Institut für die Wissenschaften vom Menschen, Vienna. We would also like to thank TARKI, and Matilda Sági in particular, for making 1993 and 1996 data on Hungarian business ownership available to us.

All errors of fact or judgement are those of the authors.

Gil Eyal, Iván Szelényi, Eleanor Townsley
June 1998

Introduction

This book offers a new theory of the transition to capitalism, by telling the story of how capitalism is being built without capitalists in post-communist Central Europe. We theorize *capitalism without capitalists* as a distinctive new strategy of transition adopted by technocratic–intellectual elites in societies where no class of private owners existed prior to the introduction of market mechanisms. Note, however, that capitalism without capitalists is not necessarily capitalism *without a bourgeoisie*. If one thinks of the bourgeoisie as plural – thus, if one conceives *bourgeoisies* as a social group composed of both possessors of material property (the economic bourgeoisie) and possessors of culture or knowledge (the cultural bourgeoisie) – then one can claim – and we do so in this book – that post-communist capitalism is being promoted by a broadly defined intelligentsia which is committed to the cause of bourgeois society and capitalist economic institutions.

This approach to analyzing the transition to capitalism in Central Europe necessarily differs both from the classical social and economic theories of Adam Smith and Karl Marx and from twentieth-century visions of corporate, managerial, or other kinds of post-capitalist societies, such as those proposed by Ralf Dahrendorf, Berle and Means, or Daniel Bell. On one hand, classical theorists assumed that there must have been *capitalists before capitalism*. For this reason, these theorists expended much scholarly effort investigating the process of the 'original' or 'primitive accumulation' of capital. The rationale was that both logically and historically, private capital accumulation must have occurred before market institutions could operate.[1] On the other hand, a recurrent theme in the study of existing capitalist systems, particularly since the 1930s, has been that the importance of individual private owners is waning. Observing the growth of large corporate organizations, the increasing role of financial institutions, or the

1

growing importance of science/knowledge, varied theorists of 'late' capitalism have argued that the role of capital as the main source of economic growth is ending.[2] There is little doubt within this group that the capitalist system itself remains robust; what is in contention is the shape of *capitalism after capitalists*. Our theory of the transition to capitalism in Central Europe borrows from both these theoretical traditions, but differs from and builds upon them by imagining the historical possibility of *capitalism without capitalists*.

First, like 'capitalists *before* capitalism', ours is primarily a theory of transition. Our central aim is to understand and explain how capitalism can emerge in an economic system with no propertied bourgeoisie. We want to know what agents are building post-communist capitalism, and on whose behalf and for what purposes they act. One possibility is that the technocratic elite of former state-socialist societies may turn itself into a new propertied bourgeoisie and thereby fulfil the classical condition for capitalist development. Indeed, some analysts claim – rather prematurely, in our view – that such a transformation has already occurred. Another possibility is that the liberal intelligentsia will act as an 'intellectual vanguard of the economic bourgeoisie', creating a new class of proprietors from agents other than itself. Having fulfilled its historic mission, the intelligentsia may then return to creative writing, research, or teaching, or it may keep managing capitalist enterprises owned by others.

Within this field of possibilities, however, it is not inconceivable that capitalism will be built without a class of individual proprietors. In this case, we would expect an economic system which looks like those envisioned by twentieth-century theorists of 'capitalism *after* capitalists'. If it is true that the future of capitalist economies will be systems in which individual proprietors do not play a major role (and this proposition has been forcefully challenged by Zeitlin, Domhoff and others[3]), it is possible that Central European societies will emerge as corporate or post-capitalist societies without the historical intervention of a *grande bourgeoisie*. In other words, it is conceivable that post-communist elites will take a historic short cut and move directly to the most 'advanced' stage of corporate capitalism, never sharing their managerial power (even temporarily) with a class of individual owners.

At the current moment, all these possibilities remain open. Indeed, our originating premiss is that the rapidly changing world of property rights in Central Europe is contested terrain where intense social struggles take place with an as yet unknown outcome. This observation is central to the burgeoning field of *comparative capitalism* which, since the advent of post-communism, has subsumed the comparative study of socialism and capitalism.[4] Our ambition is to contribute to this emergent field of social science; thus we hope that this book will not be read narrowly as 'transitology' or as something of concern only to 'East European area specialists'.

Indeed, we believe that as a research site, Central Europe provides strategic research materials for exploring the development of new capitalist possibilities all over the world and into the twenty-first century. To put it even more boldly: the fall of communism can be understood as an invitation to sociologists to revisit those old sites which were investigated by classical sociological theorists like Marx and Weber. As neoclassical economics emerged with the demise of the welfare state, so the fall of communism offers the opportunity to launch a new research program, to set the research agenda for a neoclassical sociology. Neoclassical sociology, much like the classics of sociological theorizing, will be primarily concerned with the origins and character of modern capitalism. With the fall of communism, however, there is an important shift in emphasis. For Marx and Weber, the question was: what are the preconditions which give rise to modern capitalism? They assumed that the destination was given. The only question was whether or not the preconditions would be met. Today, however, capitalism is being made within the ruins of socialism, and the transition is being led by former communists. Neoclassical sociology is less concerned with preconditions, then, since it appears that the most unlikely agents, starting from the most inconceivable point of departure, are the ones who are building capitalism. What neoclassical sociology emphasizes is the diversity of emergent capitalisms – in short, the subject matter of neoclassical sociology is comparative capitalism*s*.

In an endeavor to pursue these possibilities without being overburdened by inherited theoretical viewpoints, we pursue a threefold analytical strategy. First, we begin from the observation that there are different paths leading towards capitalism. Therefore, we compare transitions to capitalism in different times and places to discover what, if anything, is particular to the Central European case. Second, we argue that capitalism has never been, and will never be, a single destination. Capitalism will always be a generic term describing a diverse set of social actors and institutions. For this reason, we contrast different types of capitalisms to explore the range of possible actors and institutions that can sustain a functioning capitalist system (including a capitalist system without capitalists). Third, we believe that the social attributes of actors, their class capacities, and the historically contingent outcomes of struggles between them, are likely to be decisive for explaining the particular kind of capitalism which is being built in Central Europe. We are interested, therefore, in a comparative study of various kinds of capitalists, or bourgeoisies.

Comparing our research site of Central Europe with other sites – other conditions for capitalisms and bourgeoisies – we find two unique features which we believe will be deeply consequential for the kind of capitalism that will be built in the region. First, we find that the transition from socialism to capitalism has very different dynamics from the classical transition from feudalism to capitalism. Although the institution of private property in feudal societies was far from identical to that of capitalism, in both systems property rights were sufficiently similar, and the transition to capitalism sufficiently lengthy, to allow the growth of a propertied capitalist class and a gradual 'blending' of the aristocracy with the bourgeoisie.[5] This was inconceivable in the abrupt transition from socialism to post-communist capitalism. Under socialism, property was fully socialized, and even in the most liberal reform communist countries, private property ownership was marginal. Thus it was not surprising that former second-economy actors did not claim political or economic power when the communist system broke down. Instead, power was grabbed by the technocratic fraction of the former communist *nomenklatura*, or by former dissident intellectuals, or by an uneasy coalition of the two. This is not to suggest that second-economy actors did not play important roles in the delegitimation and gradual erosion of the state socialist system – they did.[6] However, it does imply that those who had enjoyed success in the second economy were not the main beneficiaries of system breakdown. Indeed, more recent analysis shows that a significant proportion of former second-economy actors are among the big losers of the post-communism transition.[7] In this context, the transition to capitalism in Central Europe clearly could not follow the classical, West European path of 'capitalists *before* capitalism'.

The second distinguishing feature of our research site is that despite the absence of a propertied class in Central Europe, the transition to capitalism was undertaken in the context of a relatively highly developed 'civil society'. The building of capitalism was begun under the leadership of an intelligentsia which continues to believe that its historic, ethical mission is to create capitalist institutions under the watchful eye of democratically elected parliaments, exposed to the scrutiny of free media. In this context, the making of a class of private proprietors appears to have fallen substantially behind the growth of new market institutions. To explore this point further, and to inquire why the growth of a class of proprietors after system breakdown has been slower than expected by classical and neoclassical theorists, we note that 'capitalism *without* capitalists' appears to be particular to Central Europe. It runs counter to the theoretical expectations of political capitalism in the region, and it does not seem to characterize the social systems of Eastern Europe/Russia.

From about the middle of 1988 onwards, as the old communist elite prepared itself for the system breakdown they knew was to come, a broad range of commentators suspected that communists would enact privatization laws to enable them to convert *nomenklatura* positions into new forms of post-communist privilege.[8] In this book we offer evidence that in contrast to the Russian case, there is relatively little evidence of this sort of political capitalism in Central Europe. While there have been instances of the successful conversion of political capital into individual private wealth in all Central European societies, they seem to have been the exception rather than the rule. By contrast, the evidence from Russia and China suggests that the political capitalism hypothesis has greater explanatory power for these cases than in Central Europe.[9] In Central Europe the evolution of market institutions appears to have outstripped the development of private property, but in Russia the accumulation of wealth in private hands is far ahead of the establishment of market institutions. Unlike 'capitalism *without* capitalists' in Central Europe then, Russia might be cited as a case of *capitalists without capitalism*.

It is possible that the growth of civil society – and, in particular, the earlier development of parliaments and free media – made institutionalized, widespread corruption in Central Europe less likely than it was in Russia. Some analysts even attribute this difference to the greater moral integrity of Central European elites. But this is speculation, of course. It is challenged by widely held public perceptions of a 'great robbery' by the Central European *nomenklatura* which is supported by extensive anecdotal evidence, and even some statistical data.[10] Indeed, for this reason, when we began our investigation of post-communist capitalism in Central Europe, we, too, proceeded from the political capitalism hypothesis. As we began to gather and analyze more systematic data, however, we were forced to reformulate this initial hypotheses.[11] We were struck by how many members of former communist elites had lost their grip on power in Central Europe, how modestly they now live, how little business activity they report, how limited managerial ownership appears to be, and how little concentration of property in individual private hands we found. Of course, it is possible that our respondents did not tell the truth about these highly politicized issues, and for this reason we have tried to keep an open mind about the validity of our data. At the same time, however, we observe that the evidence offered in support of the political capitalism thesis is even less systematically collected. There is little reason to suspect, therefore, that our data are any less reliable, and a number of good reasons to believe that they are far more representative and systematic. The punch-line is that more systematic research is needed in Russia (and also in Central Europe).

Despite these qualifications, then, we believe that the distinctiveness of the Central European case and the quality of our data have much to contribute to theories of capitalist transition in general, and to an understanding of the contemporary possibilities for capitalist development in Central Europe in particular. What evidence we have supports a *prima facie* case that there is a distinction between the two post-communist regions: 'capitalism without capitalists' in Central Europe, and 'capitalists without capitalism' in Russia. Moreover, 'capitalism *without* capitalists' suggests a range of intriguing possibilities for capitalist organization, and challenges many of our deeply held assumptions about transitions to capitalism. For this reason, in what follows we outline our theory of 'capitalism *without* capitalists' in more detail before proceeding to an analysis of the actors and institutions of this historically novel strategy of capitalist transition.

Thesis 1. Post-communist society can be described as a unique social structure in which cultural capital is the main source of power, prestige, and privilege. Possession of economic capital places actors only in the middle of the social hierarchy, and the conversion of former political capital into private wealth is more the exception than the rule. Indeed, the conversion of former communist privilege into a post-communist equivalent happens only when social actors possess the right kinds of capital to make the transition. Thus, those who were at the top of the social hierarchy under state socialism can stay there only if they are capable of 'trajectory adjustment', which at the current juncture means if they are well endowed with cultural capital. By contrast, those who relied exclusively on now devalued political capital from the communist era are not able to convert this capital into anything valuable, and are likely to be downwardly mobile.

Chapter 1 offers a comparative analysis of post-communist, communist, and pre-communist societies in Central Europe. In this analysis, our aim is to develop a structuralist theory which is dynamic and can be cast in historically specific, conjunctural terms. Our point of departure is Bourdieu's theory of social structure, which we reconstruct using Weber's distinction between rank and class societies.[12] In this way, we hope to bring a comparative-historical dimension into Bourdieu's framework, which was designed initially to explain reproduction rather than social change. (No criticism is implied here: Bourdieu's research site is contemporary French society, where reproduction is the overwhelming trend; we study the recent social history of Central Europe where turbulence and large-scale social change have predominated.) From Bourdieu we borrow the ideas of three forms of capital, social space, and habitus. On this basis, we distinguish between social, economic, and cultural capital, and we conceptualize social structures as 'spaces' which are differentially stratified by various distributions of these types of capital. Individuals 'travel' in these spaces, and if changes in the relative importance of one or another type of capital occurs in their lifetimes, they try to reshuffle their portfolio of different types of capital and convert devalued forms of capital into revalued forms in order to stay 'on trajectory'. On this basis, there are several specific innovations we propose to explain the nature of social change in Central Europe.

1. *We conceptualize pre-communism, communism, and post-communism as three different stratification regimes defined by the dominance of different types of capital.* While Bourdieu used the three types of capital to describe contemporary French society, where economic capital is dominant and the other

forms of capital are subordinate, in the ever-changing landscape of Central Europe during the past fifty years we distinguish three qualitatively different social spaces, each of which is defined by the dominance of a different form of capital.

2. *We claim that post-communism is a historically unique system of stratification in which cultural capital is dominant.* This enables us to develop a new theory of post-communist social structure which is consistent with our argument about the crucial roles played by the technocracy and former dissident intellectuals in the transition from socialism to post-communism. We define capitalism as a class-stratified system in which economic capital is dominant, and communism as a system in which social capital – institutionalized as political capital – was the major source of power and privilege. With the decay of state socialism and the rise of post-communism, the importance of political capital is declining, the role of cultural capital is increasing, and economic capital is sufficient only to locate its possessors in the middle of the social hierarchy.

3. *The transition to post-communism is a shift from socialist rank order to capitalist class stratification.* Drawing on Weber, we conceptualize communism as a society based on rank order. Social capital was dominant, and resulted in a socialist form of patron–client relations. Compared to societies where economic capital was dominant – which we understand, with Weber, to be class-stratified societies – communist societies were examples of modern rank order. With this understanding, we can argue that the transition from communism to capitalism is, in principle, a transition from rank order to class society, and thereby introduce the dynamism of Weber's historical sociology into Bourdieu's structural analysis. Actually existing post-communism, however, as a system of 'capitalism *without* capitalists', occupies a middle position on this scale from rank to class. The *Bildungsbürgertum* is neither a rank nor a class. Rather, it combines the characteristics and contains the possibilities of both logics of social stratification.

4. *Converting devalued forms of capital into new, more valued forms is the preferred way individuals cope with changes in social structure.* In analyzing social change, we want to move agents to the center of our analysis; therefore we invoke Bourdieu to enrich Weber's analysis. We proceed from the observation that individuals, or groups of individuals, try to stay on trajectory and maintain their relative social positions in the face of massive social change. Each individual possesses a portfolio of 'stocks' of different forms of capital, and when they confront social change they try to reshuffle this portfolio to get rid of forms of capital which are losing value, and convert them into forms of capital which are more valuable. The conversion of one form of capital into another is a tricky business. One has to time it well, and one is usually in a much better situation to

convert a devalued form of capital if one is *already* well endowed with a revalued type. In the post-communist transition, for example, those who are well endowed with cultural capital may be able to convert their former political capital into informal social networks, which can then be usefully deployed to take advantage of new market opportunities. By contrast, those who do not possess much cultural capital may find that their former political capital is a disadvantage to them.

5. *There is a dialectical interaction between habitus and institutional position: new positions change incumbents, but new incumbents rely on their habitus to interpret how an institution ought to operate.* When the objective characteristics of social space change, the value of one form of capital is reduced, the value of another form is increased, and the criteria for recruitment into a new position or for the retention of an old one change. Confronted with this kind of pressure, individuals who try to stay on trajectory – who try to keep their positions, or gain a new position with the same power, prestige, and privileges as the one they lost – will pursue a dual strategy. One is adaptation to the new challenges. Individuals will reshuffle their portfolios to get rid of 'stocks' which have lost their value, and try to acquire other capitals which have gained in value. Second, people also try to learn the new rules of the game and adjust their habitus in order to fit new positions in new institutions. Habitus, however, has a certain degree of 'stickiness', and in every society – and especially in small ones like those of Central Europe – there is a limited pool of individuals who can possibly occupy key positions. The result is a creative interactive relationship between the characteristics of individuals who are recruited or retained in various institutional positions and the characteristics of those positions. This is a fundamental process which underlies the process of social change: the new positions change the habitus of individuals, but individuals who are recruited into those positions also affect the way institutions operate.

6. *Social change can be understood as a process of trajectory adjustment. This implies that evolutionary adjustment to new challenges and the path-dependent transformation of previous institutions / behaviors occur simultaneously. Furthermore, individuals whose habitus may not serve as a reliable compass in times of social change may also invoke 'archeology' – that is to say, in the process of trajectory adjustment, precommunist social experiences, which were repressed in the collective subconscious during communist times, are also recalled.* This last innovation highlights the value of 'archeological knowledge' in the interaction between individual habitus and the characteristics of the positions individuals occupy. On the basis of this observation, we offer a synthesis of two competing theories of social change. The first is evolutionary theory, which underpins both neoclassical economics and rational choice Marxism. The assumption of these two schools of thought is that if you create the proper

institutions, they will shape the individuals who occupy them so that individual behavior will conform to institutional constraints and imperatives. In the context of the post-communist transformation, this is the idea of capitalism-by-design: you destroy the old state-socialist institutions and replace them with institutions that are known to work in advanced market economies. In this way, actors will learn how to operate within new constraints: cadres will become entrepreneurs, clients will be transformed into wage laborers.[13] The second theory of social change which dominates current scholarship on Central Europe is involutionary theory, or the theory of path-dependent transformation.[14] This approach assumes that post-communist institutions are created out of the ruins of state-socialist institutions. The transition is not from plan to market, but from plan to clan. Our theory of trajectory adjustment makes three propositions which, we believe, offer a synthesis of these competing theories while minimizing their contradictions. First, the individuals who will be able to stay on trajectory in times of change are those who are capable of learning; the individual who is able to reshuffle their portfolio of 'stocks' and alter their habitus is indeed a part of a process of social evolution, adapting to meet social change. Second, however, this learning is not copying. When individuals adjust their social trajectory, they do so in a path-dependent way. They collectively reinterpret the roles they have to play, and in so doing they draw on shared experiences, ways of knowing, and common understandings. Third, when individuals are confronted with abrupt breaks, such as the one which occurred in 1989 in Central Europe, they realize that the habitus they carry from the immediate past is not appropriate to altered circumstances, and look for other models of behavior and society which are accessible to them. In this process, the logic of the 'negation of negation' often operates: pre-communist ways of doing business are invoked. The logic is that if communism got it wrong, we should go back to the way things were done before communism, especially if those ways of thinking and behaving were rejected by communism.

Thesis 2. Since state socialism constrained the development of a class of private proprietors in Central Europe, it is a cultural bourgeoisie (the 'second Bildungsbürgertum*') which has assumed the historic mission of creating bourgeois society and a capitalist economic order. So far, however, it appears to have been more successful in establishing the market institutions of modern capitalism than in creating a class of individual private proprietors, especially in the corporate sector.*

Chapter 2 traces the strategy of 'capitalism without capitalists' to the late eighteenth and early nineteenth centuries, analyzing its roots in the relationship between Central European intellectuals and bourgeois society.

Inspired by the work of the German social historian Jürgen Kocka, we observe that Central European intellectuals have been attracted to various ambitious historical projects to reshape their societies, and we argue that whatever else they may be, the power bloc that rules contemporary post-communism is heir to these projects. There have been at least three of these historical projects.

In the first project, nineteenth-century Central European intellectuals defined themselves as a *Bildungsbürgertum*. That is to say, they viewed them-selves as part of the bourgeoisie, and believed that their historic task was to promote the ideals of bourgeois society and to foster the growth of the weak Central European propertied class. It was well understood at the time that those countries east of the Elbe in the German sphere of influence were eco-nomically backward, and had relatively underdeveloped business classes. At the same time, however, these countries boasted relatively large and Westernized educated middle classes, who were seen – and viewed them-selves – as part of the bourgeoisie. In this context, it was argued that the task of modernization might be carried out not only by the class of proprietors (the economic bourgeoisie, in German the *Wirtschaftsbürgertum*), but also by the educated middle classes (or the cultural bourgeoisie, the *Bildungsbürgertum*). During most of the nineteenth century, then, the Central European intelli-gentsia saw itself as a *Bildungsbürgertum* which, in alliance with an enlightened civil service bureaucracy, would implement what was seen as the *utopian project* of bourgeois society.[15]

The second project of the Central European intelligentsia was, in large part, a reaction to the slow pace of modernization in the region. Ever more disenchanted by the ideals of bourgeois society, the core opinion-making leaders of the intelligentsia became interested in anti-bourgeois ideas. Motivated either by altruism in bringing about modernization, or by self-interest to enhance their own social positions, key segments of the intelligentsia began searching for short cuts to modernization which would bypass capitalist development.[16] By the beginning of the twentieth century the *Bildungsbürgertum* project was all but abandoned. Instead of viewing them-selves as the historic agents who would promote the spread of bourgeois values, intellectuals turned increasingly to right- and left-wing radicalisms, and became hostile to the very term 'bourgeois'. Indeed, by the 1920s the term *Bildungsbürger* was used pejoratively to mean bourgeois philistine.[17] Key segments of the intelligentsia began to style themselves the 'vanguard of the proletariat', or at least as the possessors of a rationality which could supersede the irrationality of the 'invisible hand' of capitalist markets. Despite less than uniform support for such ideas among the intelligentsia, by the end of World War II, as is well known, anti-bourgeois ideologies were hegemonic in Central Europe.

The third intellectual project undertaken by Central European intellectuals was born of the communist era. With the defeat of right-wing radicalism in World War II, and in the face of Stalinist censorship and counterselection, dissident intellectuals slowly rediscovered bourgeois liberalism. By the end of the communist period, dissidents had joined forces with the technocratic fraction of the communist ruling estate in a commitment to transform the socialist economy and build capitalism. Their aim was to overthrow the communist order and try to make capitalism without capitalists. Although the anti-bourgeois project among Central European intellectuals lasted well into the 1960s, and despite the fact that it took more than a decade for the originally left-radical dissident intelligentsia to begin to see itself as a new *Bildungsbürgertum*, by the end of the communist era this third project – which we interpret as a *second Bildungsbürgertum* project – was well under way.

In some respects, however, the second *Bildungsbürgertum* faces even more formidable challenges than the bourgeois educated middle class faced two hundred years ago. It has to promote the utopian project of bourgeois society with an even smaller and weaker propertied class than the pre-communist one. Moreover, with the collapse of communism it has also become obvious that no single intellectual fraction can undertake this project alone. Different segments of the intelligentsia are learning to form alliances across the old divisions within the intellectual elite. The second *Bildungsbürgertum* reflects this in its composition as an uneasy alliance of former dissidents and former communist technocrats. It is a marriage of convenience rather than love at first sight, but – as Chapter 2 shows – this post-communist project to build capitalism has deep historical roots in the collective biography of the Central European intelligentsia.

Thesis 3. The spirit of post-communism can be traced back to the times when the second Bildungsbürgertum *was formed, thus to reform communism and anti-communist dissent. As the second* Bildungsbürgertum *emerged as the alliance of dissident intellectuals and reform communist technocrats, this spirit found its roots in the idea of civil society on the one hand and economic rationalism on the other. It was in this way that managerialism became the ideology of the new power bloc. Managerialism does not simply or primarily imply that managers or technocrats rule. Rather, managerialism is a mentality, or govern-mentality, which cements the diverse fractions of the post-communist elite into a hegemonic power bloc.*

Chapter 3 begins with an analysis of the ideology of the post-communist technocracy. We claim that the core of this ideology is monetarism. Confronted with the challenges of post-communist institutional restructuring, however, the technocracy has had to reinterpret its monetarist ideals. The reality of post-communist economic policy is budgetary restraint which, instead of distant guidance by an invisible hand, demands close, hands-on management of economic processes. We suggest that such a reinterpretation of monetarism into a policy of budget cuts comes easily to former communist technocrats. They are accustomed to running the economy this way, and the resulting system of subterranean redistribution also creates spaces for enterprise management to engage the technocracy in the practice of budget-bargains, reminiscent of the plan bargains of communist times. This sort of bargaining is important for building cooperation between technocrats and enterprise managers, since firm-level management is usually suspicious or resentful of monetarism, and is most comfortable with a government which offers subsidies and has industrial, employment, and foreign trade policies.

The former dissidents – who have constituted themselves as the opinion-making intelligentsia of post-communism – have also traveled a long way from their starting point to broker a common cause with technocrats and managers. The point of departure for former dissident intellectuals is the idea of civil society. Like technocrats, dissidents believe that an invisible hand can regulate the economy. To this belief they add the idea that social control can be exercised from a distance rather than 'up-close', as in the communist system. As the reality of governing has shaped them, however, former dissidents have developed a range of hands-on strategies of social control. Specifically, because civil individuals and civic culture must be created from a polluted communist reality, the intellectual vanguard of the post-communist revolution has developed rituals which serve as tools to manage the social and cultural matters of a society during the process of transition. Chapter 4 identifies three such rituals: purification, sacrifice, and confession. These rituals were cast initially in anti-communist terms: the communist system was impure, it had to be purged to create civil individuals; this would demand sacrifices from all, and would work only if those who lived under communism confronted their collective guilt in the ritual of public confession. Understandably, this latter ritual did not appeal to former communists at the core of the new power bloc. As a result, in post-communist practices of social management the anti-communist overtones of these rituals have been muted and redeployed as tools to legitimate the policies of budgetary restraint pursued by the technocracy. These recast rituals no longer call for purification from communist officials, but emphasize instead the need to purge the population of non-market modes of behavior, such as dependence on government assistance. Sacrifice has also been reinterpreted in economic terms. Former dissidents now preach that market transition requires the postponement of gratification: communism was a system in which people lived beyond their means, and now they have to learn not to spend what they have not earned. This economic reconfiguration of the rituals of purification and sacrifice also have the benefit of making dissident discourse about civil society palatable to the former communist technocracy. Indeed, these reconfigured rituals now serve technocratic purposes. The managerialist ideology of post-communism was thus born of the contradictory social practices of remaking societies and individuals in the process of transition. Eventually, it was adopted by actors with diverse interests who arrived at post-communism from very different intellectual origins, and traveled very different intellectual trajectories. Managerialism works, however, because the govern-mentality of the society in transition demands that the ethos of close hands-on management be shared by those who remake the economic, political, social and cultural institutions of former socialist societies.

Thesis 4. The general theory of political capitalism does not offer a compelling explanation of the class dynamics of post-communist transition. Contrary to its predictions, many members of the former communist elite have not retained their positions in the post-communist transformation. If they possessed only political capital and no cultural capital, they lost their privilege, power, and prestige. At the same time, however, if former cadres possessed cultural capital, they were likely to be among the winners of the transition. Indeed, most of the economic command positions in the post-communist corporate sector are occupied by former communist technocrats who were younger and much better educated than senior cadres. Even this group, however, has not pursued political capitalism: former communist technocrats exercise managerial authority, but there is little evidence to suggest that they have acquired substantial private wealth. Moreover, this group of former communists is unable to exercise power alone; and therefore it has formed an alliance with the new politocracy and the opinion-making intellectual elite, many of whom are former dissident intellectuals.

Contrary to our original expectations, and the predictions of the theory of political capitalism, we present evidence of substantial downward mobility among former communist elites. Many of those in very high positions during communist times took early retirement and quit the workforce before they reached the age of sixty or sixty-five. Moreover, former political capital – that is to say, membership of the Communist Party – seems to have exercised a negative effect on the survival chances of *nomenklatura* members, with those who were not members of the Communist Party being more likely to keep their jobs during the transition. It is also difficult to substantiate the claim that early retirees entered private businesses in large numbers. In fact, we found that those who were able to keep their jobs reported more business ownership than those who opted for early retirement. In short, substantial numbers of former *nomenklatura* members are among the losers in the transition; the conversion of political capital into economic wealth has been less than automatic. These findings cast doubt on the validity of the political capitalism hypothesis formulated by Staniszkis and Hankiss, which argued that the communist *nomenklatura* was establishing itself as a new *grande bourgeoisie*.

The next finding presented in Chapter 4, in a way, contradicts the first one: while there were losers among former members of the *nomenklatura*, it is also true that the big winners of the post-communist transition are former communists – specifically, the technocratic fraction of the communist ruling estate. The contradiction, however, is more apparent than real. Our data provide strong evidence of the fragmented nature of late state-socialist elites, a characteristic of late communism first theorized by Erzsébet Szalai.[18] Indeed, 1989 might best be understood as the successful revolution of the technocratic fraction of the communist ruling estate against its bureaucratic fraction – it was a victory of 'experts' over 'reds'. The overwhelming majority of the incumbents of economic command positions during the post-communist epoch come from the ranks of former management, especially middle-level management. Most of these managers not only possessed political capital but were also well endowed with cultural capital.

In one respect, however, our findings diverge from Szalai's predictions. Staniszkis and Hankiss anticipated that former communists would use their power to become the new corporate owners of post-communism, while Szalai argued more specifically that the technocratic–managerial elite was the most likely candidate to achieve this aim. Our data suggest, however, that both these predictions miss the mark. Managerial ownership, or the management buy-out of state-owned firms, is not the major story in post-communism. Indeed, the majority of corporate and industrial managers have acquired no business property at all. Furthermore, fully half of those who own businesses possess stakes not in the firms they manage, but in small subcontracting firms. Finally, we find that those who own shares in the businesses they manage are likely to be managers of smaller firms, and typically own only a small fraction of the assets of these firms. In other words, the former communist technocracy do not hold ultimate economic decision-making power as owners, as Szalai predicted; rather, they exercise power as experts and managers.

While data available to us on ownership relations in large firms are sketchy and may not be sufficiently representative, the evidence at our disposal supports hypotheses put forward on the basis of ethnographic observations by David Stark and Larry King.[19] Stark found that ownership in Central European corporations is 'recombinant', that is, it is neither private nor public. King found firms with 'recombinant' property, too, but he also identified a number of alternative strategies of privatization, most of which have not led to ownership by identifiable individuals. Our data on property also document diffuse patterns of ownership in post-communist Central Europe, and with the exception of foreign-owned firms (which are really significant only in Hungary), it is not easy to tell who the real owners are. Direct or indirect public ownership, institutional cross-ownership,

ownership by banks that are owned by the government or state privatization agencies, and self-ownership (firms owning firms, which own them) are all typical. Together, this creates the material base for the substantial autonomy and power exercised by non-propertied technocrats and managers.

Finally, while the big winners of the post-communist transition are former communist technocrats, we find that they cannot rule by themselves. They have been forced to create a hegemonic power bloc together with the new politocracy and the opinion-making intellectual elite, and these two groups are composed largely of former dissident intellectuals.[20] Immediately following the fall of communism, the new politocracy and opinion-making intellectual elite made an attempt to squeeze the former communist technocracy out of power. They soon learned, however, that neither fraction of the intellectual elite could rule alone. During the second post-communist elections, many former dissidents were dropped from the politocracy, and the late communist pragmatists joined the new political elite. These are strange bedfellows indeed, who form the 'unholy alliance' of post-communism.

Thesis 5. The formation of classes under post-communism is a highly contested process. There are diverse candidates who could constitute a new propertied class – the technocratic–managerial elite, foreign investors with their compradore intellectual allies, and the new entrepreneurs who are starting small businesses in the hope that they will grow big.

It is possible that post-communism will culminate in a system in which a class of private proprietors is formed. At the present time, however, the formation of such a class is highly contested. Its members may eventually be recruited from among former communist technocrats and managers. Alternatively, new private entrepreneurs may give former apparatchiks a run for their money, or these socioeconomic systems may operate, in the long run, with a marginal domestic bourgeoisie and with the key productive assets owned by foreign investors. It is also conceivable, as we have argued, that technocrats and managers will successfully reproduce diffuse property relations and retain economic control without ownership. At the very least, we expect that the nature of the bourgeoisie-in-the-making will be deeply affected by the fact that the transition project was invented and implemented by a post-communist power bloc with deep roots in historical struggles between fractions of the intellectual elite. What the outcomes of ongoing struggles for ownership and control will be, however, are as yet unclear.

In a casual conversation once, we tried to explain the punch-line of this book to an old friend, an Australian Labor Party faithful. He listened attentively to the story of former communists now busy making capitalism. He shook his head in disbelief: 'Are you telling me that those characters who screwed socialism in Eastern Europe are now going to screw capitalism too?' Trendy sociologists like to say nowadays: agency matters. This is what our friend meant. You do not have to accept the implied Left Labor Party political message (socialism was screwed because the wrong people tried to implement it) to be receptive to the substantive point: not only do institutions shape actors, the collective biographies of actors who make history will also leave their imprint on the institutions within which they are compelled to operate.

Chapter 5 concludes that capitalism can be most fruitfully perceived as a variety of possible destinations. The reality of the world after the fall of socialism is not the making of a unitary system from the Chicago School's economic textbook. Rather, it is a world of capitalisms – that is, a world of socioeconomic systems with a great diversity of class relations and institutional arrangements.

This concluding chapter is a call for a study of comparative capitalism. It is a call for something which could be called 'neoclassical sociology'. This is a research program which, like classical sociology, views its main task as the exploration of the origins and nature of capitalism. Classical social theory focused its attention on the 'preconditions' for making modern capitalism. Since those preconditions were numerous and precarious, capitalism was thought to be a miracle – it was a miracle that all these conditions could be met at the same time in the same place. The neoclassical project, however, begins its analysis by observing how capitalism is being made by the most unlikely agents in the most inconceivable sites. In our case, capitalism is being made within the ruins of socialism by former communist apparatchiks and their former left-wing critics. Classical sociologists from Marx to Weber conceptualized capitalism as a single (though in the Marxist tradition not the final) destination. With the disappearance of any feasible alternative economic system, however, it has suddenly become clear to the neoclassical sociological commentator that actually existing capitalism is a mosaic of the most diverse socio-economic structures and institutions. Thus, the task is not to explain why capitalism emerged 'in the beginning'. Instead, the question before us is: how do the initial conditions of capitalist transformation affect the kind of capitalism that will be made, where it will be made, and by whom it will be made?

1

Classes and Elites in the Changing Structures of Twentieth-Century Central European Societies

This chapter develops a conceptual framework to study the dynamics of social structure in rapidly changing societies. Focusing on Central Europe as our case study, we redevelop Bourdieu's ideas of 'capital' and 'habitus' to analyze how people have navigated rapid and massive changes in social structure. Our approach is ironic in this sense, since Bourdieu is usually viewed as a theorist of social reproduction whose ideas are marked by the context of social stability in which they were constructed – namely, capitalist France. None the less, we think Bourdieu's ideas are useful for our research site because although there is massive social change, *plus ça change, plus c'est la même chose*.

In what follows, we attempt to unpack this common wisdom – that 'the more things change, the more they stay the same' – by critically invoking the notion of habitus which Bourdieu defines as a 'generative grammar of practices'. We understand habitus as 'knowledge' of the 'rules of the game' which allows diverse actors in different sorts of relationships to navigate the rapidly changing social spaces they confront. So, although the idea of habitus can be read in several ways, we want to distance ourselves from an understanding of habitus as formed *simply* by the positions actors occupy in stable social spaces. Instead, we emphasize the *dialectical interaction* between agents (their dispositions, habits, biographies, collective memories) and their positions (in institutions, class relations, and networks). Using this understanding, we build a theory of social change which places agents and their life strategies at the center of analysis. We focus on how people have tried to stay 'on course' in the face of massive social changes in Central Europe – that is to say, how they have reinterpreted their experience and reoriented their world-views to make sense of, and conform to, rapidly changing social logics.

17

Before turning to the theory of social change, however, we require an understanding of the social 'spaces' or social structures which Central European actors have confronted in the last six or seven decades. In the lifetime of a single generation, the criteria defining what is 'up' and 'down' in the social structure have been radically reconfigured several times. To understand these changes, we develop a framework which combines Weber's distinction between 'rank' and 'class' with Bourdieu's theory of 'forms of capital', and on this basis, we compare the 'space structures' of precommunist, communist, and post-communist societies in Central Europe.

Note however, that the purpose of this book is much more modest than analyzing the totality of these structures. This book focuses on the top of the social hierarchies. To put it in neo-Marxist terms, we are focusing not on inter-class but on intra-class or, more precisely, inter-elite struggles. This does not imply that inter-class conflicts will not be of vital importance in shaping the characters of these societies. Rather, it is to say that in this historical conjuncture, where old class and elite constellations are dissolving, and new classes are not yet formed, looking at these inter-elite struggles is theoretically and historically justified. Indeed, one of the fundamental points of this book is that the post-communist power elite is busily engaged in making classes – it is in search of the new bourgeoisie (and, by implication, of a new proletariat, properly speaking). The main dynamic shaping these struggles, however, is not that between the bourgeoisie and the proletariat. The main dynamic is the struggle over the making of those classes which they eventually seek to represent; classes for which they wish to become the organic intellectuals.

The central argument of this comparative analysis of social structures is that the social 'space' of post-communist capitalism is distinguishable from the stratification regimes which preceded it because it is a system in which cultural capital (education, skill, credentials) is more important than economic capital (property ownership) or social capital (social network ties) for attaining elite status, power, and privilege. However, we also emphasize that the *particular* shape post-communist social relations will take in different countries remains an open historical question. The elites that govern these societies are composed primarily of agents with biographies and repertoires of life strategies developed as dissidents, or as socialist technocrats and managers; and we think this is likely to be deeply consequential for the kind of capitalism post-communist agents will implement.

Continuity and change

In prewar Central Europe, being wealthy, a good Christian, or of noble origin was a source of pride and prestige. At that time, you were called a 'smelly peasant' or a 'rotten proletarian' if others wanted to insult you. If you were a communist, you were a criminal. It was enough to be a socialist, a 'lefty', or an atheist to be suspect. By the late 1940s, however, former family wealth or noble origins had become a handicap. You were discriminated against if you happened to be from the wrong – formerly rich – family. As the Maoists put it a few thousand miles away, you were 'a rotten egg from the wrong basket'. You were likely to lose your job, or you needed to work twice as hard as anybody else to get a promotion. You were advised to find or invent poor peasants among your grandparents, and to remove the photograph of your clergyman uncle from your bedroom. Combined with your own Communist Party membership and loyalty, poor peasant or proletarian origins were the express elevator to the heights of power and privilege. Even being an 'expert' was suspicious during the Stalinist period of the early 1950s: expertise was forgivable only if you were 'red' beyond doubt.

As Stalinism relaxed into the reform communism of the 1960s, however, status hierarchies became more balanced. Now it was not enough to be of humble origins and a Communist Party member. If you wanted to hold on to the job you were promoted into during the revolutionary period, you went back to school to get proper educational credentials. At the same time, loyalty to the party and to party bosses remained of considerable importance. You were proud if you knew important people in the party, and you showed off how well connected you were. As state socialism neared its end, however, education and diligence mattered more and more, and politics less and less. It began to seem as if people's pasts – even people's current practices – would no longer be held against them. If you were religious, you were no longer embarrassed to be seen by your colleagues entering a church; the clergyman uncle's photograph reappeared among the family pictures in the living-room, along with other memorabilia of the bourgeois past.

Then, in 1989, the world turned around once again. Now it is the 'negation of negation', and the pre-communist pecking order seems to be returning with a vengeance. Once again 'communist' is a swear word. You suddenly forget you ever joined the party or, if you are reminded of having done so, you compensate for it by being more Catholic than the Pope. You no longer remember the names of your friends on party committees, but you have a clear recollection of all the heroic anti-communist acts for which you were punished. If you cannot hide your party past, or if you find it out of character to do so, you are once again discriminated against. Again, you are likely to lose your job, especially if it is an important one and/or your political past is suspect. Again, you are denied a promotion which is granted to a co-worker who has no party past (or is better at hiding it). Again, being wealthy is more respectable and useful than being poor. Once more, you show off your distinguished family origins. All the turbulence of the past decades was in vain: history has come back; the past half-century was only a 'detour'. Revolutions and counter-revolutions created big waves on the surface, but in the deeper layers of individual and collective experience, silence – continuity – reigns.

So, indeed, *plus ça change, plus c'est la même chose*! As the impressionistic account above conveys, what has remained constant in Central Europe is an enduring preoccupation with social origins in the face of massive social change. In particular, the categorical division between the politically correct and the politically suspect continues to inform the way agents perceive and classify the social world. At the same time, however, the fundamental alterations in behavior and beliefs that this anecdotal history chronicles suggest that human society is endlessly plastic: a great many people radically changed their life strategies as the institutions and rules of the game changed around them.

The organization of this chapter mirrors this dialectical interaction between agents and structures. In the first section we focus on social structure, expanding Bourdieu's notions of 'social space' and the 'forms of capital' to examine how the 'social logic' or the 'rules of the game' have changed in Central Europe in the last six or seven decades. Although Bourdieu has never used the different forms of capital to analyze modern capitalist society systematically in comparative-historical perspective, in our reading such an analysis is implicit in his approach. We think that the three major forms of capital – economic, cultural and social – play different roles in shaping social structures in different social formations. We suggest that it is capitalism in which economic capital is determinant; in pre-capitalist economies, social capital is more important; and in socialist society – where 'politics is in command' – a special form of social capital – namely, political capital – is the dominant form. Using this logic, we present snapshots of social structure in Central Europe, comparing pre-communist, communist, and post-communist societies. In the second part of the chapter we focus on agents as we discuss the historical transitions between these different space structures in Central Europe. It is here that we present our theory of *transitions* to capitalism as an extension of Bourdieu's theory of habitus, posing it against the antinomies of neoclassical economic theories and path-dependence explanations of social change in contemporary Central Europe.

Different types of capital

Bourdieu's conceptualization of the forms of 'capital'[1] is helpful for thinking about the connections between changing social structure and the strategies and choices of agents in Central Europe. While we rely on Weber's distinction between rank and class,[2] we also suggest that some of the changes in Central Europe have been more complex than a two-dimensional metaphor can convey. Bourdieu's differentiation of different kinds of 'capital' helps us to conceptualize more fine-grained differences in the social logic of Central European societies.[3]

Our analysis begins from Bourdieu's understanding of different types of 'capital'; primarily economic, cultural, social, and symbolic capital (although occasionally he uses even more types: 'artistic' or 'academic capital', etc.). The importance of the notion of 'capital' is in specifying the concept of social structure as a set of social relations which define what Bourdieu calls 'social space': as in a magnetic field, locations in space (positions and agents) are defined by their 'charge' – by the amount and composition of capitals. With quite a bit of simplification, we suggest that economic capital can be measured by property ownership, cultural capital by educational credentials, social capital by network extensiveness and centrality, and finally, symbolic capital by the facility with which different kinds of capital can be converted into other advantages (for example, how easily can 'expert' status be converted into financial luxury, or can one 'buy' a place in the elite?).

In this schema, modern capitalist societies like France are conceptualized in terms of the possession of two types of capital: economic and cultural. While both types of capital are useful for getting ahead in the French social hierarchy, possession of economic capital is of particular importance. At the very top of French society one finds those who have a great deal of economic capital: wealthy members of the propertied *grande bourgeoisie* and managers of large corporations. In contrast, those who have acquired more cultural than economic capital – for example, doctors, academics, or senior professionals – belong, according to Bourdieu, to the 'dominated fraction of the dominant class'. By extrapolating this hypothesis, we can envision the whole class map of contemporary French society. Below the dominant class, which is well endowed with both economic and cultural capital, one expects to find the 'middle classes'. These are composed of individuals who have either cultural capital but no economic capital (for instance, routine professionals and white-collar workers), or economic capital but not much cultural capital (the self-employed petty bourgeoisie). Finally, at the bottom of the social hierarchy one finds the popular classes, deprived of both economic and cultural capital.

In contrast to capitalist societies, in state-socialist societies economic capital was of minimal importance (indeed, during the early years of socialism pre-communist ownership of economic capital was a handicap rather than an asset). Instead, social capital, which was highly institutionalized in the form of membership in the Communist Party, was predominant. Given its highly institutionalized form, we propose specifying the notion of 'social capital' by introducing the concept of 'political capital' for the former state-socialist societies of Central Europe. We do not intend to imply that 'political capital' is reducible to party membership, although party membership remains a particularly important variable in the study of socialist social structure. Rather, political capital is interpreted here as a special case of social capital – that type of social capital which was institutionalized through the practices of the Communist Party. In the following analyses, party membership is a proxy for membership in an extremely powerful and influential network. Formal office-holding stands for both formal and informal ties that were extremely productive under state-socialist conditions. One could even compensate for the lack of party membership with such networks. For example, cadre-kids were forgiven much, and people who collaborated with the intelligence services got ahead in their careers, without party membership. The police were not supposed to recruit Communist Party members as informants. And while party members 'informed' on their co-workers through party channels, the domestic intelligence services were allowed to recruit only non-party members. Being a police informer, then, was the functional equivalent of party membership in terms of political capital. Other, more generalized forms of social capital may also have affected stratification in Central Europe, but political capital was clearly the most important form throughout the communist period.

In what follows, we use this reworked understanding of the distributions of capital to describe the societies of Central Europe, and how they changed over time. Our central claim is that those who maintained their relative social trajectories in the face of change were those who possessed more than one kind of capital, and were able to convert resources when the social assets defining 'success' were altered. Recall that the logic and laws of Central European social stratification have changed profoundly in this century. People who are now over fifty or sixty years of age have lived in at least three distinct social structures: in pre-communist society, under communism, and since 1989 – or in Russia since 1991 – in post-communism. These three different 'space structures' were characterized by strikingly different criteria of ascent and descent, so a person would have had to possess quite different types of capital to remain successful over time. Indeed, in order to stay on a trajectory traveling to the 'top' an individual had to learn to navigate these changing 'space structures': they had to learn how to dispose of devalued types of capital and acquire those types of capital that had increased in value; they also had to learn how to convert old, now devalued capital into a new, more valued type. So while markedly different principles of social organization characterized the three periods, they were by no means discontinuous. Each multidimensional 'space structure' was connected historically by a transition in which elements from the old social structure were preserved, new rules of the game were introduced, and people tried to connect both in an effort to stay 'on course' in the new social space.

Differences in the logic of social structure are summarized in Table 1.1. Following Weber, we believe that pre-communist societies were dual-

Table 1.1 Determinants of social structure in different types of societies

| | Types of Capital | | |
Types of Societies	ECONOMIC	CULTURAL	SOCIAL
Baseline model: 'ideal type' of modern capitalism	+++	++	+ (Rational social network)
Pre-communist Eastern Europe (–1948)	++	++	+++ (Traditional status honor)
Classical (Stalinist) model of socialism (1949–mid 1960s)	– | | | V	+	+++ (Institutionalized as political capital)
Reform model of socialism (mid 1960s–1989)	+	++	+++ (Institutionalized as political capital)
Post-communism: managerial society (1989–)	++	+++	++ (De-institutionalized and rationalized as social networks)

stratification systems, characterized by the competing logics of traditional feudal rank order and modern economic classes.[4] The communists abolished this system decisively in the late 1940s and 1950s, but their rule was deeply affected by the fact that revolutions occurred in societies without fully developed modern class relations. Indeed, at the same time as the communists destroyed feudal client ties based on status honor, the state-socialist system reinvoked the logic of rank in a qualitatively different way. In this case of modern rank order,[5] a system of socialist patronage was institutionalized via political capital in the form of Communist Party membership. At the same time, the relative status of economic and cultural capital was decisively devalued. As the Stalinism of the 1950s relaxed into the reform communism of the 1960s, however, cultural capital became an increasingly important secondary form of capital, signifying mastery of the symbolic code of Marxism–Leninism in the first place, and the goals of scientific and technical excellence under socialism in the second. The reforms of the state-socialist system in the 1960s also permitted a resurgence in the importance of economic capital, but its significance was clearly third, after cultural capital. Politics remained 'in command' in Central Europe until the 'revolutions' of 1989, when the logic of social structure was again reconfigured. In contrast to the preceding social structures of Central Europe, post-communist societies are dominated by the logic of cultural capital.

Political capital has been de-institutionalized and devalued, and a large propertied bourgeoisie has not emerged from the ranks of either state-socialist entrepreneurs or former cadres. In this context, we argue that those who possess cultural capital are in command. Post-communism presents a novel set of social relationships with an as yet unknown potential.

Changes in the social structure of Central Europe during the twentieth century

Social structure in pre-communist Central Europe: the duality of rank and class

Our central hypothesis for pre-communist social structure in Central Europe is that it was organized on the basis of two competing logics of social stratification: class and rank order. Money mattered, but so did education, bloodline, and gentry lifestyle. Specifically, we argue that power and privilege were based on possession of traditional social capital, but this state of affairs was constantly being challenged by an emergent bourgeoisie (defined by possession of economic capital) and a modernizing intelligentsia (defined by possession of cultural capital). The results of struggles and bargains between each of these groups of social actors produced variation in the extent of modernization and 'openness' in different countries.

Table 1.2 describes our hypotheses for specific countries, highlighting variation in the extent to which different societies in Central Europe were dominated by the social logics of rank and class during the pre-communist period. We believe that the logic of class was probably strongest in the Czech Republic at this time, characterized by a reasonably well-formed proletariat and bourgeoisie. And while Czech intellectuals sometimes saw themselves as a *Bildungsbürgertum*, their organization as professionals was more advanced than in Hungary or Poland.[6] At the other end of the continuum, pre-communist Poland was characterized by a pervasive logic of rank and the endurance of traditional feudal relations, particularly in the countryside. Hungary, by contrast, comes closest to what Weber meant by a dual-stratification order. In all these countries there were concerted attempts to form capitalist classes, and in each case they were met with strong gentry organization. In these conditions, the closed logic of rank society continued to block upward mobility and class formation, especially in the countryside, while a relatively closed stratum of intellectuals, reproducing itself over time, formed the conditions for the creation of a *Bildungsbürgertum* project among the educated middle classes.

Despite the development of capitalist class relations throughout the region, then, some version of traditional social capital played an important role in all the pre-communist societies of Central Europe. In Hungary and Poland – and, we would suggest, to an even greater extent in pre-

Table 1.2 *Characteristics of social structure and economic development after World War I, in four Central European Societies: hypotheses*

Country	CHARACTER OF STRATIFICATION SYSTEM	DEGREE OF ECONOMIC DEVELOPMENT
Czech Republic	Weak rank order, well-formed proletariat and bourgeoisie, some professionalization under way	High
Hungary	Well-defined dual-stratification system, weak propertied class, intellectuals constitute a *Bildungsbürgertum*	Low/Medium
Poland	Weak propertied class, endurance of traditional feudal relations, especially in the countryside, smaller and weaker *Bildungsbürgertum* in the absence of a Polish nation-state	Low

revolutionary Russia – social capital was of a traditional type, based on feudal social rank, and the power of the gentry remained unbroken throughout the pre-communist era. As a result, the process of embourgeoisement in these countries was blocked, subverted, or slowed down. A sizeable, traditional peasantry was reproduced at the margins of society, with little chance of upward mobility. The gentry occupied some of the key command positions in the state and economy, and to some extent they succeeded in gentrifying members of the educated middle classes and the nascent propertied bourgeoisie, attracting them to gentry lifestyles and locking them into a traditional system of patronage. A similar situation probably held for pre-independence Czech society, but during the interwar years the Austrian and German gentry were dispossessed, and a modern capitalist class and proletariat began to form. None the less, it is probable that even in the first Czechoslovak Republic the logic of rank – of clientelism – may have survived into the interwar period.

For these reasons, we emphasize that the pre-communist stratification system in this part of the world cannot be described *only* in terms of traditional authority in Weber's sense of the term. To the extent that the logic of class operated, the social space of the interwar years was characterized by the increasing importance of economic and cultural capital, and can be described by the schema Bourdieu uses to analyze social stratification in contemporary France. The relative importance of these two forms of capital, however, was not the same in different parts of Europe: in Germany – and to an even greater extent in non-German Central Europe – economic capital played a more modest role, and cultural capital was of greater significance than in Western Europe properly speaking. In Bourdieu's terms, this can be interpreted as a difference in the weight attributed to economic and cultural capital. In England and France, economic capital was clearly determinant, and cultural capital was only complementary. In Germany and Central Europe, by contrast, economic and cultural capital were of roughly equal importance, and operated in a context marked by the continuing importance of traditional social capital. And in so far as the logic of rank – or *Stand* in Weber's terms – continued to shape the dynamics of social inequality in Central Europe, traditional semi-feudal social networks based on gentry lifestyles were dominant. To sum up: these societies were on their way towards legal-rational domination prior to the advent of communism, but the process of modern class formation was sufficiently delayed, and the logic of rank sufficiently strong, to justify the claim that these were dual-stratification systems. Figure 1.1 presents our ideal type of pre-communist social structure, stratified by the competing logics of rank and class.

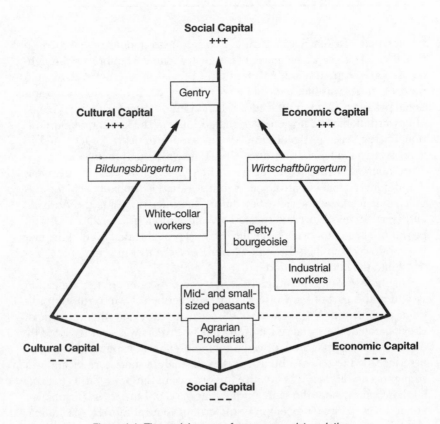

Figure 1.1 The social space of pre-communist societies

Communist social structure: the primacy of political capital and the growing importance of cultural capital

The communist revolutions of the late 1940s abolished feudal rank order, and blocked the processes of embourgeoisement and proletarianization which had been under way in Central Europe during the interwar period. In the qualitatively new system of stratification that emerged in the 1950s, economic capital lost its significance and became a handicap. Members of the former propertied bourgeoisie became 'class enemies'. Similarly, communists eliminated the feudal landowning class, and broke the political and cultural hegemony of the gentry.[7] Even those with cultural capital from the pre-communist era were suspect during the classical period of state socialism, despite the fact that intellectuals were at the forefront of the communist transition. Only those who joined the Communist Party had a chance to climb to the top of the social hierarchy. Only those whose loyalty to the political boss was unquestionable, and whose dedication to the Marxist–Leninist world-view was beyond doubt, could be successful. In short, those with political capital were at the top of the communist hierarchy. If those possessing other forms of capital wanted to stay 'on course', or stay 'on top' (or even stay alive) in the new system, they had to acquire some of the newly appreciated form of capital – namely, political capital, that is, party membership and position in powerful communist networks. This was particularly true for those who had formerly possessed economic capital or who came from distinguished gentry families.

In this context, the role of cultural capital took on particular significance. Since loyalty to the party and the charismatic leader were such intangible phenomena, educational credentials became an important indicator of political value and affiliation. Educational credentials – a university degree or, in its absence, completion of party school at the University of Marxism–Leninism – were useful, if not necessary. They indicated not only the possession of human capital (specific skills and technical knowledge) but also mastery of the new hegemonic symbolic code of Marxism–Leninism. For those who were promoted into positions of authority without adequate credentials in the early communist period, completing a degree at least at a party school, or an evening course designed for 'working class cadres', was essential for maintaining political position. Those who possessed *only* cultural capital of the pre-communist kind, however, had little chance of getting to the top in the Stalinist era. There were few exceptions. Until the middle or end of the 1960s, even the best medical doctors were not appointed as hospital directors unless they were ready to join the party. This phenomenon, called counterselection, meant that competent people were rarely appointed to positions of authority unless they were party members. To sum up: although cultural capital was a useful asset in the early communist period, it was secondary to political capital: cultural capital could usually be valorized only if one also possessed political capital, usually in the form of party membership.

For this reason, we argue that early communist societies, like pre-communist societies in Central Europe, were also based on rank order. Indeed, the early communist system has been called 'feudal socialism' because loyalty to patrons and faith in the proper world-view recall the logic of feudal rank order and clientelism. Notwithstanding the fact that socialism was a thoroughly modern ideology, and the *nomenklatura* system was imbued with the rationality of that ideology, this analogy is useful because it highlights how the top of the state-socialist social hierarchy was like a 'ruling estate' rather than a 'ruling class'. Indeed, the social structure of classical Stalinism could probably be described with some accuracy as a dichotomy comprising a dominant, caste-like ruling estate confronting a relatively immobilized, passive 'mass'. Djilas's analysis of the Stalinist bureaucracy as a 'New Class' was innovative precisely because it captured this fundamental conflict of interest between the party–state bureaucracy and the rest of the population for the first time.[8] The use of the term 'class', however, was somewhat imprecise. The Stalinist bureaucracy fell short of being a class in more than one sense of the term. It was not constituted in a fully 'rational' manner. Its cohesion and authority were based on patron–client relations, so it was more a rank, or an estate, than a class – at least in the Weberian sense of the term.

Moreover, like the medieval clergy, this estate recruited broadly from all ranks of society in Central Europe, and it appears to have had difficulty reproducing itself intergenerationally. In the context of pervasive non-rational relations, issues of intergenerational reproduction highlighted the inability of Stalinist ruling estates to establish hegemony on the basis of the rational, scientistic foundations of the socialist project. These reproduction problems were an important source of instability in the state-socialist social order. Many cadre children did not want to become cadre members themselves: some became dissidents; many opted for professional careers; and most did so with the approval of their parents. The *nomenklatura* in most state-socialist countries, therefore, was continuously recruited from the lower ranks of society. The result was an ongoing 'circulation of communist elites' in the Paretoian sense of the term. The former Soviet Union was probably an exception to this rule, with the *nomenklatura* successfully passing their bureaucratic privileges on to their children. Leon Trotsky captured this characteristic of the Soviet *nomenklatura* quite accurately with the idea of a bureaucratic caste. Without accepting the whole ideological baggage of Trotsky, we concede that in Soviet Russia the bureaucratic ruling estate separated itself from the rest of society by caste-like barriers. As we shall see, however, in Central Europe there were limits to the ability of such closed bureaucratic castes to reproduce themselves.

The nature of the ruling estate, and in particular the degree of social clo-sure it achieved, varied across countries in ways that were consequential for the transition away from Stalinism. In some countries, such as Hungary, the ruling Stalinist estate was like the clergy in medieval times: it was relatively open to upwardly mobile individuals. This relative openness possessed the twin advantages of maintaining legitimacy by preserving the image of the ruling estate being 'from the people and for the people', and ensuring inter-nal discipline by fueling the insecurities of new members, many of whom were promoted quickly on the basis of their political capital, but often with-out proper credentials or training. Patronage characterized not only relationships between the ruling estate and the 'masses', then, but also rela-tionships within the ruling estate. In other countries, such as Stalinist Russia, and probably to some extent in Romania and North Korea, the ruling bureaucracy began to reproduce itself. The children of the *nomenklatura* began to fill *nomenklatura* positions, and social closure developed between the bureaucracy and the masses. As a self-reproducing ruling caste, however, such bureaucracies suffered from legitimation problems, and encountered difficulties maintaining internal discipline and popular legitimacy.[9]

Reform Communism

Stalinist rank order began to weaken in most of Central Europe after the mid 1960s, and with the modernization of the stratification system that ensued came the gradual appearance of class relations. Here again we see a tension between a dominant rank order and the emergent forces of class stratifica-tion. This tension recalls our discussion of pre-communist dual-stratification systems, and the Weberian analysis of the conflicting logics of rank and class: in both pre-communist and reform communist times, the dominant rank order and the forces pointing towards class formation and the rationalization of stratification systems were counterposed. However, this similarity should not be exaggerated. The state-socialist bureaucracy, unlike the Junkers, did not co-opt and distort market forces. Rather, it restricted second economy activity legally, and used the existence of the second economy for political legitimation. In retrospect, we can also see that when the socialist bureau-cracy was faced with the challenge of rationalization, it proved much less resistant than the Central European gentry of the interwar years. The rule of the gentry was overthrown only after two world wars and revolution, while in 1989 the rule of the socialist bureaucracy just melted away.

The emergent new class formations of late Stalinist state socialism took two different trajectories. First, by the early to mid 1960s, meritocratic prin-ciples of recruitment to prestigious and powerful occupations gained ground. While political capital remained the dominant resource for upward mobility, more importance was attached to the possession of cultural or human capital than before, and it increased in value proportionately. Second, by the mid to late 1970s, newly acquired economic capital began to play a role in shaping social inequalities.

Both these processes of change were particularly evident in Hungary. After the mid 1960s, the Kádár regime went out of its way to recruit the most competent and talented young university graduates for party and state bureaucratic positions. Membership of the Communist Party, associated networks, and loyalty remained important, but social ascent without political capital now became possible. One could become a director or a full professor without joining the party, and the proportion of well-qualified professionals increased even among political cadres.

Other countries varied in their similarity to the Hungarian model. Poland – and to some extent Yugoslavia – were closest to the Hungarian model, and Romania and Russia were the most different. During the first years of the rule of Gierek, in the 1970s, the Polish system approached the Hungarian model most closely. This was the time when the technocratic intelligentsia was co-opted most successfully by the ideology of the 'second Poland', or the 'second industrialization of Poland'. Czechoslovakia was moving in the Hungarian direction in the 1960s too, but in 1968 the Czech technocratic reform intelligentsia was crushed, and never quite recovered. In Russia there were numerous attempts to co-opt the technocratic intelligentsia. The first attempt came shortly after the October Revolution, during the early and mid 1920s. Khrushchev's measures opened a second chapter in the reforms designed to win over the intelligentsia, and while they were eventually abandoned by Brezhnev, reforms were resumed vigorously by Gorbachev. What were the consequences of these post-Stalinist reforms in Central Europe?

The first consequence was a weakening of socialist rank order. While the socialist bureaucracy reached a *modus vivendi* with the new socialist petty bourgeoisie, it had a much more difficult time coping with the challenges posed by the holders of cultural capital – namely, the intelligentsia. The Stalinist bureaucratic estate relied heavily on pure coercion and the charisma of the leader to maintain its power. The reforms of the post-Stalinist epoch that resulted in the increased value of cultural capital began to undermine both these sources of bureaucratic authority. In a search for legitimacy, the post-Stalinist bureaucracy reached out towards the increasingly powerful technocratic intelligentsia, much in the way Alvin Gouldner predicted in *The Future of Intellectuals and the Rise of the New Class*.[10] The bureaucratic ruling estate attempted to recruit technocratic intellectuals – indeed, to draw in the whole of the intelligentsia – in a search for competent cadres who could justify the rational, scientistic nature of the socialist social project and make it their own. To the extent that intellectuals accepted the overtures of the bureaucracy, there was a New Class in formation in the state-socialist societies of the mid to late 1960s. However, this New Class was not rooted solely in the Stalinist bureaucracy, as Djilas had expected. Instead, the New Class began to form within the merger between bureaucracy and technocracy, and started to redefine the project of 'scientific socialism'. Its aim was the 'rationalization of the redistributive economy' of state socialism through a 'scientific-technological revolution'. The New Class sought to build a 'socialism with a human face' with which to replace Stalinist bureaucratic despotism. It was not unreasonable to speculate in the late 1960s and early 1970s, then, that a transition from socialist rank order to socialist class stratification was under way.[11]

The forces pointing towards the formation of this New Class and the transition from socialist rank order to a class-stratified socialist society were real, but eventually the project failed. A bureaucratic counteroffensive against the technocrats in the late 1960s and early 1970s blocked or destroyed the New Class project everywhere in Central Europe. This was most evident in Czechoslovakia following August 1968, but similar trends prevailed in East Germany and in Poland, and eventually even in Hungary. The rigidity of the neo-Stalinist rank order in Brezhnev's Soviet Union may have been ultimately responsible for the defeat of New Class projects throughout the region. These failed projects left their mark, however, since the bureaucracy could not avoid relying on credentials as criteria for recruitment to elite positions. Thus, in some respects, the bureaucratic victory proved Pyrrhic, as state-socialist elites became increasingly 'intellectualized'.

Other post-Stalinist reforms outlived the failure of the New Class project. From 1963 to 1964 the Kádár regime in Hungary not only tried to co-opt the intelligentsia, but offered concessions to the working class as well. The most important concession to workers was the tolerance the regime extended towards the second economy. State employees were permitted to engage in market-like business transactions after official working hours, and were also allowed to work in private family work organizations. As a result, by the mid to late 1970s two alternative trajectories of social ascent existed: one could move ahead by climbing the bureaucratic ladder, but one had the alternative of learning to master the rules of the emergent market. The best villas in Budapest's upper-middle-class districts, and the nicest of the many new family homes built in rural communities at this time, were inhabited by two types of people: by cadres, specifically senior bureaucrats or successful professionals; and by small part-time private entrepreneurs. A new social 'class' was forming. New agents, located between a traditional self-employed petty bourgeoisie and a classical proletariat, appeared on the scene. These were people who typically kept full-time employment in the public sector but earned significant incomes from part-time private activities as well. One could observe similar trends after Martial Law in Poland, when Jaruzelski attempted to co-opt the technocratic intelligentsia into the power elite, successfully promoting a semi-private sector, and tolerating a large second – or underground – economy.

Czechoslovakia after 1968, in contrast to Hungary and Poland, can be characterized as a neo-Stalinist social order.[12] After the crackdown on the Prague Spring – which was similar to the reform communist movements in Hungary and Poland during the late 1960s – the bureaucratic estate re-established its hegemony forcefully. The bureaucracy made it very clear that it was not willing to compromise with the intelligentsia, and the Czech regime, unlike other countries in the region, did not make concessions to the working class by opening up the second economy. Instead, the Czechoslovakian system of domination between 1968 and the late 1980s can be characterized as 'neo-Stalinist paternalism'. Social peace was achieved by coercion on the one hand, and by state-guaranteed full employment, price stability, and a reasonable supply of basic goods for consumption on the other. Commentators usually emphasized the coercive nature of Czechoslovak society at this time, and indeed, it was much harsher on dissidents and far less concerned about violating civil rights than the regimes in Hungary and Poland. The stability, security, and relative equality that the Husák regime was able to provide, however, did form the basis for a relatively legitimate exercise of neo-Stalinist authority. By contrast, as market reform progressed in the reform regimes of Hungary and Poland, social inequality grew, inflation was significant, and poverty spread. Czechs and Slovaks looking at their neighbors believed that they were better off, and in some ways they were.

So, by the end of the 1960s the structure of state-socialist societies had become rather complex in comparison with the classical state-socialist model. In most countries, the possession of political capital remained the major source of power and privilege, but the relative importance of cultural capital grew, counterselection was greatly reduced, and ownership of economic capital began to play a role in shaping life chances. Note that economic capital was still only weakly associated with the distribution of political power, and remained a clear 'third' in terms of importance among the factors that shaped social ascent and descent in reform communism. Despite this complexity, however, these were still dual-stratification systems with a dominant logic of rank order and a subordinate class-stratification logic. Figure 1.2 presents our ideal type of state-socialist societies.

Post-communist social structure: political capital is devalued and cultural capital becomes primary

There were a number of schools of thought about which social groups would be best placed to take advantage of market reform after the fall of communism. Market transition theory[13] and research on socialist

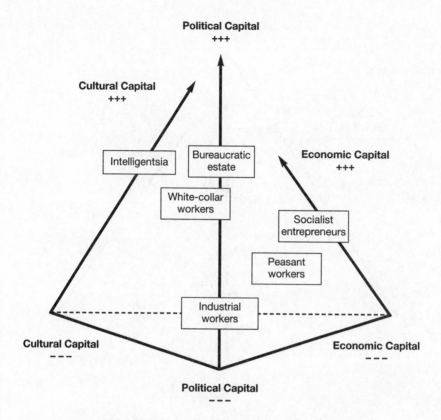

Figure 1.2 The social space of reform communism

entrepreneurs[14] suggested that those who had been successful in the second economy during the late communist period would benefit most from the transition to capitalism. In contrast, theorists of political capitalism argued that former cadres were best placed to convert state-socialist privilege into economic capital.[15] Against both these theories we contend that cultural capital became the dominant form of capital in post-communism. The coalition that governs post-communist societies is comprised of technocrats and managers – many of whom held senior positions in communist institutions – and former dissident intellectuals who contributed to the fall of communist regimes at the end of the 1980s.

Figure 1.3 presents our ideal type of post-communist societies. It suggests that while economic capital has increased in importance since the fall of communism in 1989, it still does not approach the significance of cultural capital in determining who holds power and privilege in the new post-communist social formations. In addition, we find clear evidence that

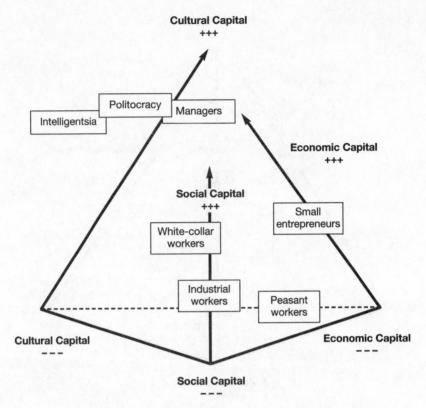

Figure 1.3 The social space of post-communist society

political capital has been decisively devalued during the transition. Although de-institutionalized political networks from the communist era can help one to rise to the top of the post-communist social structure, they are useful only if one also possesses cultural capital. In other words, positions in former communist networks operate as a secondary and dependent form of capital in post-communism, much as cultural capital operated to complement political capital in the communist period: a person could valorize their secondary form of capital only if they were well endowed with the primary form as well.

These changes – the de-institutionalization of political capital and the revaluation of cultural and economic capital – characterize societies where a substantial readjustment of social structure has taken place to meet the imperatives of a market integrated economy.[16] The main winners in the transformation so far have been highly educated middle-aged men. Members of this group are the least likely to be unemployed and the most likely to be self-employed. Furthermore, if these educated men come from families which operated businesses in the pre-socialist period, or if they occupied positions of bureaucratic authority in 1988, they are very likely to have established small businesses with employees, thereby entering that category of self-employment where incomes are high and capital accumulation takes place. In addition, middle-aged, educated men are greatly overrepresented within the top income categories. While these are the kind of people who were doing well before 1989, the post-communist transformation has increased inequalities, which means that the relative advantages of this group have also increased.

In this connection, one of the most controversial findings of this book is that there is little evidence to support the 'political capitalism' thesis. Former Communist Party membership does not seem to matter much, and if one controls for other determinants of success, such as education, former party membership either does not matter or is a disadvantage for those who wish to succeed. In this context, we observe that the major losers in the transition have been those who were 'clients' under the state-socialist system. Less educated people in their fifties, especially those who were employed in sectors of the economy which were highly subsidized under state socialism, faced serious difficulties by 1993. Incomes under post-communist conditions are peaking for people in their forties – unlike market capitalist or state-socialist economies, where incomes peak a decade later – and many men and women in their fifties have found it difficult or impossible to adapt to the demands of the market economy. In other words, without education, these state-socialist clients find it difficult to convert their previously valuable political capital into currently valuable cultural and economic capital. The fact that these people were members of the Communist Party, then, makes little difference; their party comrades can help them only if they have skills which are useful under market conditions, because former party membership *per se* is not an asset any more.

In addition to state-socialist clients, the state-socialist 'middle-class' – those who benefited from participation in the second economy – have also lost their relative advantages in the transformation following 1989. The share of total income captured by those in the middle three or four income deciles has declined substantially since 1989. Furthermore, the gap between the middle and the bottom has narrowed, while the gap between the middle and the top has widened. The poor have become poorer, but the most striking development of post-communism is that the not-so-poor have become poor too.[17]

Turning finally to those who were the most powerful and privileged in communist times, we find that they are divided among the winners and losers in the transition. The biggest winners have been those with high levels of cultural capital. If these people also happen to have occupied elite offices during the communist period, if they are young, and particularly if they never joined the party, they are likely to have done very well indeed.

Even former party members can compensate for the shadows which party membership now casts if they are well trained. By contrast, however, older members of the communist-era elite are likely to be among the biggest losers. It is not that they have become poor, but they have certainly become much less influential and somewhat less privileged. These were the members of the elite who often did not possess proper educational credentials. They were the ones who were promoted to office from working-class backgrounds, receiving 'soft' credentials from special party schools. By 1989, most of this group had reached retirement age, and even if they had not, many were sent or went voluntarily into retirement, despite the fact that they would have served for many more years had communism not collapsed.

To sum up: cultural capital dominates the social structures of post-communist societies. Overall, the winners are better-educated middle-aged men, especially those with training in engineering and economics. Of these, the biggest winners are members of the technocratic fraction of the old communist ruling estate, particularly those who were promoted into office during the 1980s, when technical competence took precedence over party loyalty in the recruitment of administrators. These individuals possess the dominant capital of post-communism – cultural capital – and with this, they have been able to convert their former political capital into valuable post-communist resources. In combination with their de-institutionalized (but still powerful) social networks from the communist era, these individuals have succeeded in maintaining their social trajectories particularly well. By contrast, the big losers are the clients of the state-socialist order: people who did not develop marketable skills, or exploited the loopholes created by the softness of budget constraints in the public sector during the state-socialist period. These people are very poorly placed to compete in the new market conditions. Their bureaucratic patrons are also among the losers. These bureaucrats may not have slipped to the very bottom of the social hierarchy, since there appears to be a safety net in the form of party networks, wealth accumulated legally or illegally during communist times, and occasionally, respectable pensions. None the less, it is clear that with the disintegration of the system of state socialism, many are finding it increasingly difficult to convert old political capital into a new, more valued kind.

So far we have compared 'snapshots' of Central European social structure at different time points. Now we turn to a discussion of transitions, offering a theory of social change to capture the multiple transitions between strikingly different social spaces in Central Europe over time.

Theories of social change

The social facts of continuity and change in the face of social transformation in Central Europe raise fundamental historical questions which have yet to find satisfactory answers. Which individuals and groups have successfully negotiated the transitions between social structures over time? And how and why have they been successful? In particular, who ascended to the top of the social hierarchies across time, and who was downwardly mobile? These questions are of deep political import for the post-communist transformation: they inform what paths will be taken; what choices and decisions will be made; and who will win and lose in the struggles to build capitalism out of the ruins of communism. Moreover, as sociologists, we believe that unless we understand the 'how' and 'why' of social change in Central Europe during this century, we cannot even begin to grasp what the future might hold.

As we said at the outset, although social structure changes, there is an element of continuity through these changes. We begin with the understanding that people want to stay 'on trajectory'. That means that in the context of rapid social change, people are interested in diversifying their portfolios and converting their capitals into new, more valued kinds. In this process, people mobilize their implicit understandings of what the rules of the game are – that is to say, their habitus guides them as they try to make sense of changing social structures. And as our snapshots showed, the most enduring feature of Central European social structures has been the relative dominance of social capital in all its different forms up to the post-communist era. This is what accounts for the obsession with social origins in Central Europe. Even though the rules of the game have changed over time, in each successive social formation the question of social origins – past alliances, past complicities, and often unspoken understandings – has emerged as the predominant way to 'make sense' of change, to understand new criteria of privilege, and to plot the safest social trajectory in new and changeable conditions.

Evolution or involution: theories of social change

Existing theories of social change in Central Europe do not even begin to grapple with the characteristic paradox we describe above, that is, the eerie continuity in the midst of massive social change. Instead, we find that the dynamics of social change in Central Europe are viewed *either* as evolutionary *or* as involutionary, but never as both. On one side, neoclassical economists – but also many journalists working for Western newspapers – and many, if not most, post-communist politicians believe that the region is on an evolutionary trajectory, leading from backward communism to advanced capitalism. This belief proceeds from the observation that state property has been privatized, markets in labor and capital have been established, and the economies of Central Europe have been opened up to foreign markets. Proponents proclaim that capitalism is being made by design, and that there will be no more social 'experiments'. It is now simply a matter of carefully copying the well-functioning institutions of Western market capitalism. Central Europe may not yet have arrived at the common destination of all societies, but the train to liberal capitalism is already on the right track. With the 'right' institutions in place, there are no barriers to the development of a Western-style market society. The premiss of this argument is that humans learn and adapt, they are rational and they evolve. It follows that with the 'right' incentive structure, people will become entrepreneurial market actors. While the shock of transition may produce temporary downturns in some social indicators (employment, wages, etc.), this transitional period, it is promised, will soon end; Central Europe will very shortly enjoy all the benefits and advantages of healthy, vibrant capitalism. The end of history is in sight.

Other observers of the post-communist transition emphasize continuity. Xenophobic nationalists, such as Csurka, Milosevic, or Mecar, do so with pride. Contending that Central Europe will resist the virus of cosmopolitanism, they argue for the preservation of its culture, which is superior to Western commercial civilization. Yet others – liberals disenchanted by the slow pace of change – make the same point with skeptical overtones. According to Timothy Garton-Ash, 1989 was only a 'refolution'; or, to use David Stark's formulation, Central Europe is not on a path from redistribution to market, but has experienced a shift 'from plan to clan'.[18] The old power structure has also been reproduced. The 'usual suspects', the old communists, have retained power and privilege into the post-communist transformation. This view is supported by analyses showing that cadres rather than capitalist entrepreneurs have been the main beneficiaries of privatization,[19] despite prior theory which suggested that second economy entrepreneurs were best positioned to take advantage of market reform.[20] Post-communist societies are building capitalism not 'on the ruins of socialism', then, but 'with the ruins of socialism'. This is what David Stark means when he proposes that the post-communist transition is path-dependent.[21] He contends that if we begin our analysis with the teleological assumption that a 'transition to market capitalism' is occurring, we may ask the wrong questions about the dynamics of transformation. Instead of looking for an emergent capitalist class, he suggests analyzing the particular processes of privatization in each country, and identifying which elements from old ownership structures and institutional arrangements have been incorporated into the new. In short, Stark emphasizes that although a communist legacy remains in Central Europe, major institutional change has also occurred. Instead of moving along a straight evolutionary line towards a common and well-defined destination, Central European societies are following a path-dependent involutionary route.[22] Involution does not imply that there is no change. It only suggests that rather than experiencing progress, or evolution, societies and social actors use old ideas, behaviors, and social logics to adapt to new conditions.

Our observation on the ongoing debate about whether post-communist social change is evolutionary or involutionary proceeds from Stark's observation that it is consequential for the post-communist transition that capitalism is being built in a society with a recent history of communist rule. In the controversy between neoclassical evolutionism and path-dependency, we are closer to the path-dependency position, but we also try to move beyond it in several ways. Specifically, we try to develop a synthesis of the neoclassical and path-dependency accounts of change by placing actors at the center of our analysis. We conceptualize individual and collective actors, such as members of classes or elites, as actors whose behavior is affected by the nature of the institutions they used to operate in under communism (hence change is path-dependent), but who have also learned to adapt to challenges which come from externally imposed changes (thus these agents are also exposed to evolutionary pressures). The life trajectories of these actors are shaped by their ability to position themselves against other actors whose positions may be up for grabs, and who will also make a bid to move into a desirable new social position or a recently vacated one. This is our recommendation for studying social change: to examine what we call 'trajectory adjustment', or to analyze the process of 'trajectory correction'. And in this connection, we think that those who are able to adjust their trajectories to meet social change most successfully are those who possess the most diverse portfolio of different kinds of capital. Along with the neoclassical theorists, then, we agree that there are indeed evolutionary pressures: there are models of institutions and behaviors which offer themselves to be copied or adapted in the new post-communist situation. We also agree with the fundamental insight of the theory of path-dependence: that the heritage of past institutions and behavior is consequential. Social actors are tempted to go back to 'what they know' when they are confronting new situations. In short, people adapt in path-dependent ways. The idea of trajectory adjustment, therefore, sees both forces at work simultaneously, and emphasizes the importance of actors, or agency, in this connection. We think that actors confronted with new challenges, and operating within old institutional constraints, come up with innovative answers.

It follows from this understanding that what kind of capitalist social structure will emerge in post-communist societies remains an open question. It will be decided by the historically contingent struggles of social actors with deep roots in socialist ways of doing business. For this reason, we suggest that even the most common assumptions – namely, that a class of private proprietors is bound to emerge in Central Europe, and that it will perform functions identical to its counterparts in the West – should be subjected to critical scrutiny. Indeed, the process of privatization may be a *sui generis* phenomenon, distinct from the making of early capitalism, and more intimately connected with pre-1989 bargains and struggles between powerful social actors. On this basis, we observe that the literature focusing on the path-dependent development of post-communist *institutions* rarely inquires into how the *agents* of the transition have approached the task of building post-communist societies. It is agents other than capitalists who are making capitalism in Central Europe, agents who share biographies as communist managers and technocrats, or as former dissidents.[23] We believe this is deeply consequential for how they will conduct the post-communist transformation. In addition to analyzing property rights or tracing the origins of current arrangements to state-socialist institutions, then, we also suggest examining these *agents* of transition, and how they negotiated the fall of communism and the rise of post-communist institutions. In short, what is central to our approach is a historical emphasis on the *interaction* between agents and structure in the post-communist transformation: agents matter as well as institutions.

From this perspective, the central weakness of neoclassical economics and its rational choice underpinnings is its ahistorical conception of human action. In the neoclassical economic view, people are stripped of their biographies and prior experiences. They are posited as self-interested and rational automatons, gathering information on costs and benefits, and acting to maximize returns for minimal effort. If you want to build capitalism on this premiss, the policy prescription is to change the opportunity set that actors confront so that it becomes rational for them to be entrepreneurial, market-oriented, and profit-motivated. The idea that there may be historically shaped, socially embedded understandings that provide non-rational motivations for individual choice in the post-communist transition is not considered.[24]

With the path-dependence model, the problem is quite different. Theory and research in this tradition have been relatively sensitive to the continuities between state-socialist and post-communist social structures. However, in its emphasis on institutional continuity and variation, the theory of path-dependence has tended to underestimate the role of actors in shaping institutional change in novel and historically contingent ways. Political capitalism theory takes this tendency even further, pointing to corruption and dishonesty as the defining features of the transition.[25] Although corruption has undoubtedly occurred, we doubt that it is the main story to be told about the post-communist transformation. What is neglected when the focus is on social reproduction is the question: what are the institutional and historical conditions for the conversion of communist into post-communist privilege? In neither the theory of political capitalism nor the path-dependence model has sustained analytical attention been paid to the dynamics of the *interaction* between agents and social structures. So although we agree in broad outline with Stark's critique of 'transitology', we want to add another dimension to the idea of path dependence in which people's world-views, biographies, and social structure are viewed as fundamentally connected.

In what follows, we develop such a theory using Bourdieu's ideas of habitus and capital in an attempt to grasp this fundamental connection between practice, world-view, and social structure. We want to chart the continuity stretching 'underneath' the ideologically informed 'revolutions' of Central Europe; we want to tell the story of how people struggled to stay 'on course' in a rapidly changing social space.

Habitus

Surviving in Central Europe in the past half-century can be likened to traveling in outer space and trying to plot a safe course; you did not always know where 'up' and 'down' were, or where your 'destination' was, or indeed if there was one at all. Learning how to navigate in this strange, ever-changing environment eventually reinforced your self-confidence. You stayed on course no matter what. If necessary, you rewrote your biography, much as Schweik wrote the pedigrees of the half-breeds he sold. In this process, people reinterpreted the apparently objective categories of social judgement that constrained their lives. In our attempt to conceptualize this process for Central Europe, we found Bourdieu's approach to the dilemma of objectivism and constructivism appealing. Bourdieu's vision of social structure as a 'traveling space', through which social actors navigate, trying to stay on course without necessarily having a 'correct' perception of their destination, fits the empirical phenomena we are trying to describe particularly well.[26]

On the one hand, Bourdieu conceptualizes social structure as a multidimensional space through which individuals in possession of various types of capital travel on different trajectories, engaging in classificatory struggles with each other to negotiate the social meanings of positions, boundaries, and collective identities.[27] It follows from this that what sociologists call classes are usually only 'paper classes', boundaries drawn on class maps by sociologists: at best, they are *hypotheses* about where collective actors or identities are likely to form. In this way, Bourdieu attempts to transcend the conventional 'objectivist' way of thinking about class, which, according to him, is particularly characteristic of Marxism. On the other hand, however, Bourdieu also wants to avoid the trap of 'constructivism', wherein social phenomena such as classes exist *only* 'in the eye of the beholder'. While he emphasizes that the class boundaries drawn by the sociologist exist only on paper, Bourdieu also argues that the social spaces we study are *real*: there are real positions and dispositions around which the formation of classes can occur. It is this idea of the *interaction* between social agents and the social relationships they *both constitute* and *confront* which makes Bourdieu attractive to us in an attempt to conceptualize the dynamics of changing social structure in the biographies of the actors who lived through this turbulent century in Central Europe.

The idea of *habitus* is crucial to Bourdieu's attempt to avoid the pitfalls of objectivism and constructivism and, we believe, it is particularly useful for thinking about the mutual interdependence of agents and structures in an innovative and empirically rich way. Bourdieu defines habitus as a 'structuring structure'.[28] On the one hand it is an embodied internalization of objective social relations, as experienced from a particular position in social space. On the other, these relations become a 'generative grammar of practices' – that is to say, the source of coherence in the lifestyles and judgements of classes and populations.[29] Habitus guides individuals in social life by supplying them with an implicit grasp of the 'rules of the game'. An individual's habitus begins to form in early childhood, as they internalize the 'objective' position of their family in social space, their 'class origin'. As deeply ingrained predispositions, habitus helps people to navigate social life in a non-conscious or non-rational way: we are guided by our habitus precisely when we do not think about choices, when we just listen to some 'inner voice' which clearly tells us right from wrong.

The theory of habitus represents one of the most formidable challenges to 'rational choice' explanations of social action. Rational choice theory assumes that individuals make rational calculations when they make choices. Yet if, in our mundane practices, we are guided by habitus, we may not actually try to gather all the information which is necessary to make rational choices. We may just listen to our 'inner voice': we fall in love with the person we marry; we buy a house because we like it; we take a job because we cannot resist the temptation. All these examples indicate the non-rational (though far from irrational) elements of social action. When I decide whom to marry, I do not even consider making an attempt to assess who is available on the marriage market. I trust my habitus to guide me in the right way. In purchasing a house I may pretend to behave as a rational actor, but more often than not I will buy a house which resembles the place where my father or grandfather – whom I would like to resemble – lived. The point is that we may not rationally assess the costs and benefits of alternative outcomes as often as we believe. Many of the most important choices in our lives are made by following our 'instincts' – our 'habitus' – rather than by assessing our options in a cool and rational way. Yet from a probabilistic point of view, the sum total of these choices reflects the fact that we are determined social creatures: often, our choices re-create the environment of our nativity or, more often than not, the desired surroundings to which we are 'destined' by virtue of the prevailing social logic.

For this reason, habitus should not be viewed as simply subjective. The dispositions of a player in the social game are hierarchically distributed: how to get things done, how to get out of trouble, what to like and what to dislike, what to avoid and what to aspire towards – all these skills differ according to one's 'starting point' in the game, and are closely tied to family occupational and educational origins: that is to say, habitus is shaped by class structure. This is not to say, however, that habitus is inflexible or completely rigid. As a product of early socialization it is relatively stable, but habitus can also change over time as institutional conditions alter, as class relations develop, or as one's social standing changes. In short, the idea of habitus connects social structure to individual motives, world-views, and actions in a *determining yet relatively autonomous* relationship.

With this understanding it becomes clear that the habitus of agents occupying positions in social space is also a generative principle according to which they reproduce or change the objective relations making up the 'social space' they inhabit. In the context of comparatively stable societies, this idea is useful for capturing the relationship of reinforcement between agents' predispositions on the one hand, and the social positions and relationships they inhabit on the other. Indeed, in some cases this interaction can produce an almost unbreakable circle: if agents with anti-modernist dispositions occupy positions in a pre-modern social structure, social change becomes virtually impossible.

More often, however, change does take place, but not 'according to plan'. In societies undergoing social structural changes, we think the idea of habitus may be even more useful because it provides analytical leverage for examining how the interaction between agents' predispositions and changing social logics might generate historically novel life strategies and choices as people try to stay 'on course' and maintain their social trajectory. In this case, the interaction between habitus and social structure is somewhat of a *bricolage* (to invoke Lévi-Strauss's famous metaphor). 'New' social structures are built out of what is available to agents, by using whatever materials are 'out there' as well as ideas and practices deeply sedimented in their habitus. It is not simply that institutional forms are reproduced during social change, as the path-dependence model would have it, but that social actors build and/or change institutions and social relations in their attempts to stay on their social trajectory – to follow their habitus and preserve as much of their identity as possible – in a rapidly changing social space.

This conceptualization can help us to understand, for example, why the elaboration of socialist rank order was deeply affected by the fact that socialism was attempted in societies which had never experienced bourgeois hegemony, and were still deeply embedded in systems of patronage. Some communist cadres behaved like pre-communist gentry simply because this was one of the few models of behavior available to be emulated. The gentry style was an idea of governing behavior which survived the communist revolution in the form of the practices and understandings (habitus) of the social actors whose biographies spanned the transition from the pre-communist to the communist worlds. On the basis of this logic, we suggest that it is not unlikely or surprising that post-communist entrepreneurs resemble communist functionaries in some respects, since it is significant that bourgeoisification has been attempted in societies emerging from social-ist clientelism, marked by the disintegration of the intellectuals' New Class project. At the same time, the idea of habitus can help us to conceptualize why, in some cases, post-communist actors draw on pre-communist under-standings and world-views to inform institution-building.

It follows from our argument that we disagree strongly with those who think that if the 'right' institutions are implemented, the 'appropriate' behav-iors will inevitably emerge.[30] We think, rather, that institutions and incumbents of institutional positions shape each other in unpredictable ways. For example, we know that communist revolutionaries were mistaken when they believed they could create collectivists by eliminating private property and instituting the 'appropriate' property relations. Older forms of behavior and prior ideas continued to shape individuals' actions within the new collectives. Given such historical precedent, why should we believe the ideologues of *laissez-faire* capitalism when they claim that by instituting iden-tifiable proprietors they will instantly create *Bürgers*: capitalist entrepreneurs and citizens? The habitus of post-communist agents may subvert, constrain, or obstruct radical institutional change. The point is that habitus links indi-vidual actors to social-structural determinants, and in this interactive process, *both are likely to be altered*.[31] Our theory of social change, which we call trajectory correction, is contrasted with the models of social change under-lying the theory of path dependence and neoclassical models in Figure 1.4.

Social change and capitalist transitions

This book is about the post-communist transition as a form of trajectory cor-rection. It is also a book about the *transition to capitalism*. We are conscious, therefore, that our theorizing is heir to a long sociological tradition, since we are returning to some of the great originating questions of classical sociology. Like Marx and Weber, we are asking: what are the origins of capitalism; what are the dynamics of capitalist transition? However, we approach these questions from a very different historical vantage point, and with very dif-ferent analytical tools, from our illustrious classical forebears.

While Weber also focused on actors and their ideologies, and while he also pursued a comparative analysis of capitalism, comparing ancient and modern forms, his view of modern capitalism was that it was a single desti-nation, miraculously born in a unique historical constellation comprised of the 'right' agents, with the 'right' world-views, in conducive socioeconomic conditions. Weber did not conceive of the multiplicity of possible *capitalisms*

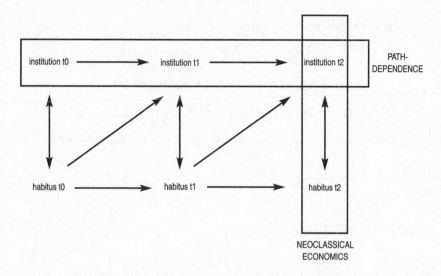

Figure 1.4 The Trajectory Correction Model of Social Change

that have developed in global modernity. And we do not believe he could have imagined our research site which, from any classical perspective, is constituted by the 'wrong agents' with the 'wrong dispositions' at a very different historical juncture. In all probability, Weber could not have imagined a project of building capitalism out of the ruins of communism. None the less, we follow in Weber's footsteps, since we believe that actors and their ideas matter. We simply do not think that the building of capitalism in the late twentieth century is a miracle, although it is certainly a theoretical and empirical puzzle of the first order.

The single most important concern of this book, then, is how capitalism can be made from a socioeconomic system where private property does not exist and in a social structure where there is no class of private proprietors. Because we start from this position, we radicalize some of the classical questions of sociology. We are asking not only: what is the genesis of capitalism?, but also: what are the different types of capitalisms? In other words, the novel historical conditions which we analyze call for a new approach. First, we have to consider different kinds of capitalist societies comparatively, and we have to place our analysis of the agents of transition in a comparative framework. Hubris aside, it is in this sense that we see ourselves as *neoclassical sociologists*, revisiting the core questions of the sociological tradition at the same time as we radicalize them. With this in mind, in the next chapter we turn to a comparative analysis of bourgeoisies, placing the Central European intelligentsia in comparative and historical perspective.

2

The Second *Bildungsbürgertum*:
Intellectuals in the Transition from
Socialism to Capitalism in Central Europe

The central paradox of the 'great transformation' currently under way in East Central Europe is that a capitalist society is being created without a propertied bourgeoisie. By now, it is impossible not to recognize that the most important capitalist institutions – namely, labor and capital markets – are firmly in place. At the same time, a class of property owners, the 'principals' whose irreplaceable role in the great transformation is assumed by virtually all advisors and analysts, is nowhere to be found. The aim of this chapter is to diffuse this apparent paradox. We argue that the transition from socialism to capitalism – which in Chapter 1 we conceptualized as a transition from a socialist 'dual-stratification' system to a class society – has been orchestrated and led by a 'cultural bourgeoisie'. This bourgeoisie is a 'second *Bildungsbürgertum*' composed of the most unlikely allies – former dissident intellectuals and the former communist technocratic–managerial elite. Strange bedfellows indeed, but these two fractions of the intelligentsia have assumed the historic task of a bourgeoisie: civilizing their societies and creating market institutions. Together with the managers of large state or semi-privatized enterprises, they have succeeded in forming themselves into a 'power bloc' controlling all the major command positions of post-communist society.

Such a thesis naturally begs the question: in what sense is capitalism without a propertied bourgeoisie conceivable at all? How can the paradox be diffused? In the first section of this chapter, we try to establish the legitimacy of such a concept. Our central point is that the generic analysis of capitalist economic institutions should be kept conceptually distinct from the genetic analysis of capitalist agents and classes. We consider several historical 'strategic research sites', in periods and regions other than contemporary Central Europe, in which capitalist institutions were either built or managed by agents other than a propertied bourgeoisie.

The second section of the chapter develops a conceptual framework for a historical sociology of capitalist agents: of bourgeois classes and class fractions. The elements for such a sociology already exist in the work of Central European social historians, especially in Jürgen Kocka's distinction between the propertied and educated middle class, an economic bourgeoisie [*Wirtschaftsbürgertum*] and a cultural bourgeoisie [*Bildungsbürgertum*]. Drawing on Weber and Bourdieu, we build on this work to develop a tighter conceptual typology of bourgeois classes. We define the cultural bourgeoisie as a historical coalition of groups and class fractions, whose power and privilege are based on the possession of cultural capital and whose project is to foster the transition from rank order to a system of class stratification. This definition allows us to compare and contrast the 'first' *Bildungsbürgertum*, composed of the nineteenth-century 'educated middle classes', with the 'second' *Bildungsbürgertum*, composed of the post-communist coalition of dissidents, technocrats and managers.

The third section tracks the historical genesis of the post-communist power bloc and its strategy for making capitalism. Here we move away from a typological comparison of the 'first' and 'second' *Bildungsbürgertum* to a historical analysis of their similarities and differences. While we argue that the post-communist power bloc is a direct and conscious heir to the nineteenth-century intelligentsia – a fact which explains many of the similarities between the two groups – we also emphasize a crucial historical distinction between the two: the second *Bildungsbürgertum* emerges from the ruins of the 'New Class' project – that is, the historical detour of the Central European intelligentsia between its two attempts to build a capitalist society. It is marked by the experience of this failure, which forms a paradoxical and somewhat shaky bond between its different fractions.

Thus, this chapter lays the foundations of an analysis of the post-communist transition, along the lines suggested in Chapter 1. The first step in such an analysis is to identify the *agents* of change, and to chart their trajectories. This is precisely what we aim to do with the concept of the *Bildungsbürgertum*.

Is 'capitalism without capitalists' conceivable?
Historical analogies and predecessors

The initial scholarship on the origins of capitalism (Smith, Marx, and to some extent even Max Weber) concentrated almost exclusively on Western Europe, and in particular on England and France. These scholars all assumed – and to some extent demonstrated – that the emergence of a propertied bourgeoisie was the first necessary step in the transition to capitalism. It was self-evident for all of them that an original accumulation of capital in private hands had to take place before market capitalism could emerge. Although they disagreed about the sources and mechanisms by which the original accumulation of capital was accomplished, they all took it to be the natural starting point for their analyses. Nor did any of the participants in the early or later debates about 'the transition from feudalism to capitalism' question this assumption. Instead, historians of the transition have shown that the social origins of the propertied bourgeoisie can be traced to a variety of social groups, such as the gentry in England and artisans and merchants in the Netherlands and France.[1] These findings, however, did not alter the central, self-evident thesis of 'capitalists before capitalism': regardless of their social origins, these agents had to be transformed into individual property owners before feudalism could be torn down.

Marx's theory of the transition pushed this idea even further, arguing not only that the bourgeoisie is formed within the womb of feudalism, but also that the social force which led the anti-feudal revolution was the bourgeoisie. In Marx's analysis, the propertied bourgeoisie *had* to be the revolutionary class, since it was the 'universal estate' of the feudal order; it was the only historic actor interested in the end of the feudal order who was also capable of carrying out a successful revolution. Only the bourgeoisie could have brought the rule of the estates to an end, since this was the only way it could become a dominant class ruling a class society.

More recent scholarship, however, has begun to cast doubt on the assumption that there must be 'capitalists before capitalism'. Over the past decade, historians and sociologists have identified a number of strategic research sites where it can be shown either that capitalism emerged without the leadership of a propertied bourgeoisie in the transformation process (i.e. it was 'capitalism before capitalists'), or that capitalism currently functions in the absence of clear individual owners (in this version it is usually 'capitalism after capitalists'). Let us present these strategic research sites in logical order, moving from those supporting the weakest claim – that the bourgeoisie does not necessarily play an important role in the 'bourgeois revolution' which destroys the feudal order – to the strongest – namely, the 'managerialist thesis' according to which advanced capitalism is marked by the disappearance of the class of private owners in favor of impersonal capital and its agents, the managers.

The revisionist reading of the French Revolution

Even in the 'classical case' of the transition from feudalism to capitalism, in eighteenth-century France, there are scholars who question the importance of the role played by the propertied bourgeoisie in the break-up of the *ancien régime*. French 'revisionist' historians argue that the revolution was neither conducted nor led by the bourgeoisie. Their research shows that struggles between different fractions of the state elite, the aristocracy, the gentry, and the clergy were at its heart. They also document the formidable role played by intellectuals, but nowhere do they find evidence that the urban bourgeoisie was leading the crowds or resisting the power of the monarchy.[2]

Of course, this interpretation has not gone unchallenged, but in the great debate which followed, even more questions were raised. In particular, some historians observed that the French bourgeoisie *could not* have led the revolution against the old order, since it was deeply embedded in feudal relations and co-opted by the feudal state elite.[3] This challenge prompted some Marxists, notably Perry Anderson, to rethink the concept of 'bourgeois revolution'.[4] Anderson criticizes the Marxist theory of the bourgeois revolution as it was formulated by theorists such as Plechanov and Lenin, arguing that their primary concern was to elaborate the strategies of the coming socialist revolution. For this reason, Anderson argues, the Marxist theory of the bourgeois revolution missed the essential difference between the transition from feudalism to capitalism and the transition from capitalism to socialism. The former transition is between two (albeit different) economic systems based on private property,[5] while the latter is from private property to 'socialized property'. Consequently, Anderson argues, it is quite probable that the transition from feudalism to capitalism looked very different from the violent upheaval envisioned by Russian socialists. Given the similarity of property relations in feudalism and capitalism, a propertied bourgeoisie could develop under feudalism without challenging the feudal order. Indeed, in 'mutually advantageous transactions' between the bourgeoisie and landowning nobility, the nobility gradually transformed itself into a part of the propertied bourgeoisie.[6]

Anderson's reformulation of the Marxist theory of bourgeois revolution appears, then, not so much a response to the French revisionists as a rather ingenious reinterpretation of Marxist tenets to accommodate the new evidence put forward by the revisionists. The result is that the concept of 'the bourgeois revolution' is pushed to the background, in favor of a strong distinction between 'pre-industrial' and 'industrial' transitions, which closely resembles Weber's distinction between 'rank order', and 'class stratification'.[7] We are not historians, nor do we specialize in French history; hence we are not prepared to take sides in this debate. In this context, however, we simply note that the 'weak' revisionist claim becomes plausible: the breaking of the feudal order and the legislation of capitalist social relations may have been carried out not by a propertied bourgeoisie, but by other agents. Moreover, this claim is plausible even in the classical case of capitalist transformation. The French revisionists have successfully disputed an important element of Marx's method – that is, deriving the historical action of collective actors from interests imputed to them by virtue of their position in production relations. The revisionists suggest that the 'contradictory class location' of the bourgeoisie within the feudal order was not enough to make it a revolutionary agent – or, to put it more methodologically – that the theoretical analysis of class relations cannot be substituted for the empirical analysis of the historical formation of the identities and interests of collective agents.

Latecomers to modernization

As the capitalist system began to extend all over the globe from the late nineteenth century onwards, the challenge of 'catching up' was faced by many countries that found themselves at the periphery or semi-periphery of the world system: countries with relatively underdeveloped market institutions or archaic, traditional social structures. The drive to 'catch up' and modernize powered numerous attempts, in many different countries, to introduce capitalist economic relations and industrial technology, to create classes of private owners, and to foster capital accumulation, all with a view to improving the country's standing in world trade, and to breaking out of the 'cycle of backwardness'. Some famous cases of successful capitalist transformation occurred this way, and also some notorious cases of failure. Regardless of their success or failure, however, our observation is that practically all these attempts to 'catch up' were initiated by agents other than a capitalist class. Be they enlightened gentry, civil service bureaucrats, or intellectuals trained in the West and committed to Western values, all these agents took upon themselves the task of social and economic modernization in the absence of a class of private proprietors. Indeed, they saw the absence of such a class as something they needed to remedy.

The Meiji Restoration in Japan can be cited as the most successful case in which a Western-trained professional class used government institutions to implement capitalist transformation.[8] Similarly, Gerschenkron argues that during the late nineteenth century, the Russian state was conducting a reasonably successful 'revolution from above', in which economic and social institutions were modernized.[9] In these cases there was either a weak domestic bourgeoisie, or none at all. After World War II in post-colonial Africa there were similar – albeit eventually unsuccessful – projects to build capitalism, usually led by civil service bureaucracies or the military.

What is common to most of these latecomers to modernization is the pattern of 'political capitalism' – that is, the implementation of capitalist institutions 'from above' by the state and by 'enlightened' state elites. Typically, the absence or weakness of a class of private proprietors is perceived as an obstacle on the road to modernization. Indeed, the role of a propertied bourgeoisie is often perceived from the state's point of view as a resource for augmenting state power. Our point is that with latecomers we are no longer analyzing the emergence of capitalism, but its 'diffusion' across the globe. In this sort of analysis the major questions are not about capital accumulation but about the imitation of existing models of capitalism, and the identity and consciousness of the agents who recognize the 'need' for such imitation. We contend that in most cases of the diffusion of capitalism, the need for imitation is recognized by elites interested in protecting and developing the 'national economy' (although in some cases they turn out to have used political office merely to accumulate private wealth). In other words, 'reasons of state' rather than the requirements of a domestic capitalist class were often the major factors behind the diffusion of capitalism. Thus an even stronger version of the 'capitalism before capitalists' claim becomes plausible: capitalist transformation is often managed by the state with a view to creating a class of private proprietors who will contribute to the general development and power of the national economy.

The Central European Bildungsbürgertum

A particular case of latecomers to modernity is that of Central Europe during the nineteenth century.[10] Thinking about the peculiarities of this case allows us to move away from the state-centered model of 'political capitalism' towards a more sociological account of the social actors who take the lead in the process of modernization. Although the model of 'political capitalism' is arguably Prussian, it is also true that in this region of the world, political capitalism found a formidable ally in the form of the educated middle classes. They, not the weak propertied bourgeoisie, were the social agents who took upon themselves the task of building capitalism, and they were interested in far more than augmenting state power.

The work of Jürgen Kocka is particularly useful in this respect.[11] Rather than assuming that capitalism can only follow the emergence of a propertied bourgeoisie, he poses the question of the transition empirically: he asks who are the social actors who are interested in putting an end to the old rank order, and also capable of leading a modernization project to establish a class society? Kocka develops an ambitious, tripartite comparative framework contrasting Western, Central, and Eastern Europe, in terms of the distinction between two types of bourgeoisie: the propertied capitalist class, or economic bourgeoisie [*Wirtschaftsbürgertum*] on the one hand, and the educated middle class, or cultural bourgeoisie [*Bildungsbürgertum*], on the other.[12] Both classes have their own reasons to be dissatisfied with the existing rank order, and both are interested in a more rational, meritocratic system of class stratification. In Western Europe, capitalism was built principally by the economic bourgeoisie, which explains why the West European cultural bourgeoisie, which arrived on the scene when market capitalism was already well established, is best described as a 'professional class'.[13] By contrast, if capitalism had to be made in nineteenth-century Russia, Kocka argues that it could have been built only by the cultural bourgeoisie. The economic bourgeoisie in Russia was minuscule and composed mostly of foreigners, whereas the Russian intelligentsia was growing rapidly in the late nineteenth century, and it was interested in modernizing and Westernizing Russian society. Finally, in contrast with Western Europe and Russia, Kocka argues that Central European capitalism was 'blessed' by an alliance between the educated middle class and a relatively well-formed propertied class. In this alliance the cultural bourgeoisie was the leading partner, since it was older, more numerous, and well positioned in the state apparatus and the universities.[14]

On the basis of Kocka's analysis, we argue that the Central European research site allows us to formulate a much stronger hypothesis about 'capitalism without capitalists' than the other research sites we have explored. Kocka's analysis suggests not only that the breaking of the feudal order and the transition to capitalism can be initiated by agents other than a propertied class, and that propertied classes are, in some cases, the product of conscious efforts by state agents to create capitalist development, but also that the very meaning of the term 'bourgeoisie' should not be equated exclusively with the image of propertied capitalists. We explore this claim and its ramifications in the next section. Here we simply note that this claim is still rather limited since, in Kocka's account, capitalism cannot develop 'without capitalists' altogether. For Kocka, the Central European *Bildungsbürgertum* could be successful only with the assistance of a propertied class, albeit a weak one. Moreover, Kocka suggests that the further the *Bildungsbürgertum* proceeded in the task of capitalist transformation, the more likely it was that the *Wirtschaftsbürgertum* would supplant it.[15] Without an alliance with a propertied class, as in Russia, the capitalist project was much less attractive to the intelligentsia, which was much more likely to abandon it in favor of populist or statist projects. In short, all the research sites we have explored so far are 'weak' inasmuch as they do not allow us to envision a functioning capitalist economy run by somebody other than a class of private proprietors. This difficulty, however, may be simply due to the fact that up until now we have been examining relatively 'underdeveloped' cases of nineteenth- and early-twentieth-century capitalism.

Advanced capitalist managerialism

One of the major debates regarding the development of advanced capitalism revolves around some analysts' claims that we are witnessing the gradual separation of ownership from control, and the concomitant rise of a new class of managers and technocrats.[16] These analysts argue that with the spread of the modern corporation, individual private owners begin to own smaller and smaller portions of stock, and thus begin to cede to managers not only control of the day-to-day management of productive capital, but also strategic decision-making power.

Indeed, theorists of advanced capitalist managerialism suggest that to some extent we already inhabit a 'capitalism without capitalists'. This time it is not because capitalism has been imposed on a relatively underdeveloped society, but because capitalism itself has developed beyond its reliance on individual capitalists. In such a system, authority and effective power are exercised by actors other than private proprietors. These actors legitimate their control of productive assets not through the institution and ideology of private ownership, but through a claim to technical or managerial know-how. Although early analysts argued on this basis that managerialism represented a transcendence of modern capitalism and the beginning of post-capitalist society, later formulations have focused on managerialism and the decline of the capitalist class as part of the ongoing rationalization of the capitalist order. It is in this respect, then, that managerialism is a theory of 'capitalism without capitalists'.

Note, however, that the managerialist claim that ownership and control have been separated in advanced capitalism has been effectively demolished by Maurice Zeitlin.[17] Not only did he show that the weight of the evidence was in favor of the thesis of continued control of American corporations by 'family spheres of influence', but he also argued convincingly that managerial motivations and policies were no different from those of capitalists – that is to say, ruthless profit-seeking was characteristic of managers as well as owners. Although the debate continues,[18] we think that most of Zeitlin's arguments remain valid. For present purposes, however, note that Zeitlin's critique was about the *actuality* of the managerialist thesis, not about its *possibility*. In other words, the managerialist thesis can be reinterpreted as arguing that advanced capitalist institutions offer the *potential* for managerial control, while Zeitlin's critique can be shown to refer to the historically specific reaction to growing managerial authority by the American capitalist class. Indeed, Zeitlin's own critique demonstrates that capitalism is able to function 'without capitalists', since he shows that managers have been successful in maintaining high profit rates. Moreover, recent analyses of the transformation of the American corporate structure point to the hegemony of financial capital within that structure, and the concomitant development of a 'financial conception of control' among corporate managers.[19] These analysts argue that the growing power of finance managers, for whom the corporation is primarily a bundle of financial assets, can guarantee the continued coordination and functioning of the capitalist economy even without a class of private owners. In the context of this literature, our point is much more modest. We claim that in a class constellation different from the American one, it is not inconceivable that managers will be able to control productive capital and coordinate investment decisions without the intervention of private owners. Indeed, this is precisely what we claim is taking place in post-communist Central Europe.

The transition from socialism to capitalism in Central Europe: post-communist managerialism?

During the transition from socialism to capitalism an unprecedented historical situation was created. On the one hand, market institutions have emerged reasonably quickly, and they are increasingly modeled after those in the advanced West. This, as we have noted above, leads to the hegemony of financial capital, and creates the potential for managerial control. On the other hand, the development of a propertied domestic bourgeoisie has been relatively slow, and the project of capitalist transformation has been led by former communist technocrats and managers in cooperation with former dissident intellectuals. These groups control state institutions *and* productive assets; they are conscious followers of the nineteenth-century Central European modernizing intelligentsia, and they bring with them technical knowledge and social prestige accumulated under communism. Thus, two conditions which have never coexisted before – in our terms, 'capitalism before capitalists' and 'capitalism after capitalists' – now characterize the post-communist situation in Central Europe. This is why we have conceptualized the current system as 'capitalism *without* capitalists'. The term 'post-communist managerialism' captures the other essential feature of this historically novel situation. It describes the agents who have led the process of modernization and capitalist transformation – technocrats and managers – and it also describes the basis of their power and authority – managerial know-how and executive position.

We conclude this section with two interrelated points. First, by identifying various strategic research sites and locating our case in relation to them, we have suggested that capitalism can be made – and may even be able to operate – without a propertied bourgeoisie. If this point is conceded, then our hypothesis concerning post-communist managerialism deserves to be tested. Second, while the post-communist system is similar to other cases of 'capitalism without capitalists' we emphasize that this similarity is, at best, only a historical *analogy*. There are some outstanding differences between our cases and their analogues.

First, as Anderson argued, the constellation of actors in the transition from socialism to capitalism is essentially different from the constellation of actors in the transition from feudal or pre-modern society to capitalism. In most transitions from feudalism, a class of proprietors exists. In some cases it has been too weak or too deeply entrenched in feudal social relations to lead the transition, and the task of breaking the old order has been performed by modernizing fractions of the feudal elite in lieu of the bourgeoisie.

No propertied class, however, exists in the post-communist transformation. So, although its name is constantly invoked, it cannot be relied upon to assist in establishing capitalist institutions.

Second, compared with latecomers to modernity, post-communism is blessed (or cursed, depending on one's point of view) with a high level of capital accumulation achieved during the socialist period. Consequently, even though the elites managing the transition may be somewhat similar to those in countries coming late to capitalism – civil servants and intellectuals in the latecomers' case; technocrats, managers, and intellectuals in the Central European case – their typical consciousness, and hence the alliances they are likely to make, are utterly different. Central European technocrats and managers are not imbued with 'reasons of state', and therefore do not seek to concentrate productive resources for the purposes of empowering the nation. Instead, they construe their task as the dismantling of centralist redistribution, and their typical approach has been 'managerialist', consisting in a careful, hands-on fine-tuning of the transformation process.

Finally, post-communist managers may appear similar to managers in advanced Western capitalism, both in terms of the way they legitimate their authority and in terms of the structural potentialities of their positions in large industrial enterprises. We would emphasize, however, that these similarities are more apparent than real. Post-communist and advanced Western managers occupy positions in capitalist institutions at different stages of development, and they act in strikingly different class contexts. Post-communist managers have been schooled in socialism, not in Ivy League business schools; they manage former state-socialist firms, not multinationals; and they are under neither the discipline nor the tutelage of a propertied bourgeoisie, since none currently exists.

All these differences derive from the specific historical genesis of the social agents who are engaged in the project of capitalist transformation in Central Europe. This is the conclusion we would like to draw from this section: if one aims to understand the concrete results of capitalist transformation in Central Europe, one cannot work with an abstract model of 'capitalism' based on a generic analysis of capitalist economic institutions as they 'should' be, or as they are 'in the West'. One needs, first, to recognize that capitalism is not only a 'system', but also a *class society* composed of differing constellations of classes and class fractions. Additionally, we argue that the characteristics of these classes and the alliances between them, as they are historically, conjuncturally, and contingently formed, are highly consequential for the end result. Thus one cannot escape the need for a genetic analysis of capitalist agents and classes.

Which bourgeoisie? A conceptual framework for a historical sociology of capitalist agents

The best historical analogy with the post-communist transition to capitalism is the nineteenth-century *Bildungsbürgertum* project of the Central European intelligentsia. In fact, in the next two sections we argue that there are stronger theoretical and historical affinities between these two than mere analogy. In the next section, we tell the story of the Central European intelligentsia: how the educated middle classes of the nineteenth century embarked on a project of embourgeoisement; how they took long detours in their almost fatal love affairs with fascism and communism; how they aspired to become the 'New Class', to replace both the bourgeoisie and the communist ruling estate as the enlightened rulers of an engineered society; and finally how, by the mid 1980s, they had returned to their nineteenth-century trajectory and once again adopted the role of a cultural bourgeoisie. Before we plunge into these historical waters, however, we need to clarify the theoretical framework which allows us to identify the essential similarities between the two periods.

The problem can be stated first in simple terms. The apparent similarity between the two epochs is that some of the major actors in both cases are intellectuals. Analytically speaking, one can also see similarities in their peculiar social position as 'socially unattached'. The sort of positions these intellectuals claimed to deserve, on the basis of their education and knowledge, were not offered to them by society in either epoch. Consequently, their consciousness was similar. They were bitter, since they felt excluded from political power; while at the same time they thought they were better qualified to rule than those who occupied political office, be they aristocrats or communist apparatchiks. Hence there was a similarity in their interests and conscious projects: both groups of intellectuals were interested in the transformation of the old order (be it gentry-ruled or communist) into civil society. Finally, their claims were not based merely on the fact that intellectuals had better credentials than the incumbents of political office (although they did not neglect to mention this). In both cases, their claim to power and entitlement was based on the unique prestige accorded to 'men of ideas' in Central Europe. These intellectuals were far more successful than their Western counterparts in persuading society of their role as moral and spiritual leaders. They were never perceived as mere 'professionals', with a monopoly over technical knowledge, but as 'intellectuals' with a special ethical responsibility for society as a whole. They were supposed to be the searchlight into the future, the soul of the nation.[20]

The similarities in the roles of these two groups of intellectuals notwithstanding, there are also fundamental differences between the two epochs. After all, and almost by definition, intellectuals are but one fraction, and not necessarily the dominant fraction, of either the post-communist intelligentsia or the nineteenth-century educated middle class. The groups with which the intellectuals allied themselves differ across the two periods. Professional civil servants – a social category that was destroyed by the communists – formed an important part of the modernizing intelligentsia of the late nineteenth century. Technocrats and managers – a social category that did not exist at the time of the first *Bildungsbürgertum* – have played major roles in the transition from communism to capitalism. Why, then, do we call the post-communist intelligentsia 'the second *Bildungsbürgertum*'? What are the grounds on which we claim that despite the differences in the composition of the two alliances, there is a similar project and a similar coherence to these two groups from these different time periods? To answer this question, we begin by clarifying the concept of *Bildungsbürgertum*.

The meaning of Bürgertum

The term 'bourgeoisie' is reasonably straightforward in English, and even more straightforward in French.[21] Its meaning, at least for social scientists, refers unambiguously to a class of private proprietors. Similarly, 'bourgeois society' in these languages is synonymous with capitalism. Modern social life, of course, cannot be reduced to economic interests and institutions, but since the eighteenth century, French and English social scientists have been well equipped with terms to conceptualize 'politics' and 'culture' as relatively autonomous from 'economics'. The most useful conceptual tool for this purpose has been the idea of 'civil society' (and of citizenship). It denotes a social reality which has strong historical and theoretical affinities with markets and capitalist class relations, but cannot be reduced to these and remains, therefore, analytically separable from capitalism and the bourgeoisie.

Those who had to write social science in German (and other languages whose social science logic was shaped by German[22]), however, were blessed and doomed by the fact that the neat distinction between the bourgeoisie as a class of proprietors and the bourgeoisie as citizens, and thus between capitalism and civil society, could not be made in this language. The German concept of *Bürger* or *Bürgertum* is fuzzier, and at the same time richer, than the concept of the 'bourgeoisie'.[23]

For example, the double meaning of this concept has created a space of ambiguity in the work of Marx, which has been exploited by latter-day Marxists to interpret the founding father in diverse ways. In the early works, prior to 1845–46, Marx used the term '*bürgerliche Gesellschaft*' to describe modernity.[24] In later works, and especially where he strove to achieve analytical rigor, he switched to the term 'capitalist society'.[25] '*Bürgerliche Gesellschaft*' could still be found in the *Grundrisse*,[26] but it was rarely used in texts 'authorized' by Marx. Arguably, the mature Marx decided to abandon the notion of *bürgerliche Gesellschaft*, since he was irritated by the ambiguity of the concept. With his theory of historical materialism fully developed, he could no longer see the benefits of its richness. In the theory of historical materialism, the political and cultural phenomena captured by the notion of 'civil society' were subordinate and secondary to underlying economic institutions and class relations. A concept which fused these two disparate orders of phenomena served only to mystify the determinate relations between them, and the mature Marx had no need of such mystifications. The 'young Marx', of course, later became a source of endless quarrels among Marxists, partly because the term '*bürgerliche Gesellschaft*' could be translated either as 'civil society' or as 'capitalist society', a choice of words which was far from innocent ideologically or politically.

But to choose between the two translations, as some Marxists did, is to abandon the insights one can gain from the inherent ambiguities of the term *Bürgertum*. Precisely because it is 'ambiguous', we argue, the idea of *Bürger* and *Verbürgerlichung* (poorly translated as embourgeoisement), captures the meaning of 'the great transformation' of modernity more precisely.[27] Moreover, it is a more accurate description of the process of modernization in Germany during the eighteenth and nineteenth centuries. The apparent 'double' meaning of the term *Bürger* derives from a concrete social context, not from some inexplicable German attraction to analytical imprecision, as Marx and many Anglo-American social scientists would have it.

The term *Bürger* signifies at one and the same time the class of proprietors and the category of citizen. Indeed, it probably emphasizes the idea of citizenship a little more than the idea of property. After all, the term was coined initially to describe those 'who live in cities'.[28] It is meant to describe a form of life distinct from that of the landed classes – that is to say, of both the gentry and the peasants. *Bürgers* are somewhat more affluent than peasants, and certainly better educated. At the same time, they are distinct from the nobility because they are sober and utilitarian, while nobles are obliged to engage in 'conspicuous consumption' to maintain their status honor. Thus, gentry education (which may be considerable) is construed by *Bürgers* as 'useless' in comparison with their skills-oriented learning. Members of the gentry pursue art rather than mathematics; philosophy rather than science; rhetoric rather than law.[29] The most important feature which distinguishes *Bürgers*, however, is that they are free – or, to be more precise, that they have gained certain political rights. *Bürgertum* implies 'urban autonomy': the right of cities to govern themselves; the right to pass their own laws and have their own courts; and the right to collect their own taxes, rather than be subject to direct taxation by feudal lords.

As Weber explained, the significance of this all-important autonomy was that it shifted the determination of identity from lineage, or bloodline, to territoriality.[30] *Bürgers* are those who reside in cities. Even escaped serfs could become 'citizens', solely by virtue of residence, if they dwelled long enough in the city. Urban residence broke the power of the bloodline and obliged the lord to forgo his claim on the serf. This is why 'Stadtluft macht frei' – 'urban air sets you free' – and this, incidentally, is why Weber called the authority system of cities 'non-legitimate'. It was non-legitimate precisely because it challenged the core institution of traditional authority, the personal master–serf relation assigned on the basis of lineage.

Hence, the term *Verbürgerlichung* denotes not only, or even principally, the development of markets and capitalist private property, but the diffusion of a form of life associated with the civil liberties enjoyed by *Bürgers*. It refers to the modernization of social relations, the breaking of rank order, and its replacement by a logic of class stratification. Associated with *Verbürgerlichung* is not only 'possessive individualism', but also the values of civil rights, autonomy, meritocracy, self-mastery, culture and credentials.

This understanding of *Verbürgerlichung* is specifically Central European. It reflects the region's uneven process of modernization.[31] During the late eighteenth and early nineteenth centuries, Central Europe was clearly economically backward: market institutions and industrial development lagged far behind post-revolutionary France, the Netherlands, or England. Moreover, the economic and political clout of the class of private proprietors was nowhere near as developed as that of their more prosperous West European peers. At the same time, Central Europe was already 'modernized' in the sense that a bourgeois form of life was well advanced. The educational system was large and well established, and the Central European educated middle classes were as numerous and probably even more influential than Western intellectuals and professionals at the same time. It is in this context of 'uneven modernization' that the idea of a uniquely Central European *Verbürgerlichung* was formulated. Slowly but surely, Central European intellectuals and 'mandarins' began to recast the meaning of *Bürgertum*. It no longer denoted merely the autonomy of the city-dweller, but the culture and education [*Bildung*] of the educated classes.[32] After all, the heroes of this culture – Goethe, Schiller, Kant – were eminent *Bürgers* themselves, prototypes of what being 'modern' meant. The members of the educated class were thus decidedly on the side of modernity, civil society, and the *Bürger* form of life.

Education and educational reform were the Central European substitute for what the English or French Revolutions achieved in the West: the diffusion of the bourgeois form of life. During the late eighteenth and early nineteenth centuries, school curricula were changed to include a far greater emphasis on the sciences. History teaching no longer focused on the tales of kings and queens, but in a grand bourgeois way reached back to Cicero, the Roman Republic, and the notion of 'civic education'. One of the most

telling reforms was the relocation of many boarding schools from the countryside to the cities, into the strongholds of the *Bürgers*. Originally, the
children of the aristocracy received their education at home from private
tutors who were usually treated as servants. In the new urban boarding
schools, children of the urban bourgeoisie, the gentry, the clergy, and artisans
roomed together, studied together, and were taught the value of education
and respect for the 'man of culture'. This was the nursery of the emergent
Bildungsbürgertum, where children from diverse social origins were brought
together and taught a new *esprit de corps*, a way of 'being modern' through
culture and education.[33]

Here is the essence of our argument: we define the bourgeoisie not 'struc-
turally', by its position in the relations of production, but 'historically', as the
class whose historical project is to modernize society.[34] A historical sociology
of the bourgeoisie should not solve its comparative puzzles by force of definition – by defining the bourgeoisie according to purely economic criteria.
Instead, a historical sociology of the bourgeoisie should seek to identify collective agents who are the bearers of the project of modernization. Nor do
we believe that the reader should entertain even a 'weaker' version of the
above economism: that the *Bildungsbürgertum* is a 'substitute bourgeoisie', a
secondary replacement of the 'bourgeoisie proper', the economic bourgeoisie. As we have learned from the French debate, the class of proprietors
can be deeply embedded in feudal relations, content in its role as a *rentier*
class and financier for the monarch. Consequently, the educated middle
classes may be a far more effective agent of modernization than the members of the economic elite. We argue, following Kocka, that this is what
happened in the Central European transition to modernity: instead of being
led by the weak and traditional economic bourgeoisie, the 'Great
Transformation' was led by the cultural bourgeoisie.[35] After all, the transition from rank order to class stratification is about as important to the
making of modernity as the accumulation of private capital. In this task, the
cultural bourgeoisie was frequently a far more effective agent of
modernization.

The meaning of Bildung: *culture as capital and symbolic domination*

So far we have explained why it is meaningful to use the concept of the
bourgeoisie in the plural, especially in analyzing Central European societies.
Not one bourgeois class but multiple bourgeoisies were standing at the
cradle of modernity in these societies. Moreover, we have argued that *which*
of these bourgeoisies was the driving force behind the Great Transformation
is an empirical question. In this context, we now turn to the issue of what it
means to argue, as we have, that the Central European intelligentsia was a
'cultural bourgeoisie'.[36] The *self-definition* of the modernizing class of Central

Europe revolved around culture and education [*Bildung*], but is it possible to use this 'folk' category to answer the question of 'classness' – that is, can we understand this assembly of actors as a collective agent organized on the basis of a shared relation to 'culture'?

Our answer to this question is a qualified 'yes', and it is based in large part on the work of Pierre Bourdieu. After all, Bourdieu earned early fame by introducing the notion of 'cultural capital', though – as we noted above in our discussion of 'habitus' – he used it primarily for the purpose of analyzing social reproduction rather than the transition to modernity.[37] For this reason, we suggested that we need to supplement and historicize his conceptual framework using Weber's historical sociology of forms of stratification. In this way, we can redeploy the concept of 'cultural capital' as a key building block for our theoretical definition of the *Bildungsbürgertum*, since it allows us to appraise the 'classness' of the educated middle classes – that is to say, the degree to which they are capable of acting as a collective agent entrusted with the task of building modern civilization.

Bourdieu's definition of 'cultural capital' is complex, and relies on an analogy with Marx's analysis of economic capital and the dialectic of alienation it embodies. The essence of his argument is the distinction between two forms of knowledge: a 'practical mastery' of practices, which usually takes the form of tacit, everyday, habitual, and even embodied knowledge; and a 'symbolic mastery' of practices, which is the discursive capacity to codify, theoretically or abstractly, what others are doing or saying.[38] 'Cultural capital' is the sum total of dispositions, positions, and titles which allows individuals and groups to appropriate the discursive mechanisms of 'symbolic mastery'. The effect of using the mechanisms of 'symbolic mastery' in general is to create a social distance between those who engage in everyday practices, and those who can formulate the 'principles' of these practices.[39] The effect of using these mechanisms within a school or a school-like environment, however, is much more devastating, since the social distance becomes a hierarchy of excellence and receives the institution's seal of approval. Thus, the accumulation of cultural capital is dependent on the institution which deprives 'practical mastery' of its efficacy (in the same way as the accumulation of economic capital is dependent on the expropriation of workers from the means of subsistence): the institution, in the case of cultural capital, being the modern school and the modern education system in general.[40]

We would emphasize, however, that the accumulation of cultural capital should not be understood as literally analogous to the accumulation of economic capital. Certainly, the education system creates a situation in which individuals can get ahead to better-paid jobs and positions of influence by appropriating the mechanisms of 'symbolic mastery'. But this is a relatively insignificant consequence in comparison with the general effect of the education system, which is to reproduce the 'symbolic domination' and social distance ('distinction') between those who 'know' and those who 'don't know'. As with capital accumulation for the economic bourgeoisie, 'symbolic domination' constitutes the collective project of the educated class.

In this sense, the collective project of the educated tends to make them bearers of modernity – that is to say, a cultural bourgeoisie. As they build new educational institutions, like modern universities, and as they create universal education, they turn what was always implicit in the position of the 'men of knowledge' – the rejection of 'practical mastery' – into a postulate of modernity. As they strive to distinguish themselves from the rest of society, the mandarin intellectual glorifies the value of education as spiritual nobility, and rejects all forms of knowledge which are merely 'practical'. As is the case for the economic bourgeoisie, however, this collective project does not make the cultural bourgeoisie inevitably or wholly on the side of modernity. In their quest for cultural prestige and distinction, the educated create credentials and titles for themselves. They strive for 'spiritual nobility', which is equivalent to the distinction of the temporal nobility. As we shall see below, such intellectuals are easily seduced by the prospect of gentrification.[41]

Forms of capital in the social spaces of traditional, capitalist, and socialist societies

Thus, just as it is possible to think of economic capital as material wealth, in particular as ownership of productive assets such as a business, or stocks and bonds, it is also possible to think of educational credentials as the best approximation of what cultural capital signifies.[42] For our purposes, the crucial point is that Bourdieu argues that these two forms of capital are alternative sources of power and privilege, and that cultural capital is at least 'relatively autonomous' from economic capital in shaping the system of social stratification.[43]

According to Bourdieu, position in social space is determined by the volume and composition of the capitals one holds. Thus, whether one is 'on top' or at the bottom, whether one is at the 'center of power' or at its margins, is to a large extent a reflection of whether one possesses capital and, if so, how much, and what kind. We have already discussed Bourdieu's empirical observation that in the social hierarchy of French society, possession of economic capital is generally the most useful, and that cultural capital plays an important but secondary role in determining one's position in that hierarchy.

The actual analysis is more complicated, however, and also more realistic, since Bourdieu discusses other forms of capital which play a role in structuring the social hierarchy. The most important of these is 'social capital' – social ties and networks which, independently of one's credentials or money, can help one gain power and prestige. The better networked one is – the more people one knows and, more importantly, the more people who know *about* one – the more influential one is, the more obligations are owed to one, the more 'trust' one can rely on in one's negotiations with others. In other words, the more 'social capital' one has. Bourdieu claims that in French society, social capital generally plays a marginal role in structuring social hierarchies within classes and class fractions. Social capital distinguishes those individuals who are more successful than others or have managed to become 'representatives' of these groups. Simply by virtue of belonging to the dominant class, elite individuals possess more social capital than others, but no important class distinction can be made on the basis of social capital; no class fraction is structured by it. This is because social capital, unlike cultural and economic capital, is only weakly *institutionalized* in contemporary France.[44]

To summarize: modern capitalist societies are characterized by a class structure or a stratification order in which economic capital is dominant, while cultural capital is relatively autonomous but plays a secondary role in stratifying the dominant class. Social capital is subordinate and de-institutionalized. Personal networks, of course, matter a great deal in a modern capitalist society, but one's position in social space is defined mostly by wealth, and additionally by one's certificate of education. So although personal connections may mediate the effects of wealth and credentials by facilitating the smooth functioning of the other forms of capital, social capital rarely supersedes or counteracts economic and cultural capital.

To complicate matters even further, it might be useful to think about advanced capitalist societies from a comparative perspective. It may be that Bourdieu emphasizes the relative autonomy of cultural capital because he is describing the particularities of French society. It is difficult not to notice that his thinking has been greatly influenced by the extraordinary role 'Les Grandes Écoles' (École normale supérieure, École Nationale d'Administration, École des Hautes Études Commerciales, École Polytechnique, etc.)[45] play in France. Virtually the entire French elite is channeled through these schools, which together comprise a unique system of indoctrination in 'symbolic domination', and serve as exemplary markers of distinction. At the other end of the scale, Japan is probably the best example of an advanced capitalist country where social capital is the most influential and relatively autonomous. Japanese capitalism is structured by extraordinary networks which connect firms both vertically and horizontally, and by networks within enterprises which tie employees and employers together through bonds of loyalty and responsibility. One's position in Japanese social structure is thus dependent not only on one's wealth or education, but also on one's place within these networks.[46] The point is not that cultural capital in France or social capital in Japan can override the primacy of economic capital, but that within advanced capitalist societies the importance of education and social networks is variable, and tends to distinguish one form of capitalism from another. American capitalism, for example, may be conceptualized as a middle case between France and Japan in this respect. Degrees from Ivy League schools, and prestigious business and law schools, are immensely important for the reproduction of the American business elite, but their effect is more than explained by the upper-class origins of candidates to these schools, and their personal network connections.[47] Credentials are necessary for getting ahead in the United States, but they are not as consequential as they are in France; network ties are also essential for conducting business, but they are not as vital as they are in Japan.

The three forms of capital provide us with relatively simple but potent tools for representing and comparing diverse orders of stratification, and also for analyzing the transition from one such order to another, such as the transition to modernity, or the post-communist transition. In this way, we can further clarify the concept of the 'cultural bourgeoisie' and the similarities between the post-communist intelligentsia and the nineteenth-century Bildungsbürgertum.

Specifically, it is our suggestion that traditional, pre-capitalist societies are usually marked by the dominance of social capital. If this argument seems far-fetched at first, it is probably because we tend to understand social capital as interpersonal networks, and fail to see how a whole stratification order could be built on such a flimsy basis. But this understanding derives from the fact that we live in capitalist societies, societies in which social capital is at its most diffuse, in its least *institutionalized* state. In a feudal society, however, the holders of social capital do not need to rely on the constant, laborious mobilization of personal obligations and debts. Rather, the obligations owed to them are guaranteed by their titles, by their position in the traditional order of estates, by the personal fealty owed to them by their subordinates. In short, social capital is highly institutionalized in feudal systems, and – to put it in Max Weber's terms – it takes the form of *status honor*. In feudal society, institutionalized social capital is not only the single most important indicator of privileged status, it is also the principle according to which the other forms of capital are valued. Thus, the possession of economic and cultural capital provides important resources even in feudal society, but within limits carefully circumscribed by the estate order.

We have already suggested that it is also possible to consider state-socialist societies as societies in which social capital, albeit in a modern form, was dominant. The ultimate source of power and privilege under communism was the *party*, and the highly institutionalized network of ties and obligations the party constituted. The capacity to command this network and to appropriate the powers and benefits it produced was given not in the traditional form of the bloodline but in the quasi-modern, quasi-rational political organization of the 'office' a person occupied. Hence social capital was institutionalized as 'political capital': as membership of the Communist Party, or of the *nomenklatura* or the central committee. Devotion and loyalty to the party, the bosses, and communist ideology on the one hand, and the willingness to implement the work necessary for the functioning of the party network machine on the other, were the main criteria determining position and promotion in the social space of communism.

Herein lies one of the important similarities between the post-communist intelligentsia and the nineteenth-century *Bildungsbürgertum*. Both embarked on a strategy of embourgeoisement and attempted to valorize their own cultural capital in a struggle against the holders of institutionalized social capital. But herein also lie some of the important differences between these two groups. We are not the first to have emphasized the analogies between feudalism and communism, but in following Bourdieu we hope our comparison is more conceptually rigorous, and consequently better attuned to nuances. Thus we argue that characterizing communism as 'feudal–socialism' or 'neo-traditionalism', as some analysts have,[48] overlooks important differences between the two periods. First, social capital is institutionalized quite differently in socialism and in feudalism. Feudal social capital was institutionalized as traditional status honor; thus the only way in which it was detached from the person of the noble was through inheritance and the bloodline. As Mark Bloch has shown, this was precisely how feudal stratification evolved. As social capital was institutionalized, the relatively merit-based system of chivalry was restricted to legal inheritance.[49] Communist political capital, by contrast, was institutionalized as modern-rational organizational membership. Hence not only was it not attached to the person of any single individual, but it did not preclude an element of achievement and mobility.

A second – and related – difference is that the roles played by the two other forms of capital also differ in feudal and communist systems. Under communism, political loyalty could not be guaranteed by the traditional mechanisms of kinship and fealty, as it could in feudalism, so credentials tended to become an additional, reliable indicator of loyalty. Thus, 'the party' expected individuals, even if they were promoted on the basis of their political capital, to acquire the appropriate educational credentials if they wanted to maintain their new offices and positions of authority. In this sense, cultural capital played a role under communism which it did not have under feudalism. Credentials were required as further demonstrations of loyalty – that is to say, cultural capital was subordinate to social capital – but at the same time cultural capital became an increasingly important determinant of life chances, and tended to become 'relatively autonomous' of party membership. The same cannot be said of economic capital. Its position in communist society was probably analogous to the position of social capital in Western capitalist societies. It was subordinate, unimportant, and de-institutionalized. Moreover, in the post-revolutionary phase of early communism, former possession of economic capital was a handicap rather than an asset. Former members of the propertied bourgeoisie were either downwardly mobile, or they had to compensate for their bourgeois past by demonstrating their possession of highly desirable *cultural capital*. Sometimes they even had to outbid communists in demonstrating their ideological commitment and loyalty to the party.[50]

In feudal society, on the other hand, the situation was precisely the opposite: credentials hardly existed, and they certainly did not play the role of additional indicators of loyalty. Nobles were educated, but the content of education was determined largely by the 'third estate'. In short, cultural capital was subordinate, insignificant and de-institutionalized. Economic capital, on the other hand, played a much more important role, since – as Perry Anderson argues – both feudal nobles and proto-capitalist bourgeois were individual property owners. The flow of money gradually came to function, in part, as a substitute for the flow of loyalty. Not only did it become possible to 'buy' noble titles and offices, but from the start, feudal alliances were held together by ties of money and monetary obligations.

A reinterpretation of the Weberian distinction between rank [Stand] and class [Klasse]

The analogy between the dominant position of social capital in both feudal and socialist social spaces sheds a new light on Weber's distinction between 'rank order' and 'class stratification'. It allows us to preserve some of the more instructive elements of this distinction, while going beyond the antinomy between 'traditionalism' and 'modernity' with which it was infused. This antinomy, which Weber shared with most other nineteenth-century intellectuals, has been discredited by more recent scholarship, and we ourselves are uncomfortable with it. To our minds, to collapse the phenomenon of twentieth-century socialism into this nineteenth-century distinction overlooks what was a most significant part of the socialist project: the fact that it attempted to overcome this antinomy. After all, socialism was unmistakably a modernization project, the progeny of Enlightenment ideas. Nobody believed more ardently in Enlightenment values than Karl Marx, although the same cannot always be said of his followers. And despite the fact that Central European socialism replicated many of the features of the quasi-traditional society which preceded it, it is also true that 'real socialism' in practice put a great deal of emphasis on meritocracy over the tyranny of ascribed characteristics. Socialist regimes initiated a veritable revolution in elite recruitment processes when they first came to power, and they effectively criticized capitalism and private property precisely for not being meritocratic enough.[51] At the same time, socialism possessed many traits which are analogous to those Weber and his followers regularly classify as 'traditional': the embedding of the economy in political and social relations; the emphasis on substantive rationality; the important role played by world-views and ideologies; and the leading role of the Communist Party.

To state it bluntly: our point is that the distinction between tradition and modernity is unhelpful in understanding what socialism was. We believe, however, that by bringing in Bourdieu's theory – and especially the concept of 'social capital' – to inform Weber's distinction between 'rank' and 'class', we go a long way towards overcoming this archaism, thus rescuing the 'rational core' of Weber's analysis.

Our theoretical ambition is to develop a concept of 'rank' which does not necessarily describe a traditional social order. Weber's theory of social structure has been interpreted in different ways. Some – most eloquently Runciman – read Weber as if he were proposing a multidimensional approach to stratification analysis.[52] According to this view, Weber's 'class, status and power' are three dimensions of social inequality. In our interpretation, however, Weber is a historical sociologist who describes two distinct logics of stratification: rank order [*Stand*] and class stratification [*Klasse*]. In this interpretation, power is not a third dimension, but the dependent variable. The key question is: what is the social basis of the power exercised in a given society – is it class, or is it rank?

If we do not interpret the two logics as an evolutionary movement from traditional to modern, then the crucial variable here is 'embeddedness': in Weber's work, 'class' presumes a social structure in which the economy has been disembedded, and could be conceived as a sphere of social reality in and of itself. Once this happens, the inexorable operation of economic institutions begins to determine the life chances of individuals, and hence also their identities and the groups they form. Of course, as many analysts have pointed out, the political center, as well as ethnic groups and interpersonal networks, play an important role in determining the distribution of power and the outcome of social actions,[53] but they do so principally as 'secondary characteristics'.[54] We suggest thinking of individuals and groups as holding bundles of different stocks, or as wielding card 'hands' with different colors. Among these stocks, or cards, or 'capitals', there is always one which is dominant, and our only claim is that in class stratification the 'trump' stock or card is economic capital. Social and cultural capital play only complementary roles. As in the stock exchange, people are, of course, careful not to put all their eggs in one basket. They invest in the most profitable stock, but also take care to invest in other, less profitable, but maybe more secure stocks, in case something goes wrong. Social capital in particular is the 'pension fund' of individuals under capitalism; it is a survival strategy when everything else fails.

Looking at the other side of the distinction, we find that Weber's idea of 'rank' stands for a logic of stratification in which economic institutions are still embedded in feudal political and legal structures. In this order, the distribution of power and life chances is determined primarily by the structure of interrelated obligations, in particular the obedience owed to a personal master, whose claim to authority is based on age-old rules and on 'status honor'. There are two elements in this conceptualization: first, the suggestion that the basis of social power is in a network of social ties and obligations; second, that the capacity to monopolize and accumulate this power is justified by reference to 'traditional authority'. If we discard this second, historically specific, element included in the notion of 'rank', an analogy with socialism becomes possible. Socialism represents a qualitatively new type of rank order, in which economic institutions are re-embedded in the political structures of the Communist Party–state. As with feudalism, politics is in command, and loyalty to the master is all-important. The differences between the two have more to do with the mode of justification of this power network, and less with its structural properties. The politics which is in command in a communist society is justified according to rationalistic criteria, not tradition. The party is a political master, not a personal one. The party–state is not an ascriptive order, but a voluntary one. The party–state certainly attempts to legitimate itself by claiming that joining it is a matter of 'choice' – it is a voluntary organization.

But if the ideal-typical notion of rank order is based on social capital, and the ideal type of class stratification is based on economic capital, how does cultural capital fit into this analysis? Historical experience seems to indicate that hitherto no stable stratification order has ever existed in which cultural capital was the dominant form. There was no lack of intellectuals who dreamt about a 'good society', in which the major source of honor and power would be knowledge, but they never had enough clout to achieve this ideal.

Consequently, the dominance of cultural capital has appeared historically as a transitory phenomenon. It is dominant only when one logic of stratification crumbles, and another has not yet been established. The role of cultural capital in our theory is not unlike the role of 'charisma' in Weber's theory of social change. Indeed, we may even be so bold as to suggest that in using it as we do we resolve several ambiguities and difficulties noted in relation to the concept of 'charisma'.

According to Weber: 'the term charisma will be applied to a certain quality of an individual personality by virtue of which he is considered extraordinary and treated as endowed with supernatural, superhuman or at least specifically exceptional powers or qualities'. Thus at one and the same time Weber claims that charisma is a quality of an individual, but also that it has to be 'attributed' to this individual, which means that it is not quite an objective attribute of the person who is perceived as charismatic leader.[55] Similarly, cultural capital has to be 'recognized' in order to become effective. Those who exercise symbolic mastery can do so only if they manage to persuade others of the validity of their truth claims, or of the usefulness of their knowledge, neither of which can really be judged according to objective criteria.[56]

In the case of 'charisma', however, it is always an individual who is supposed to carry these superhuman characteristics, and Weber can never really escape the insinuation that this is indeed an exceptional individual. Thus, the idea of the *Übermensch* floats around in Weber's theory of charisma. These connotations are, to say the least, a source of discomfort for the late twentieth-century reader, who knows that Weber is located in time halfway between Nietzsche and Hitler. In this context, the concept of cultural capital is attractive because it dislocates this problem from the individual to the *discourse*. What has to be recognized are not individual characteristics, but the validity of truth claims and the discursive procedures for producing and manifesting validity.

What sort of stratification logic, then, does cultural capital represent? We would argue that a system where power and privileges are derived primarily from the possession of cultural capital can be represented only as some sort of 'mix' between the ideal types of 'rank order' and 'class stratification'.[57] Such a society would be based on neither rank nor class, but would be characterized by attributes of both logics of stratification. This is evident in the most common institutionalization of cultural capital as 'credentials'. We can express this observation in the following theorem, derived from the work of Randall Collins: *The more disembedded economic institutions are from social relations, the easier it is to accumulate and convert economic capital, but the same does not hold for cultural capital. The more disembedded credentialling institutions are from social relations, the harder it is to accumulate and convert cultural capital.*[58] Thus, the more socially dominant credentialling is, the more reminiscent it is of the process by which one enters a status group, rather than a class: it involves rituals and initiation ceremonies, such as examinations, and the conferring of degrees, which are calculated to maximize social recognition for the discourse of the group, and to create community and solidarity among its members. Additionally, a host of 'irrelevant' social characteristics – such as membership in ethnic and racial groups, lifestyles and tastes – are usually of great importance in defining social groups constituted by cultural capital, and for distinguishing the 'genuine intellectuals' from the rest. At the same time, the more disembedded cultural capital is, the more it functions in a 'pure' way approximating the logic of class stratification, the more it tends to develop mechanisms of de-institutionalization and delegitimation, which render recognition difficult and contentious. The victory of the 'enlightened' over their opponents represented by the universalism of truth, the culture of critical discourse, or the force of the better argument, also represents their inevitable undoing.

A stratification regime in which cultural capital is the dominant form, then, plays the same role in our theory of social change as charisma does in Weber's theory. With some immodesty, we would claim that this is a superior theory to Weber's because it allows us to explain social change not by relying on the appearance of unique individuals but by identifying the specific social mechanisms by which epochal change is induced. These mechanisms are the delegitimation of hegemonic ideologies which justify particular logics of stratification, and the production of counter-hegemonies, which are probably the most important revolutionary acts in history. To put it differently, and within the Marxist tradition: those intellectuals who constitute themselves as a cultural bourgeoisie are the most likely to be a 'universal estate', since they represent the development of a class logic of stratification. However, although they are the status group which has an interest in eliminating 'rank order' and establishing a logic of class stratification, because they are a group organized on the basis of cultural capital, they are unlikely to establish their own class rule.

The genesis of the post-communist strategy of capitalist transformation

In the previous section we made an attempt to offer a tighter conceptual foundation to distinguish between different types of bourgeoisies. We attempted to show how a cultural bourgeoisie defined by the possession of cultural capital might make a believable attempt to lead the process of transition from a society rooted in rank order to one stratified by class. By conceptualizing socialism as a modern rank order, we suggested that the agents who transformed socialism in Central Europe could be seen as a 'second *Bildungsbürgertum*', and that their efforts could be seen as analogous to those of the 'first *Bildungsbürgertum*' of the late nineteenth century. In this section, we would like to tell the same story historically. To this end, we trace the social history of the Central European intelligentsia as a process of 'interrupted embourgeoisement' – 'interrupted' not so much because of the intervention of an external force, but because the first *Bildungsbürgertum* could not sustain the project of capitalist transformation, and began a long love affair with left- and right-wing radicalisms. This love affair culminated in the failed 'New Class' project of the middle communist period. With their aspirations crushed, Central European intellectuals then reinvented their legitimate marriage with capitalism, and returned to the trajectory of capitalist transformation as a second *Bildungsbürgertum*. Let us compose the social history of the Central European intelligentsia as if it were a sonata in three movements.

First movement: the nineteenth-century project of embourgeoisement

One distinguishing characteristic of modern Central European history is that from the mid-nineteenth century onwards, the expansion of the education system preceded the development of markets. For historical reasons, the economic bourgeoisie was small, and both urbanization and industrialization were rather slow.[59] At the same time, for economic reasons, the aristocracy had little incentive to turn itself into a profit-seeking capitalist class. It retained its Junker character, and agrarian development remained on a 'Prussian road', oriented towards extensive production with cheap labor.[60] In this context, the relatively large and well-developed university system was the major avenue of social mobility for those social groups dislocated by the emancipation of the serfs and the abolition of the guild system – that is, the smaller landed gentry (who were excluded from the Junker class), artisans and Jews. This relatively large class of the university-educated, however, could not be absorbed as professionals by the fledgling market economy. Under these circumstances, the educated middle classes were doubly 'dislocated': recently cut off from the old order, but with no clear place in a new one.

This was the empirical phenomenon Mannheim called the 'socially unattached intellectual'.[61] As a general proposition about the social role of intellectuals, this concept is rather unpersuasive, but as a description of late nineteenth-century Central European Jewish and gentry intellectuals it is insightful. If they were not of independent means, they were often hard-pressed to find employment. Since there was a very limited demand for professional expertise in these relatively underdeveloped economies, the predicament of being 'unattached' was forced upon many intellectuals. It could also have been a matter of choice, as with those intellectuals of gentry origins who possessed sufficient family means to enable them to avoid employment. For these 'gentlemen intellectuals', being 'unattached' was a privilege. They could lead their lives 'in search of truth' rather than in the service of employers. Regardless of whether their 'unattached' condition was by choice or default, the educated were searching for a role and position for themselves: therefore they were the class of actors with the highest incentives to transform society. They were to be the agents of change in Central Europe – not the relatively small bourgeoisie or proletariat, which were well contained within the existing order; nor the aristocracy, which was the main beneficiary of this order.

What sort of change did the Central European intelligentsia seek? As we shall see, their project kept changing over time, but at least at the outset they were interested in embourgeoisement – in the making of a capitalist class and a market economy – because they were interested in Westernization. After all, in the distinguished universities of Central Europe students were socialized in the principles of modern science and the values of Western enlightenment. It was only natural that they aspired to transform their own societies along these lines. To describe the nature and activities of these Westernized and Westernizing groups, then, the concept of a *Bildungsbürgertum* project is quite accurate.

The concept of *Bildung* expressed the specific aspirations of this class, and its transformation reflected the processes of its formation and disintegration. In its first phase, with Kant, it expressed the vision of a history of reason moving along the lines of rationalization towards a well-defined destination – in short, it stood for 'enlightenment'. At this time, in the late eighteenth century, it was not linked at all to the idea of '*bürgerliche Gesellschaft*'.

It is only with Goethe, a generation later, that the two ideas were linked, as the Central European *Bildungsbürgertum* began to form and to formulate its project. Goethe, however, had an acutely tragic perception of the antinomy between the two ideas.[62] Although he was firmly committed both to the Enlightenment and to the development of a bourgeois society, he emphasized that *Bildung* was initially an aristocratic ideal of a well-rounded and harmonious development of the personality, which could not be sustained in bourgeois society. In Goethe's words, the bourgeois had to adapt to the '*Zeit der Einseitigkeiten*' (the times of one-sidedness); thus *Bildung* became *Ausbildung* (training) or *Berufsbildung* (professional training). Thus Goethe had a tragic perception of the transitory role of the *Bildungsbürgertum*: if it wished to carry through its project of capitalist transformation, it would have to abolish itself.

This tragic understanding of *Bildung* disappeared after Goethe. For mid-nineteenth-century Central European liberals, *Bildung* was a synonym for the German *Sonderweg* to bourgeois society.[63] They argued that German development, especially from the middle of the century onwards, was on the 'golden middle road' between culture and civilization, between the cultural and economic bourgeoisies, and between social stability and rapid industrialization. Evident here was the self-assurance of a rising class, the claim that it had managed to achieve a new 'synthesis'.

Indeed, from 1870 to roughly 1890, there was substantial modernization in the Central European region, along lines consistent with the vision of the *Bildungsbürgertum*. Society was being rapidly bourgeoisified, in the sense that the processes of urbanization and industrialization were accelerated, and the Prussian and Austro-Hungarian regimes began to experiment with cautious extensions of citizenship rights and the formation of public cultures. We do not claim, however, that the *Bildungsbürgertum* ever attained a hegemonic position in Central Europe. It had a formidable enemy in the aristocracy, and it never succeeded in imposing its way of life and values on society. Additionally, its relatively meager political power and influence could be obtained only by virtue of an uneasy and self-limiting alliance with the civil service bureaucracy.

Indeed, it is our claim that the nineteenth-century Central European *Bildungsbürgertum* was constructed by an alliance between humanistic intellectuals and that portion of the intelligentsia which chose a civil service career. This alliance is best represented by the ambivalent position of German 'mandarin' professors, who at one and the same time were intellectuals of significant stature and also held civil service rank. Consequently, they were rather conservative, and their lifestyles were much more similar to those of high-ranking civil servants than to those of *avant-garde* intellectuals. But it is also true that these mandarin intellectuals served as role models and tutors for a substantial portion of Prussian and Austro-Hungarian civil servants; hence the identities and world-views of these officials are not easily described as 'bureaucratic', at least not in the colloquial sense of the word. The notion of the 'educated middle classes' is a better approximation.

In what sense, then, is it possible to think of this social group as a group of *Bürgers*? Was the fact that they were at the service of the state directly antithetical to their role as citizens? The basis of their legitimacy was not the knowledge they possessed but their office, and the authority delegated to them by the state. None the less, it is clear that in order to gain access to civil service office they usually had to hold credentials, and to have acquired significant university education, during which they came into contact with mandarin intellectuals, and learned to recognize their cultural authority. This influence and the common bond of *Bildung* explain why the social type of the Prussian or Austro-Hungarian civil servant had strong affinities with the 'bourgeois' form of life. Generally, these civil servants presented themselves as 'enlightened'; they shared bourgeois lifestyles with most humanistic intellectuals; they were committed to procedural rationality, to the values of efficiency and predictability; and they believed that the governments under which they served were vehicles of reform, change, and modernization.

This proceduralism and rationalism characteristic of nineteenth-century Central European civil service bureaucracies may explain some of the complexities in Weber's controversial theory of bureaucracy. Without taking into account this specific historical group, with its deep ties to the *Bildungsbürgertum*, Weber's belief that the bureaucracy is the purest form of legal-rational authority seems rather confusing.[64] For many scholars, and especially students of socialism, this assertion seems nonsensical. It also runs counter to the common wisdom which associates bureaucracy with 'red tape' and inefficiency. Indeed, nineteenth-century Central European bureaucracies themselves were sometimes sufficiently 'Kafkaesque' to merit this common wisdom. None the less, the 'rational core' of Weber's ideal type – or, for that matter, of the Hegelian theory of the bureaucracy as the universal class – resided in the generally 'enlightened' character of these bureaucracies, and in their capacity to enlist the educated middle classes in the civil service as a 'vocation'.

It might be useful to keep these civil service actors conceptually distinct from the members of the *Bildungsbürgertum*, and to label them a *Beamtenbürgertum*, or 'bourgeoisie of officials'. The important point is that they were part and parcel of the Central European project of embourgeoisement, and thus served as natural allies of the *Bildungsbürgertum*. There was a fair amount of personnel circulation between humanistic intellectuals and officialdom, since there were relatively few employment opportunities for the educated middle class outside the public sector. Moreover, without this representation in the civil service, the *Bildungsbürgertum* project would have lacked any real possibility of materializing. The bottom line of the *Beamtenbürgertum* concept is that in so far as it is meaningful to identify a 'first *Bildungsbürgertum*' project, it is only as a core alliance between the humanistic intelligentsia, whose lifestyles and values gravitated towards a bourgeois form of life, and the civil service, which possessed some capacity for political action and institution-building, and was deeply committed to procedural rationality.[65]

It is also true that when this alliance broke up and the humanistic intelligentsia adopted 'counter-cultural' lifestyles, and began to ridicule rather than admire the civil service (roughly from the early 1910s), this also indicated the end of the 'first *Bildungsbürgertum*' project and the beginning of the Central European humanistic intelligentsia's love affair with right- and left-wing radicalisms. 'Real intellectuals' in the 1920s no longer perceived themselves as bourgeois, and they invented the term *Bildungsbürgertum* as a pejorative synonym for *Bildungsphilister*.[66]

It is impossible, however, to understand the breakdown of the embourgeoisement project without taking into account its greatest enemy – the aristocracy – and the countervailing pressure and temptation of gentrification they represented. Indeed, there is some evidence that even before World War I, instead of aristocrats gradually being turned into proper bourgeois citizens, the *Bildungsbürgertum* of those ethnic groups who were in political power (mostly Germans and Hungarians) was gentrified. Ironically, even assimilated Jewish intellectual families were not immune to the appeal of the gentry way of life. After all, Georg Lukács authored his first book as Georg von Lukács, and the Polányi household at the turn of the century, as we know it from contemporary interior photographs of the family home, was identical to any urban gentry household of the period. The civil service bureaucracies were not immune to gentrification either, as we know from Germany. Senior civil servants and mandarin professors, if they were not of Junker families themselves, avidly sought to belong to that class, either by marriage or by imitating its lifestyle.

What we see by the turn of the century, then, is the growing polarization

and disintegration of the formerly fairly homogeneous 'cultural bourgeoisie'.[67] There are several opposing trends pulling this group apart: the
growth of markets and industry offer some of the educated, who possess
marketable skills, the prospect of professionalization in the private sector.
Other educated people, who are becoming marginalized by these developments, are attracted by anti-capitalist 'radical' ideas. Finally, another
segment of the educated middle class, especially from the older and more
prominent families, are gentrified, or at least adopt high-bourgeois lifestyles.
These social schisms within the educated middle classes manifested themselves in bitter ideological disputes, especially around the issues of capitalism
and 'modernity'.[68] Thus the disintegration of the cultural bourgeoisie coin-
cides with the loss of the utopian project of making bourgeois society.

Second movement: the magic of right-wing and left-wing radicalism and the
attraction of the New Class project

While the extent of gentrification before World War I is a subject of some
dispute among social historians,[69] none denies that by the end of the Great
War the *Bildungsbürgertum* project was dead. Its disintegration was not due
primarily to declining aristocratic power, although the aristocracy was
greatly weakened by the war. Rather, support for the *Bildungsbürgertum* project was eroded by a growing disillusionment with capitalism, which was
precipitated by the war. The Central European intelligentsia first lost enthu-
siasm for the economic bourgeoisie, which it viewed as responsible for the
war. From this point the intelligentsia began to question the viability and
desirability of capitalist transformation itself. The war also destroyed the
alliance between intellectuals and civil servants, since civil servants remained
committed to the interests of the state, even at its most belligerent and non-
rational, while at the same time the war destroyed the old empires and, with
them, the power base of the civil service.

Ironically, the collapse of the *Bildungsbürgertum* project occurred just as
capitalist transformation was taking hold of Central European societies.
During the last decades of the nineteenth century, substantial urbanization
and industrialization took place in the region. Berlin and Budapest were the
fastest-growing metropolises in Europe, with growth rates comparable to
those of Chicago and New York at the same time. While Central Europe
remained in the semi-periphery of the capitalist world system, it was probably never closer to the advanced capitalist core than during the first years
of the twentieth century. Indeed, the western regions of Germany and
Bohemia were at the same level of economic development as the core at that
time.

None the less, the tone of the liberal intelligentsia during this period, even
before the war, had changed to one of disappointment and 'despair'. They

blamed the aristocracy and its continued rule for what they saw as the inevitable failure of modernization. Max Weber was one of these 'liberals in despair', and his intellectual development is instructive from this point of view. The early part of his work, written and published during the nineteenth century, is typical of the reflections of a *Bildungsbürger*. At this time Weber was firmly committed to the ideal of capitalist transformation, while he was impatient with the archaic and reactionary nature of the Prussian social and political order. Before his nervous breakdown, Weber was a reformer who knew exactly what the destination of German society should be. The Weber of the twentieth century, however, was in many ways a different person. In his first substantial work after his recovery, *The Protestant Ethic and the Spirit of Capitalism*, modernity has become an 'iron cage', and the story of modernization is one of 'disenchantment': the rationalistic world of capitalist modernity is dehumanizing, but it is also without real alternatives. While Weber remained a committed liberal all his life, the experience of the war, with its unprecedented irrationalism and cruelty, made him painfully aware of the price that had to be paid for capitalist transformation. He began to view this price as more and more taxing, though he never reached the conclusion that it was too high to be worth paying at all.

Some of Weber's contemporaries, however, did reach this conclusion. In their eyes, the operetta world of Kaiser Franz Josef and the iron cage of Prussian bureaucracy were reproducing themselves endlessly. As a result, radicalism spread, in both its right-wing and left-wing forms. While it is undeniable that right-wing ideologies attracted some prominent intellectuals, to our minds the radical, revolutionary Left had a stronger, more irresistible appeal. The main reason for this appeal, of course, was that it offered a historic mission to the socially unattached Central European intelligentsia, which not only matched but outbid the cultural bourgeoisie project. Additionally, left radicalism appealed to the lasting misgivings many intellectuals held about the economic bourgeoisie. They were uncomfortable with the hegemony of instrumental reason, and less than thrilled by the prospect of being professionals, whose knowledge is reduced to technical know-how. Left radicalism, and in particular the Marxist-inspired project of socialism, promised an alternative role for the 'men of knowledge': intellectuals could become the vanguard of history, the theorists of the revolution who would 'ascribe' to the proletariat its historic mission.

The intellectual trajectory of Georg Lukács is instructive in this respect. During his Heidelberg years he was close to Weber – not only as a friend of the family, but also as a thinker. Indeed, it is clear that during this period Weber and Lukács had substantial impact on each other's thought. It is equally likely either that Weber's notion of 'disenchantment' was the first incentive for Lukács to begin the line of thought which eventually concluded in the theory of reification, or that Lukács's interest in the problem of alienation stimulated Weber to formulate the antinomies of modernity with the concept of disenchantment. Whatever the case, it is clear that even during this early period, Lukács was already more radical than Weber. While they shared the perception of modernity as a disenchanted reality, a world in which men became homeless, Lukács also searched for a solution. From his perspective, although modernity fractured the totality of human existence, regaining it was still a historical possibility. Lukács found totality in Greek art, for example, and in *The Theory of the Novel* he also discerned the possibility of totality in the Russian literature of his time.

In short, what was a productive antinomy in Goethe – namely, the tension between 'culture' and 'civilization', and the ambivalent meaning of *Bildung* – had, by the early twentieth century, begun to acquire a different value and import. Instead of culture being seen as an important element of modernization, partly in tension and partly consonant with the growth of markets and private property, it began to imply the notion of the '*Sonderweg*' – that the Central European road, with all its relative economic backwardness, was not only different from but also superior to the Western path of modernization.[70] In the terms we have been developing in this chapter, we can say that for earlier men of ideas it was almost self-evident that they were part of a cultural bourgeoisie, as allies or even as the vanguard of capitalist transformation; but for Lukács, even in his pre-Marxist period, this identification was fraught with contradictions. Lukács represented a growing anti-bourgeois sentiment, which equated the advent of capitalist society with the degradation of culture, the commodification of human relations, and the hegemony of instrumental reason. And for Lukács and his contemporaries, the only hope of escaping this hegemony lay with culture. For them, culture was a refuge, a 'home', or even a revolutionary force. Indeed, long before Lukács became a Marxist revolutionary he was a 'cultural revolutionary' who believed that totality could be achieved in culture. Only at the end of 1918, did he make his quantum leap: his yearning for a 'home' led him to Marx and the Communist Party. He became a Marxist, joined the party, and – like Saul, who was transformed into Paul on the road to Damascus – Lukács the counter-cultural bourgeois intellectual was converted into a 'proletarian' virtually overnight.

Lukács's trajectory, like Saul's, became the site of repeated pilgrimages by Central European intellectuals from the turn of century until the 1950s. Indeed, this was true not only in Central Europe but also in Western Europe (especially in France and Italy), where if one was to be a genuine intellectual, at least a short adventure on the revolutionary Left was a 'must'. In this context, the 'bad news' about Stalinism was suppressed for as long as possible, and many a messenger was intellectually 'killed' (basically until the Twentieth Congress of the Soviet Communist Party and the Russian repression of the Hungarian popular uprising of 1956). What is unique about Lukács's biography is his fidelity to the doctrine and the party. While for most intellectuals left radicalism was a rather brief encounter, Lukács remained loyal to the party until the end of his life. So intense was his anxiety about homelessness in the modern world that he could never leave the home he found.

While the adventure with left radicalism did not unfold particularly happily, as the brief excitement of the Russian Revolution turned into the massacres of Stalinism, Central European intellectuals (like Lukács) found it difficult to give it up. The core of their commitment, until the late 1960s, was the belief that the reform of state socialism was possible and imminent. Reform offered them the role which had been promised but denied to them by the communists: the role of teleological intellectuals. Thus they typically foresaw the reform of socialism as a process of rationalization, in which the ruling communist estate would eventually be made to share power with the intelligentsia as a whole. It took another decade, and the drama of the suppression of the Prague Spring, for intellectuals to realize that no power-sharing with the bureaucracy was possible. This, in turn, quickly led to the conclusion that socialism had to be overthrown rather than reformed.

At this point, let us note that left-wing revolutionary anti-capitalism was only one of the roads open to the Central European intelligentsia as it lost faith in capitalist modernity. Typically, it was the road traveled by humanist intellectuals rather than civil servants or the rank and file of the educated middle classes. Many of the latter opted for a populist anti-capitalism, which occasionally had left-wing overtones and converged with revolutionary Marxism, but more commonly converged with the goals and practices of the radical Right. While the left intelligentsia carved out a social function for itself by becoming the 'organic intellectuals' of the working class, the populists were speaking for 'the people', and became leaders of peasant parties, fascist movements, or authoritarian military dictatorships. The dividing line between Left and Right, then, was actually a rather narrow one: for some, 'the people' were the workers; for others, they implied the unspoiled soul of the nation, primarily the peasantry, which was counterposed to the sinful and often alien or 'ethnic' elements which dominated urban life.

The chapter of right-wing adventures was rather short for the Central European intelligentsia, and ended in World War II. The left-wing love affair was more protracted and, as we have explained above, had its own insidious appeal. Especially for the younger generation who came of age during the war, the call emanating from the Left was much more attractive than a resumption of the cultural bourgeoisie project. Let us not indulge Central European intellectuals in the reinvention of history they have been engaged in during the last decade, and especially since the fall of communism: let us not accept the suppression of the memory of their collective biographies, and their story that the intelligentsia, as a whole, was from the beginning, always and already, on a collision course with communism. The truth of the matter is that around 1945 liberalism was a weak ideology in Central Europe. It held little appeal for those under thirty or thirty-five, most of whom found the Marxist revolutionary project much more appealing. Nazism was perceived not as the twin brother of Stalinism, as some intellectuals claim today, but as the logical outcome of capitalist development. Consequently, for the younger generation of intellectuals, anti-Nazism went hand in hand with anti-capitalism.[71]

It is difficult to judge now how widespread left-wing radicalism was during the postwar years. Since the region was occupied by the Red Army, anti-communist intellectuals were silent, silenced, or left for the West (especially the more bourgeois among them). Our only claim is that among those who stayed behind, and whose voice was heard, the hegemonic ideology was not the nineteenth-century cultural bourgeoisie project but, rather, that ideology which ascribed to young intellectuals the historic mission of leading society.

Only very gradually did this cohort of intellectuals begin to drift away from communism. For some, disillusionment began as early as 1953; indeed, in 1956, former young communists played crucial roles in the anti-Stalinist movements in Hungary and Poland. But the story is more complex. The anti-Stalinist intelligentsia of the late 1950s was more prone to perceive Stalinism as a deformation of the idea of socialism, rather than its most consistent expression. Thus Stalinism was rejected from what was perceived to be a 'genuine' socialist standpoint.

In this respect, 1956 in Hungary is illuminating. In retrospect, we know that the uprising brought together very different elements: some were 'reform communists', typically young communist intellectuals who wanted to replace Stalinism with 'real socialism' (no pun intended); others were 'freedom fighters', often descendants of privileged pre-communist families who wanted to restore the pre-communist social order. With the defeat of the uprising there was an intense classificatory struggle over how the movement should be labeled. The neo-Stalinists who tried to restore the communist order insisted on calling it a 'counter-revolution' – which, ironically, was viewed as the proper term by many of the 'freedom fighters'. After all, the Horthy regime, established on the ruins of the 1919 Communist Republic, proudly called itself counter-revolutionary. The reform communists, however, could not accept this label. Since they were still committed to a Marxist theory of socioeconomic evolution, they insisted that they were the 'real revolutionaries', the agents of real progressive historic change.

Intense as these classificatory struggles were, they have not survived the test of time and the evolution of the Central European intelligentsia. While many people during the 1960s were ready to lose their jobs, or even go to jail, over the issue of whether 1956 was a 'revolution', this was a non-issue for the young intellectuals of 1989. When Imre Nagy, the reform communist hero (whose last recorded words, before he was executed, expressed the desire that his historic role be judged 'by the international proletariat'), was reburied in June 1989, the event was attended by relatively few people, mostly middle-aged or older. For the younger generation, this was nothing but an internal communist dispute. They were not prepared to embrace it as their own cause. The reburial of Nagy also marked the final divorce between the 'reform communists' and the 'freedom fighters'. The latter wanted 1956 to be recognized as a nationalist movement, whose aim was to restore the role of the Church, religion, and traditional Hungarian cultural and social values. The former began to label their old allies as proto-fascists, and were re-interpreting their own movement as a fight for civic values and liberal democracy.

The key point is that the collective transformation of former communist intellectuals into bourgeois liberals, although it was a matter of intense classificatory struggles, did not take place before 1968. During the early 1960s, intellectuals were much more likely to have espoused the idea of technocratic socialism or the market reform of state socialism, and to perceive themselves as socialists or democratic socialists rather than liberals. In some cases they even viewed themselves as 'left' of the neo-Stalinist order. To put it simply: the road of Central European intellectuals from their adventure with left-wing radicalism to their new identities as neo-liberals passed through what in retrospect appears to have been the cul-de-sac of reforming socialism. The ruling ideology of the day was reform communism – that is to say, the idea that socialism could be turned into a democratic political system and could function relatively efficiently as an economic system. An important part of this vision was the desire to see Stalinist bureaucratic 'counterselection' eliminated, so that intellectuals could occupy the key command positions of society by virtue of their claim to expert knowledge.

The different fractions of the Central European intelligentsia had diverse reasons for being interested in reforming socialism. Some, especially from the 'Old Left', were attracted by the possibility that reform would finally deliver on the promises of the socialist revolution, which were betrayed by Stalinism. The renaissance of Leninism in the late 1950s was a direct result of this ideological interest. For others, especially technocrats, 'reform' carried the connotation of a more rational social order, one in which science would be the major productive force, and reason would overcome the anarchy of the market. The slogan of the 'new economic mechanism' captured this vision of reform as the creation of a perfect redistributive mechanism, which they would administer on the grounds of their expert knowledge. Others still, especially younger intellectuals of the 'New Left', were drawn to the promise of a 'socialism with a human face'. Like Lukács, they were interested in 'totality', in turning socialism into a home where the evils of the

West – consumerism, alienation, egoism – were avoided, while at the same time the supremacy of culture was recaptured. In their critique of Stalinism, which they sometimes construed as the twin brother of capitalism, one can hear echoes of early-twentieth-century intellectual resentment against 'civilization'.

Despite their differences, however, what all these groups had in common was the belief that rational intellectual discourse would play a leading role in social change and the management of society. They shared the belief that 'civilization' was 'at the crossroads' in the 1960s, and that they were the actors destined to steer it towards a better future. In hindsight, this belief may sound naive, but at the time it was not that unrealistic. Following the death of Stalin, Central European communism underwent a legitimation crisis, and the Stalinist bureaucracy was desperate for allies, for legitimacy, and for new ideas. All these groups represented viable candidates who would bring science, humanism, or revolutionary radicalism into such an alliance.

With the reforms of the early 1960s, the two new agents mentioned above appeared on the scene: technocrats, and what may be called a Central European 'New Left'. Both groups were generally younger than the 'reform communists' and the 'freedom fighters' of 1956. The technocrats were relatively non-ideological. They were interested in making socialism work, and they believed this could be achieved if proper meritocratic selection procedures were implemented – that is to say, if the incompetent Stalinist bureaucracy would surrender or, at least, share its decision-making power with them.

The Central European New Left also flirted with the idea of compromise, but this flirtation did not last as long as the one between the technocracy and the bureaucracy. Many members of the New Left were children of former communists, some of whom were victims of purges, some of whom were the purgers themselves. These children eventually came to the conclusion that pragmatic reforms of the technocratic type betrayed the real objectives of socialism. In a way, their revolt against the regime was a revolt against their fathers. First they joined the Communist Youth League or the Communist Party, and tried to promote change from within. As they realized how difficult it was to implement change in this way, they entered into direct confrontation with the bureaucracy. The examples of Kuron and Modzelewski in Poland, Kis and Bence in Hungary, or Kavan and Uhl in the Czech Republic, are typical in this respect.

During the mid and late 1960s, there was substantial competition and positioning among these various groups – hard-line bureaucrats, young technocrats, New Left intellectuals, 'reform communists' and 'freedom fighters'. The open historical possibility at this juncture was that these groups would renegotiate the distribution of power among themselves, and hence the course and character of the reforms. Despite the wrangling between the different factions, we argue that in the community formed by this struggle we can identify something which may be labeled a power project of intellectuals, or a 'New Class' project. In the context of reform, the possibility existed that these diverse fractions of intellectuals would take over the command positions of the political and economic system.[72]

Our central claim is that from the early twentieth century onwards, for some fifty to sixty years, the hegemonic ideology of Central European intellectuals was anti-bourgeois. Before the fall of Nazism, they fluctuated between left- and right-wing radicalism. After World War II, they positioned themselves decidedly on the left, even after they turned anti-Stalinist. Finally, they were attracted by the possibility of bringing anti-capitalism to its logical conclusion by carving out a position for themselves not as '*Bürgers*' but as teleological intellectuals, becoming a 'New Class' rather than a cultural bourgeoisie.

The crucial turning point in this historical journey of Central European intellectuals was 1968. With the events in Poland and the suppression of the 'Prague Spring', the Central European intelligentsia began to doubt whether a compromise with hardline bureaucrats was possible at all. If the essence of the intellectual power project of the 1960s was a *rapprochement* between hardline bureaucrats, technocrats, and critical humanist intellectuals, this project clearly could not be sustained following the events of 1968. This lesson was not learned everywhere immediately. It was probably learned most quickly in Czechoslovakia, though even there many of the activists of 'socialism with a human face' remained loyal to the dream for a long time (some to this very day). In Poland, disenchantment was also quite rapid, but it was much slower in East Germany and in Hungary. For some years, in these two countries, many intellectuals continued to think that the events of 1968 were only a temporary setback in the 'reform process'. None the less, in all these countries it was not until the late 1970s that a sizeable group of intellectuals became radical. At this point, they reached the conclusion that socialism was not reformable, and began to view themselves as part of a new project. The banner under which they gathered was – not surprisingly – that of 'civil society'; indeed, in some cases, where the disenchantment with socialism was most thorough, the project was viewed as 'embourgeoisement' – the project of a transition from socialism to capitalism.

*Third movement: the Central European intelligentsia returns to the
project of embourgeoisement*

In the late 1970s, when Central European intellectuals once again assumed their historic role as leaders of a bourgeois transformation, they did so with a markedly different consciousness and set of alliances from the first *Bildungsbürgertum*. The second Central European *Bildungsbürgertum* is composed of dissidents, most of whom come from the 'New Left' of the 1960s; and technocrats, some of whom were active in the 1968 reforms, but most of whom belong to a younger generation. These two groups traveled different trajectories during the 1970s and the 1980s, and began to merge together only around 1988–89.

There were many tensions between technocrats and New Left intellectuals during the 1960s, but throughout the reform process they were united by the perception that the real cleavage was not among themselves, but between them and the bureaucracy. One important reason for this was that they were both attracted to what Gouldner has called 'the culture of critical discourse'.[73] Both groups valued the reasoned, discursive validation of truth claims, rather than the resort to authority. To some extent they also formed common social networks, since both were attracted to high culture, and could be found fraternizing in crowded concert halls and theaters, or in the 'salons' of literate society in Prague, Budapest, or Warsaw.

The events of 1968 shook this precarious unity of technocrat pragmatists and New Left ideological critics. The New Left proceeded rapidly down the road to dissent and towards a direct confrontation with the regime. For those among them who were 'purged' in the aftermath of the Soviet intervention in Czechoslovakia, or during the crackdown in Poland, dissidence became a way of life – one might even say a 'vocation'. By this time they were no longer afraid of the police state, and no longer interested in gaining political influence. The dissolution of the intellectual class project may also have dissolved their belief in ideology, but they found in dissidence a way of recapturing the lost purity of their souls, reminiscent of the voluntary 'unattached' status of prewar gentry intellectuals. Hence they did not mind if they were arrested and imprisoned for a few weeks, since this was an initiation ceremony into the dissident 'community of saints'.

The technocratic fraction of the intelligentsia, in contrast, watched the development of dissent with alarm. They were still committed to pragmatism, to compromise, to reform rather than revolution, and they did not care much about their souls. Thus, after 1968, technocrats and dissidents proceeded along divergent trajectories. Dissidents increasingly considered the technocrats no better than collaborators, while the dissidents were shunned and dismissed by reform-minded technocrats as irresponsible 'troublemakers'. Even the social networks, which during the 1960s brought the two closer together, were broken. The dissidents were engaged in underground activities, circulating *samizdat*, huddling in secret apartment seminars, learning the art of conspiracy. As a result, they were ghettoized in their relatively small circles. The technocrats, for their part, did not want to risk what they perceived as their possible positive impact by being seen to be associated with the dissidents. Hence they took pains to demarcate themselves clearly from 'ideologues' and 'dissidents'.

Technocrats and dissidents also differed from one another in terms of lifestyles and tastes. The dissidents came of age during the 1960s, and were socialized in the 'New Left'. Consequently, they had a particular 'counter-cultural' mentality. In terms of their lifestyles, artistic tastes, sexual mores, and attitudes towards authority, family and religion, they were about as anti-bourgeois as the 'beat generation'. Thus, when they finally began to formulate a project of embourgeoisement, it took them almost a decade to reconcile the antinomies of their explicit ideologies and their immanent values and lifestyles. The technocrats, on the other hand, were 'good socialist citizens', valued family life, and to the extent that they were coming of age during the sober 1970s, they moved the most rapidly and easily towards bourgeois lifestyles. Their eyes were turned to the West, and in many respects they sought to imitate Western conservatives.

The historical irony is that precisely as they became isolated from one another, both fractions of the intelligentsia began to change, mostly in response to the shock of 1968, in ways which eventually made *rapprochement* possible and even necessary. In the case of the dissidents, this happened as they broke with Marxism and with ideology altogether, and with all forms of grand theorizing. Their unique invention during the late 1970s was the discourse of 'anti-politics'. It meant that the culture of critical discourse, this method for 'thinking differently', which had served to formulate alternative ideologies, took center stage. The ideological content was discarded, but the new 'grammar' was utilized as a weapon that could delegitimize the regime. Hence they were ready to put ideological differences aside, and embrace all those who would submit to this new grammar.

As far as the technocracy was concerned, their conflict with the bureaucracy was intensifying, and their faith in the reformability of socialism was wavering. They began to search for weapons in their struggle against the bureaucracy, and discovered that they, too, knew how to use the culture of critical discourse, especially in its new dissident version, bereft of ideological content. So by the 1980s, technocrats could be found reading the underground *samizdat* press and conducting secretive seminars on the work of Hayek, Milton Friedman, and the like. It is important for us to note that the common bond between intellectuals and technocrats was again, as it was for their nineteenth-century predecessors, *Bildung*, the culture of critical discourse.

The dissident intelligentsia began to draw even closer to the technocrats with the reinvention of the idea of 'civil society'. In its first stage, during the late 1970s, this was clearly not a capitalist project. Indeed, it had little to do with economics, and therefore held very little appeal for the technocrats. It was primarily an anti-bureaucratic program, with an emphasis on the 'social contract' and human rights and liberties as 'against the state'. Some of the dissidents even believed in the possibility of a 'socialist civil society' – hence in liberty not only in the formal, bourgeois sense, but also as economic liberty or – dare we say it – 'freedom'.

So although it appeared that the dissident emphasis on civil society and the technocrats' interest in free markets and monetarist discipline had little in common during the 1980s, as soon as they both reached the conclusion that socialism was dead, they also realized that what seemed so different were merely two sides of the same coin – that is, liberal capitalist society.[74]

It was really in the period between 1985 and 1988 that the second *Bildungsbürgertum* emerged, composed of dissidents and technocrats coming at it from different directions. Like their nineteenth-century predecessors, they formulated a utopian vision of capitalist transformation, and reinvented their own role as leaders of that transformation. The evidence for this is overwhelming. For example, Kocka's evidence for the prominent role of the *Bildungsbürgertum* in capitalist transformation partly relied on a study of the social composition of the Frankfurt national assembly in 1848–49. Three out of four delegates had academic degrees, but only 7 percent of them came from the propertied class.[75] In comparison, practically all the delegates in all the new parliaments created in Central Europe after the fall of communism possessed university degrees, and many of them held Ph.Ds. Importantly, too, virtually none was a property owner. If the early nineteenth-century Central European road to capitalism was exceptional because it was attempted with a weak economic bourgeoisie under the leadership of a cultural bourgeoisie, how much more exceptional and intriguing is the post-communist project to create 'capitalism without capitalists' under the leadership of a second *Bildungsbürgertum*?

The Ideology of the Post-Communist Power Elite

Searching for a term to denote the bonds that hold the different fractions of the second *Bildungsbürgertum* together, we would like to reinterpret the term 'managerialism'. By managerialism we mean a mentality – more specifically, a 'govern-mentality': a vision of how society, markets, firms and individuals can be led, coordinated and monitored. This mentality is not the exclusive property of CEOs; it is shared equally by all fractions of the post-communist power bloc, although it certainly testifies to the dominance of the managerial habitus within the power bloc alliance. Intellectuals and technocrats acquire this mentality reluctantly, sometimes with embarrassment, as they face the task of making 'actually existing post-communism' work. Indeed, the origins of the managerial mentality are not simply in the realm of ideas, but precisely in the painful meeting between ideology and reality. Its dual origins are in the failure of monetarist prescriptions to address the problems of the post-communist economy, and 'the disenchantment of the dissident world' effected by post-communist realities.

This disenchantment is a well-known 'modernist gloom'. As Peter Wagner notes, modernity projects like that of the Central European *Bildungsbürgertum* always begin as a discursive rupture, creating new 'imaginary significations for individuals and society'. The requisite modern institutions, however, always take much longer to develop, if they develop at all. Hence 'the relation of affinity, but non-identity, between ideas and institutions of modernity that is at the root of most of the problems in analyzing the history of modernity'. It is precisely this relation of affinity but non-identity between ideas and institutions in post-communism that we try to capture with the notion of the 'managerial mentality'.

The material embodiment of the managerial mentality is in rituals meant to reconcile ideology and reality, and to exorcize the demon of

86

disenchantment. It is in the course of these rituals that the vision of a society governed 'from afar', through the intermediary of monetary means, is reinterpreted and transformed into the reality of hands-on management of daily economic affairs, and a very close supervision of people's minds. The second – no less important – achievement of these rituals is in cementing the alliance between different fractions of the post-communist power bloc. None of these fractions is happy with every aspect of this bargain, but they all pay homage to the rituals of managerialism, and in this way they profess their allegiance to the imaginary significations of the post-communist transformation and the very real status quo of elite power-sharing and bargaining.

We begin this chapter by examining the ideologies of monetarism and civil society – the ideologies, respectively, of the technocratic and intellectual fractions of the power bloc – in their 'pure' form. We describe the 'elective affinity' between these ideologies, which consists in similar visions of the role of knowledge in society, and corresponding understandings of how society should be ruled. Next, we describe how these ideologies were transformed into a 'managerial govern-mentality', as dissidents and technocrats recognized the need to strike an alliance with the managers of state enterprises. This compromise with reality meant that intellectuals and technocrats began to negotiate key tenets of their ideologies, and the charismatic vision of post-communism began to be routinized and secularized. In this interaction with managerial habituses, monetarists reinterpreted their ideology as budgetary restrictionism, and former dissidents reinterpreted the idea of 'civil society' as civic education. We describe the result of this reinterpretation, the managerial mentality, as a peculiar mutation wherein control from afar becomes micro-management. Finally, we describe the rituals associated with these reinterpretations, and demonstrate how they achieve the simultaneous preservation of the imaginary significations of the post-communist transformation and the welding together of the interests and identities of the different fractions of the power bloc.

The monetarist ideology of the technocratic fraction of the elite

Since the technocracy's flirtation with monetarism began as part of its fascination with Western economics, we begin by offering a brief history of monetarist ideology as it developed in the West.

Monetarism in its classical form, as propounded by Chicago School economists, was an economic theory and a set of economic policies which challenged mainstream Keynesian theory and practice in the early 1970s. The most important of its policy recommendations were: (1) to reduce inflation and/or to control it strictly (since inflation distorts the capacity of markets to provide accurate *information*), even at the expense of permanent unemployment; (2) to reduce the discretionary jurisdiction of government in favor of fixed policy rules, which are known to all, and can therefore guarantee stable expectation-formation; (3) to maintain a tight-fisted fiscal policy and a 'monetary rule of steady growth in the money stock'; and, (4) to establish flexible exchange rates, and open the national economy to international competition.[1]

Thus monetarism aims to reduce the government's economic role, and creates a situation in which governments are limited to the use of monetary means in the regulation of the economy. Even these activities, monetarists argue, should be limited by law to avoid excessive attempts at 'fine-tuning'. Governments do not need to formulate specialized industrial or employment policies, since these will only confuse economic actors, interfere with the natural equilibrium of the market, and achieve the opposite of what they set out to do. Worst of all, governmental intervention encroaches upon the freedom of individuals, and for this reason alone it is undesirable.[2]

The success of monetarism in the West is not due only to its emphasis on 'freedom', however, but also to the vision of *order* it offers. This is why we call it, following Foucault, a 'govern-mentality'.[3] To understand this point, we need merely to recall that the term 'economy' itself only recently came to mean a 'sphere of society'. Early in the eighteenth century it still referred to an economizing art of government, a way of putting things in the right order.[4] We retain this sense of the word when we say that someone does something 'with economy' – that is, properly, frugally, and so on. It is only with nineteenth-century liberalism that 'the economy' came to signify a sphere of society, for the very reason that this sphere of society was thought of as the source of a naturally arising order. Thus liberalism itself was an 'economizing' art of government, with the proviso that it attempted to exploit the capacities for natural order inherent in what it ruled.

Monetarism, too, is such a liberal art of government. Monetarists have rediscovered in the workings of the market, and especially in flows of money, the possibility of a social order governed 'from afar' (distance being the technical correlate of freedom). Such an art proceeds by imposing monetary representations on social phenomena, which can then be expected to become 'self-regulating'. They never really do, but the monetarist art of government consists in carefully cultivating the natural self-regulation tendency of social phenomena by avoiding gross interferences as much as possible. Monetary representations, like all other representations – maps, charts, statistics, reports and forms – open up the possibility of regulating the conduct of individuals and populations 'from afar', because they can 'mobilize' distant phenomena, and bring them closer into 'centers of calculation'.[5] Moreover, monetary representations of populations and individuals (such as 'the money stock' or 'human capital') have the added advantage of precise calculation, and they exploit a tendency of markets to self-regulate. With this thinking, it is possible to imagine that social problems might be regulated or pacified without direct government intervention.

Take 'accident insurance', for example. Before it was introduced, accidents at work were an area of bitter conflict between employers and employees. Insurance was a technology which allowed actors to regulate this social problem because it objectified the possibility of accident as 'risk', which could then be represented by money. Henceforward the self-regulation of the market was entrusted with containing this problem, making it governable. Employers, so the reasoning went, would have a financial incentive to provide safe working conditions, because otherwise their premiums would be higher. Supply and demand would determine what was defined socially as an 'accident' and what an accident would be worth. This is not necessarily how accident insurance works in actuality, of course, but this was certainly the 'govern-mentality' behind its introduction, and the consequences are indisputable: a domain of social life which was ill-defined and could be controlled only by direct intervention, or even force, was now given the 'constitution', so to speak, for self-governing.[6] Similar suggestions for dealing with 'problems' surrounding immigration, marriage and divorce, punishment and prisons, soon followed, and can be found not only in the work of theorists like Gary Becker, but also in Clinton's 'New Democratic Party' as well as in the 'contract with America'.

Once social activities are monetized in this way, the 'center of calculation' – the point from which they can be regulated – is no longer the state budget. In fact, the budget – and especially budget deficits – interfere with such control, since they distort the workings of money. The new centers of calculation, and the increasingly dominant hub of the new monetarist technology, are banks – especially central banks, and in a sense financial markets, and the financial system as a whole. It is in this sense that we can claim that monetarism is more than just an ideology in Western countries. It is a mentality of governing that is well endowed with a variety of technical tools which make it superior to older forms of governing, such as Keynesianism. For this reason, as Neil Fligstein has shown, monetarism has absolutely transformed the corporate world. Corporate headquarters have become 'profit centers' peopled by finance managers, who control the corporation's 'capital units' 'from afar' (i.e. via monetary representation rather than 'planning').[7] Supported by the growing power of financial markets and world financial institutions (like the IMF and the World Bank), this approach to governing has become the *sine qua non* all over the world, and is even seen as a means of encouraging democratization in such places as China's countryside, Bangladeshi villages, and Middle Eastern cities.

The moment, however, that monetarism becomes this kind of a political–utopian program, it faces a mounting problem – it creates a sisyphean stone with which it is doomed to grapple. This is the problem of individual responsibility and initiative. In the words of Milton Freedman:

> Freedom is a tenable objective only for responsible individuals. We do not believe in freedom for madmen or children. The necessity of drawing a line between responsible individuals and others is inescapable, yet it means that . . . paternalis[t government] is inescapable for those whom we designate as not responsible.[8]

In other words, monetary control from afar depends on individuals being entrepreneurial, efficient units of human capital so that they will react appropriately to the opportunities offered by monetization. Hence a variety of problems which haunt monetarist theorists as well as policy-makers: the problem of an 'enterprise culture' and the problems of 'trust' and 'malfeasance'.[9]

However, these issues were not the aspects of monetarism which originally appealed to the Central European technocracy. Monetarism appealed mostly to the heterodox fraction of the technocracy – to those economists, social scientists and other professionals who were blocked in their careers, and interested in a radical overhaul of the system. They were not dissidents, but career civil servants who were frustrated in their striving for greater rationality. In their frustration they began reading, and then secretly translating and discussing, Hayek and Friedman. They were attracted to monetarism's sharp rejection of a 'Third Way', a stance which set them apart from 'reform communists', and often from their superiors. Most of all, they were attracted to monetarism's promise of greater freedom coupled with greater control and predictability. Monetarism offered a simple and fast solution for the two ills of communism. It also provided a formula for managing the post-communist transformation: marketize, monetize, and restore money to its status as universal currency, and then you will be able to know what is going on in society.[10] All this could be done in 'five hundred days' or less. One needed only precisely what monetarism offered: 'simple, general, fixed rules . . . improvements in the strength and quality of markets and rational macro-economic policy'.[11]

Václav Klaus, future Finance Minister of the first post-communist government in Czechoslovakia, spoke for the new breed of technocrats at the beginning of 1989: 'They believe in certain general principles of monetary economics which are relevant across many different types of institutional arrangements and they advocate an orthodox public finance approach and monetary restraint.'[12] As we can see, Central European technocrats were not so much interested in the utopian side of monetarism, they were looking for principles of economic 'shock therapy'; indeed, they went about their business with the self-confidence of 1950s psychiatrists.

Soon, however, Central European technocrats were grappling with the same problems of trust and malfeasance which baffled monetarists in the West. Indeed, the problems of the post-communist monetarists were far more difficult. While one may be skeptical about the wisdom of the monetarist vision, it is clear that such policies are at least conceivable where market institutions are already well formed, and economic actors already have predispositions which enable them to navigate an environment shaped by monetary policy. However, these conditions did not exist in Central Europe in 1989. It was at this point, then, that the technocracy became interested in the utopian side of monetarism, since – as we shall see – the political dimension of the monetarist ideology has strong elective affinities with the critique of state socialism developed by the dissidents: the ideology of 'civil society'. This critique problematizes responsibility and initiative in much the same way that utopian monetarism aims to inculcate them through financial discipline. Moreover, in the Central European context, the ideology of civil society drew on the considerable symbolic capital accumulated by dissidents during the late communist period.

The dissident's vision of life beyond socialism: The ideology of civil society

For dissident intellectuals, the society beyond socialism promised to be a rationalized yet enchanted garden. Their project was no less ambitious than overcoming the antinomies of rationalization: society and community, truth and virtue, responsibility and conviction, individuation and authenticity – all these conflicts were to be superseded. They have achieved none of this, of course, but in the process of struggling towards this vision, dissidents thoroughly delegitimated state socialism, accumulating a significant amount of symbolic capital in the process.

The ideology of civil society was rationalistic in several respects. For example, the society beyond socialism was to be civil rather than military, a society of contract rather than a society of command. There were to be no commanders and no privates, no rulers or ruled, no soldiers whose job was to obey commands mindlessly, without reflection. Rather, post-communism was to be a society in which people would negotiate deals with each other as equal partners, where they would finally take responsibility for their own lives. Thus the ideology of 'civil society' was formulated as a powerful critique of the irrationality of communist paternalism. In place of a society of minors, who are in constant need of protection, nurturing, and fatherly discipline, proponents of civil society posed the vision of a society of adult citizens.[13] At least in this respect, 'civil society' was to be 'the rule of reason', reason in the form of procedure.

The slogan of 'anti-politics',[14] however, attempted to reconcile this rational side of the dissident critique with the promise of enchantment. It was rationalistic, even procedurally rational, to the extent that it represented a demand for separating spheres of society from one another as a way of putting the political 'back in its place'. In a sense, it was an attempt to carve out a realm of freedom, where intellectuals would be left to their own devices, and could practice art and science without political interference. All they wanted was to be allowed to live their 'civil' lives without interference; to write their novels or essays, without being worried that domestic intelligence would confiscate their manuscripts or put them in jail for their work as intellectuals. Socialism was identified as a form of 'hyperrationality', a world not yet rationalized because substantive rationality or 'totalitarian ideology' pervaded all spheres. By contrast, civil society signified procedural rationality, a world where one could not use the magic of ideological incantations to overcome the rules specific to each sphere.

However, to the extent that 'anti-politics' meant 'living within the truth',[15] dissidents revealed an unmistakable penchant for life in an enchanted world. Socialism was to be resisted and overcome, so that an 'authentic community' could be created in its stead.[16] We can hardly think of any concept in modern philosophy which is less self-reflexive than this dissident concept of 'civil society'. None of the antinomies, ironies, or even the realism of the old concept was retained in this modern version of 'having your cake and eating it too'. These ideologists of civil society were proud that their theory of civil society contained a vision of society governed by procedural rationality which was also a 'real community', a task which all nineteenth-century thinkers (with the possible exception of Karl Marx) knew was the 'squaring of the circle'.

The reason that dissidents could so easily overlook the enchanted nature of the task they set themselves under socialism was that instead of envisioning a community of real individuals with conflicting interests, they viewed their community as a 'community of saints' – that is, of dissident intellectuals. This community was understood to possess a peculiar spiritual power by virtue of the example it set for the rest of society of how to live a moral, authentic life. The moral force of this example was underlined, in the eyes of dissidents, by the fact that they *sacrificed* – or, at least, were willing to sacrifice – all they had in the name of truth and morality. It was this moral authority which, dissidents believed, possessed the power to transform society into a community of responsible, moral individuals.[17] In this respect, dissidents were laying claim to an ancient form of power, which Foucault has termed 'pastoral power'. It is a form of power modeled after the authority of the Christian pastor, the 'good shepherd', who takes care of his flock and thereby claims their submission. The ultimate basis for the authority of the pastor is his willingness to 'be prepared to sacrifice himself for the life and salvation of the flock'.[18]

This notion of community[19] also meant that in the world foreseen by dissidents, truth and virtue were fused. This is another aspect of the enchanted nature of dissident thought. The distinction between truth and virtue has haunted Western rationality since its inception, and is one of the more productive antinomies informing its development. Of course, many Western theorists have been critical of this distinction, especially when it has resulted in a radical separation between truth and virtue. For the Frankfurt School, such a separation represented the root cause of some of the ugliest features of modernity. But in dissident discourse this antinomy was dissolved in the enchanted world of 'civil society'. The dissidents imagined a world after socialism in which people would 'live in truth', which was understood to mean that they would also lead virtuous lives. Indeed, they argued that the only way to be virtuous is to 'live in truth', and the only truth there is consists in virtuous, moral existence.[20] Virtue and truth were fused beyond recognition in the term 'civility' (in Czech, *kulturnost*), of which the dissidents were so fond: it referred to the ideals of charity and compassion, of neighborly love and respect, and also to the ethos of individual autonomy, the pursuit of self-interest, and self-realization. Being compassionate and responsible would not prevent one from fully realizing oneself, it would not require any concessions. Truth would be one at long last, and it would also deserve to be called 'true', because it would not be true unless it was also ethically correct.

The world beyond communism, civil society, was enchanted because it was *authentic*. Authenticity implied that the individuation which takes place with civil society would not separate the individual from his/her *aura*, because inner and outer selves would coincide. The irony of this rediscovery of authenticity is that such authenticity was precisely the aim of Stalinism, which wanted to abolish the private sphere, so that inner and outer selves would coincide. Later communist rulers abandoned this attempt to intrude into the sphere of private selves, as long as communist rituals were properly attended and respected in public life. For the dissidents, however, this communist compromise was 'living within a lie' *par excellence* – it was the essence of the lie that public and private selves did not coincide.[21]

It is impossible to understand dissident ideology, and particularly the enchanted nature of the dissident vision of 'civil society', without taking into account the social function of this ideology in cementing the provisional alliance between different fractions of the dissident community. By the late years of communism, intellectuals were becoming increasingly diverse in terms of their critiques of socialism and, as a result, in their visions of post-communist society. The division between liberals and the patriotic–religious Right, which emerged into full-blown conflict after 1989, already existed *in embryo* in the late 1970s. It was not recognized, however, because it was swept under the carpet by the all-encompassing notion of 'civil society'.

With hindsight, we could say that one of the social functions of the dissident discourse of 'civil society' was precisely that it papered over the differences between the two groups, and allowed them to think that they were speaking about 'the same thing'. Not only did it serve as a powerful critique of the state-socialist rank order, articulating the position of social groups that no longer found their place within it: it also served as the basis for a *rapprochement* between diverse opposition groups, who could not otherwise have entertained the notion that they had shared interests.

In the concept of 'civil society' two heterogeneous standpoints were fused. At the core of the liberal standpoint was the issue of human rights – a concept of citizenship derived from the theory of social contract. On this basis, liberal dissidents attacked socialism as a mode of rule which was far too authoritarian and repressive, and treated individuals as subjects rather than citizens. The patriotic–religious opposition, on the other hand, saw in communism a secular, godless, cosmopolitan ideology, which neglected the *natural* community of 'the nation'. On this basis, patriotic right-wing dissidents accused communist rulers of betraying the nation, of being the henchmen of the Russian empire, and of undermining ethnic Polish, Hungarian, Czech or Slovak interests and culture for the sake of the Russian Tsar. Hence the patriotic opposition adhered to a notion of citizenship, but it was very different from the liberal meaning of the concept, since it was cast in terms of ethnicity.

The importance of 'bloodline' and the 'natural community of the nation' in constructing the ideology of 'civil society' was particularly obvious in the Hungarian and Slovak cases. One major reason why Hungarian 'patriots' were anti-communist was because they believed that communist rulers had neglected the cause of Hungarians living abroad. There was little doubt in their minds that Hungarians living abroad were part of Hungarian society, and thus of 'civil society'. Hence they demanded that Hungarian authorities defend the 'citizenship rights' of expatriate Hungarians against other rulers. Regardless of how uncomfortable the liberals may have felt about this patriotic construction of national–ethnic citizenship, their commitment to the language of civil society made it impossible for them to articulate their disagreement before communism fell. When the first non-communist Hungarian Prime Minister, Antall, called himself 'the Prime Minister of fifteen million Hungarians', however, the differences between the two groups could no longer be contained. What the patriotic–religious Right considered obvious – that the Hungarian government should defend the cause of those of Hungarian ethnicity even if they resided in Romania or Slovakia – was perceived by the liberals as irresponsible chauvinism. The liberal concept of citizenship, of course, referred to a political, territorial nation, not to notions of ethnicity and bloodline.

Similarly, even though few Slovaks signed 'Charter 77', Czech dissidents – and particularly the Protestant intelligentsia – were quick to point to the activities of the Catholic Church in Slovakia as a sign that 'civil society' was resurgent there. But for Slovak Catholics, the call for 'civil society' meant a revival of *Slovak* society, even a continuation of Hlinka's 'people's Republic'. Again, the differences emerged directly on the heels of the communist system breakdown, coming to a dramatic conclusion in the break-up of Czechoslovakia.

The later fortunes of the nationalist–liberal coalition, cemented by the discourse of civil society, reveal all too clearly that the discourse of civil society reconciled the fundamental antinomies of modernity only in the *minds* of some dissident intellectuals. In reality, the disagreements among different wings of the dissident coalition were irreconcilable. As socialism collapsed and the dissidents were confronted with the difficult task of building 'actually existing post-communism', they had to be reconciled with the *world*. In particular, they had to find the means through which a society, approximating to their vision of 'civil society', could be brought into being, educated, civilized and, most importantly, controlled.

The elective affinity between monetarism and the discourse on civil society

We summarize the elective affinity between the ideologies of monetarists and dissidents in five points, the first four of which demonstrate how they converge on a certain – rather utopian – vision of how society should be ruled, and what their role within it should be. Although this vision is in sharp tension with the realities of post-communism, it is none the less true that monetarists and dissidents have found a common response to the task of negotiating the disenchanted reality of post-communism. This common response demonstrates the working of 'habitus' rather well, since it shows how these two very different groups of intellectuals, faced with different predicaments, developed reasonably homologous responses by creatively applying their old ways of knowing to their new situation. This common response emerges as the final, fifth, affinity between dissident and monetarist visions of the role of intellectuals in society, and describes the new historical project of the Central European *Bildungsbürgertum*.

We call the first affinity 'the Cassandra complex'. As the reader is well aware, Cassandra, daughter of the King of Troy, was cursed by being able to foresee the future without anybody ever believing her. Similarly, following the demise of the New Class project, neither the dissidents nor the technocrats assumed the role of 'teleological intellectuals'. Instead, the dissidents strive for pastoral rather than temporal power, while the technocrats perceive themselves as the technicians of the transformation, and characteristically adopt a conservative ideology (monetarism) which limits their role in such a process. Both groups reject as 'totalitarian' the suggestion that intellectual knowledge could be the basis for planning society, and point to 'perverse effects'. For example, monetarists argue that policy-makers should refrain from 'forecasts' and planned 'targets', and be bound instead by a fixed rule, because otherwise individuals are likely to expect them to renege on their promises, counteract, and create perverse effects such as inflation.[22] Like Cassandra, nobody will believe them; hence they can only predict misfortune. Similarly, dissidents as pastors do not claim to know the future, nor even to have a political program.[23] They contend that any attempt to plan a moral society is bound to bring its opposite, since emancipation is an inner process, one that cannot be prescribed from above.

Both dissidents and technocrats seek to create the conditions under which individuals will govern themselves. In other words, the second affinity between their respective views of how society should be ruled concerns their common effort to create the conditions for 'living within the truth'. Individuals will be able to make meaningful decisions about their actions if they can measure them by something, and if this measure holds good in all realms of life. For the dissidents, this measure is truth/morality/authenticity, and it requires a constant struggle to maintain. For monetarists, however, the problem of 'information' is a technical problem, and monetization provides a solution. If you let the market work, if you have the correct price for everything – if, that is, you have a 'rational' price structure set by the market – then you 'live in truth'. You live in truth because your conduct is governed by cues (prices) set naturally (by the market), which reflects their value truthfully (in money). You can then make meaningful choices, calculate your steps rationally, and behave responsibly. If, on the other hand, as in socialism, you do not monetize or balance your budget (which amounts to the same thing), then you 'live within a lie'. Similarly, inflation means living within a lie, since it distorts prices.[24]

A third affinity between dissident and monetarist views of how society should be ruled is their preference for 'action from afar'. The dissidents envisioned a society ruled by 'pastoral power' – not, that is, by command or repression, but by a government operating 'from afar'. The monetarists supplied them with a technology – monetarism – to achieve this goal, although this technology has been really successful only in the corporate realm. Privatization should be understood not only from the point of view of property rights, then, but also from the point of view of 'governmentality'. Instead of finding capital to purchase state firms, monetarists were interested first and foremost in corporatization and in creating a market for trading shares in these firms, because in this way they could divest the state of direct control – that is to say, they could divest the state of direct economic control of firms, and submit post-communist enterprises to a structure of financial control through the banks.[25]

The fourth affinity between the monetarist and dissident conceptions of how society should be ruled is their interest in the rule of law. This was a major part of the dissident program to create a civil society. If the rule of law is not observed, individual responsibility is corrupted, and the excesses of rule are liable to turn into their own undoing, a state of ungovernability. If, on the other hand, the rule of law is observed, individuals can be responsible and civil. Similarly, Milton Friedman argued for a fixed rule of slow monetary growth and a fixed rule of budgetary balance; and Václav Klaus echoed this prescription with a call for 'fixed, clear rules'. Otherwise, they warn, there are likely to be excesses of interference in the economy, and it is likely to 'get out of hand'.

The preceding discussion has sought to show that monetarism and the dissident discourse of civil society address a common problematic. This problematic is best described as 'government' – as finding the correct method by which the conduct of individuals and populations can be guided, so as to cultivate their natural propensity for order and progress. It is at this rather utopian level that they first discover an 'elective affinity' between their respective projects. While 'monetarism' offers a range of tools with which to 'act from afar' on the conduct of individuals and populations, the dissident discourse produces the requisite symbolic resources for such applications.

Unfortunately, however, as these two fractions of the burgeoning post-communist power elite approached the task of making capitalism from above, they were confronted with the disenchanted realities of post-communism. The advocates of anti-politics and monetarism found themselves deeply involved in political struggles. Their central problem was that post-communist society was anything but civil, especially in the context of 'austerity measures' and 'shock therapies'. Very quickly the new power elite realized that however formidable the task of changing property relations and restructuring economic institutions was, it paled in comparison with the task of making the kinds of people who could operate within these institutions. The new leaders of post-communism realized that before they could govern from afar they had to attend to the task of civic education, of creating the social actors who could be thus governed.

It is here that monetarist technocrats and dissident intellectuals found the final affinity between their respective ideologies. Both these fractions of the power bloc came to perceive their role as that of pastors and 'civilizers'. Monetarists tended to emphasize the role of the market as an 'impersonal' educator for greater responsibility,[26] while dissidents placed more value on education for civility, obviously conducted and led by intellectuals. Despite these differences, it is clear that both groups viewed their task as one of 'governing' rather than commanding. Their role model was no longer Joseph in Egypt but Moses in the desert, as he led the people of Israel away from Egyptian slavery and the fleshpots of Goshen towards the Promised Land.

Like Moses, they found that their task was more complicated than they had anticipated. They thought initially that it was to lead the people towards freedom and, in the course of the (as they thought, rather short) journey, to rule by gentle admonition rather than coercion. Alas, also like Moses, they discovered that it would be a longer journey than they had anticipated. Forty days turned into forty years, primarily because the people were not ready for freedom.[27] Hence they redefined their task as turning slaves into free individuals by giving them laws and educating them to become law-abiding citizens.

Like Moses, the Central European post-communist *Bildungsbürgertum* took upon themselves the role of lawgivers, shepherds and civilizers. Also like Moses, they told people that the road to civilization could be traveled only through sacrifice and submission to a new code of law. They have to pass through the Vale of Tears, as Ralf Dahrendorf put it so eloquently.[28] Ironically – at least for the current transition – the making of capitalist man requires that people turn away from material values, from 'consumerism', from the fleshpots of Goshen, and towards 'spiritual civilization'.

In the course of finding themselves a new role, dissidents and mone-tarists have transformed the discourse of civil society and abolished two hundred years of the secularization of 'pastoral power'. In the eighteenth century, 'civil society' meant a natural order, a naturally self-governing soci-ety. This was an ideology particularly suited to the emergent bourgeoisie. Instead of absolutist power, the bourgeoisie introduced legal–rational authority, a type of domination in which power was exercised from a dis-tance, a form of government which utilized a pastoral function, but without the archaic exchange of sacrifices between a pastor and his flock. As the economic bourgeoisie was coming into its earthly dominion, it searched for a 'positive' anchor for its rational authority, and rejected the mysteries of sac-rifice.[29] After all, the agents were already there, in the form of self-sacrificing entrepreneurs imbued with 'the spirit of capitalism'. The task was to create the *institutions* of a capitalist market and a bourgeois democracy. By contrast, during the transition from socialism to capitalism the task is a dual one: both the institutions and the *agents* with appropriate habituses have to be pro-duced. Hence we see a peculiar twist in the Central European discourse on civil society, which is detectable in dissident debates as early as the late socialist period: civil society cannot be counted upon to organize itself; it must be civilized. It is not a natural order, but one that has to be created by moral example and, most importantly, by sacrifice.

This is because, from the point of view of the new power bloc, new post-communist citizens are nothing but 'the generation of the desert'. It is a generation corrupted by decades of socialist slavery, paternalism, excessive dependence, and an unrealistic sense of security, egalitarianism, and consumerism. Civil society, therefore has to be created, nurtured, and defended not only against the state, but against society itself. This is an idea which never crossed the minds of eighteenth-century anti-feudal, anti-aristocratic contractarians. But it is precisely this notion which has gained prevalence as communist rulers disappear and the only obstacle on the road to civil society is society itself.[30]

What sets eighteenth-century contractarians and post-communist intellectuals apart then, is that the former were the ideologues of an emergent *Wirtschaftsbürgertum*, while the latter are members of a *Bildungsbürgertum*. The former were content to create the economic institutions which would guarantee their class rule, while the latter have to create an economic bourgeoisie and other classes before civil society can be developed.

The managerial mentality and its reinterpretation of monetarism and civil society

The other disenchanted aspect of post-communist reality with which the new alliance of technocrats and dissidents had to come to terms was the resistance of industrial managers. Technocrats and dissidents quickly discovered that their plans for economic transformation stood little chance of materializing without the support of the managers of industrial firms. Industrial managers possessed one of the most valuable commodities of post-communism: close, hands-on knowledge of state firms, their assets, liabilities, commercial partners, and so on. Monetarist knowledge, which the technocrats were quick to pick up, is highly abstract and is particularly silent about what goes on inside firms. In fact, part of its unmistakable force as a form of 'symbolic mastery' is due to the fact that it treats the firm as a 'black box'. In the monetarist night, all black boxes look alike, and all are subject to the same mechanisms of financial control. This knowledge gives technocrats an edge over managers, but it also makes them inescapably dependent upon them, since knowledge of inner firm workings is essential for anybody who wants to draw up a privatization project, or buy a firm.[31]

Managers of industrial firms, however, were less than thrilled by the prospect of monetarism. They would have liked to see a government which had industrial and employment policies, subsidized exports, and defended them against unfair competition from abroad. Hence they created 'industrial lobbies' and pressure groups, some of which are rumored to be so powerful that they belong directly to the private circle of the Slovak Prime Minister.[32] The compromise and the resulting coalition with the managers necessitated a transformation of the ideology of dissidents and technocrats. The best way to describe this transformation is as a 'managerial mentality', a reinterpretation of the theories of civil society and of monetarism in the context of a habitus which was formed during years of service as communist bureaucrats, technocrats, and managers.

Up until now we have described the ideology of the new power bloc as if it were formed only by a reconciliation with outside reality – the reality of a society that was not really ready for the task of making capitalism. The truth is, however, that the managerial ideology has also been shaped by the process of coming to terms with itself and its own shortcomings. As we shall see in Chapter 4, the overwhelming majority of post-communist technocrats, and particularly post-communist managers, are former communist functionaries. They were as much part of socialism as anybody else. The very fact that they have opted for 'capitalism from above' can be attributed to their inclination to draw on their past experiences to solve the new tasks of the post-communist transition. In this process, they have developed three practices which reflect the combined effects of monetarist ideology, habitus, and the need for compromise between managers and technocrats.

The first such practice, and the most important element of post-communist economic policy, is the 'budget-bargain' between managers and technocrats. During the communist period, it was well known that the 'plan' – the blueprint supposedly drafted by central redistributors and imposed on enterprise managers – was actually the subject of intense negotiations between managers and central planners. The process by which managers disputed certain elements of the 'plan', and maneuvered to set production targets for the factories, came to be known as a 'plan-bargain'.[33] This generation of managers and technocrats were socialized by the plan-bargain institution never to accept central decrees at their face value, and to look for 'strings' to pull to manipulate the plan to their own advantage. This is precisely the same generation that is reinterpreting the monetarist canon of fiscal and monetary discipline. The result is that in the post-communist setting, technocrats offer policies of budgetary restriction, which are interpreted by managers as the cue to begin intense negotiations, in a process that looks very much like a 'budget-bargain'. This negotiated budget-bargain creates a space, which on the surface seems to satisfy the requirements of the IMF or the World Bank, but at the same time makes it possible for managers to engage the financial technocracy in making deals which resemble the 'plan-bargaining' process.

The second practice which combines monetarists and monetarism with managers and their managerial habituses is the practice of close hands-on management of firms and other institutions. Nowhere is the transformation of monetarism more evident than in the changed role of the 'national privatization fund' (NPF). This institution was created by the first post-communist governments as a transitional tool. It was understood to be a mere 'fictional owner', needed only until actual private owners could be found. Indeed, the impetus for its creation was sheer monetarist peculiarity, since it was conceived as a means of getting 'the state' out of the process so that privatization could proceed in the most neutral, market-like space conceivable. Moreover, it was also thought that if the proceeds of privatization were deposited in this newly founded body, they would not be immediately usurped by budget-hungry bureaucrats.

Seven years after the fall of communism, however, in virtually every Central European country, a substantial portion of previously state-owned firms remain in the hands of the NPFs. Moreover, most of these firms are in debt and require assistance. Monetarist prescriptions are of no help in this situation because they are contradictory. On the one hand, they would require NPF officials to play the role of 'real owners', to watch the market for cues, and to be ready to take action to respond to these cues. On the other hand, however, monetary prescriptions also absolutely oppose any form of state ownership. NPF officials, and technocrats in the ministries of finance – few and overburdened as they are – cannot play the role of real owners. At the same time, however, they control funds (proceeds from the privatization of other firms) which could be used to benefit the state firms remaining under their supervision. Under these conditions, NPF officials have reformulated their task in accordance with the principle of budgetary restrictionism, and become involved in the daily affairs of the institutions and firms they control – at least to the extent that issues of fiscal discipline are concerned.[34]

The resulting situation is one in which structures of control over firms by the NPF far exceed the control exercised by communist authorities in the later phases of communism. As Kare Dahl Martinsen noted, the post-communist state has moved from a position of impotence *vis-à-vis* enterprises, which was characteristic of the late communist state, to a position of omnipotence. All roads lead back to the state. Its capacity for controlling firms is greatly enhanced owing to the adoption of monetarist methods, but – ironically – state officials continue to engage in close, hands-on supervision of enterprises under their jurisdiction.[35] One good example of this is the Hungarian Ministry of Finance which, instead of cutting university budgets and leaving it to individual institutions to decide how to cope with the cuts, told each institution how many people to lay off.

Finally, even the 'vanguard' of monetarist change, the finance managers, do not let their monetarist urges get the better of them. Faced with the overwhelming problem of bad debts, they reinvent redistribution, in the form of 'the consolidation bank' in the Czech Republic, or as 'subterranean redistribution' in other countries.[36] This subterranean redistribution is the third practice reflecting the encounter between monetarist ideology and managerial habituses.

The rituals of post-communist life

The need to impose their program on society, and to come to terms with managerial power, has also left its imprint on the ideology of 'civil society'. This imprint can be seen in the rituals of the post-communist *Bildungsbürgertum*, in which practical acts like cutting the budget take on symbolic meanings derived from the enchanted vision of civil society. The function of these rituals is not only as collective representations meant to civilize society, but also as last-ditch attempts to save some modicum of the vision of civil society from disenchantment. The post-communist *Bildungsbürgertum* is engaged in saving its collective biography, and protecting itself from doubt, by the most ancient method known to humankind: repetition.

There are two types of ritual that attempt to stave off post-communist disenchantment. The first type follows directly from the world-view of former dissident intellectuals, and their claim to pastoral power; the second type follows directly from the managerialist interpretation of monetarism. The former are rituals of civic education; the latter are rituals of budgetary restriction. Both refer to the same symbolic complex of sacrifice, purification and confession.

Sacrifice

While the contractarians and the nineteenth-century Central European *Bildungsbürgertum* promised affluence, the post-communist *Bildungsbürgertum* calls for sacrifice. In Weber's *Protestant Ethic*, the call was directed towards the individual entrepreneur, who was required to delay consumption for the sake of accumulation.[37] By contrast, the post-communist 'spirit of capitalism' extends the call to the whole of society, requiring everyone to sacrifice for the sake of 'the future': society lived beyond its means under socialism; now it has to come to terms with reality.[38]

The irony is that as long as socialism existed, it was frequently criticized for 'production for production's sake', 'dictatorship over needs' – in short, it was perceived as interested only in accelerated industrialization, not in the consumption needs of individuals.[39] Socialism demanded collective sacrifice in no uncertain terms – a collective postponement of consumption for the sake of societal accumulation – and the achievements of this policy were spectacular. From the vantage point of post-communism, however – both to those who yearn for its golden years and for those who see it as the cause of all the shortcomings of contemporary society – socialism now looks like the fleshpots of Goshen.

As we saw above, the idea of sacrifice was very important for the dissidents during late socialism. Indeed, many displayed remarkable courage at that time in acts of self-sacrifice. To be a dissident meant to sacrifice oneself, because only the act of self-sacrifice could challenge the regime's corrupt cynical pragmatism.[40] In a curious reversal of socialist ideology, where the proletariat was the universal class, the sacrificial lamb that saved humanity,[41] the dissident intellectuals threw themselves at the regime's altar and offered their bodies for sacrifice. The most moving example of this was the self-immolation of Jan Palach in Václavske Square. Now the dissidents are members and ideologues of the new power bloc, and as they are confronted with the task of post-communist transformation, they invoke the idea of sacrifice again. This time, however, self-sacrifice no longer suffices; now they ask society to be the sacrificial lamb for the sake of the future economic bourgeoisie.

As we shall see in Chapter 4, members of the post-communist power elite are among the big winners of the transition to capitalism in Central Europe. Some may accuse them, therefore, of being somewhat hypocritical, of demanding sacrifice from society while they enjoy the sunny side of post-communism. Managers and technocrats can say very little to counter these accusations, but former dissident intellectuals have a credible defense against this kind of criticism. They can point to sacrifices already made during the late communist period. For this reason, former dissidents are invaluable to the new power bloc, since they can very legitimately ask that those who sat around the fleshpots of 'goulash communism', should now make sacrifices.

In this context, note that budget cuts and budget-balancing acts often do not serve primarily economic purposes, but represent similar ritual calls for sacrifice as exercises in civic education. In Hungary, for instance, the government introduced a tuition fee of $15 a month at universities. Nobody in their right mind thinks that this tiny fee will make any difference in financing tertiary education. Rather, the reason for its introduction is to educate citizens in civic responsibility. The new tertiary fee does not serve to finance education; rather, it is intended to be an education in finance. Similarly, in the Czech Republic, the government announced with great ceremony that it finished the 1991–92 fiscal year with a surplus. A small ceremony was conducted to mark this achievement, and it was televised nationally. The Prime Minister and the Minister of Finance participated in this ceremony, in which the surplus was written into the budget for the following year, which was then ceremonially signed by the two politicians. Note that the economic rationality behind this ceremony was dubious: a government which did not spend its money is a government which overtaxed the population. Clearly, the ritual nature of this event was much more important; it sent a message to the population: 'Balance your checkbooks, and save a little – this is what virtue means.'

Purification

This, then, is the first purpose of sacrifice: it is a way of saving for the future and building proper, virtuous citizens. At the same time, however, the ritual of sacrifice is also oriented to the past. Sacrifice is a means of atoning for the sins of the past, and thus purifying individuals and society of the corruption suffered under communist rule. This is another novelty of the ethics of the post-communist *Bildungsbürgertum* – the rhetoric of purification. While for Adam Smith or Benjamin Franklin the natural human propensity to 'truck, barter and trade' was given (i.e. the stuff of civil society was given; it was natural; it was pure and ready to be taught), and what was needed was merely to inculcate the merits of the business ethic, the post-communist reformers proceed from the assumption that the human material they have inherited is thoroughly polluted. Sacrifice is thus a means not only of securing the future, but also of erasing the past. Socialist industrialization polluted the environment, they argue, but this was trivial in comparison with the pollution of minds and souls wrought by communist politics and communist education. The souls are probably the worst problem: it is not only that individuals have the wrong ideas, they have the wrong motivations as well.[42]

Post-communist reformers proceed from the dissident critique of state socialism, and from their point of view as pastors, they denounce the whole communist period as one of bad education. Before the corruption of minds and souls, there was 'the closing of the socialist mind'.[43] It began with the school curriculum. People were taught Russian instead of English, Marxism– Leninism instead of neoclassical economics, welding instead of computer programming. The closed mind then became impoverished, since it was detached from its natural context. Solzhenitsyn said that the official Soviet language was a degenerated form of Russian, which used an extremely restricted vocabulary and a simplified grammar, did not allow people to express their authentic selves or their national identity, and did not allow them to think properly. This also meant that people did not know their history. They were taught a false history of their nation, and they were taught to forget even what they themselves personally experienced of their own national history. For these reasons, the dissidents argue, both individual consciousness and collective consciousness were polluted and deficient.[44]

The impoverished mind created by the school curriculum was an easy target for the corruption process which continued outside schools. People were socialized to 'live within a lie', to play the game of 'as if' as if they believed in it, to participate in public rituals whose sole purpose was a display of conformity.[45] Thus they were taught to disrespect the value of public speech, to suspect all politicians as power-hungry, corrupt liars. They were taught to suspect and disrespect all intellectuals, especially the sacrificing types. They were even taught to steal: they were allowed to collect an income without working hard for it. The whole society was allowed to live beyond its means, to consume more than economic efficiency allowed. People's bodies were polluted as well: they overate, drank and smoked too much, and were biologically destroying themselves and society.[46] Even what appeared to be the marketplace – namely, the second economy – was turned into a school of parasitic values.[47] Most importantly, communism failed to teach people how to be responsible for their own lives.[48] People became addicted to and dependent on state redistribution: a sort of socialist welfare dependency. Cutting the welfare budget, therefore, is simultaneously a call for sacrifice from the population, and an attempt to purify the population of welfare dependency. Post-communist intellectuals never miss an opportunity to draw out these meanings. The point is that post-communist reformers do not trust these people whom socialism has produced. They do not believe that a civil society can be made from such raw material, or that these socialist dependants will be able to navigate the complexities of market capitalism, or even obey the law. Former socialist citizens have to be purified first.

This task of purification and of making the new 'capitalist man' is relatively easy (though not unproblematic) when it comes to young people.[49] According to post-communist reformers, the major problem here is that the teachers of this new generation cannot be trusted. They are the polluters of old. So while teachers in Western democracies usually have a great deal of autonomy in deciding what they teach and which books to use, post-communist curricula are hand-managed by opinion-making intellectuals, just as they were in the Stalinist period. In their concern for the souls of their young students, these intellectuals write new textbooks, and require that teachers teach only these certified texts in the same way all over the country.

Moreover, the task of purification is even more serious and difficult when it comes to the older generation. It may even be hopeless. If, in the 1960s, the 'New Left' radicals thought that everybody over forty was suspect, now intellectual members of the post-communist elite – themselves refugees of the New Left, and well over the requisite age – think that everybody over forty is hopeless. In this context, economic policies like 'downsizing' and layoffs are not merely technical steps required to restore the economy to health, but also ritual sacrifices meant to purify society and individuals. In most Central European countries, for example, about 10 percent of the labor force opted for early retirement in 1989. This was not the 'golden handshake' of large Western corporations or universities; early retirement typically took the form of disability pensions. This was a symbolic 'disabling' message: these people who spent most of their lives under communism are 'beyond help' – they are no longer fit to work, they cannot be trusted to work, or to participate in society. They might as well lie down and die . . . which they do: the symbolic figures being pathetic old communist leaders, passing away one after the other, immediately after their ouster in 1989.

With a similar logic, unemployment is perceived as 'purgatory'. People are being laid-off not only for the sake of the firm, but for their own sake as well. They are being given a chance to 'retool', acquire 'human capital', and work on their résumés. This logic conveys the message that things cannot be done the old way any more. People have sinned – they will have to atone for their sins by becoming more efficient, flexible, responsible, and skilled. Indeed, unemployment breaks the relationship of dependence between the individual and the state, and teaches individuals that they have to be responsible for themselves. In fact, in the name of inculcating responsibility, the most bizarre measures have been taken. The reform of the dental system in Hungary, for example, has eliminated all free dental care except extractions. Now patients are faced with the choice of being responsible or becoming toothless. This is the post-communist version of preventive care – to prevent irresponsibility rather than cavities.

This ideological interest in 'purification' explains why post-communist technocrats, who claim to adhere to the monetarist canon, have actually devised policies which imply a great deal of government intervention in the economy, and involve hands-on management of economic processes. Behind the façade of monetarist rituals, we have argued, post-communist managerialism concentrates on budgetary restrictionism as a means of gaining a foothold in the daily workings of state firms and institutions. This is precisely because the technocracy believes that people's minds are polluted, that they cannot be trusted to do what they are supposed to do in a capitalist economy. Consequently, the technocracy sees its task in educational–pastoral terms: it has to instruct, supervise and monitor individuals; it has to instill the requisite initiative in agents who are not entrepreneurial enough; it has to inculcate self-discipline and responsibility in subjects who routinely break the rules, or search for ways around them. Even if you cut their budgets, they cannot be trusted to 'slim down' and become more efficient. For example, instead of laying off workers, the university may decide to institute an across-the-board wage cut. This misses the point, so the technocrats must intervene and guarantee that the point of budget-cutting gets across – it is meant to *purify*. It is meant to rid the university of former communists or 'parasites'. If a false sense of solidarity and a retrograde 'egalitarianism' prevents university rectors from taking the rational and efficient road of purification, it is up to the technocrats to instruct and supervise them, to make sure that they implement budget cuts in a way which purifies the institution and makes it more efficient.[50] Indeed, in the budget-cutting ritual the meanings of de-communist purification and economic efficiency are fused together, and serve to legitimate one another.

Confession

In the rituals of purification, the post-communist *Bildungsbürgertum* went well beyond its original intentions. The role originally envisioned for its pastoral art was a mild one: in a civil society composed of confessing individuals, purification would have been unnecessary. The intellectual fraction of the power bloc would have been able to exercise power as the moral guides of subjects interested in the care of their own souls. Unfortunately, the bulk of Central Europeans have not confessed. Having lived through socialism, they cannot even comprehend what their crime could possibly have been.

Confession, however, is necessary. No amount of sacrifice and re-education can make the polluted 'socialist man' pure, without a confession of the crimes and misdemeanors of the past. One cannot live an authentic life, the Central European reformers believe, unless one confronts one's past. With the exception of dissident intellectuals, probably everybody in Central Europe has something in their past to confess. As Havel's greengrocer metaphor suggests, the most ordinary people going about their daily business, not suspecting that they have committed any sins, were actually deeply and mortally implicated in the workings of the communist system.[51]

To see the gravity of their sins, post-communist citizens have to appreciate the enormity of their crime of not resisting the system. This is the point that intellectuals attempt to impress on the public. They recall the executions, torture, and imprisonments of the Stalinist period to make this point, even though Stalinism lasted for only about four to five years in the early 1950s, and anyone younger than forty could not possibly have witnessed or condoned Stalinist policies. But more importantly, post-communist intellectuals recall all those 'crimes against human nature' which marked the socialist era: all those acts which prevented people from living authentic lives, crimes which ranged from the activity of censors to the cashier at the supermarket, who made you wait unnecessarily long in line until you lost your temper, started swearing and were embarrassed before your own authentic self.[52] The example of the cashier, like Havel's greengrocer or head waiter story, may sound trivial, but it is not. During the long decades of post-Stalinism, people were not executed; few spent time in jail for political acts. People suffered mostly from the general inefficiency of the socialist system; they spent their lives waiting in queues, trying to get things done. So we are talking about wasted lives. What is unusual about these crimes, however, is that virtually everybody engaged in them. The victims of today's queue were typically tomorrow's criminals. This is the stuff of which collective crimes were made. If people recollect themselves as victims, they still feel irritation, but if they remember themselves as former perpetrators, they tend to dismiss these acts as petty and unimportant. It is generally difficult to impress upon Central Europeans that they were participating in an enormous collective crime.

But impressed they must be, and confess they must, if they are to be purified. Hence the intellectuals have done everything humanly possible to uncover the sins of the past. Chief among these confession rituals has been the drive to open secret police files, to release the names of agents and collaborators, and even to make the complete files public, as monuments to the extent of collective guilt. This post-communist process of confession has some similarities to the Inquisition, in the sense that the real purpose is not punishment but to make the accused confess in order to save their souls – to purify them. In the Czech Republic, this process was called 'lustrace', a term adopted from the Latin, which Siklova renders as 'purification by sacrifice, purging'.[53]

And, it is true: if one confesses, forgiveness is granted. The case of István Csurka, the *enfant terrible* of Hungarian politics, illustrates this point well. When Csurka first clashed with Prime Minister Antall and called for his resignation, Antall counterattacked by hinting that he had evidence of Csurka's affiliation with communist internal security. Csurka's (rather savvy) response was to publish a 'self-lustration', in which he described how he was recruited and what he did as an informer.[54] Public reaction to this confession was telling: many people were moved by his 'courage' in confessing – it was evidence that his soul was 'saved'. After this confession, not even his most bitter enemies could use his informer past against him. The confession purified Csurka.[55] The opposite happened to Jozsef Torgyán – a somewhat less extreme politician than Csurka – and also to the Slovak Jan Budaj, a well-known liberal dissident. Both men were accused of being informers for the secret police. They never confessed, and are still under fire for their assumed ties with the police during the communist era.

The ritual nature of confession, which reminds one of communist 'self-criticism', also serves to forge a moral community. Without it, the dissident intelligentsia would have disintegrated in a war of accusations. Instead, the public confession dramatizes the message of collective guilt, but also indicates the means of atonement and reintegration. It is proof of the generosity, leniency, and forgiveness of the post-communist inquisition. Persuading individuals to confess is not an act of revenge. Rather, it serves to demystify the evil nature of the previous regime, and provides a way of saving the souls of sinners, enabling them to rejoin the community of saints. Even if there are only a few public confessions, the result is likely to be cathartic. The other guilty individuals, all those who 'lived within a lie' (practically the majority of ordinary people), can identify with the negative hero of the confession drama, and without going on public display themselves, they can at least confess to themselves and receive absolution.

The post-communist power bloc is heavily invested in the public ritual of confession. Indeed, to the extent that it is impossible to prosecute people who acted within the law, they resort to extra-legal spectacles, such as mock trials conducted by historians and other researchers to promote and validate confession. If the gaze of the prosecutor cannot penetrate the guilt of these individuals, and if they do not confess, then it should be left to the historian. True, many famous Czech dissidents have come out in public against the practice of 'lustration', but they did not do so because they wanted to put an end to the confession process. On the contrary, they protested because 'lustration' was not confession enough. They were irritated when journalists, and other irresponsible demagogues, usurped 'lustration' for their own purposes, especially when these individuals pursued scandal and accusation rather than the confession. Worst of all, of course, journalists often directed their attack at the dissidents' midst. The Kavan affair in the Czech Republic was a prominent example, which prompted Havel and Siklova to denounce the publishers of 'wild lists' and explain that the point of lustration was not vengeance.[56] Similarly, others have suggested collecting secret police files in special archives accessible only to historians and other researchers, not to journalists or the general public. Regardless of their protests against sensationalism, and despite suggestions to curb the furor surrounding confession, the post-communist power bloc in the Czech Republic remains so deeply invested in the ritual of confession that the Czech parliament extended the process of 'lustration' into its sixth year.

Since people do not confess, the opinion-making intellectuals engage in an escalation of the scale of the crimes for which people are held culpable. One such form of escalation is the analogy between communism and Nazism. After all, many Germans never committed crimes themselves, but they were guilty because they never raised their voices; they knew but never dared to resist – or, if they did not know, they are guilty because they did not make an effort to find out. The same structure of argument is used about communism: those who did not resist were co-conspirators. Post-World War II West Germany is pointed to as an example to follow. It is emphasized that a successful post-Nazi civil society was built quickly in West Germany, precisely because Germans were made to confront their collective guilt and confess it. East Germany, on the other hand, is proffered as the counter-example, a case in which the ghost of Nazism has never disappeared, because no confession has ever been made. On this basis, the argument is made that the ghost of communism will disappear only if people can be made to confess.

A no less insidious form of escalation is to explain how the petty crimes and sufferings of the communist period were a punishment for the 'original sin' which preceded communism. In the Czech case, this original sin was the expulsion of the Sudeten Germans. It is precisely because the Czechs did not atone for this original sin that they suffered under communism. There

is a direct line from the looting which followed the expulsions to the abolition of private property under communism; from the disrespect shown
towards the human rights of the Sudeten Germans to the show trials and
executions of the 1950s; from the relocation of Czechs into German homes
to the 'communist constituency' which made Czechoslovakia the only country in Central Europe where the communists won the democratic elections
in 1948; from the principle of 'collective guilt' employed in the expulsions to
'socialist justice' – in short, from the immorality of the expulsions to the
moral decay of the Czech nation under communism.[57] The Czechs will
never be able to overcome their moral decay, argue the intellectuals, if they
will not confess to the original sin. This is why one of the first acts of
President Havel was to apologize to the Germans. His intention was osten-
sibly to start a chain of confessions which would encompass all those who
were moved into German property by communist authorities and, well
beyond them, all those who collaborated with communism in matters totally
unrelated to the German question.

In addition to the original sin, there is also the issue of continuity between
Stalinism and post-Stalinism. Since the enormity of post-Stalinist crimes can
be perceived only in their totality – since each single act was usually quite
minor – it is necessary to emphasize the continuity between Stalinism and
post-Stalinism to invoke a heightened collective guilt. Specific public rituals
are devised to dramatize this point. The reburial of Imre Nagy and his
comrades was such a ritual. The casks containing the remains of the fallen
heroes, the solemn music played while the long list of names of the executed
was read over the loudspeaker – all these powerfully proclaimed that an
unpunished crime had been committed. It turned out that the essence of the
Kádárist regime was contained in these executions, not in the long decades
of goulash communism. Hence all the beneficiaries of Kádárist paternalism
were called upon to confess. Although they had not spilled blood, they were
sojourners in the house of the murderer. And, like ordinary Germans in
Nazi times, they saw nothing, said nothing, and did nothing.

Finally, the confession ritual also has its monetarist forms. Legislating
wealth declarations has been debated in Hungary, for example, as a means
of making sure that tax evasion is prevented. Since there has been strong
opposition to requiring people to make an inventory of their assets public,
there is now a move to make this declaration voluntary. This impresses us as
similar to the confession which is expected of former police agents. If you
confess now about the wealth you accumulated during late communism or
early post-communism, you will not be asked where this wealth came from,
or whether you attained it by legal or illegal means. Even if you committed
crimes in the past, with a simple confession they will be forgiven; the point
being that from now on you can and shall lead a virtuous life, 'living in
truth'. This is different from the idea of a tax 'amnesty' in Western countries,

because the purpose is not to recover past revenue but to establish a baseline for a confessing population.

To conclude this chapter: the post-communist mentality has been conceived in the womb of the ideas of civil society and monetarism, and the post-communist power bloc has benefited from the elective affinities between these ideas, which contribute to its own authority. The post-communist mentality, however, is also a disenchanted one. Its making required a fundamental reconstruction of both economic and political philosophies, and especially the reformulation of the ideal of 'action from a distance'. A close hands-on management and supervision of the economy was called for, and rituals of civic education had to be imposed on society.

The different fractions of the power bloc view this development with differing attitudes. As former communist functionaries, managers have benefited greatly from the subversion of monetarism. They were accustomed to conducting business in the context of budget-bargaining, and they could accept the rituals too. After all, as former communist functionaries they were used to negotiating their way in an environment in which ritual affirmations were the order of the day. The managers swim in this new post-communist society like fish in water, and this is why we have called the mentality which results from the reconciliation between civil society, monetarism, and managerial habituses a 'managerial govern-mentality'.

Many of the technocrats were also communist functionaries at earlier points in their careers, and to this extent their response is quite similar to that of managers, since their habituses are quite similar. None the less, those technocrats who are committed to the monetarist vision are also sensitive to the discrepancies between their *modus operandi* and monetarist orthodoxy. They adopt a defensive tone: after all, they are technocrats; their sole task is to make the system work, in whatever conditions prevail and however it is required of them. Society may not yet be ready to be entrusted with self-regulation; it is still in 'transition', it has to be regulated and fine-tuned a little more.

The most disaffected fraction of the new power bloc is the former dissident opinion-making elite. This group accepts the managerial mentality with reluctance, disenchantment, and often with a great deal of guilt. Indeed, feelings of guilt have been so intense that many intellectuals have dropped out of power altogether, returning to their professional and literary activities. Even these 'dropouts', however, rarely manage to distance themselves from the rituals of post-communism. It is just too much to ask of them to subject these rituals to critical scrutiny when they were so active in creating them, and are so deeply committed to the noble ideas behind them. Moreover, the intellectuals who remained in power are their friends and former comrades in arms. To criticize their practices now is tantamount to betrayal. This is the reason for the unidimensionality of the post-

communist mind. Only the affirmative dimension of the mind has survived – the critical imagination has been lost, and it is virtually impossible to
resuscitate it.

To sum up: in this chapter, we offer a description of the ideology of the
post-communism power bloc. This ideology has its origins in the elective
affinity between the dissident theory of civil society and Western monetarist theory. The managerial mentality which developed out of this elective
affinity, however, was also shaped by the task of building and governing
'actually existing post-communist society' and by the compromise with
socialist enterprise managers that this task necessitated. After all, the theory
of civil society was worked out as a critique of state socialism, and was never
a blueprint for the transition from socialism to capitalism. Similarly, monetarism was a proposal for governing the institutions of advanced Western
capitalism, not post-communist institutions. When socialism collapsed, then,
the ideologues of 'civil society' and monetarism were confronted with fundamentally new tasks. They did what the theory of 'trajectory adjustment'
would lead us to expect: they took their old ideas and used them to make
sense of the new realities, modifying those ideas a great deal in the process.
This is how the mentality of post-communist managerialism was born, and
although it fails to meet the goal of 'action from afar' sought by the dissidents, it is none the less capitalism, a decisive break with the redistributive
control of state socialism.

4

Post-Communist Managerialism:
Theoretical Controversies and Social Struggles Over the Making of the New Propertied Class

How is the making of a propertied bourgeoisie happening in Central Europe? Is it happening at all? Has the second *Bildungsbürgertum*, or any component of it, successfully converted itself into a class of private proprietors? In Chapter 3 we introduced the idea of managerialism as a cultural phenomenon – as the *Weltanschauung* of the post-communist power bloc. In this chapter we extend this analysis by using the idea of managerialism to explain some of the novel features of the political economy and class relations of post-communist societies.

As we have emphasized, the unique feature of making capitalism from the ruins of state socialism in Central Europe is that it is happening without a propertied bourgeoisie. In all other historical sites where modern capitalism has developed, some form of private property and some class of private proprietors – no matter how embryonic, and no matter how different from modern capitalist entrepreneurs – already existed. In the classical case of transition, feudal landlords gradually converted their property into private ownership and began to be recruited into the new *grande bourgeoisie*. Urban artisans and merchants were busily accumulating capital, and were well positioned to transform themselves from the third estate of a feudal order into one of the fractions of the new dominant class in a capitalist mode of production. Post-communism is the first situation where the transition to private property from a collective form of ownership is being attempted. Moreover, as we observed in Chapter 2, this project is being led by the second *Bildungsbürgertum* – by an uneasy alliance between former communist apparatchiks, technocrats, managers and their former left-wing critics, the dissident intellectuals. In short, capitalism is being made by a coalition of propertyless agents, who only yesterday outbid each other in their anti-capitalism.

113

In 1988 two leading sociologists of the region, Jadwiga Staniszkis and Elemér Hankiss, formulated a provocative hypothesis, which we have discussed previously as the theory of political capitalism.[1] According to Staniszkis and Hankiss, the former communist *nomenklatura* knew by 1988 that the destruction of the old communist order was inevitable. They therefore designed a scheme to convert political office into private wealth, and attempted to transform themselves into a new *grande bourgeoisie*. Indeed, many commentators on the Central European transformation think that this is what happened after 1989: communist officials used political office to convert public goods into private individual wealth – *de facto*, they stole state property and became a 'kleptocracy'.

We were also among those who were fascinated by the theory of political capitalism. In the light of the so-called 'spontaneous privatization' legislation passed in Poland and Hungary in 1988–89, this hypothesis sounded plausible. We were intrigued by the idea that communist apparatchiks had started preaching capitalism. The notion that they would rule as private owners also appealed to our ironic sense of history. In this context, in 1990, we launched a survey in six East and Central European countries – Russia, Poland, the Czech Republic, Slovakia, Hungary and Bulgaria – to assess the empirical support for Staniszkis's and Hankiss's forecasts. In 1993, in each country, we interviewed 1,000 people who were members of the 1988 *nomenklatura*, 1,000 people who belonged to the new economic, political, and cultural elites at the time; we also conducted personal life history interviews of 5,000 adults randomly selected from the population.[2] In this chapter we present data from three Central European countries: the Czech Republic, Hungary, and Poland. We ask: what happened to the old *nomenklatura*? What are the social origins of members of the new elite? Is there any evidence for the existence of a propertied bourgeoisie by 1993? If so, how is this new class of domestic proprietors constituted? How much, and what, do they own?

Our search for answers to these questions transformed us from empirical sociologists into detectives. As we gathered and began to analyze data, our list of suspects began to grow, but the culprits continued to elude us. We kept reformulating our hypotheses, and we are still in the process of doing so. We invite our readers to join us for an hour or so – or for however long it takes to solve this mystery – in our search for Whodunit (and what did they do)? To put it in Goffman's terms: although books usually present readers with the 'front stage' of the drama – usually orderly, clean, and well acted – we would like to invite you to come 'backstage'. We want you to see the messy behind-the-scenes labor which is necessary for the performance to unfold smoothly on the 'front stage'. Instead of showing you the most polished theory supported by the data available to us, we want to document the process of how one theory after another collapsed, as we dug deeper into the data, and as suspect after suspect was eliminated. Indeed, as we write this chapter we are still digging. We do not claim to have arrived at the final truth. To be frank, we do not believe in final truth. The great historical transformation we are studying is still unfolding. The stakes of this transformation are still being fought over. The scene is changing as we write and as you read. With this in mind, let us anticipate the plot of the drama, and tell you what this chapter tries to accomplish.

Act I. The *nomenklatura*:
The thief of Budapest and Warsaw

The story begins with our confrontation with political capitalism theory, which states that people who were in *nomenklatura* positions prior to 1989 were able to retain power and privilege through the post-communist transition by converting political office into private wealth. The analysis which follows casts doubt on this prediction. To our surprise, we find that a substantial circulation of elites took place during the post-communist transition. The first section of this chapter documents massive downward mobility among members of the old *nomenklatura*. Moreover, we find little evidence to indicate that the *nomenklatura* was successful in acquiring private property. These revelations require us to reformulate the theory of political capitalism, since by 1993 the old communist *nomenklatura* had not established itself as a new propertied *grande bourgeoisie*.

Act II.
The victorious technocracy

The second theory we confronted was Erzsébet Szalai's theory of 'technocratic revolution', which in some ways, can be viewed as a refinement of the general political capitalism thesis.[3] Szalai's argument is that the late state-socialist *nomenklatura* was highly fragmented, and that the dynamics of social change should be understood as an intense struggle between the bureaucratic and technocratic fractions of the old ruling estate. In this view, 1989 was a successful revolution of the late state-socialist technocracy against the bureaucratic fraction of the communist ruling estate. And, indeed, the data we analyze in the second section of this chapter support this contention. In all three countries, a significant proportion of the top economic command positions in 1993 were occupied by those who had belonged to the technocratic–managerial elite during the 1980s. Rather than the *nomenklatura* as a whole grasping power, one of its fractions – the technocratic-managerial elite – appeared to have established itself as the new propertied class.

Act III. The cautious managers

In the third section of the chapter, then, we set out to describe what we thought was the new propertied class, recruited from the ranks of former socialist technocrats and managers. Our analysis confirmed the argument that former technocrats were prominent among the new political elite of post-communism, while former socialist managers and deputy managers occupied the top economic positions. However, we also found, to our surprise, that these post-communist managers did not exercise their economic power as *private owners*. Managers owned little property, and they exercised decision-making power in the absence of capitalist proprietors. In other words, although it is true that managers were extremely successful, it was not the kind of success that theorists of political capitalism expected. We believed that we had finally isolated the right suspect – the managers who had retained position, power and privilege into the post-communist transition – but we began to doubt if a crime had been committed at all. Indeed, if managers were culpable of anything, it was of failing to appropriate public goods as private property. In an ironic twist on the twist, we were *disappointed* that managers had not done what we had formerly *feared* the *nomenklatura* were doing after 1989! In the light of these findings, we began to build our own theory to explain the power of these managers.[4]

Act IV. The Great Bank Robbery of 1993–96

Finally, we arrive at the last scene of our detective story – at least, the last scene for the time being. We would remind our readers that the curtain is still up in Central Europe; the drama is still unfolding. Our initial survey was fielded at a relatively early stage in the post-communist transformation, being completed by 1993. Since then, we have acquired more recent data on changes in property relations, and although they are limited to Hungary for 1995 and 1996, they raise the possibility that similar trends characterize the rest of the region. These data reveal a marked change in patterns of property ownership. The most striking development is a dramatic decline in public ownership and a correspondingly large increase in private ownership among domestic individuals. Of particular importance is the growth in private ownership of middle-sized firms between 1993 and 1996. In the light of these data, the final section of this chapter explores the question of whether or not a propertied class is now emerging in Central Europe. We ask: who are these owners? Are they *our* managers? If so, does our theory of post-communist managerialism fall? Or is this recent round of 'privatization' consonant with our analysis of the balance of class forces at the top of Central European societies?

Whatever happened to the *nomenklatura*?

Downward mobility among former nomenklatura *members*

Political capitalism theory expects to find that the old communist elite has turned itself into the new propertied bourgeoisie of post-communist society. Its most general proposition is that people who were in *nomenklatura* positions prior to 1989 were able to retain their power and privilege through the post-communist transition by converting their political capital into private economic wealth. Our data cast doubt on these predictions.

Table 4.1 describes the 1993 post-communist occupational destinations of those individuals who occupied *nomenklatura* positions in 1988 in Hungary, the Czech Republic, and Poland.[5] While there is some variation across the countries, the main finding in the table is one of massive downward mobility among *nomenklatura* members during the first five years of post-communism. Only half of those who occupied *nomenklatura* positions in 1988 were still in positions of authority in 1993, and this includes rather minor positions in low-level management. Indeed, the proportion of former *nomenklatura* members who occupied *any* authority position in 1993 was rather low. And – rather surprisingly – in Hungary, which boasted the most advanced market reform policies of the late communist period, the loss of authority positions among former *nomenklatura* members has been even more marked than it has in the other countries:[6] only 43.1 percent of the Hungarian *nomenklatura* retained jobs in which they have subordinates.[7]

Table 4.1 Occupational destinations in 1993 of people who were in nomenklatura *positions in 1988 by country*

Occupation in 1993	Czech Republic	Hungary	Poland
All in position of authority	**51.7**	**43.1**	**51.2**
High political office	3.0	6.4	9.0
High manager – public	16.2	11.2	13.4
High manager – private	12.8	2.4	9.1
High cultural office	1.1	4.4	7.1
Low-level managers	12.6	13.0	8.6
Entrepreneurs	6.0	5.7	4.0
Professionals	**12.2**	**19.9**	**13.9**
Workers	**12.6**	**5.5**	**9.5**
Retired early (younger than 65)	**15.4**	**19.1**	**17.2**
Other retired and unemployed	**8.1**	**12.6**	**8.2**
All respondents	**100%**	**100%**	**100%**
(n)	**(468)**	**(803)**	**(849)**

Note: Numbers may not add up to 100 percent due to rounding.

Critics might argue that we overstate the extent to which *nomenklatura* members have been 'losers' in the post-communist transition. After all, some of the *nomenklatura* were very old, and would have retired anyway.[8] We think this is a reasonable concern: the amount of downward mobility attributable to retirement, and especially to early retirement, is non-trivial. So, to investigate whether or not retirement indicates downward mobility, we examine age at retirement, patterns of property ownership, and the occupational trajectories of former *nomenklatura* members.

Trends in retirement and private business ownership among former nomenklatura *members*

Early retirement is a good indicator of 'being out of favor' in the new post-communist order, so it is important to get a sense of how widespread it is. Although the official retirement age in the Czech Republic and in Hungary was sixty for men and fifty-five for women, in fact, for people at the very top of the communist social hierarchy, retirement occurred much later, usually around the age of seventy. For this reason, we chose sixty-five as the boundary year indicating early retirement. In Table 4.1, it is clear that rates of early retirement among former *nomenklatura* members have been relatively high in Central Europe, ranging from 15.4 percent in the Czech Republic to a high of 19.1 percent in Hungary. Moreover, a substantial proportion of former *nomenklatura* members under sixty in 1993 were also among these early retirees: 7 percent of 1988 *nomenklatura* members under sixty had retired by 1993 in the Czech Republic; there were 14 percent in Hungary, and 16 percent in Poland (these data are not shown in the table). These findings support our contention that there has been massive dispossession, downward mobility, and circulation out of the labor market among former *nomenklatura* members during the post-communist transition.

The second major finding in Table 4.1 is the extremely low proportion of former *nomenklatura* members who reported moving into private business by 1993, either as owners or as managers of privately owned firms. This finding is also at odds with political capitalism theory which predicted that cadres would quickly transform themselves into private-sector entrepreneurs, given the opportunity to do so. Our data show, however, that only about 6 percent of former *nomenklatura* members in Hungary and the Czech Republic had become private owners of businesses by 1993, and the rate was even lower in Poland: 4 percent. In fact, the proportion of *nomenklatura* members opting for early retirement was higher (17.2 percent) than the proportion moving into private business (4.0 plus 9.1 = 13.1 percent) overall. Furthermore, only about 8 percent of all *nomenklatura* members across the three countries reported *managing* a privately owned firm in 1993. There is significant cross-country variation here, with a higher proportion of *nomenklatura* members moving into the private sector in the Czech Republic than in the other countries: 18.8 percent (12.8 plus 6 percent) of former Czech *nomenklatura* members owned or managed a private firm in 1993, compared to 8.1 percent (2.4 plus 5.7 percent) in Hungary and 13.1 percent (9.1 plus 4 percent) in Poland. This difference might be attributed to the Czech policy of 'lustration' – in the Czech Republic, former leading communist cadres were legally prohibited from holding public office, and may have 'escaped forward' into private business as a result. Whatever the case, the comparatively small proportions of former *nomenklatura* in the private sector by 1993 in each of the countries, suggests that the political capitalism hypothesis needs to be reformulated.

Occupational destinations of different fractions of the former nomenklatura

If we dig deeper into the data, the problems with the political capitalism thesis become even more serious. In its original formulation, this theory stated that political office had been used for the accumulation of private wealth in Central Europe. In order to test the accuracy of this statement, we need to disaggregate the '*nomenklatura*' category further. There were very different kinds of *nomenklatura* positions in the communist system, and good reason to think that they were divided among themselves.[9] For this reason, a fair test of political capitalism theory should investigate whether or not any particular component of the *nomenklatura* has successfully negotiated the post-communist transition and become private proprietors. After all, some of our *nomenklatura* members in 1988 were top managers of large firms – thus they were 'technocrats', or what we term the 'economic elite' of the late communist period. In their case, it is not obvious that becoming a manager of a privately owned firm is a conversion of political capital into private wealth – managers and technocrats may simply have used their human capital and their managerial experience to maintain senior economic positions in the post-communist transition. Other former *nomenklatura* members belonged to the 'cultural elite' – they were rectors of universities, Members of the Academies of Sciences, or editors of daily newspapers – and these jobs in the cultural sector were not positions from which one could easily generate vast amounts of private wealth. Thus, political capitalism theory would not necessarily expect former members of the communist cultural elite to be those most able to convert political office into private wealth. Arguably, however, the political capitalism thesis should hold for members of the 'political elite'. These were people who held positions in the Communist Party apparatus or in the civil service, and of all the members of the *nomenklatura* they were the best placed to use their 'office' to enrich themselves through the mechanism of 'spontaneous privatization'.[10] With this disaggregation of the *nomenklatura* into its economic, cultural, and political components, we are now in a position to offer a crucial test of Staniszkis's and Hankiss's version of the political capitalism thesis by asking: to what extent has the 'bureaucratic' fraction of the ruling estate – the 'political elite' – benefited economically from the post-communist transition?

Table 4.2 Occupational destinations in 1993 of people who were in economic, political and cultural nomenklatura *positions in 1988 in all three countries (Czech Republic, Hungary and Poland)*

Occupation in 1993	Economic elite, 1988	Political elite, 1988	Cultural elite, 1988
All in position of authority	**70.7**	**39.3**	**44.2**
High political office	1.5	10.8	1.3
High manager – public	33.4	5.9	7.8
High manager – private	19.2	4.0	1.4
High cultural office	0.4	1.8	19.3
Low-level managers	10.8	11.0	11.8
Entrepreneurs	5.4	5.8	2.5
Professionals	**4.7**	**16.9**	**27.4**
Workers	**2.2**	**13.4**	**3.3**
Retired early (younger than 65)	**14.7**	**20.9**	**11.1**
Other retired and unemployed	**7.6**	**9.4**	**14.1**
All respondents	**100%**	**100%**	**100%**
(n)	**(536)**	**(1,186)**	**(398)**

Note: Numbers may not add up to 100 percent due to rounding.

Table 4.2 documents the 1993 occupational destinations of former *nomenklatura* members for each component of the *nomenklatura*: the economic fraction, the cultural fraction, and the political fraction. It shows, first, that the political fraction of the *nomenklatura* was the least successful in weathering the post-communist transition. Only 39.3 percent of the political *nomenklatura* retained positions of authority between 1988 and 1993, compared to 44.2 percent of the cultural elite and 70.7 percent of the economic elite. Second, early retirement was also much more common among the political fraction (20.9 percent) of the *nomenklatura* than among the economic and cultural fractions (14.7 and 11.1 percent respectively). This suggests that political capital was much less useful than cultural capital, and particularly cultural capital in the form of managerial expertise, for successfully navigating the pitfalls of post-communism. Third, Table 4.2 suggests that former Communist Party and state officials who comprised the political fraction of the *nomenklatura* in 1988 had less success in entering new private-sector positions than former communist managers. Among the former members of the economic *nomenklatura*, 24.6 percent (5.4 plus 19.2 percent) either owned or managed a private business in 1993, compared to only 9.8 percent (5.8 plus 4.0 percent) of members of the political fraction. These findings indicate that it was more advantageous to be a manager than a party or state official if one wanted to enter the new economic elite of post-communism. Moreover, these findings directly refute arguments by Staniszkis and Hankiss that it was the political fraction of the former communist elite who were best placed to take advantage of post-communist market reforms; rather, we find that members of the economic *nomenklatura* were much bigger beneficiaries of the post-communist transition than members of the political *nomenklatura*.

Business ownership among different fractions of the former nomenklatura *and the post-communist elite*

The response of political capitalism theory to our findings might be, however, that it is irrelevant who is *managing* firms in the new post-communist private sector. Rather, political capitalist theorists might argue that their theory predicts that political cadres will become business *owners* in post-communism. To address this issue, Table 4.3 presents data on business ownership among different fractions of the former *nomenklatura* to investigate whether or not the political or the economic fraction was more likely to own businesses in 1993. And in an effort to assess whether or not 'old communists' or members of the new post-communist elite have benefited the most from the transition to capitalism in Central Europe, Table 4.4 presents data comparing levels of business ownership in 1993 among former *nomenklatura* members and members of the new post-communist elite.

Table 4.3 Number of businesses owned by people who were members of the 1988 economic, political, and cultural elites

Number of businesses owned	Economic elite	Political elite	Cultural elite
Owns no business	77.1	82.0	88.5
Owns one firm	15.2	13.4	8.8
Owns more than one firm	7.6	4.5	2.8
All respondents	100%	100%	100%
(n)	(538)	(1,191)	(400)

Note: Numbers may not add up to 100 percent due to rounding.

The first conclusion we can draw from Tables 4.3 and 4.4 is that the distribution of post-communist business ownership among different fractions of the former *nomenklatura* runs in a direction opposite to the one predicted by the theory of political capitalism. Table 4.3 shows that former members of the political fraction (13.4 plus 4.5=17.9 percent) were less likely to report business ownership than former members of the economic fraction (15.2 plus 7.6=22.8 percent). Second, Table 4.4 shows that members of the new post-communist elite (22.2 percent) were more likely to report business ownership in 1993 than former members of the *nomenklatura* (18.4 percent).[11] In the context of our prior discussion about early retirement, these findings on business ownership suggest that those who were better able to retain their positions during the post-communist transition – namely, the economic fraction of the *nomenklatura* – and those who were upwardly mobile into the new elite during the post-communist transition, were more likely to acquire business ownership than those members of the old *nomenklatura* who were downwardly mobile at the end of communism. This supports our argument that the basis of business ownership seems to be more closely linked to technical–managerial know-how (cultural capital) than to the office held during the communist period (political capital).

Table 4.4 Business ownership among members of the 1993 post-communist elite and by members of the 1988 nomenklatura

Business ownership	1993 post-communist elite	1988 nomenklatura
Owns business in 1993	22.2	18.4
Does not own business	77.8	81.6
All respondents	100%	100%
(n)	(2,898)	(2,139)

Third, Tables 4.3 and 4.4 suggest that business ownership is not a major dimension of elite status and/or recruitment among former *nomenklatura* members or among members of the new post-communist elite. Although we lack detailed information on the size of firm and size of the ownership stake elite members hold in firms, these general data show none the less that only about a fifth of those who were members of the *nomenklatura* in 1988 reported business ownership in 1993. This proportion translates into about 500 former *nomenklatura* members in Hungary and the Czech Republic, and about 800–1,000 in Poland (a much larger country). If this business ownership among former *nomenklatura* members is in large corporations, then these findings provide strong *prima facie* support for the revised political capitalism hypothesis outlined above. However, we reiterate that the data in Tables 4.3 and 4.4 describe only business ownership *in general*. Our survey asked whether former *nomenklatura* members, or any member of their family, owned any part of a business of any size.[12] Thus, included in the 20 percent of former *nomenklatura* members reporting business ownership are those with very small ownership interests, and those with interests in very small firms.

Although business ownership data are poor on this score, according to the available evidence most of the ownership reported by former *nomenklatura* members in Hungary, the Czech Republic, and Poland is in very small firms. Many of these enterprises are tiny subcontracting units with little fixed capital, or they serve only as tax havens.

We return to this issue later in this chapter, using more detailed and reliable Hungarian data on business ownership collected by TARKI. Simply note at this point that the TARKI data confirm our general suspicions. About half of the TARKI respondents who reported any business ownership reported ownership in small businesses. Moreover, the other half of respondents who reported an ownership stake in a firm with more than ten employees held only a tiny stake in these larger firms. Only about 7 or 8 percent of the former *nomenklatura* reported ownership in firms with more than ten employees, and only 3 or 4 percent of these owners reported more than a 10 percent share in these businesses. If we generalize to the population, this translates into approximately 90–100 former senior cadre families in Hungary and the former Czech Republic, and about 150 senior cadre families in Poland, who may own 10 percent or more of a business with more than ten employees. Among these senior cadre families with 10 percent or more ownership stakes in actual private businesses, about half are families with a member from the political fraction of the former *nomenklatura*.[13]

These findings on business ownership among former *nomenklatura* members are in line with other research which shows that a great deal of business ownership among former cadres in Central Europe is really petty-bourgeois ownership.[14] Such ownership does not indicate the formation of a propertied ruling class. Eric Hanley shows, for example, that one of the best predictors of becoming a small business operator, with a small number of employees, is managerial position prior to the fall of communism. Once managerial position is taken into account, Communist Party membership does not affect the odds of small business ownership in 1993 at all. This finding is consistent with what we have been arguing about business ownership among former *nomenklatura* members. That is: the most probable post-communist destination for former cadres who entered into private business is the occupation of small employer, and they typically own businesses with very few employees.[15]

Note at this point that we are not suggesting that none of the old communist elite successfully exploited public firms to enrich themselves in a big way. We are sure that this has occurred to some extent, and Hankiss and Staniszkis are persuasive when they argue that the former communist elite planned to appropriate state firms as private property from as early as 1988. What we are arguing, however, is that the successful conversion of communist political capital into post-communist economic capital has been the exception rather than the rule among former *nomenklatura* members in all three countries. There is a 'kleptocracy' to use the terminology of Frydman and his co-authors, but the number of really successful 'kleptocrats' appears to be very small; the kleptocracy does not appear to be running any of the countries we are studying.

Retirement, business ownership and the economic well-being of members of the former communist nomenklatura

Although the conversion of communist political capital into post-communist economic capital was not impossible, our data suggest that it was a great deal more difficult than most people thought it would be. Data on Communist Party membership provide further support for this argument. Table 4.5 returns to the question of early retirement, examining the effects of Communist Party membership on retirement behavior. In this way, we try to get a sense of *which* former communist elites were the biggest losers in the transition, and which members weathered the changes following 1989 particularly well.

Table 4.5 shows, first, that the incidence of Communist Party membership was considerably higher among members of the Czech *nomenklatura*

Table 4.5 The effect of party membership on early retirement among former nomenklatura members, by country

	Czech Republic	Hungary	Poland
% of CP members among all *nomenklatura* members, 1988	91.7	82.4	80.5
% of CP members among those *nomenklatura* members who had retired by 1993	96.8	90.1	86.8
% of CP members among those *nomenklatura* members under 60 who were still economically active in 1993	90.7	82.8	81.1
% of CP members among those *nomenklatura* members under 60 who had retired by 1993	94.1	90.9	86.2
% of CP members among those *nomenklatura* members, aged 60–69, who who were still economically active in 1993	86.5	69.2	76.9
% of CP members among those *nomenklatura* members, aged 60–69, who who had retired by 1993	97.3	90.7	91.2

Source: Hanley and Szelényi, 'Changing Social Structure During Market Transition'.

than among members of the Hungarian and Polish *nomenklatura*. Second, note that among those *nomenklatura* members who were under sixty in 1988, there was a higher proportion of Communist Party members among those who retired than among those who remained economically active in 1993. There was also a disproportionate representation of Communist Party members among retirees between sixty and sixty-nine. In short, among former top-ranking communist officials the chances of keeping one's job after official retirement age were much better for those who were not members of the Communist Party. We think that being an expert helped a person to retain their job. If a person was only 'red', they were in trouble.

Note, too, that it seems that people were 'punished' more heavily for party membership in Hungary than in the Czech Republic or Poland. This may be because Communist Party membership was less of a prerequisite for a top job in Hungary in the late communist period. In the Czech Republic, by contrast, if one wanted to get to the top, there was little chance unless one joined the party. This was true even in the final years of state socialism. Thus in Hungary, Communist Party membership was viewed as more of an indication that someone was indeed a communist, while in the Czech Republic it was seen by many people simply as 'opportunism'. The greater chances of former Communist Party members being squeezed out of jobs in Hungary compared to the Czech Republic, then, indicates that party affiliation was more of a liability in post-communist Hungary than it was in the Czech Republic (it may also indicate that Hungarian Communist Party members had a deeper ideological commitment to socialism, and many of them therefore withdrew voluntarily with the fall of communism, acknowledging that their time had passed).

We have tried to get a lot of mileage out of early retirement as a measure of who the losers in the post-communist transition have been in Central Europe. We have shown that market transition was not always kind to those who held positions of high authority during communism; we found that early retirement hit the bureaucratic fraction of the former communist ruling estate more heavily than the technocratic fraction; and we have also shown that possessing a lot of political capital during communism did not always help people to avoid early retirement. An objection to our analysis, however, could be that early retirement is not the disadvantage we claim it is. Critics may argue that early retirement is a mechanism through which former communists have preserved their privileges. Former top-ranking cadres may have cashed in their political power for private property and then, with their new economic capital, they may have opted for early retirement to 'cover' how they acquired their new wealth, or because they no longer needed their incomes to survive. This is a reasonable objection to our analysis, and it requires us to explore whether or not early retirees are those who accumulated substantial private wealth during the transition.

Specifically, we need to examine whether or not people took early retirement because they no longer needed their salaries, or because their working lives became uncomfortable because of their communist past.

Table 4.6 Business ownership among different fractions of the 1988 nomenklatura by their 1993 occupation[1]

	Owns business	Does not own business
1988 economic elite		
in elite position in 1993	26.3	73.7
in sub-elite position in 1993	27.0	73.0
retired by 1993	10.9	89.1
1988 political elite		
in elite position in 1993	29.8	70.2
in sub-elite position in 1993	12.6	87.4
retired by 1993	9.4	90.6
1988 cultural elite		
in elite position in 1993	14.9	85.1
in sub-elite position in 1993	11.0	89.0
retired by 1993	7.0	93.0
All respondents	18.1%	81.9%
	(380)	(1,719)

1. We define sub-elites as those who were professionals without supervisees, or those who had lesser jobs. The elite is defined broadly, including not only those in positions which were formerly *nomenklatura* positions, but all positions in which people had subordinates.

To assess these possibilities, Table 4.6 presents data on business ownership and retirement among different fractions of the former *nomenklatura*. The table shows that roughly 90 percent of retirees from the economic, political, and cultural fractions of the *nomenklatura* reported no business ownership in 1993. By contrast, for those former *nomenklatura* members who managed to retain their jobs throughout the post-communist transition, the incidence of 1993 business ownership was two to three times higher than it was for retirees. The trend which emerges from this table is powerful evidence that retirement among *nomenklatura* members represented significant downward mobility in the post-communist transition.

In the light of these findings, we must also ask about the reliability of these data. If the old communist political elite is a kleptocracy, as political capitalism theory suggests, then it has good reasons for not reporting business ownership to a survey-taker, particularly if that business was obtained illegally. Since our data are the products of survey research, we have no way of checking the reliability of answers given to individual questions. One hedge against this kind of reliability problem is to check for consistency in reporting across a range of economic indicators (like income, aggregate value of all real estate and movable property) and then to compare these indicators to see whether or not they are consistent. Because reliability questions can also be raised about these other economic indicators, however, we analyze the number of rooms in the house/flat that people live in to assess the economic well-being of former *nomenklatura* members. The number of rooms in a house impresses us as the most 'objective' measure of economic well-being, because we think it is the question to which our respondents were the most likely to have given a truthful answer.

Table 4.7 Number of rooms in the house/flat among different fractions of the 1988 nomenklatura *by their occupational destination*

	3 rooms or fewer	4 or more rooms
1988 economic elite		
who are in elite position in 1993	39.8	60.2
who are in sub-elite position in 1993	37.8	62.2
who were retired by 1993	60.5	39.5
1988 political elite		
who are in elite position in 1993	52.6	47.4
who are in sub-elite position in 1993	60.9	39.1
who were retired by 1993	65.3	34.7
1988 cultural elite		
who are in elite position in 1993	51.5	48.5
who are in sub-elite position in 1993	52.9	47.1
who were retired by 1993	67.3	32.7
All respondents	54.6%	45.4%
	(1,107)	(920)

Table 4.7 presents these data on the number of rooms in the house/flat in which former members of different fractions of the *nomenklatura* lived during 1993. These data tell us that there is little reason for concern about the economic well-being of former *nomenklatura* members. These people obviously took good care of themselves during state socialism, and by

Central European standards they live in good housing. The average size of a house/flat in our general population sample is about two rooms, so it is rather impressive that nearly half of our former *nomenklatura* members live in houses or flats with four rooms or more. Table 4.7 shows that a greater proportion of the economic fraction of the old ruling estate enjoys the biggest houses and flats compared to smaller proportions of former political and cultural *nomenklatura* members. Note, however, that in contrast to former *nomenklatura* members who remained economically active, and who have retained a position of relative advantage into the post-communist transition, those former *nomenklatura* members who took early retirement before 1993 are significantly less likely to enjoy superior housing. Early retirees are clearly worse off on this measure than those who remained employed.[16] Together with the data on business ownership, these data on size of residence support our contention of downward mobility among many former *nomenklatura* members into the post-communist transition, and highlight our argument about the relative advantages enjoyed by former members of the economic fraction of the *nomenklatura*. It is to this issue that we now turn.

Act II in our unfolding drama explores the dynamics of system breakdown in the final years and months of communism. We tell the story of a successful revolution by the technocratic elite at the expense of the old bureaucratic order, showing why it was managers, rather than high political office-holders, who were the most likely to benefit from the new opportunities provided by the emerging post-communist market.

The victorious technocratic–managerial elite

In this section, we explore the extent to which the technocratic fraction of the former communist ruling estate can be viewed as the big winner in the post-communist transition. Although the *nomenklatura* as such cannot be understood as the clear winner – many former *nomenklatura* members have been downwardly mobile – the technocratic fraction of the former communist ruling estate certainly appears to be victorious. The sources of technocratic power, however, remain unclear. While political capitalism theorists would expect to find the roots of technocratic–managerial power in private property, the foregoing data on retirement, occupational trajectories, and patterns of property ownership should suffice to show that the theory of political capitalism requires substantial reformulation if it is to capture the dynamics of post-communist transformation.

So far, we have examined only rather crude versions of the political capitalism thesis. The roots of this thesis are traceable to 1988, a time when the communist elite was still in charge, and a 'political capitalism' project may well have been under way among members of the *nomenklatura*. Scholars like Staniszkis and Hankiss probably played a role in preventing the success of the political capitalism project because they demystified the new power game of the old elite. Indeed, Hankiss and Staniszkis showed a great deal of intellectual courage and theoretical foresight in 1988 when they observed that spontaneous privatization had been conceived as a vehicle for retaining communist privileges after the fall of communism. As Hankiss argued, by offering private wealth to the political elite, the reform communists tried to forge a 'grand coalition' – in this way they hoped to diffuse resistance to the transition by creating stakes in the new capitalism for the old guard.[17] Our point in this chapter is that the 'grand coalition' identified by Hankiss did not hold together during the transition. We do not question the fact that it existed; we simply think it failed: by the summer and autumn of 1989, the forces of market reform in Hungary and Poland did not need the assistance (or the permission) of the bureaucratic fraction of the ruling estate to pursue new market opportunities.[18] In fact, we think that an important obstacle to the enrichment of the old elite through the process of spontaneous privatization was the intense public scrutiny they endured during the transition: the new, post-1989 anti-communist political elites, the free media, and academics like Hankiss and Staniszkis, were highly suspicious and vocal critics of the old elite.

Having acknowledged Hankiss's contributions to the development of political capitalism theory, we would also like to observe that Erzsébet Szalai had already modified the crude or generalized form of the political capitalism thesis in the late 1980s. Szalai studied the economic behavior of large firms during most of the 1980s, and very early in the process of market reform under late state socialism she realized that the dynamism of social change was rooted in the internal fragmentation of the communist elite.[19] Rather than thinking about the *nomenklatura* as a homogeneous category, Szalai argued that at least since the late 1960s, a 'new elite' had begun to emerge to challenge the old bureaucratic fraction of the ruling estate.[20] She eventually identified this new elite, with great precision, as the 'late Kádárist technocracy' which, she argued, was moving increasingly rapidly towards a confrontation with the communist bureaucracy.[21]

Szalai's early reading of the events of 1989 in Hungary was that this technocracy had managed to defeat the bureaucratic fraction of the ruling estate. This victory, however, was not one in which the technocracy aspired to replace the bureaucratic elite. Rather, the technocracy sought to alter the nature of socialist domination. Technocrats were ready to move towards a separation of political and economic power; they were also supportive of free elections and a multiparty system. In this effort, the victorious technocracy opened up a dialogue with the dissident intelligentsia. And in the so-called round-table negotiations of late spring and early autumn 1989, in both Hungary and Poland, the separation of the polity and economy, and the issue of free elections, were the main items on the agenda. One might even say that the price the technocracy had to pay for its victory over the bureau-cracy was to give up its claims to political monopoly; it had to allow the rise of a new politocracy, a new political class. The members of this new poli-tocracy in 1989–90 were recruited largely from among former dissidents, and other intellectual strata.

The transition from bureaucratic state socialism to a post-communist formation, however, turned out to be a good deal rockier for the technoc-racy than they had anticipated. Since the transition was a 'negotiated one' – indeed, if it was a revolution, it was a 'velvet one' – it ran into problems of power-sharing. Less than twelve months after the round-table discussions of 1989, it became abundantly clear to the former state-socialist technocrats that the transition was not going to work as they had expected. As 1989 pro-gressed, the technocracy's political position weakened, and by the end of the year it was the former dissident intelligentsia, constituted as a newly formed political elite, which was calling the shots.[22] Instead of amicable cooperation between former communist technocrats and the new political elite, the first post-communist electoral campaigns witnessed bitter recriminations and vitriolic anti-communist rhetoric. Indeed, the new political elite played the anti-communist card – not only against hardline communist bureaucrats, but also against the technocrats with whom they had sat down to broker the transition in the autumn of the year before. With hindsight, we might observe that this sort of political toing and froing was only to be expected in the context of political competition in an emergent multiparty system. And so it followed that as the Berlin Wall came down, the new, non-communist parties of Central Europe tried to outbid each other in the virulence of their anti-communism. It is important to note that it was in this context that the disintegration of the communist political and economic system took place.

In this rapidly polarizing political space, the process of system break-down did not proceed along 'evolutionary' lines towards a Western-style market economy, as the reform communist technocrats had originally intended. Even in Hungary, where the non-communist Democratic Forum had presented itself as willing and able to govern in coalition with the former Communist Party, such a coalition did not materialize. After Democratic Forum won the 1990 elections, they took an increasingly hos-tile anti-communist stance. Strong anti-communism was dominant in Czech and Polish politics during this period as well. Moreover, a common feature of anti-communist rhetoric in all these countries was a failure to dis-tinguish between the reform communist technocracy which had been instrumental in bringing about the transition from communism, and the conservative bureaucratic fraction of the dominant communist estate which had been ousted. In a whirlwind of overblown political rhetoric, the previ-ous forty years were dismissed out of hand: socialism was not only a failure, but a Gulag. In this conflation, no distinction was made between the (rather brief) Stalinist period and the much more benevolent, paternalistic post-Stalinist epoch of socialism. Thus the reform communist technocrats were caught by surprise: the former dissidents, whom they had learned to appreciate and viewed as their allies against the bureaucracy, had turned against them.

In the Czech Republic, the lustration law was passed. In Poland, Wałęsa won the presidential campaign by accusing Mazowiecki of being too soft on communists and allowing them to benefit from privatization. In this context, Wałęsa promised legislation which would make it illegal for former leading communists to privatize public firms. Similarly, in Hungary, the government led by Democratic Forum began to dismiss some of the leading reform communists from their positions, replacing them with their own followers. Prime Minister Antall even sacked the President of the National Bank, Surányi, who had earned professional respect during reform communism. Surányi was replaced by a Democratic Forum Cabinet minister, Bod, who did not have much of a reputation in banking circles.

As Szalai and others have pointed out, by 1990 it appeared that the victory celebrations of the late state-socialist technocracy were to be short-lived. The new political elite appeared to be squeezing old state-socialist technocrats out of power. Data from 1993, however, testify to the tenacity of the technocrats, and to the new politocracy's inability to govern without them.

Tables 4.8 and 4.9 document the occupational origins of members of new elites in 1993 by different fractions of the elite, and by country, respectively.

Table 4.8 Occupational origins in 1988 of members of the new economic, political and cultural elites in 1993 in the Czech Republic, Hungary and Poland. (Social stratification in Eastern Europe after 1989 survey, 1993–94, New elite samples)

	Occupation in 1993		
Occupation in 1988	**New economic**	**New political**	**New cultural**
Elite/*nomenklatura*	31.9	15.3	18.8
Lower-level managers	41.0	14.0	15.9
Entrepreneurs	1.1	1.9	0.2
Professionals	12.9	52.8	56.6
Workers	11.3	12.0	4.9
Not in labor force	1.8	4.0	3.6
All	100%	100%	100%
(n)	(1,793)	(642)	(464)

There are three main findings. First, these data show that many members of the 1993 post-communist elites were from non-elite occupational origins in 1988. Well over half of all the members of the new political and cultural elites – that is, of the members of the highest national decision-making positions during the first five years of post-communism – were only rank-and-file professionals in 1988, and only a third of the new post-communist cultural and political elites held a position of authority during communist times. This finding attests to the massive change in personnel at the top of the social hierarchy during these early years of the post-communist transformation. These data also serve to undermine the generalized political capitalism hypothesis which assumed that although the logic of the system changed, the personnel in the top positions would remain the same. Clearly this did not happen in either the political or the cultural realm. However, the second finding in Table 4.8 is that the new post-communist economic elites – the CEOs of the 3,000 largest firms in these countries in 1993 – were very likely to have begun their careers in top economic positions under communism. Over two-thirds of the new post-communist economic elite (31.9 plus 41=72.9 percent) had occupied positions as communist managers before the regime fell in 1989. Third, Table 4.8 shows that there was extremely low recruitment into senior managerial positions in post-communism from the ranks of those operating private businesses in the second economy of state socialism in 1988. As Table 4.9 shows, even in Hungary, where the second economy was the most developed, less than 2 percent of the CEOs of the 3,000 largest business organizations in 1993 were private entrepreneurs in 1988. This is one of the most counterintuitive findings of our survey. In both Hungary and Poland, there are a number of very prominent private businessmen who started their careers in the state-socialist private sector and who enjoyed massive success as their businesses grew in the early years of post-communism. Stories about the self-made post-communist businessmen are true. What Table 4.9 shows, however, is that these people were not typical of the incumbents of senior economic decision-making positions in 1993.

Rather, our data show that there was a high degree of elite reproduction in the economy, and a great deal of elite circulation in politics and culture in the early post-communist period. The big winners in the transition have been members of the technocratic fraction of the old ruling estate. This group shares the benefits of the transition with former dissident intellectuals who have moved in large numbers into top positions in politics, state administration, and culture.

Given these findings, and the political history chronicled above, we now ask: what accounts for high levels of reproduction among the economic elite? What explains the ability of former socialist technocrats to maintain their elite positions when we know that the dissident intelligentsia turned

Table 4.9 Occupational origins in 1988 of members of the
new economic elites in the Czech Republic, Hungary and Poland.
(Social stratification in Eastern Europe after 1989 survey, 1993–94, New economic elite samples)

Occupation in 1988	Members of the new economic elites in 1993		
	Czech Republic	**Hungary**	**Poland**
Elite/nomenklatura	19.3	31.4	48.7
Lower-level managers	47.2	42.6	31.3
Entrepreneurs	0.4	1.9	1.1
Professionals	15.4	11.6	11.2
Workers	14.8	11.4	6.6
Not in labor force	2.9	1.1	1.1
All	100%	100%	100%
(n)	(689)	(570)	(534)

against them soon after the fall of communism? Was the anti-communism of the early years only 'for show'? Was anti-communist rhetoric simply a ploy to win elections, while the new politocracy and the reform communist technocracy cut deals behind closed doors? We do not think so. As we noted in the analysis of Table 4.2, there was substantial downward mobility among the former economic elite of state socialism. Only half of the top managerial personnel of very large firms in 1988 were still top-ranking managers of private or public corporations in 1993. About a third of them were clearly downwardly mobile, and about half of these ended up in early retirement. In short, the massive reproduction of the economic elite occurred *despite* substantial downward mobility among those at the very top of the state-socialist economic system after 1989. How can we explain this puzzle? The answer is that although those at the very top were downwardly mobile out of elite economic positions when the communist system broke down, those in low-level management positions were not. Table 4.8 shows that only 31.9 percent of the new post-communist economic elite occupied high elite positions in the *nomenklatura* in 1988. Forty-one percent of them came from the levels of *lower* management. Once this dynamic of elite reproduction and circulation is understood, it becomes apparent that the anti-communism directed against the reform communist technocracy in the early years of the post-communist transition was not merely rhetorical. Some of the 'top dogs' were chased out, and after a brief experiment in trying to employ political clients as business managers – an experiment which proved to be as much of a disaster as the communist experiment of replacing capitalists with ordinary workers – the new politocracy retreated.

The compromise was to promote former middle-management personnel to positions as CEOs, since these individuals did not bear the stigma of being former communist cadres, and they possessed the managerial know-how and the social networks which are crucial for conducting business in post-communist conditions.

The data in Tables 4.8 and 4.9 are also instructive because they were collected before successor communist parties won the second round of post-communist elections (in autumn 1993 in Poland, and spring 1994 in Hungary). In both countries, the 'reconciliation' between the new politocracy and the late state-socialist technocracy took place under the first freely elected governments which were outspokenly anti-communist. This reconciliation was built on the realization that the dissident intelligentsia and the late socialist technocracy needed each other to carry out the second *Bildungsbürgertum* project of making capitalism without capitalists. This reconciliation can be seen clearly in Hungary. Following the 1994 election, where the successor party of the Hungarian Communist Party (the Hungarian Socialist Party) won an absolute majority of parliamentary seats, they opted to invite the major liberal party, the Free Democrats, to join them in a coalition government. The Free Democrats, comprised primarily of the hard core of the dissident intelligentsia of the 1970s and 1980s, accepted the invitation.[23] What a strange turn of events this was: a coalition was formed when it was not technically necessary between parties which had been the most bitter enemies only four years earlier.

On this basis, we can conclude that while Hankiss and Staniszkis were wrong in some respects, Erzsébet Szalai's predictions were largely on target. It was not the *nomenklatura en masse* who converted their political power into private economic wealth in the early years of post-communism. The bureaucratic fraction of the old ruling estate was defeated in 1989, and many of them suffered downward mobility. It was the technocratic–managerial elite – the late state-socialist technocracy, many of whom occupied middle-management positions – who defeated the bureaucratic fraction of the communist ruling estate, and then opened up round-table negotiations with the dissident intelligentsia. The technocracy was willing to let the dissidents compete for political power in free elections, and form a multiparty democracy. And although this resulted in political feuding at the beginning of the transition, eventually the technocracy consolidated its grip on economic power, and the late state-socialist technocracy and the former dissidents learned to cooperate with each other in the political and cultural spheres.

At this point, however, we must ask: is this situation simply a more sophisticated example of political capitalism? Our critics might argue that although the *nomenklatura* as a whole did not enrich itself as political capitalism theory expected, the technocratic–managerial elite has certainly managed to maintain its economic position in the post-communist transition. Only the 'relatively autonomous' fields of state power and culture have been ceded to former non-communist, dissident intellectuals. We would argue that even this statement is not adequate to capture the dynamics of circulation and reproduction that we have documented. After all, in Hungary and Poland the successor parties won the second round of post-Communist elections in 1994 outright. There was no need for them to compromise with the former dissident intellectuals at all. Moreover, the successor parties contained members of a younger cohort of communist cadres, who had cooperated with the reform communists in the 1980s against the old bureaucratic ruling estate, and they were coming back in droves in both the political and the cultural fields in the early post-communist period. By 1997, the new post-communist political and cultural elites included many people who had been middle-level cadres under communism, and even those who had been members of the Communist Party prior to system breakdown in 1989.[24] On this basis, political capitalism theory could be revised to argue that the late state-socialist technocracy used a mixture of its expertise and political networks to establish itself as the new *grande bourgeoisie* of post-communist capitalism. It also reclaimed many elite positions in politics and culture for its clients, leaving only marginal places for former non-communist or anti-communist intellectuals.

Such a revisionist political capitalism theory has great merit. But is it true that the technocratic–managerial elite has successfully established itself as a new *grande bourgeoisie*? Has the technocratic–managerial elite consolidated its hegemonic position in the economy in the form of ownership of economic capital? In the next section of this chapter we show that even this revisionist version of political capitalism theory overstates the extent to which the privatization process has been used to create private wealth among the technocratic–managerial elite. Indeed, we argue that the technocratic–managerial elite has failed to transform itself into a propertied class, and continues to exercise power on the basis of its expertise. It acts as the dominant fraction of the post-communist power bloc, but it is only one fraction. In short, post-communism has not yet produced a new dominant class.

Diffuse property relations as the context for managerial control

Managers acquire little private property; their power derives from their cultural capital

Pursuing our story further, we ask: what was the basis of the economic power exercised by the former socialist technocracy and managerial elite in 1993? Was it private ownership of capital (economic capital), or managerial know-how (cultural capital)? In other words, have managers and technocrats established themselves as a propertied class? On the basis of evidence available to us from our 1993 surveys, we believe that managers had not constituted themselves as a propertied class by 1993. To use the detective drama metaphor, we doubted that a 'crime' had taken place at all. Certainly, some management buy-out occurred during the first years of the post-communist transition, and a small number of executives acquired enough assets in the companies they managed to run them as proprietors. However, our 1993 data indicate that managerial ownership in large corporations was relatively rare. Business ownership by managers was confined to small firms, and was often in firms other than the ones they managed. Moreover, we think that managerial ownership in these kinds of small firms usually played a secondary role for managers, complementing their considerable managerial incomes and, in some cases, providing an incentive for them to run their firms efficiently and profitably. Like managers in West European or North American corporations, managers in post-communism exercised their authority on the basis of managerial know-how, business connections, and interpersonal networks.

However, the organizational settings in which our class actors and elite members live and act are quite different from those of Western managers, business owners, and political representatives. These settings and the emergent structure of class relations in Central Europe shape the possibilities for class formation, class power and class action quite differently for our actors than for those in the West. So in what follows we propose a few tentative hypotheses about what may be different – at least for the time being – in Central Europe. We proceed from the observation that what is unusual about the transition to capitalism in post-communist Central Europe is the context of diffuse property rights in which (even small and middle-sized) firms operate. In this connection, we identify three characteristics of post-communist capitalism.

First, the proportion of public ownership in 1993 remains substantial, at about 25 percent of all corporate assets. Those publicly owned firms which could be privatized have already been privatized, and the state is now stuck with many firms which are not marketable. Moreover, it is probable that if these unmarketable firms were shut down, there would be excessively high levels of unemployment. So we think that high levels of public ownership are likely to characterize the post-communist economic landscape for some time to come.

The second interesting feature of Central European property rights appears to be what David Stark calls 'recombinant property', usually taking the form of institutional cross-ownership.[25] Larry King has also found substantial 'self-ownership' and 'institutional cross-ownership' in the Czech Republic.[26] Both Stark and King have found that banks often play an important role in the chain of institutional cross-ownership, and these banks, in turn, are either directly or indirectly publicly owned. Indeed, in the banking sphere the separation of public from private seems to have been a particularly painful process.[27] Governments often use the banks they own directly or indirectly to continue their former redistributive practices – a process that King has astutely called 'subterranean redistribution'.[28] Governments put pressure on banks to keep giving loans to troubled firms to rescue them from bankruptcy, because governments fear excessive unemployment which would further burden budgets already in the red. When banks give out insufficiently secured loans under this kind of government pressure, and then get into trouble, the government is likely to bail them out. This happened on a small scale in the great Hungarian bank bail-out scheme of 1991, and on a grand scale in 1993.[29] In the latter case, the Hungarian government borrowed some 300 billion Hungarian forints – nearly US$3 billion – from the very banks they bailed out with this money, creating a major internal debt crisis.[30] The socialist–liberal government pursued a similar policy after 1994, though not on the same scale as the previous government led by the conservative Hungarian Democratic Forum. In another example from 1995, the socialist–liberal government beefed up the Budapest Bank by infusing it with billions of forints to make it attractive to foreign investors.[31] With the infusion of these funds, the government succeeded in selling the Budapest Bank for a sum which was barely enough to recover the subsidies just made to that institution.[32]

Note, however, that at the time of its privatization, the Budapest Bank unloaded some of its investments into a subsidiary, called the Citizens' Bank (Polgári Bank), and in the privatization contract there was a proviso which stated that the government could buy back the Citizens' Bank if the new owners wished it to do so. This is exactly what happened in December 1996: the Citizens' Bank was 'nationalized', and the government paid over one billion Hungarian forints to the Budapest Bank to purchase it. This appears to be a classical case of what Stark has described as the strategy of offloading liabilities and preserving assets. Firms unload liabilities into subsidiaries, bankrupt themselves, then make the government bail them out. What is unusual about the nationalization of the Citizens' Bank, however, is that it was not only bailed out, it became public property, and the government paid the now-private Budapest Bank for the honor of taking over its bad loans.[33] Government bail-outs of unprofitable corporations are, of course, far from unknown in Western capitalism. What seems to be a unique feature in Central Europe, however, is the extent to which this kind of bail-out occurs. This is not just a quantitative difference. The web of institutional cross-ownership is so dense, and the back-and-forth between the public and private realms is so frequent, that it is often impossible to tell what distinguishes public from private ownership.

Third, we think that the proportion of cases where CEOs hold ownership stakes in firms other than those they manage is rather small. Stark and King note that these firms are often small 'satellites' which act as subcontracting agencies through which managers channel substantial revenues from the 'mother firm' they manage. In Western corporations, it is inconceivable that a Board of Directors, responsible to a well-defined set of stockholders, would or could allow CEOs to operate this way. Although it is true that management everywhere uses subcontracting firms as a vehicle to organize management buy-outs, as King points out, in Central Europe management seems to operate on the assumption that these 'parasitic satellites' are permanent institutions, not just an intermediary step along the road to management buy-out. Our point in this connection is that it is not inconceivable in the context of fluid property relations, such as the one we have described in Central Europe, that managerial ownership of 'permanent parasitic satellite firms' can be established and maintained on a fairly long-term basis.

In what follows, we present evidence on business ownership among managers to assess the extent of management buy-out which had occurred by 1993.

Table 4.10 Business ownership among members of the new economic elites in the Czech Republic, Hungary and Poland (Social stratification in Eastern Europe after 1989 survey, 1993–94, New economic elite sample)

Percent of business owned	**Czech Republic**	**Hungary**	**Poland**
No business ownership	80.4	48.6	81.3
Less than 25%	9.6	30.1	7.7
25–49%	4.3	8.3	4.1
Over 50%	5.7	13.0	6.9
All	100%	100%	100%
(n)	(690)	(578)	(534)

Table 4.10 presents data from the survey of 'Social Stratification in Eastern Europe after 1989', and provides evidence that business ownership among managers in 1993 was rather limited. The table shows that the majority of CEOs in Central Europe in 1993 reported no business ownership whatsoever. Moreover, the majority of those who did report some business ownership reported relatively small shares, typically owning less that 25 percent of all firm assets.[34] Note further that there is substantial variation across countries. Business ownership among managers was much more widespread in Hungary than in the Czech Republic or Poland – 51.4

percent of Hungarian managers reported some business ownership, compared to about 20 percent of managers in the Czech Republic and Poland. This is an indication that management buy-outs and the growth of private ownership were further advanced in Hungary by 1993 than in the two other countries.[35] It remains true, however, that most Central European managers reported no business ownership in 1993, and of those who did report some ownership, the majority reported only partial ownership, often less than 25 percent.

Our next question is: was the firm in which managers reported ownership the same business as they themselves managed? Here we have to rely on the analysis of 1993 TARKI data, which are available only for Hungary. First, note that managers in the TARKI survey reported similar levels of ownership as managers in our survey: 51.8 percent of all managers reported some business ownership.[36] For statistical purposes, this is not significantly different from the 51.4 percent reporting business ownership in our survey, which bolsters our faith in the reliability and validity of our data. According to the TARKI survey, 20.5 percent of managers had ownership in the firms they managed, 21.8 percent had ownership in some other firm, and 8.5 percent reported ownership both in their own firm and in another enterprise. We cannot be far off the mark, then, when we claim that about half of the business ownership reported by managers in 1993 qualifies as management buy-out. The other half of managerial ownership was not a result of management buy-out but was likely to be ownership of the 'recombinant' type identified by Stark, or ownership in 'parasitic satellite firms' identified by King. Translated into absolute numbers for 1993 post-communist economies, managerial ownership representing management buy-out strategies describes the activities of about 10 percent of all managers in 1993 in the Czech Republic and Poland, and the activities of about 25 percent of all the managers of the largest 3,000 to 5,000 firms in Hungary. This suggests that management buy-out was not the major form of privatization in Central Europe prior to 1994.

Table 4.11 presents TARKI data for Hungary only. This table gives us a sense of the extent of managerial ownership in the firms managers administered as managers – that is to say, it presents data on the share of ownership by size of firm for those 27.3 (14.2 plus 7.6+5.5) percent of Hungarian managers who reported ownership in the firm they were employed to manage. It is intriguing that just over half of these managers owned 10 percent or less of the assets of their firms. It is even more telling that of the 1,001 managers who responded to the TARKI interview, only three owned more than 10 percent of the capital assets of a firm with at least 300 employees (0.4 plus 0.8=1.2). There were another 19 managers who owned more than 10 percent of the assets of firms employing 100–299 employees (6.8 plus 1.3=8.1), but only three of these were majority stockholders. Thus among the 1,001 managers TARKI surveyed – about 30 percent of the managerial population as a whole – we found 23 individuals with substantial ownership in firms with at least 100 employees, and only five cases where managers were majority owners. In the whole population of managers, then, there were approximately 15 majority owners of firms with 100 employees or more, and an additional 60 or so managers with between 11 and 49 percent ownership. This may represent the full extent of management buy-out in Hungary by autumn 1993. So although management buy-out may have been a more important story than the one about former Communist Party and government officials turning themselves into owners of corporate businesses, management buy-out remains a rather small-scale phenomenon. It was certainly not the big story of economic transformation prior to 1994, since on the basis of this evidence, manager-owners could hardly be seen as a new dominant class who ran the economy as their own property.

Table 4.11 Percent of business owned by managers by size of firm in Hungary (TARKI survey, 1993)

Managerial ownership	1–10 employees	11–99 employees	100–299 employees	300+ employees	All
None	53.3	64.3	78.2	88.9	72.6
1–10%	15.0	17.0	13.7	9.9	14.2
11–49%	15.9	10.5	6.8	0.4	7.6
50–100%	15.9	8.3	1.3	0.8	5.5
All	100.1%	100.1%	100%	100%	99.9%
(n)	(107)	(400)	(234)	(253)	(994)

Note: Numbers may not add up to 100 percent due to rounding.

If the owners are not managers, then who are the owners of firms in the economies of post-communist Central Europe? Tables 4.12 and 4.13 describe the extent of public ownership and ownership by foreign investors in the largest Hungarian firms in 1993. These data indicate clearly that public ownership remained the predominant ownership form in Central Europe in 1993. More than half of the largest 3,000 firms were at least partially publicly owned. Even more importantly, 65.2 percent of the firms with 300 or more employees were still at least 50 percent government owned in 1993. The decline of state ownership during the first four years of post-communism affected primarily the very small firms – those which employed ten or fewer people – though 30 percent of these small establishments were also characterized by some public ownership. This situation is the mirror-image of management ownership. While around a quarter of Hungarian managers reported ownership in their firms, over half of these firms were also publicly owned. Managers, it appears, were more likely to possess ownership in smaller firms, while the state was more likely to keep ownership in larger firms. We observe, in other words, that as the size of the firm increases, the rate of ownership reported by managers declines and the rate of public ownership increases.

Table 4.12 Percent of business owned by the state by size of firm in Hungary
(TARKI survey, 1993)

State ownership	1–10 employees	11–99 employees	100–299 employees	300+ employees	All
None	71.0	56.9	46.8	23.3	47.5
1–10%	1.9	4.0	4.7	3.2	3.7
11–49%	10.3	9.8	9.0	8.3	9.3
50–100%	16.8	29.3	39.5	65.2	39.5
All	100%	100%	100%	100%	100%
(n)	(107)	(399)	(233)	(253)	(992)

As Table 4.13 indicates, the extent of foreign ownership in 1993 fell halfway between the ownership reported by management and public ownership. A quarter of all firms reported foreign investments; in other words, foreign investment was about as widespread as the phenomenon of management buy-out. Furthermore, compared to the state, foreign investors were also likely to own smaller firms. Indeed, Table 4.13 shows that the smaller the firm, the larger the proportion of foreign ownership. In comparison with managers, however, foreign investors appear to have made deeper inroads into the large corporate sector of the economy. Among the 1,001 firms TARKI surveyed, foreign investors were majority owners in about twenty firms which employed over 300 workers. Foreign investors were particularly active in middle-sized firms: in enterprises with 100 to 299 employees. To sum up: among the 3,000 or so largest Hungarian firms in 1993, the dominant ownership form was still public, and foreign investors were ahead of managers in taking advantage of the privatization process.

In some respects, these findings make intuitive sense. Management buy-out may not be the rational strategy for managers that it at first appears to be. Although managers are in a position to rip off the government by buying publicly owned firms very cheaply, this kind of corruption may not be very profitable. Most of these firms are run down, undercapitalized,

Table 4.13 Percent of business owned by foreign firms or individuals by size of firm in Hungary (TARKI survey, 1993)

Foreign ownership	1–10 employees	11–99 employees	100–299 employees	300+ employees	All
None	71.0	71.7	74.4	83.8	75.3
1–10%	0.0	0.8	2.6	4.3	2.0
11–49%	5.6	8.8	7.7	4.3	7.0
50–100%	23.4	18.8	15.4	7.5	15.6
All	100%	100.1%	100.1%	99.9%	99.97%
(n)	(107)	(399)	(234)	(253)	(993)

Note: Numbers may not add up to 100 percent due to rounding.

technologically neglected, and without a niche in the world market. In this context, it may be far more rational for managers to find a foreign investor who is willing to purchase their company, invest in it, and use their own world market niches to sell the firm's products. The smart manager, then, may not want to acquire ownership in the firm he manages.[37] Instead, he may try to negotiate a good deal for his foreign acquaintances with the Privatization Agency, passing on inside information to his foreign partners about the real state of affairs in the firm. In exchange for these 'inside' tips, the manager may ask the foreign investor to keep him on as manager. Moreover, such a manager may now feel entitled to ask for a West German salary rather than a state-socialist one. In Chapter 5, we describe this as the 'compradore intelligentsia' strategy and we suggest that it may be more widespread than management buy-out. Foreign investors often like the idea of employing former managers because these employees have the local know-how and networks which are so necessary for business success in contemporary Central Europe. Even in East Germany, where most of the economy has been bought by West German investors, the new West German owners typically employ former communist managers to run their firms. Paul Windolf carried out a survey similar to ours in East Germany in 1995, and found that in the 288 East German firms he studied, only 31 percent of the CEOs did not have experience as state-socialist managers in 1989.[38] On the basis of these findings, we suggest that although managers do indeed exercise key decision-making power in the economic sphere of post-communist societies, they are not a classical propertied bourgeoisie – they do not exercise power on the basis of their ownership of private property. Rather, as we have argued, managers govern on the basis of their cultural capital – their technical expertise and know-how – in an uneasy alliance with technocrats and the opinion-making politocracy.

The new power bloc: the technocracy, the politocracy and the
opinion-making intelligentsia

Against our argument that post-communism is a socioeconomic system
governed by managers and technocrats in an uneasy alliance with a largely
intellectual politocracy, some may argue that real economic power in
Central Europe is not domestic at all. Critics of our analysis might contend
that social change in Central Europe is being driven by the forces of the
world market – foreign capital, multinationals, and individual foreign
investors are calling the shots. There is merit in this argument. National governments in Central Europe, financial and economic experts advising
governments, and the managers of Central European corporations have few
degrees of freedom. Much of what they can do is circumscribed by international agencies like the IMF and the World Bank. The parameters of their
action are determined by the forces of the world market, by the managers of
foreign corporations. Even if a corporation is not directly owned by foreign
investors, managers often have to sing the song for which the tune is played
by foreign owners and international techno-bureaucracies. Our focus in
this book, however, is domestic class structure. While we would not want to
underemphasize the importance of international factors, we believe it is
reasonable to assume that the domestic social structure has at least 'relative
autonomy' from international forces. If this were not the case, how could
one explain the striking differences in the recent histories of Slovakia or
Serbia, the Czech Republic, Poland and Hungary? All these countries operate in the same international environment, all have been exposed to the
same pressures from the world market and foreign investors, and they have
responded rather differently to the same challenges. Our point is that it is
important to study domestic social structure because the way classes and
elites are formed at the level of the nation, and the way their struggles
unfold, are consequential.

The point of departure for our theory of post-communist managerialism,
which we will elaborate in greater detail below, is the fact that there is no
domestic class of private proprietors who can 'call the shots' in Central
European post-communism. Rather, a technocratic–managerial elite occupies the apex of the power structure. We believe that the authority of this
elite – in the last instance – is rooted in its possession of cultural capital, and
this fact is consequential for the way it operates, and how and where it
forms alliances. This proposition is linked closely to the ideas developed in
Chapters 1 and 2. It fits the theory of the second *Bildungsbürgertum* as well as
the theory of post-communism as a social structure in which cultural capital is the dominant form of capital.

For the second *Bildungsbürgertum* theory, for the theory of post-communism
as a social structure dominated by cultural capital, and for our theory of

post-communist managerialism, then, it is a key hypothesis that the *new power bloc* of post-communist society is not exclusively constituted by the late state-socialist technocracy and managerial elite. This power bloc is a complex phenomenon, which also includes what we have called variously the 'new politocracy', 'the new political elite', the 'new political estate', the 'new political class', and finally, the 'opinion-making intelligentsia'. The purpose of this section is to present evidence which substantiates our claim that a new power bloc composed of these three components currently exists in Central Europe.

Again, survey data can shed only partial light on the question of whether or not a new power bloc exists, and which groups belong to such a bloc. It is a tricky task to find the boundaries of the power bloc and to decide where significant cleavages in social structure lie. Notwithstanding these difficulties, however, we present *prima facie* evidence first, that such cleavages indeed exist between the three components of the new power bloc on the one hand, and ordinary people on the other; and second, that these cleavages are more important than divisions between different fractions of the elite. We concede that this is rather preliminary and partial evidence for a very ambitious claim. None the less, we want to show that in terms of economic privilege, the technocratic–managerial elite is quite similar to the new political and cultural elites. Figure 4.1 compares the elite fractions with the general population in all three countries on ownership of residence, size of residence, ownership of a weekend retreat, ownership of other real estate, and ownership of stocks and bonds. On all these indicators, the variation across countries is greater than that between different fractions of the elite within each country. Similarly, the difference in patterns of ownership between the national elite and the general population in each country is greater than the variation between fractions of each national elite, although members of the technocratic–managerial elite are somewhat better off than members of the other elite fractions, as might be expected on the basis of previous analysis.

There are two major exceptions to these overall findings. First, ownership of place of residence does not explain much in the Czech Republic because home ownership is comparatively low in this country, and elite members are less likely to own their place of residence than the general population. This results from extremely low levels of home ownership in the cities, where most members of the elite live. In other words, most home ownership in the Czech Republic is rural. At the same time, however, note that among members of the Czech elite who do own a residence, that residence is much larger than those owned by members of the general population. Second, housing is not a good indicator of social cleavage in Hungary either. Here, the problem is the opposite to the one in the Czech Republic. Hungarian home ownership is almost universal; thus there is little difference in rates of home ownership between social groups. Moreover, in terms of size of

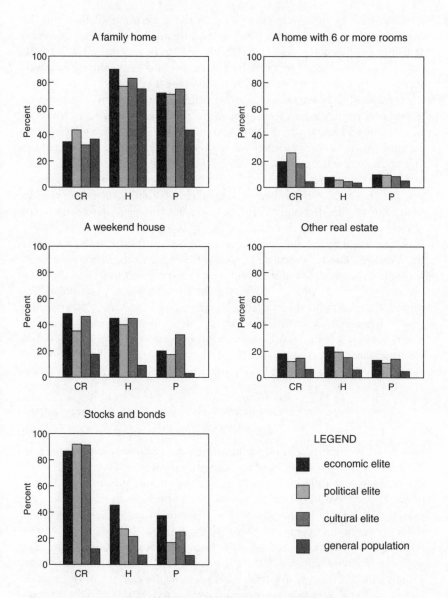

Figure 4.1 Housing ownership and ownership of other assets among members of the new economic, political, and cultural elites in the Czech Republic, Hungary and Poland (Social Stratification in Eastern Europe after 1989 survey, 1993–94)

housing, there is little difference between the general population and the members of the Hungarian elite. This can be attributed to dynamic rural housing construction in Hungary during the 1970s and early 1980s fueled by incomes generated in the agricultural second economy by peasant-workers who built very high-quality housing for themselves.

In contrast to home ownership, ownership of 'investment' real estate or a weekend retreat shows social cleavages much more clearly. In terms of investment real estate – that is, ownership of real estate which generates an income – ownership rates are much higher among all three fractions of the elite than among the general population in all the countries. Similarly, ownership of stocks and bonds sets all three elite fractions apart from the general population. On both these measures, the technocratic–managerial elite does better[39] than the two other elite fractions, but the cleavage clearly is not among elite groups, but between the power bloc and the rest of society.

This evidence suggests, then, that members of the post-communist elite – the managers and technocrats and intellectuals who figure so prominently in the politocracy and the cultural field – share a very comfortable level of economic well-being, and are distinct from the general population in this regard. As noted above, however, the evidence presented here is only *prima facie*.[40] A crucial task for further analysis is not only to document the cleavage between the general population and members of the power bloc, but also to explore the distinctions between those intellectuals who made it into the power bloc and those who were left out of it.

Cooperation and conflict between the three fractions of the new post-communist power bloc

Instead of attempting to squeeze out more support for our hypothesis from the survey evidence, then, in what follows we present other evidence about the making and functioning of the post-communist power bloc. In this effort, the analysis in Chapter 3 is crucially important. In that chapter, we presented a 'discourse analysis' of the apparently diverse ideologies of the different fractions of the power bloc. We showed that the discourse of 'monetarism', so dear to the hearts of the late state-socialist technocracy, had powerful elective affinities with the discourse of 'civil society' and 'anti-politics' promulgated by dissident intellectuals prior to the fall of the communist regime in 1989. As each of these groups confronted the task of building post-communist capitalism, these two discourses began to converge. Eventually, a shared discourse developed which combined components of both its predecessors, and served to bind the different fractions of the new power bloc together. Here, we build on the analysis in Chapter 3, highlighting other historical and political forces which brought together the former communist technocracy and its erstwhile arch-enemy, the former dissident intelligentsia.

We proceed from the perspective of the former late state-socialist technocracy. We ask: does the technocracy need an alliance with the former dissidents who made it into the new political elite, and exercise a great deal of influence through the media? If so, why?

Well before the fall of communism, the late state-socialist technocracy began to see dissident intellectuals as potential allies in their struggle against the bureaucracy. This was not 'love at the first sight', however – far from it. When dissidence emerged as a phenomenon during the late 1960s and the early-to-mid 1970s, the technocratic fraction of the communist ruling estate watched it with a great deal of suspicion. At this time, the technocrats believed that they would be able to negotiate with the bureaucracy to advance the cause of reform, and they thought that the dissidents might spoil their plan. The technocrats perceived the early dissidents as troublemakers – as irresponsible ideologues who were rocking the boat for no good reason. In the early 1970s, then, the technocrats were afraid that dissidence would undermine the relative political peace they required to cajole the bureaucracy into reforms.

The technocracy also saw early dissidents as 'left-wingers'. They observed dissident affiliations with the Western New Left with suspicion, and identified themselves, in contrast, as pragmatists who had no use for the dissidents' left-wing idealism. Anti-Semitism was also mobilized by the technocratic elite in its struggle against dissidents, especially in those cases where the technocrats wanted to appeal to that large intellectual constituency who had not yet embraced dissidence. In Poland, and especially in Hungary, there were several prominent dissident intellectuals of Jewish origins, and in attacking them the technocracy attacked 'Jews' in the hope that this would undermine potential solidarity with dissidents by the rest of the intelligentsia.

Gradually, however, the technocracy's attitude towards the dissidents began to change. There were two main reasons. First, it became clear that the bureaucracy would not and could not compromise. The technocrats began to believe that the dissidents were correct after all: the bureaucracy had to be defeated. In addition, by the early-to-mid 1980s, the dissidents began to exercise some political clout. Dissidents, it appeared, had created a weapon: the culture of critical discourse.[41] As one of us has argued earlier, from the early 1970s onward, dissidents led a 'discursive revolution'.[42] They began to break the sacred codes of communist discourse, and to identify themselves as 'those who think differently'. Soon, they became those who 'speak differently'. Dissidents rejected the abstruse metaphorical language of the technocracy, and challenged the taboos of communist discourse by trying to call things by their real names. For many years, technocrats had believed that change could be achieved by developing a metaphorical language to mask underlying fundamental reform; in short, they believed that you could engage in an effective critical analysis of the regime as long as it was couched in the linguistic codes of communism. You could be critical of the bureaucracy, as long as it was not called the bureaucracy but the 'administration'; you could talk about poverty as long as it was not called poverty, but, rather 'those who are in disadvantageous social conditions'. In sharp contrast to the technocrats, the dissidents opted for a method of verbal shock. Their aim was to undermine communist authority by developing a discourse where all topics could be discussed, brought before the tribunal of reason, and subjected to rational discourse. This new dissident language gave birth to the underground press, which the late-state socialist technocracy began to read. Eventually, the technocrats were seduced by the 'culture of critical discourse'. This dissident discourse appealed to the technocracy, in part, because many technocrats were genuine intellectuals, and deep in their hearts they resented the verbal pollution that communist discourse forced upon them. The culture of critical discourse also appealed to the technocrats as a powerful weapon with the potential to undermine the legitimacy of the bureaucratic estate. Dissidence offered a method of showing that the bureaucratic estate was 'inauthentic', that it was built on 'lies', and that the regime could not be trusted. On a strategic level, it is also probably true that the technocracy saw the power of these new ideas as they began to spread like a prairie fire, especially among the younger generation of thinkers.

After the bureaucratic estate fell from power in 1989, and as technocrats faced the task of building a new post-communist society, additional reasons for alliance with former dissidents emerged. First of all, from the mid-to-late 1980s, the technocracy realized that an irreversible destruction of bureaucratic domination required a degree of separation between economics and politics. The technocratic goal was not to replace bureaucrats with technocrats in the same institutions of the party state in which the economy was embedded. Rather, the technocrats realized that the economy must be disembedded, and a relatively autonomous sphere of politics must be created. Eventually, this led them to accept the idea of a multiparty political system and competitive elections. While most reform communists probably believed that the dissidents grabbed too much power in 1989–90, none the less the technocrats realized that sharing political power was the price for guaranteeing the permanent exclusion of the bureaucracy and the end of socialist domination. Second, dissidents, for their part, embraced the democratization of politics with all its anti-statist overtones. At the same time, however, they realized that the task of transition could be achieved only by a relatively powerful state. The institutions of the market would have to be created by legislative action and by multiple government interventions to subsidize and protect fledgling private property. In the process of transition, then, a close cooperation between the economic and political elite became a practical necessity. Finally – and for the theory of post-communist managerialism this may be the most important argument – the technocratic–managerial elite does not base its authority on private property. They have not rushed to become the new propertied bourgeoisie of Central Europe. Rather, they exercise power on the basis of their 'expert' credentials – that is to say, their possession of cultural capital. As we pointed out in Chapter 1, this is a relatively weak foundation from which to exercise authority. The technocratic–managerial elite therefore needs the ideological support of the opinion-making intelligentsia. Technocrats and politicians alike read the newspapers and watch round-table discussions on television to see what the intellectual gurus have written about them. The importance of opinion making intellectuals, and especially those in the media, is far greater in post-communist conditions than the power of similarly situated groups in Western democracies.

In an attempt to co-opt opinion-making intellectuals, technocrats began to invite members of this group to sit on a variety of government advisory boards. The advice of leading economists and sociologists is solicited and considered, and in this way key opinion-making intellectuals are caught in the power game. After all, it is much more difficult to criticize policies that you yourself appear to have shaped. A second strategy of co-optation is the system of foundations, which has been created to finance culture, science, and education. In communist times, these foundations were funded largely by bureaucratically controlled public money. Under post-communism, the technocratic–managerial elite has also channeled business funds to foundations. And, in a gesture of respect towards the role played by opinion-making intellectuals in post-communist life, the technocratic–managerial elite has handed over control of these foundations to distinguished members of the intelligentsia. Foundations have become a source of income for those intellectuals who now sit on their Boards of Directors, and most importantly serve as the major institutional base of intellectual power over culture, science and education.

Turning the question on its head, we now ask what reasons former dissidents had to enter into this 'unholy alliance' as members of the new post-communist power bloc? Their apparent political opportunism is surprising, given the courage and moral integrity displayed by many dissident intellectuals in the communist period. Dissidents made a point of insisting that they were not interested in power. They claimed that they were not interested in politics. They stated that they were only in search of truth – indeed, this is the only way, they argued, to live an 'authentic' life. How is it, then, that many of these selfsame intellectuals who resisted coercion and made substantial sacrifices before 1989 are now co-opted into power? The path to power for former dissidents reflects this ambiguity; the social trajectory which led them to their participation in the new power bloc was much longer and more conflict-ridden than it was for the technocracy.

As we saw above, the new political elite of post-communism found itself on a collision course with the technocratic–managerial elite almost as soon as communism fell. Although they entered a dialogue with reform communists at the end of the 1980s, with the disintegration of the system in 1989, dissidents and the opinion-making intelligentsia appear to have lost their ability to distinguish between reform communist technocrats and neo-Stalinist bureaucrats. Very soon after this, however, dissident intellectuals discovered that they could not conduct business against the late state-socialist technocracy. Nor could they conduct business without them, since the technocracy possessed the managerial know-how and the national and international business networks which the dissidents lacked. Regardless of how much they disliked the former communists, then, former dissidents in the politocracy had to learn to live and work with them.

For the opinion-making intellectuals – especially those from the academy and the fields of culture – this reconciliation with the technocracy was even more painful. It is notable, too, that this group of intellectuals are the weakest members of the power bloc. Their stakes in this bloc are not as high as those of other members, and their power is also rather limited. They are the 'dominated fraction' of the power bloc, and for this reason some of their prominent members have opted to exit from the game. Some have taken jobs at Western universities. Others have retreated into private life, or have become critical analysts. Others have reconciled themselves to the post-communist power game, however, benefiting from foundations which offer privileged incomes and a great deal of power to the opinion-making intellectual elite. This is undoubtedly of some importance. In our view, however, the most important force which pushes former dissidents into the new power bloc is guilt. They see themselves – and not without reason – as the architects of the post-communist project. They are the core of the second *Bildungsbürgertum*. They also see the high social cost of the post-communist transformation, and feel responsible for it. 'Reified' consciousness is the obvious way to sublimate this guilt feeling into ideology. In this permutation of their pathology, they believe that what is happening is inevitable – post-communist transformation is only obeying the 'iron laws of history'. There is no alternative. In this way, ironically, former dissident intellectuals have come full circle. Many of them started their intellectual trajectories as Marxists, rejecting the determinism of Soviet Marxism, insisting on alternatives, and arguing that the purpose of intellectual activity is precisely to map alternative social scenarios. With post-communism, these intellectuals have rediscovered the 'iron laws' of society. These are the 'iron laws' of the invisible hand, of the market. After a brief encounter with critical thought, Central European intellectuals have returned to a reified consciousness; after Soviet Marxist reification, they are now victims of bourgeois reification. To put it in Marcuse's terms, the post-communist mind is genuinely 'one-dimensional'.

To summarize: the membership of the new power bloc is diverse. Its different fractions eye one another with skepticism and suspicion. As we have argued, however, there are strong existential and ideological forces which bind them together. Until a domestic propertied bourgeoisie emerges which might have an interest in dividing this power bloc, then, we think that its members are likely to stay together.

An outline of a theory of managerial capitalism

On the basis of the analyses presented above, we summarize our theory of managerial capitalism in the following six theses.

Thesis 1. Post-communist economies are characterized by *diffuse property relations*. At the present time it is impossible to identify individuals or groups of individuals with sufficient amounts of property who are able to exercise anything even remotely similar to owners' control of economic decision-making.

Thesis 2. Ironically, it was precisely so-called 'privatization' which created these diffuse property relations. Privatization destroyed redistributive control over state firms, but it has not produced identifiable owners (yet).

Thesis 3. The dispersion of property rights is a *universal* phenomenon, but in market capitalist economies with an established propertied bourgeoisie it faces strict limits which do not exist in post-communism. Post-communist managers do not have to contend with a class of powerful capitalist proprietors; consequently, managerial power and decision-making are visible contributions to the prestige and 'distinction' of the new power bloc.

Thesis 4. Given the dispersion of property rights, the central representative of managerial power in Central Europe is not the manager of the industrial firm, but the finance manager.[43] The most powerful people of the post-communist era are bank managers, managers of investment funds, experts at the Ministry of Finance, advisors at the IMF and the World Bank, and experts working for foreign and international financial agencies. In the absence of a class of big private proprietors, the power of finance managers is not a function of how many shares they own in the banks they manage, or in the firms their banks manage. Rather, their power is a form of 'cultural capital'; it is a function of their capacity to appropriate the sacred knowledge of the workings of the world capitalist system.

Thesis 5. Even though Central European managers are not limited by the power of a propertied bourgeoisie, we would emphasize that they do not exercise power in a vacuum. Rather, they occupy a historically distinctive post-communist class context, formed by ongoing struggles over privatization and the formation of new class actors. These struggles take place among members of the power bloc – managers, technocrats, and intellectuals, in the first instance – and between this power bloc and former bureaucrats, in the second. As we have argued throughout this book, no single class fraction has emerged as the decisive victor in these struggles, and as a consequence the power of managers and their capacity to control semi-public property comes to them by default.

Thesis 6. Managerial strategies reflect their knowledge that the current balance of class forces is precarious. They understand that they exercise power by default. In order to survive, therefore, managers have developed a diverse range of strategies to navigate the political and economic uncertainties of post-communism. Probably the most prevalent managerial strategy was not managerial 'buy-out' but, rather, an attempt to stand 'on as many legs as possible'. During the process of privatization most managers acquired *some* property, but this was typically a relatively small stake, and not even necessarily in the firms they managed. Indeed, as early as the late 1980s some members of management teams were busy setting up small subcontracting firms, owned by themselves or by members of their families.[44] They subcontracted the most lucrative activities of the state firms they managed to these companies, they even sold some of the more valuable assets of the parent firms to these subcontracting units at undervalued prices. Still, it is probably the exception to the rule that these managers retired from their main firm altogether, that they 'jumped the boat' to run the subcontracting firms they own. The reason for their reluctance to do so is clear: why should they swap a *major* managerial job for the position of owner-manager in a *minor* operation which employs only a handful of people? On the other hand, managers also have an interest in being more than *only* managers. In post-communist society, the managerial elite is closely intertwined with the politocracy; hence post-communist managers are even more dependent upon politicians than are capitalist managers in the West. State bureaucracies in East Central Europe often have the power, through direct or indirect state ownership of firms, to appoint and dismiss managers. As long as their position can be threatened by the political elite, it seems to be wise for managers to have their own small private firm in the background.[45]

Postscript: The Great Bank Robbery of 1993–96

Just as we pronounced the mystery solved, and presented our theory of managerial capitalism, new evidence came to light. Data gathered in Hungary by TARKI from a random sample of 290 firms with 50 or more employees indicated a substantial increase in private ownership among domestic individuals.[46] This new evidence raised the question of whether or not managerialism was only a very brief stage in the post-communist transition. Did it mean that political capitalism would win after all? Were former communist technocrats hiding only for a short time – waiting for the anti-communist fire to burn itself it out – before they turned their 1988 dream into a reality? This is the question we investigate in the postscript to this chapter.

Our theory of post-communist managerialism was developed on the basis of data gathered early in the post-communist transition. In 1993, privatization had just begun in a serious manner, and it is possible to argue that it was far too early to find consolidated, clear-cut property relations or a fully formed propertied class at that time. For this reason, in 1996, we decided to generate the most up-to-date data on the property relations of the Hungarian firms we had surveyed in 1993. All 600 firms in our 1993 sample were also in the Hoppenstadt business register, which requires the firms it lists to release information on property relations. So, during spring 1996 we consulted the most recent edition of Hoppenstadt, which reported data on ownership for 1995, and we coded all the Hoppenstadt data available for the 600 firms in our sample.[47]

The 1996 data we generated in this way were consistent with our earlier findings about the relative unimportance of management buy-out in the early years of the post-communist transition. The data indicated some substantial changes between 1993 and 1995, but did not show any increase in management ownership, or in ownership by other domestic private individuals. We did, however, find a sharp decline in public ownership. While the TARKI survey of 1993 (see Table 4.12) showed that the government possessed an ownership stake in 52.5 percent of all firms – and usually owned a large percentage of the assets of these firms – in 1995, only 27.7 percent of the 213 firms for which we have Hoppenstadt data were owned, in part or wholly, by the government. This finding makes sense in a context of rapid privatization. The socialist–liberal government which came to power in May 1994 made privatization a top priority, and in 1995 they reported several billion dollars in privatization revenues. The other clear trend we saw emerging in the 1995 Hoppenstadt data was a rapid growth in foreign ownership. Foreign ownership grew almost as fast as public ownership declined. The TARKI data in Table 4.13 show that in 1993 only 24.6 percent of all firms reported foreign ownership. By 1995 this figure had jumped to 44.6 percent. Note, however, that for the 213 firms listed in Hoppenstadt in 1995, there was no evidence of increasing management buy-out. In fact, rates of managerial ownership in the 213 firms for which we have information in 1995 were lower than those reported for the 1,001 firms surveyed by TARKI in 1993. On the basis of these new data, then, we concluded that while privatization had progressed substantially between 1993 and 1995, it was not managers who benefited from the reduction in public-sector ownership, but foreign investors.

Thus we felt that our theory of post-communist managerialism was sustained. The 'Thief of Budapest and Warsaw' remained a myth – if any crime had been committed, it was not a systematic theft of public property. Indeed, the opposite was true. Our cautious managers seemed unwilling to take responsibility for the firms they ran, and appeared unlikely to transform themselves from socialist managers into capitalist owner-operators.

No sooner had we rested on our laurels than reality rushed ahead of our conclusions. As sociologists often are, we were reminded that social reality is far more complex than social theory. In autumn 1996, TARKI conducted a new survey on property relations in Hungary. The sample was drawn from the Hoppenstadt business register, as it was in 1993, but this time it was restricted to firms with 50 employees or more. On this basis, 290 firms were selected and personal interviews were conducted with top managers. In Table 4.14, these data are compared with data from the 1993 TARKI survey analyzed above, and they tell a drastically different story.[48]

Table 4.14 Public, domestic and foreign ownership in Hungarian firms in 1993 and 1996

	1993		1996	
	No ownership	50% or more	No ownership	50% or more
Public ownership	47.4	39.4	–	–
Government	–	–	83.6	11.3
Local gvt	–	–	86.0	2.4
Other domestic organization	82.7	9.3	67.6	20.5
Domestic bank	–	–	95.9	1.0
Workers	69.9	12.3	86.7	4.5
All domestic individuals	–	–	54.1	33.3
Managers	73.3	4.3	–	–
Their spouse	97.3	.6	–	–
Their relative	98.1	.7	–	–
Other domestic individuals	84.2	6.4	–	–
All foreign investors	75.3	15.6	–	–
Foreign firms	–	–	79.2	16.3
Foreign indiv.	–	–	95.4	2.7

The comparison of the 1993 and 1996 data, presented in Table 4.14, shows a massive increase in the proportion of firms reporting ownership by domestic individuals. As Table 4.15 shows, a no less important change took place in the size of the share typically owned by such proprietors, which increased substantially.

Table 4.15 Business ownership by domestic individuals in 1996, by size of firm

Percent ownership	1–49 employees	50–99 employees	100–199 employees	200–499 employees	500+ employees	All
None	41.7	40.0	53.8	65.6	88.5	53.8% (156)
<50%	16.6	14.6	10.3	14.0	7.7	12.7% (37)
>50%	41.7	45.4	35.9	20.4	3.8	33.5% (97)
All (n)	4.1% (12)	37.9% (110)	26.9% (78)	22.1% (64)	9.0% (26)	100% (290)

Table 4.15 shows that many firms reported some ownership by domestic individuals in 1996. This trend is particularly pronounced in smaller firms which employ 100 people or fewer. By 1996, the majority of such firms reported some private domestic ownership, and 41–45 percent of these firms had majority owners who were private, domestic individuals. As firm size increases, the proportion of firms reporting majority ownership or some ownership by domestic individuals declines, but private domestic ownership is far from trivial. In firms with 100–199 employees, 46.2 percent (10.3 plus 35.9 percent) report some private domestic ownership, and 35.9 percent report majority ownership by private domestic individuals. In firms with 200–499 employees, these numbers are 34.4 percent (14.0 plus 20.4 percent) of firms with some private domestic ownership, and 20.4 percent with majority domestic private ownership. In the case of firms with 500 or more employees, individual domestic ownership, even in 1996, remained rare, and majority ownership by domestic individuals was reported in only one case. It is quite clear from the data, however, that a fairly sizeable propertied middle bourgeoisie emerged between 1993 and 1996. And since this class of actors was nonexistent, by all indicators, as late as October 1993, their emergence and growth are impressive, if not phenomenal.

How should we interpret these new data? Should we conclude that post-communist managerialism was just a passing phenomenon? Is our theory, like most theories, the owl of Minerva that flies at dusk? By the time it appears in print, will it have become invalidated? And, more importantly, what accounts for the phenomenal growth of this middle bourgeoisie between 1993 and 1996?

We cannot offer any conclusive answers to these questions, but our suspicion is that we should not bury our theory of post-communist

managerialism prematurely. If we resume the role of detectives, we immediately note that the phenomenal rise in the number of the Hungarian
'middle bourgeoisie' took place between 1993 and 1996, precisely following
a change in government. As trained detectives we can quickly, therefore,
pronounce that a crime has been committed – the 'Great Bank Robbery of
1993–96' – and form a working hypothesis as to the suspects, motives and
means involved, a hypothesis which is fully consonant with our original
theory. The rapid increase in property ownership, we suggest, was not evidence of the victory of the entrepreneurial spirit but, rather, the outcome of
a change in the balance of those very class forces we described above.

The main point of our theory of post-communist managerialism was
that managers exercised economic power 'by default'. Their specific strategies and the positions they carved out for themselves reflected a complex
configuration of class forces at the top of the social structure – that is, the
balance of power and conditional cooperation between technocrats, intellectuals and managers. The technocratic fraction of the former state-socialist
regime allied itself with the intellectuals to depose the bureaucrats, and consequently found itself on the defensive when these intellectuals acquired
political power by means of an anti-communist rhetoric, which implicated
the technocrats as well. Thus, managers had a relatively free hand to control
the operations of state firms, but had to reckon with the intellectual 'watch-
dogs' when it came to translating this control into ownership and material
rewards.

Let us remind our readers that between 1990 and May 1994 in Hungary,
a government whose core was composed of the then vehemently anti-
communist and anti-technocratic Democratic Forum was in power. But in
May 1994, the successor to the old Communist Party, the so-called
Hungarian Socialist Party, won the elections, and Horn, who was Foreign
Minister in the last communist government before 1989, became Prime
Minister. We think that this is a crucial clue for unraveling the mystery of the
Great Bank Robbery. Although we must leave the definitive analysis to
other detectives (who would first have to establish the exact timing of the
robbery), the following sinister plot *could* fit the facts, and is in accordance
with our theory of post-communist managerialism: it was the Socialist Party,
the representative of the reform socialist technocracy, who did it. The
former communist technocracy and managerial elite felt threatened by the
anti-communism of Democratic Forum, and countered it with the rhetoric
of 'incompetence' to discredit the first non-communist government. In this
way they became the ideologues of the Socialist Party, whose slogan in the
successful 1994 campaign was: 'A vote for the socialists is a vote for competence'.[49] When the Socialist Party won the 1994 elections, the power
balance at the top shifted back towards the technocrats and managers, and
their capacity to translate managerial control into outright ownership was

greatly increased. Moreover, although the government formed by the Socialist Party did not display stunning competence, they were very efficient in rewarding the 'competent' – namely, their cadre base – with state property. This is the hypothesis we would like to advance. It is not inconceivable to think about the Great Bank Robbery of 1993–96 as the partial materialization of the 1988 conspiracy of the state-socialist technocracy, identified by Hankiss and Stanizskis.

An examination of the electoral fortunes of the Hungarian Socialist Party, lends further credence to our hypothesis. In 1990 the ex-Communist Party received approximately 10 percent of the votes, basically only from the old communist apparatchiks. By 1994, however, the Socialists had tripled their vote. They kept the former Communist Party vote, but they also added the vote of the urban working class, since as long as they were in opposition they played a 'social democratic role', presenting themselves as the advocates of the working class, the trade unions, and the welfare state. Once they began to govern, however, they implemented privatization policies which enriched former cadres and technocrats – about a third of their constituency – and adopted rather neo-liberal, anti-labor policies. As a result, they began to lose the support of the workers. If elections had been held in March 1997, the two major right-wing parties would have won 60 percent of the vote, and the Socialist Party would have been defeated with only 20 percent of the electorate behind them. Our point is simple: this party was not so much the party of labor as the representative of former cadres and the reform communist technocracy. Its rise to power tilted the scales back in favor of technocrats and managers, and allowed them, at least in some measure, to move further along the road to becoming a new bourgeoisie. But there are clear electoral limits to this project, which means that the balance of power at the top will be restored in some measure, and the 'power bloc' will be preserved as a representative of the *Bildungsbürgertum*.

These are all speculations, of course. We would need data from the Czech Republic and Poland to assess the explanatory power of these hypotheses. In principle, in the Czech Republic we would not expect to see the wave of management buy-outs we observed in Hungary, and we suspect that Poland would present a less extreme case of cadre bourgeosification than Hungary, since the Polish ex-Communist Party never had the kind of technocratic support that the Hungarian Socialists have enjoyed. Here is another puzzle that we must leave to another investigator. If that investigator finds that trends in property transformation are identical in all three countries, they may conclude that this is evidence of the 'end of history'. After all, the range of capitalisms we identify may be only a transitory phenomenon – on the other side of the bridge we may find that there was only one destination all along. In this view, historically contingent struggles between specific agents, the habituses they carry, and the path-dependent transformation of the institutional frameworks they operate within, are all fairy tales. The ultimate reality is the iron law of the logic of capitalist economy, and the rational choices individuals make within this framework.

Short of such evidence, however, all we can conclude is that for the time being, the proposition that post-communist capitalism has some novel features still holds. In the concluding chapter we summarize what these novel features are, and explore how likely they are to be reproduced across time.

5

Conclusions: The Contested Terrain of Class Formation in Post-Communist Central Europe

The process of class formation in post-communist Central Europe is highly contested. On the one hand, post-communist capitalism has been a project of the intelligentsia, broadly speaking. Specifically, it has been a second *Bildungsbürgertum* project, as we formulated it in Chapter 2. For this reason, a central question about the class structure that will emerge is: how visible and how influential will the intelligentsia be in the future? We think that they are unlikely to disappear from the political scene altogether, but they may move into the background. Some intellectuals may begin to develop a cautious critical distance from the political elite and the emerging propertied class. They are already expressing disgust with the *nouveaux riches*. However, we also believe that intellectuals are likely to remain a 'loyal opposition', because the project they have realized – the *Bildungsbürgertum* project – is one of civil society. The success of this project means that the intelligentsia is deeply entrenched in the big, weak states of Central Europe – state-run foundations are the source of intellectuals' incomes, and underpin their exercise of cultural–administrative power. On the other hand, we also think that the developing class structure of Central Europe is likely to contain a propertied bourgeoisie, since there are signs that one is slowly emerging. We argue, however, that this class is likely to be weak relative to other class and state actors. Precisely how weak the propertied bourgeoisie will be will depend on the social origins and habituses of the agents who will comprise it, and in this connection the trajectories and alliances of the intellectual fractions of the post-communist power bloc that we have identified are likely to be consequential.

That said, we should acknowledge that this book has presented an analysis of class structure 'from above'. On this basis, our readers may dismiss us as elitists, arguing that we ignore society. Against such a criticism, we would emphasize that our analytical focus on the top of society is justified by strong historical reasons. We think that the capitalism which is being made in Central Europe is being made from above. We do not think this is the only way capitalism can be built, and we are aware that in other historical sites capitalism from below has been as important as capitalism from above. For this reason, in the last section of this last chapter we examine the importance of intellectuals in the post-communist transition, and ask whether or not capitalism from above was inevitable in Central Europe. Finally, we examine the forces of change operating from below, and assess the extent to which they are likely to affect the scenario we are describing.

The 'New Class' project for the fourth time?

We have been careful not to call Central European post-capitalism a class society, and in particular we have explicitly avoided referring to technocrats and managers, or the intelligentsia as a whole, as a dominant class. Rather, the key to our theory of post-communist managerialism and the conception of 'capitalism without capitalists' is that the formation of a propertied bourgeoisie has been relatively slow: market institutions have developed much more rapidly in Central Europe than a capitalist class. It is precisely this weakness of a domestic propertied bourgeoisie which has made it possible for a power bloc, composed of different fractions of intellectual elites, to retain a hegemonic position. At the same time, our answer to the 'Whodunit'? question – that is to say, 'Whose project is post-communism'? – is that it has been the project of the intelligentsia, or at least certain fractions of the intelligentsia. So it seems that the idea of the 'New Class' haunts us – the post-communist power bloc is neither a new nor an old class, but it is composed of intellectuals, and these intellectuals are pursuing a power project.

During the last century – starting with Bakunin in the early 1870s, and stretching to Gouldner in the late 1970s – the idea of a 'New Class' of intellectuals dominating and leading society has haunted the social sciences. In the West, it was thought that intellectuals would replace the propertied bourgeoisie. In Central Europe, it was believed that they would replace the old-guard bureaucracy of communist regimes. And while successive predictions of the imminent rise of the intelligentsia to power proved false, social scientists never seemed to learn their lesson. They kept creating new theories about societies in which intellectuals would dominate. Such theorizing came in waves, was fashionable for a few years, and then discredited for a while, only to be reborn in a somewhat altered form some years later. In an essay published a few years ago, one of us suggested that the stubborn return of the idea of the New Class requires explanation.[1] We argued that while neither the intelligentsia as a whole, nor any of its strata, ever succeeded in establishing itself as a new dominant class, it was probably historically true that intellectuals formulated such 'projects' for power. On this basis, we interpreted the different waves of New Class theorizing as critical or apologetic – albeit premature – generalizations of such power projects. It may be instructive to think about post-communist managerialism from this perspective, and to contrast it with earlier intellectual class projects.

Between 1870 and 1970 we can identify at least three distinct waves of New Class theorizing, and possibly three intellectual power projects.

We identify the first wave as the 'intellectual class' theory advanced by anarchists of the late nineteenth and early twentieth centuries. This theory contended that Marxism was really the ideology of an intellectual elite, which was trying to use the working-class movement to smuggle itself into a position of class power. When a Marxism-inspired social order was established in the post-revolutionary Soviet Union – taking form as a dictatorship of the Stalinist bureaucracy rather than class rule by 'socialist scholars' – this theory died a peaceful death. However, this does not mean that the anarchist analysis of Marxism as an intellectual ideology was completely without insight. From our perspective, it helps to explain why Central European intellectuals abandoned their *Bildungsbürgertum* project at the turn of the century, and why so many of them were attracted to left-wing radicalism.

The second wave of New Class theories – fashionable in a period roughly from 1930 to the 1950s – consisted of 'bureaucratic-technocratic class' theories. In the version which addressed the social conditions of advanced Western capitalism, New Class theorists argued that the technocratic and/or managerial stratum would fill the gap created by the decline of family capitalism and individual private property.[2] We think these theorists were probably correct in identifying 'New Class' aspirations among managers and technocrats at this time, but they erred in taking the ideologues of managerialism at their word, and underestimating the power of the old moneyed class. Critics of managerialist New Class theories, like Zeitlin and Domhoff, were correct when they observed that managerialism in the United States and Western Europe failed because it confronted a strong propertied bourgeoisie.[3] We tend to side with the critics in this debate, since there is strong evidence that the old propertied bourgeoisie is alive and well. Indeed, it seems that today the concentration of wealth in the United States and Western Europe is even more marked, and fewer people own more of the productive assets than ever before.

The third wave of New Class theories, created in the 1960s and 1970s, was comprised of theories of 'the knowledge class'. In their right-wing version, these theories of the new class interpreted the radical movements of the 1960s as a power plot by the counter-cultural intelligentsia to dominate society. By contrast, social scientists on the political Left emphasized that as science became an increasingly important factor of production, scientists would begin replacing property owners as the dominant group in advanced Western societies.[4] Some of these theorists, most notably Gouldner, were not thrilled by the prospect of a society ruled by a new class coalition of the technical intelligentsia and humanistic intellectuals merged together by the 'culture of critical discourse', but given the alternatives, they believed that it might be 'our best card in history'. As the left radicalism of the 1960s faded away, however, and as counter-cultural intellectuals were replaced by Yuppies preaching neo-liberalism, this wave of theorizing also withered away.

What about post-communist managerialism? Is it possible that we are witnessing a fourth New Class project this century? Is it possible that intellectuals are indeed in power, even though it is 'by default' this time, since managers have no enemies able to resist their newly found dominance? Have the prophecies of Berle and Means actually turned out to be correct – not for the advanced West but, ironically, for Central Europe? Or is post-communism, as we have analyzed it, simply a step in the transition to market capitalism as we know it from the advanced West? Or are we witnessing the transformation of existing elements into a new *Gestalt*, of which we have no adequate conception? We know that we are shooting at a rapidly moving target, and social scientists are poor snipers even when the target does not move.

In this context, it is difficult to answer the question of whether or not managerialism will last. It is difficult to predict the chances that the post-communist power bloc will reproduce itself and the social and economic order it governs. It is unclear whether or not the post-communist elite will resist the encroachments of international capital, and the attempts of propertied middle classes to accumulate capital and take hold of the command posts of the economy. Reproduction is a possibility, however. It is conceivable that managers will consolidate their powerful institutional base by allying with national and international fiscal institutions and, with monetarism as their ideology, continue to govern post-communist capitalism as managers. The appropriate positions are ready, the adequate consciousness has been prepared, and the actors feel comfortable in their positions and are deeply committed to their ideology. Furthermore, in post-communist societies the alternatives seem to be difficult. The nationalization of property has been a process with far-reaching implications, and is possibly irreversible. As the old joke puts it: we know how to make fish soup from an aquarium, but how can we build an aquarium from a bowl of fish soup? East European economists enjoyed citing this joke before 1989, but they quickly forgot it after 1989. Indeed, one major underpinning of managers' power is their claim to be the only ones with the knowledge of how to conduct the complex task of privatization. And the more complex the task, the more it is practically impossible to convert former public property into identifiable individual private property; thus the more power managers have. Thinking about post-communist managerialism as the 'fourth wave' of an intellectual project for power is useful, then, since it helps us to ask these intriguing questions. Moreover, thinking in this way means that we do not simply assume that managerial power is a transitional phenomenon; it allows us to ask: what will society be like if managerialism reproduces itself?

To push our luck even further, we may even wonder whether or not Central European post-communist developments have any relevance for the rest of the world. To put it differently: is Central Europe the future of the West? After all, Central European managerialism may not be all that different from the way Western capitalism operates today: property rights are diffuse, managers exercise a lot of power, and monetarist ideologies are powerful and widespread. As we have already noted, however, these questions about the future are tricky ones, and social scientists are notoriously bad at answering them. Perhaps it would be best to pose the question in a different way and ask: 'If managerialism was a project during the interwar years, as Berle and Means suggested, and if it failed, why did it fail'? Approaching the issue in this way is likely to make us skeptical about the spread of managerialism around the world. Since we argued that managerialism was successful in Central Europe because it did not face powerful enemies like a large propertied bourgeoisie, we would predict that the chances for managerialism in the rest of the world, and especially in the countries of advanced Western capitalism, are slim indeed.

Furthermore, before we go very far with the analogy of post-communist managerialism and previous New Class projects, we should note that there are some historically novel characteristics of post-communist managerialism which make this 'power plot' (if it is a power plot) of intellectuals very different from other New Class projects. First, unlike the three earlier New Class projects, the post-communist power bloc has no explicit or implicit anti-capitalist intentions or ideologies. On the contrary, the post-communist power bloc sees itself as a historical vanguard whose mission is to create capitalism – even to create a class of proprietors. The post-communist power bloc sees itself as a new *Bildungsbürgertum* – the very opposite of the 'vanguard of the proletariat' which characterized intellectual identities during the first New Class project. Second, while it seems to be true that the new post-communist power bloc exercises authority unchallenged by a propertied bourgeoisie, the formation of a propertied class is under way. Indeed, although the different fractions of the power bloc watch each other to make sure that none of the others can use privatization for self-enrichment, none the less some of their members slip through the cracks and have already become rather wealthy. Many more may follow their example. There are also other candidates who might become a new *grande bourgeoisie*, so the position of the post-communist power bloc is rather shaky, and it is their own pro-capitalist ideology which is likely to undermine their power.

For all these reasons, we conclude that post-communist managerialism is unlikely to be the future of advanced Western capitalism. What is still at issue, however, is the shape of the class structure to come in Central Europe, and here a wide range of possibilities open up. In what follows we assess the current capacities and possible futures of different groups in an effort to map the widest range of futures possible in post-communist Central Europe.

The alternative futures of Central European post-communist capitalism

The social structure of Central Europe after the fall of communism is in flux. Which groups of actors will be able to act collectively, where social cleavages will stabilize, where the boundaries around classes or other social actors will form, and what kinds of actions will be taken are all still being negotiated and struggled over. In such rapidly and dramatically changing conditions, the analysis of class is the analysis of processes of *class formation*. Indeed, we think it is relatively unproductive to analyze classes by wondering if a given group of individuals constitute a class, asking what their objective class position in society is, and trying to map the class structure a priori. The reality of social change is in the formation and dissolution of classes. To put this another way, the empirical question is: 'What is the degree of 'classness' of collective actors'? Even in the analysis of classes *par excellence* – namely, the analysis of nineteenth-century capitalism – the bourgeoisie and proletariat were never really fully formed. Different fractions of the bourgeoisie have always been suspicious of one another, and during the nineteenth century they allied themselves with the aristocracy against other bourgeois fractions. In the twentieth century, by the time the capitalist class was finally as closed and as fully formed as it ever was, it had begun to disintegrate.

In this section, we examine changes in Central European social structure following these principles. In this connection, the very idea that this is 'capitalism without capitalists' has to be taken with a pinch of salt. There are, of course, already some propertied capitalists in Central Europe, and there are clear signs that a propertied bourgeoisie may form, or that a struggle is taking place over its formation. Our crucial point is that for the degree of economic development already reached, for the level of economic concentration already achieved, and given the extent of capital accumulation which occurred during the socialist period, this propertied bourgeoisie is rather embryonic. Its wealth is modest, if not trivial, and its political power is virtually symbolic. If we think about the early post-communist period as a 'transition to capitalism', then, it strikes us that market institutions are much closer to those we know from the West than property rights are. In other words, there is unevenness in the development of capitalism in Central

Europe, and this is particularly true for the development of individual private property, the evolution of class structure in general, and the development of a propertied bourgeoisie in particular.

Although the making of a *grande bourgeoisie* is certainly possible, then, we think that the question of what agents will comprise it is greatly contested. How the struggle over property and class formation unfolds, and in particular whether or not any single actor or coalition of actors will be able to form a propertied class, is not predetermined by any iron law of history. Rather, the historically contingent outcomes of struggles between actors will be consequential for what kind of society develops. From this perspective, our thesis of managerialism can be formulated either strongly or weakly. The strong hypothesis states that it is conceivable that managers will continue to operate as managers, their competitors will prevent them from becoming proprietors, and they will prevent their competitors from becoming a propertied bourgeoisie. Under these conditions, we are likely to see the reproduction of managerial society in the strong sense of the term. The weak hypothesis is that managers or their competitors will become a propertied bourgeoisie. In this eventuality, 'managerialism' will be understood as a strategy for making capitalism, and will describe how the transformation was managed. Note that even this weak hypothesis implies that capitalism was created in Central Europe without capitalists, and that the struggles between the historically specific groups identified in our analysis will leave their imprint on this region of the world for decades to come.

Political capitalism in Central Europe and beyond

In Chapter 4 we reviewed political capitalism theory at length. We pointed out that some of the most eminent observers of Central European development believed that those people who would become wealthy as the result of privatization were those who had oppressed these societies for decades: the communist *nomenklatura*. Indeed, in some cases this was not written as a forecast, but was presented as a statement of fact: the old *nomenklatura* was transformed into a new propertied class.[5] What Elemér Hankiss and Jadwiga Staniszkis predicted in 1988 – that political power was being converted into private wealth – was presented as an established fact by Frydman and his collaborators in 1996.

Our theory of post-communist managerialism fundamentally challenges this. We contend that there were clear political limits on the conversion of political power into private wealth. Some of these limits have been set by fractions of the power elite, and in particular by opinion-making intellectuals. In some ways, as we suggested in Chapter 4, Hankiss's and Staniszkis's theories became 'self-defeating prophecies' in Central Europe. Even if former party functionaries intended to steal public property and enrich themselves, theorists like Hankiss and Staniszkis alerted society early enough for the media, the parliament, its subcommittees, social scientists, and the police to start to monitor the process of privatization, making it very difficult for the *nomenklatura* simply to walk away with national property. So although any Central European can cite a case, or identify a former party official who is a rich person and a successful entrepreneur, we do not think this is the main economic story of post-communist privatization.

Let us briefly recapitulate the main findings in this respect in Chapter 4. First, our survey data showed that about 1–2 percent of the managers of larger firms in Central Europe in 1993 were party or state functionaries in 1988. Thus the phenomenon of political capitalism does exist, but it appears to be relatively small-scale. This statement, however, needs qualification. Precisely because of the public outcry against the *nomenklatura* bourgeoisie, it is safe to assume that our survey data underestimate the extent of political capitalism in Central Europe. Whatever successful conversion of political power into private wealth occurred, it is likely to have been hidden. Furthermore, some party and state functionaries were probably smart enough to jump the boat before it sank, and they were already in business in 1988. These qualifications do not undermine our argument, however, since our data, and other data colleted over the period, document that political capitalism is a much less significant phenomenon than managerial power.

The political capitalism thesis, however, may cut more ice when it is applied to Russia, Romania, Bulgaria, and Belarus. And while we do not have Slovakian data yet, events in Slovakia – for example, the cancellation of voucher privatization and the institution of direct, unscrutinized sales of state enterprises – indicate that Slovakia is on the Russian road rather than the Central European one, at least in this respect. While our data indicate that the proportion of former party–state apparatchiks among managers is under 2 percent in Hungary, Poland, and the Czech Republic, in Russia about 10 percent of enterprise managers in 1993 reported having held state or party jobs in 1988. This corresponds to the general trend in Russia, which is elite reproduction.[6] The former Russian *nomenklatura* seems to have been much more successful than its Central European counterpart in converting its political power into either private wealth, or managerial or political power. Even the new Russian politocracy has been recruited from the old guard. Moreover, the opinion-making intelligentsia is much more marginal, and the evidence suggests that it is also intimidated: there have been reports of journalists murdered, beaten, and harassed in Russia and Slovakia. The government in these countries has the key media, radio and television, under tight control.

To formulate the contrast sharply, we might say that *if we see Central Europe as a system of capitalism without capitalists, the East European post-communist regimes might be characterized as systems of capitalists without capitalism.*

The freedom of the media is crucial for the defeat of political capitalism projects among the former *nomenklatura*, and nowhere has it been born without struggle. Even in Central Europe, post-communist governments tried to reign in the media, to gain control of radio and television and even the daily newspapers. It may be coincidental, but from our point of view it is quite telling, that the same Hankiss who formulated the theory of political capitalism became the President of Hungarian Television. In this position, he fought a heroic and eventually successful battle against the attempts of the first Hungarian post-communist government to control the media.

In order to understand the prospects of political capitalism in the region, then, we argue that one has to analyze the balance of power among key actors in late socialism and post-communism. Central European elites were fragmented even before the fall of communism. As we argued in Chapter 4, bureaucratic power was challenged by a strong technocracy in late state socialism, and technocrats gradually came to view their role as different from that of the bureaucracy. With the advent of post-communism, elites diversified further, with different fractions checking the power of the others and monitoring each other's actions. The conditions for this kind of power-sharing were the victory of the technocracy over the bureaucracy, and the identification of technocrats with opinion-making intellectuals and their former enemies, the dissidents, at the end of state socialism and the beginning of the post-communist period.

In contrast, the development of elites during late state socialism in Russia and in the whole of Eastern Europe proper was quite different from that in Central Europe. Not only did the technocracy fail to depose the bureaucratic elite in Russia, it is questionable if the distinction between technocracy and bureaucracy holds for Russia at all. Both fractions come from very similar social backgrounds, and – as Eyal and Townsley have demonstrated elsewhere – both fractions of the post-communist elite were much more likely to be sons and daughters of fathers who held *nomenklatura* positions than either technocrats or bureaucrats in Central Europe.[7] Even the habituses and mindsets of technocrats and bureaucrats seem to be similar in the Russian case. And although there was a great change of personnel at the top of the social hierarchy following Gorbachev's reforms of the 1980s,[8] the relatively homogenous pool from which new personnel could be recruited limited the change that could occur. New people were promoted to top positions in Russia but they looked like the old people – they were simply younger. Indeed, it makes sense to call the *nomenklatura* the 'ruling class of the USSR', as Voslensky has suggested,[9] since it was closed to all other social classes in a caste-like manner, reproduced itself through marriage ties, and made sure that only its sons and daughters had access to positions of power.

In Central Europe this was never the case. In Poland there was always an influx into the *nomenklatura* from the popular classes, particularly from the peasantry, and in Hungary, positions of power were open to young technocrats and the children of intellectuals during the last two decades of socialism. This is why political capitalism theory makes more sense in the Russian case than in Central Europe. And while we would hesitate to say that political capitalism is the main story in post-communist Russia, the idea of a *nomenklatura*-bourgeoisie makes much more sense in Russian conditions than in Central European ones.

Our conclusion, then, is that in Central Europe the Communist Party and state apparatchiks, with few exceptions, missed the opportunity to convert themselves into a propertied *grande bourgeoisie*, and their chance to do so will never return. By contrast, in the regions further east – in Romania, Bulgaria, Serbia, and especially in Russia – it is conceivable that a substantial portion of the political *nomenklatura* became proprietors, and may constitute an important component of the propertied classes that will develop in these countries.

Managers become owners

As Chapter 4 showed, there is much more support for the proposition that managers – rather than former political bosses – acquired private property during the early post-communist transition, and that at least some of them are beginning to look like members of a propertied bourgeoisie. Our data suggest that this process is most advanced in Hungary. Almost half of the CEOs we interviewed in 1993 in Hungary reported ownership of some business property, compared to only 20 percent in the Czech Republic and Poland.

Note, however, that this managerial ownership displays some unusual features. About half the CEOs who reported business ownership own property in firms other than those they manage. Many of these are subcontracting firms which managers have created as satellites of their main company.[10] As Larry King shows, these satellites are of two types. In some cases, managers set up 'permanent parasitic satellites' owned by themselves or members of their family and/or fellow members of firm management to siphon off income from the mother firm. This sort of arrangement does not undermine post-communist managerialism. Rather, 'permanent parasitic satellites' are products of this system, since such firms can be owned and operated by managers only as long as ownership of the mother firm is diffuse – that is to say, as long as there are no owners who might closely supervise managers.[11] Furthermore, as long as managers are allowed to operate these parasitic satellites, there are no incentives for them to become owners of the mother firm. It is safer to leave ownership of the mother firm and the risks associated with it to others – ideally to the taxpayers and to the government – while profits are milked by the satellites. Of course, such managers may consider becoming full owners of these satellites and retire from their positions as CEOs altogether, but we think this is unlikely, because they would have no guarantee that their small firm would keep receiving lucrative subcontracts from the mother firm. Whatever the case, note that the system of permanent satellites constitutes a unique form of property and a novel form of capitalism in which the advantages of private proprietorship are realized only if you are also a managerial employee of a corporation, other than the one from which you gain your profit. In as much as this kind of arrangement characterizes the post-communist economy, post-communism can indeed be seen as 'managerial capitalism'. This is not the managerialism of Berle and Means, but post-communist managerialism as defined in this book.

The other kind of satellite which King identified is a vehicle for management buy-out. In this case, the CEO and/or his partners in management create a subcontracting firm in anticipation of the privatization of the mother company. They sell the most valuable assets of the mother firm to their subcontracting company at the lowest possible price, leaving all the debt and liabilities in the original company until it is declared bankrupt and auctioned off. At this point, the tiny but wealthy subcontracting firm can buy the devalued corporation cheaply. Of course, there is little about this process that is distinctively Central European, post-communist, or unique: this is the classical strategy of management buy-out in the West. The only difference is that in post-communist Central Europe, the mother firm is often state-owned (or owned by the State Privatization Agency, which is probably the loosest form of state ownership in history); hence the managers' buy-out does not take place under the scrutiny of a Board of Directors, whose personal money is at stake, nor does it occur in competition with other capitalists. Under post-communist conditions, managers who attempt management buy-out have to come to terms only with the politocracy, and the 'supervision' of the buy-out process is rather indirect, except for nosy journalists and an overworked prosecutor's office. In this context, this management buy-out strategy may be an important way in which post-communist managers become a capitalist class.

Note, however, that our data do not distinguish between permanent parasitical satellites and satellites that are part of managerial buy-out strategies. All we know at this point is that some combination of these two strategies can be detected in about a quarter of the Hungarian firms which were large enough to be listed on business registers in 1993 (and, by all accounts, occur in fewer firms in the Czech Republic and Poland). Larry King's ethnographic research in about three dozen Czech and Hungarian firms finds a similar proportion of firms engaging in one or other of these strategies. So we are probably not too far off the mark when we claim that the proportion of firms in 1993 which was subject to management buy-out or manager-owned subcontracting firms was not more than 25 percent of all firms, and may be as few as 10 percent.

Our data provide further evidence, however, that direct management buy-out also characterized the early years of the post-communist transition. About a quarter of the managers we interviewed in Hungary reported some ownership in the firms they managed (again, this proportion appears to be significantly smaller in the Czech Republic and Poland). Typically, however, these were small ownership stakes (no more than 10 percent), and they were mostly in small firms. And when we speak of large firms, we do not mean corporate giants: we mean that in firms with 100 employees or more, managerial ownership was negligible.

In addition to direct and indirect managerial ownership, about as many firms in Hungary reported employee ownership as reported ownership by CEOs in 1993. King's ethnographic work confirms that employee ownership was of some significance in the Czech Republic also. It is not known to what extent 'employee ownership' stands for ownership by fellow managers, or whether is it ownership by employees proper. Regardless, we would like to make two points about employee ownership. First, to the extent that it represents ownership by managerial personnel, this is still not individual private ownership by *the* manager. If the top five or ten people in a firm have to coordinate their action while owning 10 or 15 percent of its stock, their ability to act in unison will be limited. They are likely to be divided on a number of issues, and may search for competing constituencies among other stockholders. Second, if employee ownership represents ownership by non-managerial personnel, it is likely to increase the decision-making power of the CEO, but limit his ownership rights exactly along the lines our theory of post-communist managerialism suggests. Ownership by non-managerial employees has some analogies with socialist 'workers' self-management' in the former Yugoslavia. Critics of self-management pointed out that in this system it was managers who called the shots; workers did not have the information, the technical knowledge or the connections to offer alternatives or to overrule the decisions made by managers with reference to their competence.

To sum up: the phenomenon of managers becoming owners was real in 1993, but it was relatively insignificant. Against the common wisdom of economists and sociologists, which held that management buy-out was the royal road to capitalism, we argue that this was not the case. Although the situation may have changed since 1993, at that time managerial ownership was a relatively minor story.

Does this mean, then, that our analysis of managerialism is an analysis of only a 'transitional' – hence inconsequential – phenomenon? We do not think so. If the capitalist class which emerges is recruited from former managers, who in some way or another managed to get hold of state assets, we think that this will be extremely significant for the future of capitalism in Central Europe.

Data collected during 1996 by TARKI in Hungary indicate that individual private ownership – which probably, in the majority of cases, represents ownership by current or former members of management – grew substantially between 1993 and 1996. By 1996, a third to half of all small and medium-sized firms reported ownership by domestic individuals, or groups of individuals. To repeat our remarks in Chapter 4: we urge readers not to make too much of these findings. First, evidence of the rapid increase in domestic private ownership is for Hungary only, where it may have been caused by shifts in the balance of political power following the electoral victory of the successor party of the Communist Party. We need data from the Czech Republic and Poland to assess whether the growth of management buy-outs follows the 'iron laws' of making capitalism, or if it is the result of actions by the former Communist Party rewarding its political allies among former communist managers and technocrats. Our second observation is that our most recent data on the corporate sector – thus on firms with 500 or more employees – show that they continue to be publicly owned, or they can be characterized among Stark's recombinant property forms. Continuing high levels of public ownership are challenged by foreign investment, and there is little evidence, as of spring 1997, of the formation of a propertied bourgeoisie in this sector.

Finally, we observe that even if some managers successfully acquire substantial amounts of private property – enough to justify the label 'grande bourgeoisie' – they are likely to carry their managerial habitus with them. The establishment of market institutions will probably reshape their habitus in significant ways, but these market institutions, and the property relations in which they act, will themselves bear the imprint of the socialist–managerialist habitus of their makers. We have already seen the variety of rituals and strategies these actors have employed to negotiate post-communist conditions. They look very different from the behaviors and understandings of dynamic Schumpeterian entrepreneurs. For this reason, we think that managers who have become owners will look very different from Western capitalists. We know that the gentry habitus transformed prewar Central European economic and social institutions, and kept reproducing a 'gentroid' society, even as Central European economies were being integrated into the world capitalist economy. The managerial habitus and mentality does not, of course, have the attraction and magic of the gentry way of life, but it could operate in an analogous way, leaving a lasting imprint on social conditions well beyond post-communism.

The phenomenon of habitus is usually seen as describing the process of reproduction of social structure: individual dispositions are shaped by the structures among which they operate, while these dispositions serve to fit people into positions so that the logic of the whole structure is maintained. In short, the habitus of the incumbents of a position, and the nature of that position, are connected in an interactive and mutually determining relationship. Not only are habituses shaped by institutions, but institutions are also remade as the incumbents of positions follow their habituses to navigate their social circumstances. This is the theoretical reason why it is important to sociologists if the personnel of elite positions are changing when the logic and institutional structure of a society is also being changed. Simply speaking, it is quite reasonable to assume that capitalism run and managed by former communist apparatchiks, or their sons and daughters, will be substantially different from a capitalism which is run by the sons and daughters of Rockefellers.

So, even if Central European managers become private proprietors, the capitalism which is likely to emerge will probably be quite different from advanced Western capitalism. We think it might look like the political capitalism Weber wrote about. Weber's notion of political capitalism is quite different from the neo-Marxist one which we criticized above. The questions neo-Marxists asked were simply: where do capitalists come from, and how does original capital accumulation take place? Political capitalism is held to exist when political office-holders use their political power to appropriate private wealth. The question for Weber, by contrast, concerns the logic of the economic system and the relationship between economics and politics. Political capitalism is capitalism in the sense that it is oriented towards the rational acquisition of profits, but it is political because this happens under the tutelage of the state and/or in conditions of systematic political interference in the economic system. There are many reasons why managers who have become owners might feel more comfortable navigating a Weberian world of political capitalism rather than a world governed by the conditions of *laissez-faire* competition. As former socialist and post-communist managers, they know the rules of the game in a system in which economics and politics are interconnected. Moreover, the processes of managerial buy-out described above are likely to create clientelistic relationships between manager-owners and the politocracy.

In conclusion, it is a little far-fetched to assume that former socialist managers will become entrepreneurs in the Schumpeterian sense of the term overnight. They were managers because they wanted to acquire higher incomes for themselves than the rest of the population enjoyed, and now they use the opportunity to privatize parts of their firms because they seek to supplement those incomes. For many, the motivation for their economic action is consumption rather than entrepreneurial innovation. For this reason, we think that even if they come to constitute a capitalist class it is likely to be a *rentier* class: it is difficult to see how the future Soros of Central Europe can be made quickly from the stuff which is found among the ruins of state socialism.

Compradore capitalism: socialist technocrats become capitalist managers

There is a variety of ways in which managers could be tempted to take advantage of the post-communist transformation. So far, we have described the temptation to maximize managerial decision-making power by creating and maintaining diffuse ownership relations. This is especially tempting if it can be done through the creation of permanent parasitic satellites which allow managers to appropriate substantial incomes without taking any entrepreneurial risks. A lesser temptation – but a powerful one none the less – is for managers to become the owners of the firms they manage. These paths to managerial ownership were described above. Here, we turn to another important temptation – namely, managers facilitating the sale of their company to their old foreign business partners, demanding, in exchange for good purchase conditions or a good price, lucrative managerial employment in the new foreign-owned firm.

This managerial strategy offers high incomes as well as greater security than management buy-out. It also provides the intangible but quite powerful lure of the prestige of the West. Managers and technocrats who were dealing with Western companies during the years of state socialism may see this as the realization of a dream: finally they can run a firm which is properly managed, properly owned, and properly equipped. With the influx of foreign capital – which is frequently a condition of the privatization of state-owned enterprises to foreigners – the company can suddenly jump the queue and become the most modern in the nation.

Hiring former managers, or even former party or state functionaries, is also appealing to foreign companies and world monetary institutions. Employing these personnel as managers, advisors or consultants provides the foreign corporation with a solid and well-connected local representative. Foreign investors are fully aware of how important social networks and personal ties from the communist period are for doing business in post-communist conditions. They know that you do not necessarily hire the best and the brightest; rather, you hire the best connected. The last communist Prime Minister of Hungary, Miklós Németh, stepped out of office straight into a position as one of the vice-presidents of the European Bank of Reconstruction. Personally, we know two former senior officials of the Central Committee of the Hungarian Communist Party who now work for multinational companies – one of them half-jokingly and half-seriously calls himself a 'compradore intellectual'.

This is a useful term if we can detach it from the value judgements placed on it by neo-Marxists who despise the 'compradore bourgeoisie' of Third World countries, who, they argue, are responsible for neo-colonialism and the 'development of underdevelopment'. We would like to use the term analytically to refer to the existence of 'compradore intellectuals' who make it possible for foreign capital to penetrate post-communist markets. These intellectuals create trust and confidence so that these foreign firms will export capital to Central Europe. Whether or not the influx of foreign capital is beneficial for post-communist economies is a complex question to which no hard-and-fast answer is forthcoming. Some of the foreign investment which occurred immediately following the fall of the old regime was probably not advantageous. Some of it was predatory, aiming to eliminate competitors by dominating their domestic and foreign markets. A lot of this foreign investment was in retail, and was monopolistic in character: foreign investors bought up entire communist monopoly retail chains, filled them with cheap Western consumer goods, and damaged the domestic production of such goods, making it more difficult to break away from state-socialist monopolies or to develop alternative retail activities. Some foreign investment, however, was highly productive. It resurrected viable factories, created well-paid employment opportunities, and even brought in badly needed managerial know-how and technology.

On the whole, we are inclined to believe that in the specific Central European conditions of post-communist transformation, where one of the gravest economic problems is the lack of capital, foreign investment is likely to be beneficial rather than destructive. Even though the country in Central Europe with the highest foreign investment *per capita* – Hungary – is the country with the worst economic performance in the first six or seven years of transformation, there is evidence that most of the destructive investment took place in those first years. Moreover, Hungary's poor economic performance arguably has more to do with its foreign debt burden and incompetent domestic macro-management than with foreign investment. Indeed, how well foreign investment works depends a great deal on the character of the compradore intelligentsia and its relationship with the new power elite. A country is more likely to pursue foreign investment judiciously and beneficially when compradore intellectuals are well integrated into the power elite, rather than in conflict with those branded a 'kleptocratura'.

Note, too, that foreign investment in 1993 accounted for a rather small fraction of the economies in most Central European countries. In Hungary, which was the country most open to foreign capital, only 25 percent of firms large enough to be in major business registers reported any foreign ownership in 1993. Moreover, only 14 percent of all firms were under foreign control. Between 1994 and 1996, however, Hungary moved quickly towards a capitalist system in which the compradore intelligentsia are among the most important actors in domestic social structure. As public ownership declined, foreign ownership grew rapidly. Indeed, it seems that privatization in Hungary did not result in management buy-out benefiting managers so much as in heightened foreign investment.

Competition for private ownership between new entrepreneurs and managers

There is, however, another group of agents who may have a chance to become a member of the future propertied bourgeoisie: those new entrepreneurs who could not or did not want to take advantage of the privatization of the corporate sector, but started their own small businesses in the hope that they would grow bigger. Some of these entrepreneurs were ordinary workers during socialism, and became involved in the second economy during the 1970s and 1980s. Others were professionals; some even came from middle-level management, but opted for their own private business during the late state-socialist period or soon after the fall of communism.

Our data on the managers of larger firms indicate that new entrepreneurs were relatively rare among the CEOs of these firms in 1993. Only about 1–2 percent of the CEOs of larger firms were already in the private sector before 1989, in contrast with over two-thirds of CEOs who were managers in socialist business corporations prior to the fall of the old regime.

One should not underestimate, however, the extent and dynamism of small business in post-communist Central Europe. This is attested to by the overwhelming growth of the private sector in all these countries. The single biggest change in the social structure following post-communist transformation which is common to all these countries is the growth of self-employment. The self-employed constitute over 10 percent of the economically active population. This category doubled its size during the first five years of post-communism in Poland and Hungary, and in the Czech Republic it grew from zero.

Not all self-employment stands, of course, for dynamic economic growth and embourgeoisement. As Eric Hanley demonstrates, the category of self-employment subsumes two distinct destinations: one is only a 'refuge from unemployment', a substitute for lost jobs (this is true only for Hungary and Poland, where the number of jobs was dramatically reduced, while in the Czech Republic unemployment is negligible); the other is dynamic small businesses, the most active sector of the economy, in which some small businesses are growing big.[12] Operators of businesses in this dynamic sector are an alternative pool from which a future *grande bourgeoisie* may be drawn and, for this reason, may constitute a competitive threat to other actors, like managers, whose goal is to lead and dominate the emergent propertied class.

Who are these small business operators? Eric Hanley shows that recruitment into the two different destinations of self-employment is regulated by different social factors.[13] The first destination is primarily the route of workers faced with unemployment. The second destination, in contrast, is a channel of upward mobility and recruits people variously from among former second-economy entrepreneurs, families who were on an embourgeoisement trajectory before communism, and from the ranks of former cadres – probably former petty, local cadres for the most part.

Unlike the managers discussed above, this upwardly mobile petty bourgeoisie is likely to have a habitus which conforms more easily to the rules of a genuine market. So although very few of these individuals have made it into the corporate world to date, it is not inconceivable that they will eventually begin to compete with larger firms and with former socialist managers. This competition may intensify as privatization comes to an end. The Central European strategy of market transition has been aimed primarily at changing property relations in the corporate sector, rather than encouraging small businesses to grow bigger. This priority of privatization has tended to favor the insiders in big enterprises, namely the managers. Managers had inside information, they had the connections, and their privatization proposals were well received in the ministries and privatization agencies. This privatization game, however, is now coming to an end. It remains to be seen to what extent former socialist managers – whose power and privilege are based partly on social capital, that is, their skill in operating clientelistic networks – will be able to adapt to the competitive environment of real markets. Moreover, it is not inconceivable that those businessmen who had to start from scratch, in the basement or garage of their homes, will have an advantage. While they may have had to struggle to overcome the disadvantages they faced owing to early post-communist policies which prioritized the transformation of the corporate sector, as the privatization of the public sector comes to an end, those entrepreneurs who learned the rules of market capitalism on a competitive basis may do extremely well.

For all these reasons, we believe that the struggle between the technocratic–managerial elite of the corporate sector and the new entrepreneurs who started from scratch is far from over. Indeed, it has just begun. The outcome of this struggle is unpredictable, and it will probably be determined not merely by considerations of economic rationality but by the historically contingent outcome of the political struggles among the actors involved.

Capitalism from above and its alternatives:
The journey from civil society to capitalism

Post-communism is capitalism from above – it is a strategy used by managers to convert a state-socialist economy into a market-capitalist one.

It was relatively late in the socialist game, sometime during the 1980s, that intellectuals in socialist societies clearly formulated their goal as one of transforming their societies into capitalist ones. In previous decades, from the late 1950s to the early 1970s, a great deal of intellectual energy had been directed towards reforming socialism to make it more efficient and humane. The best minds were occupied with the tasks of 'rationalizing' the planning system, creating a mix of market and redistribution, and democratizing the party structure. None of these reforms fundamentally challenged the hegemony of public ownership, or the Communist Party. Eventually, however, Central European intellectuals lost faith in the possibility of reforming the socialist system. They were astonished to discover that at the same time as their reform scenarios were being sabotaged by the bureaucracy, other far-reaching and fundamental changes were taking place in these socioeconomic systems – namely, the emergence of a second, underground market economy. The former reform intelligentsia and the future dissidents had nothing to do with these changes; they did not foresee them, and they certainly did not plan them. Indeed, they hardly noticed them before their disillusionment with the system. But from the 1970s onward, particularly in the former Yugoslavia, Poland, and Hungary, capitalism was in the making. This was not reform by design; it was reform by default. It was capitalism from below. In agriculture, the service sector, the construction industry, and even in some of the industrial branches – part-time or full-time, legally, semi-legally or illegally – small producers began to produce goods and offer services on price-regulating markets, acting as new 'socialist entrepreneurs'. When the intellectuals first discovered these entrepreneurs, their initial response was positive. They saw a force in the 'second economy' which would eventually subvert bureaucratic power. Even at this early stage, however, intellectual attitudes towards these actors were not free from ambiguity. Intellectuals detested the new entrepreneurs for being uneducated and greedy, and wondered if this was the civil society for which they were waiting.

We cannot date precisely when the term 'civil society' was first used by Central European intellectuals as a critique of state socialism. But during the mid 1970s it caught on very quickly, substituting for the term 'democratic socialism'. As we have pointed out, Central European intellectuals were on a long journey from seeing themselves as socialist reformers to reconstituting themselves as a new, second *Bildungsbürgertum* whose mission was to make capitalism. While they were traveling on this road, civil society was the puff of smoke for which they were groping. Many intellectuals, both dissident and non-dissident, knew that they did not want socialism, but very few of them were ready to concede that capitalism was the only alternative. Indeed, when the idea of privatizing state enterprises was first suggested by a Polish economist at the national convention of Solidarity in autumn 1981, it was received with a mixture of ridicule and disbelief.

Civil society was the theory that gradually de-socialized intellectuals from a socialist, communitarian value system and reeducated them in capitalist, individualistic virtues. What was so intellectually powerful about the discourse of civil society was that it implied civility, liberty, individual autonomy and responsibility without mentioning the bourgeoisie, inequality, private property, exploitation, or domination. Civil society is a discourse about a classless society – it is a discourse of freedom which never confronts the question of inequality.

This is not the first time in the history of ideas that the notion of civil society has been used in this way. It was formulated during the eighteenth century in France and England as a critique of rank order and absolutist power from the perspective of an idealized – and, at that time, a nonexistent – market society. After that, the discourse of civil society was dormant for over a century. The term was virtually never used by philosophers or political theorists, and certainly not by sociologists. It was reinvented in Central Europe, partly because Central European intellectuals of the 1970s and 1980s faced an analogous situation to that of eighteenth-century contractarians. The Central European task was to find tools to critique a new type of status society, the absolutism of socialist rank order. The idea of citizenship and social contract was ideal for highlighting late socialist paternalism and its ambient logic of communist patron–client relations. In the early stages of the development of this theoretical tradition, Central European intellectuals vehemently rejected the accusation that civil society really meant capitalism. Civil society, they argued, was really supposed to be something which was neither Soviet-type communism nor Western capitalism. This is why the Western Left – which, by the late 1970s, began to distance itself from 'socialism' – immediately fell in love with the notion. The way the notion of civil society developed in Germany is particularly telling. While there is a precise German term – *bürgerliche Gesellschaft* – for the phenomenon of civil society, the German New Left began speaking about *Zivilgesellschaft*, making the point that they were not advocating a bourgeois society.

Central European intellectuals did not confront this ambiguity inherent in their use of the term civil society until 1988, and to some extent the contradiction between civil society and bourgeois society continues to mark intellectual discourse today. During the late 1970s, however, when this contradiction was less apparent, some thinkers conceptualized socialist

entrepreneurs not as the forerunners of a capitalist society but as representatives of an emergent civil society. Most intellectuals, however, remained
suspicious of second-economy entrepreneurs. In searching for some empirical content for the abstract concept of civil society, they usually referred to
their own activities or to the lifestyles of their intellectual parents and grandparents. Civil society, therefore, came to mean a community of those who
speak a new discourse, a community of those 'who think otherwise'.
Paradoxically, there is an exclusivity in this otherwise inclusive concept.
'They' are excluded and this 'they' might mean the communist power elite,
often conceptualized as the 'powers', but it also could mean second-
economy petty-bourgeois entrepreneurs, who were often perceived not only
as not subversive but also as complicit and co-opted, a safety-valve in the
reproduction of communist social order.

While dissident intellectuals were engaged in this somewhat narcissistic
reading of civil society, technocrats and managers in the party and state
apparatus were also becoming much more radical. Their job was to try to
make firms work, to produce, to sell their product on the world market, to
balance budgets, and to manage foreign debt and trade deficits. By the mid
1980s many of them just threw up their hands and declared that the task of
managing state-socialist economies was impossible. Socialist managers and
technocrats began to formulate the following ideas: socialism is not
reformable, state property cannot be made efficient, state firms will never
have hard budget constraints. They argued that what was needed were
hard budget constraints and the radical separation of the economy from politics, so that politicians were out of the economic process and managers
could get their jobs done. Managers and technocrats quickly recognized that
what they were talking about was capitalism. They realized that redistributive institutions would have to be dismantled, and that not only consumer
goods but also labor and capital would have to be allocated on self-regulating markets among competitive actors. Most importantly, these actors
realized that the property vacuum created by state ownership would have to
be filled with identifiable owners, preferably private and/or individual
owners.

Socialist managers and technocrats could not achieve their aims as long
as the bureaucracy was in power. In their struggle with the bureaucracy, the
major weakness of the technocracy was discursive. In the still-hegemonic linguistic code that the bureaucracy used, there were taboos (such as the taboo
on private ownership, or capitalism) that did not allow the managers to
express their new ideas. As a result, many of them were thrilled to read the
samizdat writings of dissident intellectuals and to discover the new, powerful
discourse of civil society. This discourse purported to have no taboos, and
although it did not regularly use terms like private property, capitalism,
bourgeoisie, and so on, it offered a way to speak about them. The discourse

of civil society delegitimated the discourse of communist taboos and created
a space in which an explicitly pro-capitalist language could be elaborated. At
the same time, it provided the basis for a coalition between technocrats and
dissidents.

This was the process and the context in which the project of capitalism
from above was made acceptable to managers, technocrats, and intellectuals alike. The crucial break occurred sometime around 1988–89, when the
technocracy successfully made privatization a public policy priority. Until
then, it appeared that the making of capitalism would come through the
gradual growth of the private sector and the slow development of pragmatic
mixes of property forms and mechanisms of economic integration. In this
view, there was a long timeframe for building capitalism, since it was
assumed that small private firms would grow into large capitalist ventures
only gradually. The corresponding policy was one of deregulation, which
would fully legalize private activities and would be sector-neutral, applying
exactly the same rules to public and private property, not prioritizing one
over the other.

After 1989, however, there was no pretension to sector neutrality, and
precious little gradualism. Small businesses growing big now appeared to be
the nineteenth-century road to capitalism. It was mere 'garage capitalism'.
It was the 'Third Way' leading to the 'Third World' rather than the royal
highway of privatization leading directly 'back to Europe', to the heart-
lands of the most advanced Western capitalist nations. In order to pull off
this historic coup, one needed courage and wisdom. One could not wait for
the slow maturing of small enterprises, one had to change the whole system
in one fell swoop. An economy which was 90 percent publicly owned had to
be converted in one hundred days, or five years, into an economy which was
100 percent privately owned.

Privatization itself could have proceeded in different ways. Indeed, early
in the post-communist transition one of the most prominent views was that
the reason for privatization was to find identifiable – preferably individual –
owners, and transfer state assets to them. It was believed that one should
proceed rather slowly, and wait until sufficient capital was accumulated in
private hands, so that public property could be sold at market value during
the privatization process. Privatization projects in countries like Austria,
England and Taiwan had materialized in this way, and 50 percent public
ownership – which characterized all these countries after World War II –
was reduced to 15 or 20 percent over a period of about twenty years. This
was not to be the fate of Central Europe. Instead, managers, technocrats,
and former dissident intellectuals opted for immediate corporatization. In
the process of corporatization, it was irrelevant whether the owners were
identifiable individuals or not. The important thing was that the governance structure of corporations was monetary, and that it approximated to

the form of Western corporations. As a result of these policies, former socialist firms structured themselves along the lines of Western corporate giants
overnight.

Such a vision could be formulated only by an alliance between socialist
managers and anti-communist dissident intellectuals. Privatization through
corporatization was a managerialist strategy to transform socialism into
capitalism from above. Indeed, one of the main messages of this book is
that it is a commonly held and fundamentally flawed assumption to think
of late state-socialist managers as corrupt, selfish, greedy individuals.
Obviously, privatization via corporatization served their interests – it certainly increased their discretionary power as managers and, in some cases,
greatly enriched particular individuals. But if we are to understand why
these people opted for capitalism from above, it is impossible to separate
analytically or empirically their self-interest from their commitment to professional ethics. They acted as responsible managers in the best interests of
their firms and their employees. They searched for ways to preserve the
companies they had worked in for years, and to protect their employees'
jobs. These were 'their firms' – not because they owned them or intended
to acquire ownership in them, but because they worked in them, because
they managed them.

If managers wanted to privatize their firms rather than search for identifiable owners, dissidents wanted to persuade the population that a sacrifice
was needed to purify society from the evils of communism. As Chapter 3
argued, dissidents believed that this was a task that could not wait for gradualism. The soul of Havel's greengrocer had to be rescued quickly, even at
the expense of his shop, so that he could live in truth, even though it might
also mean he would live in poverty. In the minds of intellectuals, shock therapy was not only a means of rescuing the economy, it had an important
educational value. Its goal was to transform socialist man into a citizen of
civil society – that is to say, into a private individual who was ready to take
responsibility for his own affairs. The consciousness of the people was backward. Public opinion polls indicated that majorities of the Polish,
Hungarian, and even Czech populations still subscribed to socialist values:
they wanted more equality, they were suspicious of wealthy people, they
wanted the government to guarantee their employment, and they supported
government provision of free healthcare and education. In this context,
former dissidents argued that successful capitalist transformation required
that people's consciousness be transformed first. The managers' focus on
privatization and corporatization, and the intellectuals' desire to purify society and reeducate the people, combined to produce capitalism from above.

None of this is to suggest, however, that the cooperation of former
socialist managers and former anti-communist dissidents was free of conflict. This was a sour-sweet relationship from the beginning, rooted in

mutual suspicion and deep distrust. Intellectuals could not forget the communist past of many managers. They suspected managers of belonging to a 'kleptocracy' that would steal public goods and convert them into private wealth. On the flip side, managers thought that intellectuals were rather irresponsible and unreliable, remembering that many had risked their jobs or been willing to go to jail for a good point or an idea that they thought was original. Despite their distrust, however, managers and intellectuals share the enormous task of post-communist transition to which both groups are deeply and ethically committed. This forces them to work together, since both realize that neither group can negotiate the transition alone.

Their shared and increasing fear of capitalism from below – capitalism made by the socialist petty bourgeoisie – further strengthens this alliance between managers and dissident intellectuals. Managers and technocrats, for their part, simply cannot see the point of capitalism from below. It does not have the benefit of economies of scale, small producers are not equipped to compete on world markets, and small businesses are too risky for most investments and loans. Managers also see capitalism from below as a competitor with state policies of capitalism from above, since one uses resources either to privatize state firms or to extend credit to small producers who intend to create new businesses. Pursuing both strategies at once is not considered feasible. The intellectuals, for their part, consider capitalism from below as a form of populism. They dislike the petty bourgeoisie, whom they see as money-grubbing, and they invoke the common wisdom that this group is a potential political base for populist parties.

We would like to stress emphatically that no conspiracy theory is implied here. The process we are describing is heavily contested among different class and elite fractions, and the outcome may well be one that is not desired by any of the major actors described above. For instance, another major actor in this struggle is the new politocracy, which, along with the technocrats and the opinion-making intellectuals, is one of the leading members of the new power bloc. In their capacity as politicians, members of the politocracy have mixed interests. There is a lot of pressure on them to make room for capitalism from below, and some of them may even be ideologically committed to such a project. For example, some members of the Democratic Forum (which formed the core of the first Hungarian post-communist government) flirted with the idea of the 'Third Road', which on one reading is similar to the idea of capitalism from below. Similarly, the politocracies in all Central European countries have faced tremendous pressure for restitution – a lot of it for ideological or legitimation reasons – and restitution policies have been particularly successful in the Czech Republic and East Germany. Another feature of the uneasy relationships within the power elite is the fact that during the first year(s) of post-communist transformation, the new political class made an effort to remove former communist technocrats from civil service jobs and the command posts of the economy. The lustration law in the Czech Republic and similar policies in Poland, and the sacking of many leading economic experts by the first post-communist government in Hungary, are all evidence of the power struggle that was taking place over the making of the new power elite in the early years of post-communism. Eventually, however, the politocracy learned that if it were to consolidate its power, it had to make major concessions to the technocrats and managers. After its initial hesitation, therefore, the new political class lined up behind the project of capitalism from above. How capitalism is to be achieved in this way, however, remains a matter of contestation. Arguably, the political defeat of the liberal–conservative coalition in Poland and the Patriotic–Christian regime in Hungary during the second free elections can be attributed to the fact that they were unable to come to terms with the challenges of this task, while the ex-communist parties and Václav Klaus have managed to balance those conflicting sets of interests up to this point. What are these conflicting sets of interests over privatization?

So far, we have used the terms 'managers' and 'technocrats' interchangeably, but this is something of a simplification. In addition to the fault-line separating managers and technocrats from intellectuals on the one hand, and from the politocracy on the other, there is a significant conflict of interest between managers on the one hand, technocrats and opinion-making intellectuals on the other. By managers we mean, specifically, the CEOs of corporations, and in particular the CEOs of industrial firms. By technocrats we mean social scientists, economists, management experts, and finance experts working in banks, civil service jobs, and consulting firms. While managers also have a high stake in capitalism from above, they would like to see it implemented in a more gradualist way. They are uneasy, to say the least, with shock therapy, radical monetarism, and the ideology of sacrifice and purification. They would not mind a government with well-formulated industrial policies, and instead of budget cuts and monetary restrictions they would like the state-socialist system of subsidies to be maintained.

The ex-communist parties returned to power in Poland in 1993 and in Hungary in 1994 because they were able, at least temporarily, to reconcile these different interests and visions of how to proceed along the road to capitalism. In Hungary, the communist successor party received not only the votes of the technocracy, but also their political and intellectual support. The single most important reason for the electoral success of the Hungarian Socialist Party in 1994 was that it was viewed as competent: its major electoral slogan was 'A vote for Socialists is a vote for competence'. As successors of the former Communist Party, they were able to secure the confidence of industrial managers as well. The successor party promised that it would apply as little shock therapy as was absolutely necessary, and it went without saying that they were unlikely to engage in acts of purification. The message was: pursue the radical transformation of the economy, privatization, and monetary sobriety, but with caution, and with sufficient attention to the needs of state enterprises, their managers, and even their workers.

Was capitalism from above inevitable, then? Both managers and intellectuals have claimed that it was. They point out that capitalism from below during the late socialist period was a dead-end street. The second economy and the emergent new private sector coexisted with the state economy in a symbiotic way that could not be counted on to produce dynamic evolution towards a fully fledged capitalist economy.

These are very persuasive arguments, as long as one does not consider comparative evidence. In the contemporary world there is an alternative road out of socialism, the most successful example being China after 1977. Arguably, China is building capitalism from below. The most dynamic sector of the Chinese economy is village industry. This industry is typically small-scale; it operates with new firms which are either privately owned or can be described as a hybrid property form in which elements of private ownership can be detected. According to Chinese official statistics, about 10 percent of non-agricultural GNP is produced by private firms properly speaking; another 40 percent comes from what the statistics call cooperatives or municipally owned enterprises; and the remaining half is still produced by publicly owned corporations. This may underestimate the size of the private sector, since some of the so-called cooperatives may be private enterprises. Our point, however, is that the private sector is still relatively small; it is composed of firms which employ few people; and it is extraordinarily productive. Another important feature of the Chinese path out of socialism is that privatization of public firms has not been adopted as official policy at this point. Without having privatized its public sector, the Chinese economy has been the most dynamic economy in the world for the past ten or fifteen years: it grows at about 10 percent a year, despite the fact that its public sector basically stagnates. It is difficult not to attribute China's extraordinary economic achievement to its strategy of building capitalism from below.[14] We should also add that China follows the example of Taiwan in this respect. In the early 1950s about half the Taiwanese economy was in public hands. Unlike South Korea, Taiwan based its economic development on the growth of family businesses, and only when these family businesses accumulated sufficient capital did the Taiwanese government begin to transfer public firms into private hands.

When China entered its reform phase in 1977, Chinese economic policy-makers carefully studied the economic reforms in Poland, Yugoslavia, and Hungary where, arguably, some 'capitalism from below' was taking place.

While none of the East and Central European countries opened up as much room for private ownership before 1988 as China had by the mid 1980s, there is little doubt that the initial impetus for China's move in the direction of market reform came from Central Europe. With the Chinese experience in mind, one should consider whether or not capitalism from below was doomed to inevitable failure in Central Europe. It is possible that it merely got stuck in what appeared to be a dead-end street, since communist reformers were half-hearted and did not go far enough with property reform. The key to success was making spaces for new private businesses in China; the reason for stagnation in East and Central Europe, by contrast, was that East European reformers got cold feet about allowing proper private business to get off the ground – they hoped to fix the economic problems of socialism through decentralizing decision-making and adopting market-regulated prices.

This evidence should be enough to raise doubts about whether or not capitalism from below was impossible in 1989, as technocrats and intellectuals claimed. The fact that Central Europe opted for capitalism from above cannot be attributed exclusively to its superior economic rationality. Rather, we argue that it was the constellation of class forces around 1989 which explains the choice of capitalism from above as the strategy for post-communism. The victory of the technocracy over the bureaucracy, its ability to forge a loose alliance with the intelligentsia, and the weakness of the small propertied bourgeoisie all contributed to this outcome. Analogously, in China the development of capitalism from below depends on the fact that the balance of forces between the bureaucracy and the technocracy has not been tilted in the latter's favor. If the Chinese technocracy did manage to oust the bureaucracy, China might very well adopt the policy of systematic privatization.

Having made the comparison with China, we would emphasize that it would be a grave mistake to idealize the 'Chinese way'. While its economic growth is truly astonishing, China still has a Byzantine, repressive political system, and it is unclear that this political system is in any way connected to its economic success. Indeed, it is possible that China's political authoritarianism may obstruct its economic development.[15] For this reason, Chinese economic strategies should be monitored carefully to assess what is relevant for Central European problems of the transition to capitalism.

Moreover, it is possible that not only was capitalism from above the only strategy available in Central Europe in 1989, but it may have contributed to the depth of the post-communist crisis during the transformation. Although the severity of the crisis varies across countries, it is true that GNP dropped by some 30 percent in most Central European countries during the first five years of the transition, about a third of all jobs were eliminated, and inflation raged in double digits. No single cause can be held responsible for this economic devastation. The problems inherited from socialist economies, the difficulties of reconstructing the economy to meet the demands of contracting world markets, and the disintegration of COMECON all played a role. And privatization via corporatization, implemented as the core of the shock therapy package, made its contribution to the general misery. In retrospect, it was probably not a great idea to walk into an economy which was 90 percent publicly owned and declare the public sector moribund. In declaring that all productive firms would be privatized, state privatization agencies created formidable disincentives for the management of these firms to keep investing in these ventures. Indeed, it created a major incentive for managers to rescue valuable productive assets from public companies while they were still in charge. And as we have shown, in this context some managers created subcontracting firms for themselves, their family members and friends, and sold the most valuable assets of public corporations to these firms at very low prices. As a result, the main company was devalued and moved rapidly towards bankruptcy. This was in the interests of management if they anticipated that some outside buyer would come and purchase their firms, or if they anticipated buying the firms themselves. The fact is that privatization produced disinvestment, and the destruction of jobs and productive capacities. Some of this could probably be called 'creative destruction' which cleared away the ruins of socialism and created room for modern capitalist enterprises. Some of this destruction, however, was simply a siphoning off of resources from large firms, often into private pockets or for the conspicuous consumption of managers.

To sum up: making capitalism without capitalists was a strategy to create capitalism from above. It was invented and implemented by the technocratic–managerial elite with the assistance of the new political elite and opinion-making intellectuals. Despite substantial social costs, it achieved far-reaching economic restructuring, and laid the foundations for the basic institutions of the market and parliamentary democracy. We do not believe, however, that capitalism from above was the only road Central Europe could have taken in 1989. Indeed, the purpose of this book has been to emphasize the importance of the composition of elites, intra-elite struggles, and the unevenness of class formation as factors which explain why capitalism emerged in this way in this part of the world. The social structure of Central European societies is still in flux. From this point of view, the most important issue pending is whether a domestic propertied *grande bourgeoisie* which could challenge the hegemony of the current power bloc will emerge and, if it does, on what basis it will exercise power, and which actors will comprise it. We believe that the answers to these questions will depend on the balance of social forces and the contingent outcomes of their future struggles.

Conclusion

This book does not suggest that a propertied class will not emerge in Central Europe. Nor do we doubt that fully institutionalized private property as we know it from the West is also in the making. By any definition, the countries of Central Europe are capitalist. We do claim, however, that the struggles over the formation of private property rights and class relations will be highly consequential for the nature of the capitalist agents that will emerge. This book is about transition. As we argued in Chapter 2, any society in which the holders of cultural capital are dominant is a transitional one. The historical role of cultural capital is often revolutionary, and it seems unable to institutionalize itself as the dominant logic of a stable system. Indeed, it appears to be virtually inevitable that the routinization of the charismatic rule of cultural capital leads either to the formation of a rank order in which social capital is dominant, or to a class society in which economic capital is dominant.

We have made many outrageously immodest claims in this book. First, we have presented a new theory of social change. In this we believe we 'out-Webered Weber' by replacing his theory of charisma with the idea of cultural capital as a revolutionary historical force. Second, we suggested synthesizing evolutionary, neoclassical economic theory and neo-institutionalist path-dependency theory with our idea of trajectory adjustment. Third, we claim to have reconstructed Bourdieu's theory, shifting it from a static explanation of social reproduction into a dynamic, comparative-historical theory which is able to explain social change. Fourth, we have rewritten the history of intellectuals though the prism of Jürgen Kocka's concept of the *Bildungsbürgertum*. This is a new sociology of intellectuals which conceptualizes them in search of a historical project of remaking society: from the vanguard of the bourgeoisie to the vanguard of the proletariat (to the New Class – to put it ironically), only to return to their project of making a bourgeoisie and constituting themselves as the second *Bildungsbürgertum*. Finally, our most immodest claim is that we are initiating a new sociological paradigm, *neoclassical sociology*. The reader should take this idea with a pinch of salt, but let us develop it a little to spice up the debate!

The origins of sociology can be found in the crucial question: what are the origins and character of modern capitalism? For classical theorists of sociology, the answer to this question was that modern capitalism was either a miracle or a necessity. In its most sophisticated and complex formation, in Weber, the coming together of diverse actors, conditions, and ideas to form modern capitalism was seen as amazing and miraculous. For those of us located in the late twentieth century, however, whose perceptions are informed by the fall of communism and who have witnessed the international blossoming of capitalism in a globalizing world, the making of modern capitalist socioeconomic systems appears to be the rule rather than a miracle. What would be a miracle for us would be that capitalism had converged on a single destination: that capitalism was characterized by the same property relations, identical market institutions, and exactly the same class relations everywhere. Neoclassical sociology consists in reformulating these classical questions. The question is not 'what are the preconditions of capitalist transformation?' but, rather, 'how do the various conditions of capitalist transformation shape and diversify actually existing capitalist systems?'

So the project of neoclassical sociology is to explain these diversities of capitalisms and the differences in their origins and operations. This can be done in a variety of ways. Many sociologists today focus on pre-capitalist institutional legacies, and how they shape the emergence of capitalist social relations. In this book, however, we have directed the analytical spotlight elsewhere. We have argued that the formation of capitalist classes – bourgeoisies – is deeply consequential for the type of capitalism that will develop in any particular time and place. Let us be more specific about what we mean by class formation here. What we hope to offer is a non-teleological idea of class formation by analytically distinguishing between three questions.[16] First, what is the subject matter out of which a capitalist class is formed? What different *agents*, class fractions, and alliances of agents are implicated in the formation of capitalist classes? Second, what is the mode in which these disparate groups are being drawn into capitalist class relations? In other words, what are the *positions* they will occupy as class actors? What are the characteristics of the institutions they will operate within? Finally – and most importantly – what is the spirit or *consciousness* which imbues these agents? In the terms developed in this book, what is the *habitus* of these agents?

There are novel agents struggling with each other in post-communism: dissident intellectuals, communist technocrats, petty entrepreneurs, foreign investors, technocrats of multinational financial and business organizations, and liberal-populist-ex-communist politicians. In this book, we observe shifting alliances and conflicts among these actors, and it is as yet undecided who will compose the new capitalist class, how much power that class will have, and how such a class will be related to other powerful social actors like political elites, foreign economic actors, and so on.

These unusual actors operate within an institutional context which is in constant flux. This context is one of diffused property relations. Private property with hard budget constraints exists in post-communist Central Europe, but so does state property (whose privatization potential is only nominal), and there are many organizations which diffuse property relations by transferring liabilities to the state, obscuring liabilities in complex patterns of cross-ownership, or siphoning off income through subcontracting satellite firms. There are marketplaces in which supply and demand set prices, but there is also subterranean redistribution in which shrewd former communist officials can use their old networks to protect their firms from hard budget constraints. Political institutions are also in flux. Political parties still vet members in terms of their backgrounds. The Communist Party now views itself as a Social Democratic Party, but implements the most cruel anti-labor policies, serving the interests of the cadre–bourgeoisie. Former anti-communist intellectuals claiming to have formed neo-liberal parties often find themselves advocating the causes of the oppressed and the exploited. The notions of Left and Right, conservative and liberal, are still being renegotiated. Hence the site of the formation of the new capitalist class (and all other collective actors in post-communist capitalism) remains contested terrain. In the end, the eventual shape of these institutional terrains will probably be decided by who wins and who loses in the struggles over these institutional resources in a new global capitalist context. At the same time, however, the weight of institutional legacies, or the pressures from outside to create new institutions and abolish old ones, may favor certain actors over others. The point is, as we have labored it in this book, that actors and institutions interact.

Finally, we think that the spirit which inspires these actors, the consciousness to which they subscribe, and the habitus which guides them are quite diverse, and sometimes contradictory. For example, there is the habitus formed by climbing the socialist ladder. This is the apparatchik mentality which knows how to manipulate party organization and how to use ideological slogans. There is the habitus of the reform communists – especially the technocrats – who think they know how to get things done, who do not think it is important what color the cat is as long as she catches the mouse. There is also the habitus of the pre-communist middle class who were hiding in 'parking orbits' during communism, living in 'internal exile' in their bourgeois apartments in old Prague or Buda Hill, who knew all along that the 'old ways of doing things' were the right ways of doing things. This habitus may carry gentry characteristics in Poland or Hungary, and petty-bourgeois features in the Czech case. Moreover, this habitus carries significant symbolic potency in a society which practices 'the negation of the negation'. There is also the habitus of the dissident intelligentsia, which is comprised in the mix of New Left compassion towards the poor and the oppressed and a neophyte commitment to the most doctrinaire of neo-liberal ideas. In an almost masochistic way, the intelligentsia struggle with the antinomy produced by these two commitments, convinced that both ideas are moral, both are ways of 'living in truth'.

Hitherto, we have claimed that the making of capitalism without capitalists has been consequential; and above, we have identified the mechanisms through which this is happening. At this point, our readers are

probably wondering what is at issue. In what ways is post-communist capitalism different from any other capitalism? To put it in Walter Mondale's
terms: 'Where is the beef?'[17] Who cares who makes capitalism as long as it
is made? Show us that there are indeed lasting qualitative differences
between capitalist systems.

We are not fully prepared to complete this task at this point. What we
can offer here is a preliminary research agenda for a neoclassical sociology
of comparative capitalisms, which compares different capitalist systems,
their class relations, their institutional arrangements and the characteristics
of their social structure, or the shapes of their social spaces. A library of literature exists which contrasts, for instance, Latin American, Japanese and
East Asian capitalisms with North American or North Atlantic versions.
Such work points to the difference the state plays in economic development, the unique features of property relations, and the unique features of
class structure. The kind of research on post-communism that this book
proposes builds on this tradition, extending it by moving away from identifying types of capitalism with geographic names. In Table 5.1, we offer an
extremely simplified schema which compares three types of capitalisms: the
'Classical Core', the 'New Core' and 'Post-Communism', along three
dimensions. (The table does not contain that part of the world which is usually referred to as the 'periphery',[18] or the 'Third World', or 'post-colonial
countries', since that phenomenon proved to be too diverse for us to be able
to interpret as one form even in such a schematic way.) Table 5.1 can be
read as our attempt to define the 'dependent variable' for the study of
comparative capitalism. What is that 'thing' which collective actors struggle over which defines them, what sort of habitus do actors carry within
themselves, how do they 'match' existing institutions, and how do they
reshape them?

Note, too, that Table 5.1 should be understood relationally. If we suggest,
for instance, that the working class of the 'Classical Core' is 'small and well
organized', it is meant to describe the working class in this context in comparison with the 'New Core' and with 'Post-Communism'. The working
class in the 'Classical Core' is much less organized than it used to be only
thirty years ago, but it is still 'well organized' compared to working classes in
the 'New Core' and 'Post-Communism'.

So what characterizes post-communist capitalism? In terms of class relations, these are societies with small, weak[19] domestic propertied bourgeoisies
but large intelligentsias, which have resisted historical pressures to profes-
sionalize. In terms of their institutional arrangements, post-communist
societies are likely to be characterized by big, weak states (which David
Stark has called the 'non-developmental state' of post-communism). Their
property relations are also specific. While private property properly speaking is emerging, and public ownership is rapidly retreating, privatization

Table 5.1 A research agenda for a neoclassical sociology of comparative capitalism

	Classical Core	New Core	Post-Communism
Class relations			
propertied class	large and strong	large and strong	small and weak
working class	small and well organized	small and poorly organized	large and poorly organized
intellectuals	large and professionalized	large and bureaucratized	large and non-professionalized and non-bureaucratized
Institutions			
relations in the state	small and strong	big and strong	big and weak
property rights	well-defined individual property rights	individual property is complemented with cross-ownership	recombinant property coexisting with a decaying public and emerging private ownership
Distributions of capital			
dominant capital	economic	economic	cultural
dominated capital	cultural	social	social
subordinate capital	social	cultural	economic
Examples	United States, England, France	Japan, Taiwan, South Korea	Hungary, The Czech Republic, Poland

often leads to recombinant ownership, quasi-government ownership, and diffuse ownership relations. Finally, in terms of the determinants of their social spaces, these societies are dominated by cultural capital, complemented by social capital. While economic capital is gaining rapidly in importance, it remains a clear third in terms of determining the distribution of power and privilege.

Using the comparisons in Table 5.1, let us elaborate briefly what we think the lasting characteristics of post-communist formations are likely to be. In almost any scenario we can imagine in Central Europe, the domestic bourgeoisie will be weak. The main reason is that even after the second *Bildungsbürgertum* has completed its task, and a propertied bourgeoisie is fully formed, intellectual organizations and identities will remain an important part of Central European societies. Central European intellectuals will always invent new historical projects for themselves, new missions to reconstruct society. In this respect, post-communist capitalism will be more similar to Germany and France, with long histories of strong intellectual class fractions, and very different from capitalism in Japan or the Anglo-Saxon world.

The second reason we think the domestic bourgeoisie of post-communism will be weak is that habituses from the communist past will not predispose future property owners towards autonomy. Although we do not know the social origins of the new bourgeoisie, we do know that most of the actors who aspire to this sort of position carry within themselves habituses deeply rooted in the communist past. They are about as far as they could possibly be from the ideal Schumpeterian entrepreneur. Their main creative activity is to find loopholes, to find patrons or to mobilize clients. Given the continued importance of social capital in this context, we think that post-communist capitalism will more closely resemble Japan or the United States than Western European capitalism in this respect.

The third reason we think the bourgeoisie will continue to be weak in post-communism is because we think that the Central European state is much more likely to affect the formation and development of the bourgeoisie than occurred in other countries where capitalism was born of feudal relations. In England, for example, the problem of capitalist class formation was one of accumulation. Capitalist actors accumulated resources and petitioned the state to lift legal restrictions so that they could extend and further enjoy their capital. By contrast, the task in Central Europe was privatization, not accumulation. Accumulation occurred under state socialism, and the task of post-communist capitalism is to individualize it. In this context, the state can enrich people overnight, and this is what we might be seeing with the growth of middle-level corporate ownership between 1993 and 1996 in Hungary, as the neo-socialist government rewarded its clients. And – unlike the capitalist states of East Asia, which intervene in markets to create economic growth – the neo-paternalistic states of Central Europe seem to be on an incremental growth trajectory, reinforcing their own autonomy, rather than being relatively autonomous from a powerful capitalist class. The Central European state is not necessarily strong, but it is very big. It is ironic that after the fall of *state* socialism, the anti-statist post-communist government bureaucracy continues to grow, often in the shape of 'privatization' bureaucracies. Indeed, some economists have suggested that the incomes from privatization are about as high as the cost of administering privatization – this is a good example of what we mean by a big, weak state. In short, what we are predicting in Central Europe is a small, weak propertied bourgeoisie operating within the framework of a big, weak state under the gaze of a big, strong *Bildungsbürgertum*.

Appendices

Data Sources: Social Stratification in Eastern Europe after 1989

In 1990, Iván Szelényi, Szonja Szelényi and Donald Treiman initiated a large scale comparative survey project under the title 'Social Stratification in Eastern Europe after 1989'. Funding for this study came from the National Science Foundation, the National Council for Soviet and East European Research, the Dutch National Science Foundation, the Hungarian National Science Foundation, the Czech National Science Foundation, the Institute for International Conflict and Cooperation at the University of California, the Center for German and European Studies at the University of California, the Joint Committee on Eastern Europe of the American Council of Learned Societies, and the Social Science Research Council. The study was conducted during 1993 and 1994 under the direction of Iván Szelényi and Donald Treiman.

This was a cooperative project, in which collaborators from each of the countries came together approximately twice a year to design the research, develop the questionnaire, coordinate field work procedures and post-field-work data processing, and to analyze the data. The principal members of the country teams are listed below, with the country coordinators indicated by an asterisk (*).

BULGARIA
> *Dimitrina Petrova, Institute for Social and Environmental Studies
> Tsvetan Markov, Sofia University

THE CZECH REPUBLIC
> Pavel Machonin, Institute of Sociology, Czech Academy of Sciences
> *Petr Mateju, Institute of Sociology, Czech Academy of Sciences
> Milan Tucek, Institute of Sociology, Czech Academy of Sciences

HUNGARY [country coordinator: Iván Szelényi]
Rudolf Andorka, Budapest School of Economics and Hungarian National Science Foundation
Katalin Hanák, Institute of Sociology, Hungarian Academy of Sciences
Tamás Kolosi, TARKI
Imre Kovách, Institute of Political Science, Hungarian Academy of Sciences
János Ladányi, Institute of Sociology, Hungarian Academy of Sciences
Péter Robert, TARKI
János Timár, Median

POLAND
Henryk Domanski, Institute of Sociology and Philosophy, Polish Academy of Sciences
Kazimierz Slomczynski, Ohio State University and Institute of Sociology, Polish Academy of Sciences
Edmund Wnuk-Lipinski, Institute of Political Science, Polish Academy of Sciences
*Jacek Wasilewski, Jagellonian University and Institute of Political Science, Polish Academy of Sciences

RUSSIA
*Ludmila Khakhulina, Russian Center for Public Opinion Research (VCIOM)
Natasha Yershova, Russian Center for Public Opinion Research (VCIOM)

SLOVAKIA
*Jan Buncak, Institute of Sociology, Slovak Academy of Sciences

NETHERLANDS
*Harry B.G. Ganzeboom, Utrecht University
Jan van Weesop, Utrecht University

UNITED STATES
Jozsef Böröcz, Rutgers University
Iván Szelényi, UCLA
Szonja Szelényi, University of Wisconsin–Madison
Ákos Rona-Tas, UC–San Diego
*Donald J. Treiman, UCLA

UCLA graduate student research assistants
    Gil Eyal
    Éva Fodor
    Eric Hanley
    Eric Kostello
    Matthew McKeever
    Sara Schatz
    Sergei Sibirtsev

The societies of post-communist Eastern and Central Europe have experienced massive social change since 1989. The main purpose of this survey is to document and analyze changes in the logic of social stratification during the transition to post-communism. In particular, we seek to discover whether or not the personnel of elites changed during this period. To investigate these questions, we first drew up a random sample of the adult population in six countries: Bulgaria, the Czech Republic, Hungary, Poland, Russia, and Slovakia. Second, since we are especially interested in changes at the top of social hierarchies, we drew up samples of past and current elites in five of these countries. As of spring 1997, survey data are available from all countries, except Slovakia (where an elite survey is currently under way). In what follows we give a brief description of these two sets of surveys. Note that the bulk of the data analyzed in Chapter 4 of this book come from the elite surveys of the Czech Republic, Hungary and Poland, with a few references to the general population samples for these same countries.

I General population sample

As part of the project 'Social Stratification in Eastern Europe after 1989', sample surveys were conducted in 1993 and 1994 in six countries: Bulgaria, the Czech Republic, Hungary, Poland, Russia, and Slovakia. In each country, national probability samples of approximately 5,000 members of the adult population were surveyed in personal interviews. The questionnaire reconstructed the life history of the respondents, yielding a complete activity history including information about their social origins, occupation, education, history of party membership, and the property ownership of their parents and grandparents.

Note that although country teams were free to add local questions at the end of the questionnaire, the design of the survey called for exactly comparable question wording. Variation in the response categories was permissible only where variations in national circumstances warranted it (e.g. different religious distributions). To ensure comparability, the questionnaire was translated into each local language and then translated back into English. Then the back-translated versions were compared as a group by a multilingual team, and discrepancies in wording were corrected. Despite our best intentions, minor variations crept into the questionnaire, but for the most part the instruments are highly comparable.

II The elite surveys

As part of the 'Social Stratification in Eastern Europe after 1989' survey, we also interviewed members of past and current elites in all the countries.

We drew up three random samples of elites in each country.

The *nomenklatura sample* is a random sample of 1,000 individuals who held *nomenklatura* positions as of 1 January 1988.

The *new political and cultural elite sample* is a random sample of 400 individuals who were incumbents of political and cultural decision-making positions, analogous to those defined by the *nomenklatura* lists, on 1 January 1993.

The *new economic elite sample* is comprised of interviews with the CEOs of 600 firms, randomly selected from the 3,000 largest business organizations (industrial firms, commercial and financial institutions) in each country.

1. Defining elite populations

(a) The Nomenklatura

In all communist countries, appointment to most positions of authority required prior approval of the Communist Party. The plenum of the Central Committee of national Communist Parties reviewed lists of these positions at regular intervals, usually twice a decade. In short, they controlled these lists of positions, or delegated this responsibility to the apparatus of the Central Committee. These lists were included in the minutes of the Central Committees as 'top-secret' documents, but now they can be found easily in party archives. The positions which are included on such lists are called '*nomenklatura*' positions.

The concept of the *nomenklatura* has been used in different ways in different countries and over time. Different Communist parties exercised control over different numbers and levels of positions, and the idea of the *nomenklatura* has also been operationalized in different ways in literature on Central and Eastern Europe. For these reasons, estimating how many *nomenklatura* positions existed in each country is difficult. If we define the *nomenklatura* as all those positions upon which some party organization had the right to veto appointment, then a very substantial proportion of the population would qualify as *nomenklatura*; for example, all professionals and personnel who supervised other people would be included in such a definition.

For this reason, we opted for a much narrower definition of the *nomenklatura*. We defined members of the *nomenklatura* as the incumbents of those positions for which the approval of some organ of the *Central Committee* of the Communist Party was required. This could have been the plenum of the Central Committee (a body of elected, distinguished party members, which met at regular intervals, usually more than once a year, as a sort of 'parliament' of the party), the Politburo (the executive arm of the plenum of the Central Committee, elected from among the members of the plenum of the Central Committee, which was a standing committee, which typically met weekly like the 'Cabinet' of parliamentary governments), or the secretaries of the Central Committee apparatus, or other officials of the apparatus (who were to the Communist Party what top civil servants are in parliamentary systems). It is important to note that the term Central Committee refers both to the highest elected legislative body of the Communist Party – thus to the plenum of the Central Committee – and to the apparatus of the Central Committee, including secretaries, heads and officials of different 'departments', and full-time party workers (some of whom were also elected members of the plenum of the Central Committee).

Note further that the *nomenklatura* contained two types of positions. First, most *nomenklatura* positions were 'jobs' or occupations. For example, the Secretary of the Central Committee of the Communist Party or the Division Head of a Ministry were full-time occupations. Other *nomenklatura* positions, by contrast, were positions to which the incumbents were elected, and it was not their main job. This second kind of *nomenklatura* position might not even have been a source of any income. Some Members of Parliament fall into this category, as do Members of the National Academy of Sciences. This difference between these two types of *nomenklatura* positions had interesting consequences. One consequence was that in terms of their occupation, many members of our *nomenklatura* sample were not elite at all. Among Members of Parliament, and in particular among the members of the Central Committee of the Communist Youth League, one could find individuals whose main occupation and source of income was manual work. Similarly, some Members of the Academy of Sciences held routine professional jobs without any supervisees. A second consequence was that some people were incumbents of several *nomenklatura* positions at the same time. For example, someone could be a Member of the Academy of Sciences, a member of the Central Committee of the Communist Party, and the Rector of a university. In this case, we decided that if the same person was selected more than once, we would enter their data as many times as they were selected. The interview teams in each country reported that there were dozens of such multiple selections in each country.

In October 1992, experts from all the national teams met in Budapest to review the *nomenklatura* lists. Each country team was asked to bring as many *nomenklatura* lists from different historical periods as they could find in party archives.

We reviewed these lists and found that while they were similar, there was substantial variation over time and between countries. For instance, in Hungary the longest *nomenklatura* list was in operation during the late 1960s and early 1970s, when about 3,000 positions were monitored by the Central Committee. By the mid 1980s, this was reduced to about 600 positions. Only the appointment of managers to the very largest firms required Central Committee approval. In Poland, by contrast, several hundred managerial posts were on the *nomenklatura* list as late as the 1980s. Another example: Hungary monitored appointments to the armed forces and the police carefully, while in Poland the Party had little control over personnel matters in these areas.

For all these reasons, in order to assure comparability across countries, we developed an 'ideal-typical' *nomenklatura* list. The idea was to try to capture the 'logic of the communist mind'. At the October 1992 Budapest meeting, national teams agreed on the broad outlines of what such a list should look like. We decided to cast our net broadly, and developed a list which included all the positions which were ever monitored by the Central Committee of Communist Parties in any of the countries under study.

At this point, there were a number of difficult decisions we had to make. First, we decided to omit officers of the armed forces from the population, even though they were *nomenklatura* members in most of these countries during the communist period. This decision was made on the grounds that it would be difficult to identify these members of the *nomenklatura* by name (especially in the case of KGB or the equivalent organizations in Central European countries). Moreover, we doubted that we would be able to find their addresses, and even if we did, we thought it unlikely that these individuals would be willing to be interviewed.

Second, there were relatively few guidelines for defining who belonged to the 'economic *nomenklatura*' in each country. Here we decided to use Poland as the guide since it was the country where the economic *nomenklatura* was defined most broadly. We tried to identify the most important 400–500 economic actors of the late communist period. We did this by including the three or four leading executives of about fifty of the very largest firms in each country. To this list, we added the next 200 most important national firms which were identified as those firms with 'special phone lines'. In communist countries, the telephone systems were notoriously unreliable, so major centers of power were linked by a special phone system which worked more efficiently. There was a top-secret telephone directory for special phone-line holders, which included economic enterprises. We defined the CEOs of these firms listed in the top-secret telephone directory as members of our *nomenklatura* population.

Finally, in those countries which broke up after the fall of communism – in our case in the Czech Republic, Slovakia and Russia – there was an additional problem. Which *nomenklatura* did we mean, the Czechoslovak or the Czech one, the Soviet or the Russian one? We decided to start our work from the *nomenklatura* of the Czech, Slovak and Russian Communist Parties. Thus the populations were defined as 'national', not 'federal' *nomenklatura*.

(b) Current (1993) political and cultural elites

The definition of the population of current political and cultural elites was less obvious than it was for the communist *nomenklatura*. For the *nomenklatura* we had objective manifestations of the communist collective conscience in the minutes of Central Committee meetings. We could argue that this *nomenklatura* list told us what positions the top power-holders of a communist regime thought were the most important ones in the nation. Left without such a guide to the most important decision-making jobs of post-communism, however, we decided to 'simulate' a *nomenklatura* list for post-communist conditions. Taking the *nomenklatura* list as our point of departure, we eliminated those positions which no longer existed (such as the positions in the Communist Party apparatus), then added new organizations which appeared to be of similar importance to the ones existing before (for instance, positions in the National Privatization Agency).

Such a definition of current political and cultural elites is not without problems. There were positions which gained in importance during the transition which are not included, the most important example being leading clergymen. Nevertheless, we did not include clergy in our definition of the new elite. Another troublesome category was the Members of the National Academy of Sciences. While they were part of the communist *nomenklatura* and the party closely supervised who would be elected to this body, after the transition to post-communism the power and privilege of this group declined sharply. Nevertheless, we left the academicians in our elite population for the purposes of comparability. As a consequence of these decisions, there was a major reduction in the number of slots between the *nomenklatura* sample in 1988 and the elite sample in 1993, with the *nomenklatura* population being about twice as large as the population of the new political and cultural elite.

(c) New (1993) economic elites

We defined the current economic elite as the CEOs of the 3,000 largest firms in each country. We selected the number 3,000 to ensure a large enough sample of the economic elite for analysis, since we did not think that we could rely on the general population sample to yield these data. By contrast, we believe that firms that were not among the largest 3,000 in 1993 were likely to be numerous enough for their operators to be sufficiently represented in the general population sample.

Defining the largest firms presented some problems. We asked our national teams to approach their Statistical Offices and ask for a list of the 3,000 firms with the largest turnover during 1992. We tried to avoid using number of employees as a measure of firm size, in order to avoid over-representation of moribund large state (or formerly state-owned) firms, and to ensure that we selected enough of the more profitable businesses which operated with relatively small numbers of employees. We considered the option of drawing separate samples for state-owned, privatized, and private firms (this last category would mean that the firm started as a private firm), but we abandoned the idea, since research on property relations in post-communist countries indicated that real ownership relations may be rather different from the legal ones.

2. Sampling procedures

At the October 1992 Budapest meeting it was also decided that the details of the list of different elites should be undertaken by a working group. Iván Szelényi was asked to act as head of this working group, which also included János Timár from MEDIAN and an expert from the Museum of Political History, László Hubai. This group established a 'master elite list' from the Hungarian example. The Hungarian 'Master List' is attached as Appendix II below. This 'Master List' was completed by November 1992, and was sent to each national team. Each national team, in due course, sent their national adaptation of the 'Master List' to UCLA before beginning their sampling procedure. The national adaptations were reviewed at UCLA, and sampling started after they were approved.

Preparation for actual sampling began after all the elite populations had been defined in this way. As a first step, all positions in the population were 'named' – thus each national team identified the name of the person who was the incumbent of each position. Although this was a relatively easy job for cur-rent elites, the naming of positions for the *nomenklatura* was a major task. After the naming procedure, a random sample was drawn from each population.

The elite samples were divided into strata. In the data sets for most coun-tries, these strata are coded as the variable 'Group'. Note, however, that the Polish and Russian teams used a more detailed classification, coded as 'Strata'.

For the *nomenklatura* the following variables were established:

(i)   High party officials
(ii) Lower party officials

(iii) MPs, state administrators
(iv)   Local government administrators
(v)   Mass organization
(vi)   Economy
(vii) Culture, science and media
(viii) Foreign affairs

The strata of current political and cultural elites:

(i)   MPs, state administrators
(ii)   Local government administrators
(iii) Culture, science and media

Note that by definition, the new economic elite is a separate stratum – it is in fact a separate sample

The national teams were instructed to treat each sample as a stratified one – thus in the case of missing addresses, refusal, and so on, one had to replace addresses within the same stratum. After the sample had been selected, the next step was to find the addresses of individual incumbents of positions. For the *nomenklatura*, this was a major research task in itself. In the case of current elites, we used the official addresses as contact addresses and made appointments to conduct the interviews when and where it suited the respondents.

3. Fieldwork

Fieldwork was carried out in Hungary and Poland during the late spring and early summer of 1993; in Russia the fieldwork extended into the autumn and early winter of 1993. Interviews were conducted in the Czech Republic and Bulgaria during 1994. The fieldwork in Slovakia is currently (April 1997) under way.

Our understanding is that the interviewers who did the fieldwork also interviewed the general population sample; thus they were already well trained when the elite study began (all countries were instructed to start their research with the general population sample). However, we do not have detailed fieldwork reports at our disposal, and without written reports we do not have precise data on response rates. Our understanding is that the success rate was around 50 percent.

The majority of failures are attributable to incorrect addresses; changes in addresses; and the inability of the survey firms to find current addresses. We were told that finding addresses for lower-level *nomenklatura* was particularly difficult – the most difficult cases cited were those of party secretaries of very large firms. While the stratification of our sample should ensure that differences in response rates between strata will not affect the representativeness of our sample, it is possible that our results are biased towards the higher levels of the *nomenklatura*. Actual refusal was around 10 percent, comparable to refusal rates in the general population. We have no evidence that there was any special group in which the refusal rate was particularly high. The agencies who carried out the fieldwork insisted that once they found addresses, they had a good chance of completing interviews. In the case of the new economic elite and people in high positions in 1993, it took more time to arrange the interviews, but willingness to give interviews was surprisingly high in all strata. The Czech Republic seems to be an exception from this point of view. They reported a 30 percent refusal rate among economic elites and an 80 percent refusal rate among civil servants (although surprisingly, in the Czech Republic, the response rate among elected officials was close to 100 percent).

4. Problems of cross-country comparability

Economic elites

As far as we can judge, the most serious deviations from sampling procedure occurred in the case of economic elites.

(a) Old economic elite

Our partners in the Czech Republic did not follow our instructions and they did not establish who the economic elites were in 1988. They selected a sample of currently existing enterprises, and defined as 'old economic elite' those managers who were managers in the same firm in 1988. As a result, it is not possible to estimate outflow from the 1988 Czech economic elite.

Russia produced a very small sample of the old economic elite, and it is not clear why this happened. A possible explanation lies in the size of the Russian *nomenklatura* population. In other countries, the size of the *nomenklatura* varied between 3,000 and 5,000 individuals, but in Russia it was just over 10,000. Because the number of firms sampled was the same in all countries, but the *nomenklatura* was much bigger in Russia, there might have been a lower probability of selecting a member of the old economic elite in Russia. Whatever the case, there is no reason to believe that the Russian sample is not representative of high economic *nomenklatura*.

(b) New economic elite

Poland deviated the most from the proposed procedure. The Poles selected 200 enterprises from a list of only 600 large enterprises, and interviewed the three top officials. As a result, the Polish new economic elite sample is a sample of managers of much larger enterprises than the samples in the other countries.

The definition of size of firm also varied across the countries. Only Hungary defined the 3,000 largest firms in terms of annual turnover. In the Czech Republic, size was defined by number of employees, and in Poland and in Russia a combination of annual turnover, profit and number of employees was used. Our understanding is that each national team made an earnest effort to try to identify the largest firms in their countries, but statistics available to them varied, and they had to work with the information at their disposal.

Nomenklatura *and current political and cultural elites*

These elite populations seem to be sufficiently similar in all countries. The only major difference we can detect is the absence of foreign service officials in the Czech elite population, but since this is a very small category, it does not seem to affect the comparability of old and new political and cultural elites in any major way. Note, too, that the *nomenklatura* in the state bureaucracy is greatly underrepresented in the Czech Republic. While in other countries *nomenklatura* in the state bureaucracy constitute about 10 percent of the total elite sample, in the Czech Republic this figure is only 2 percent.

A final note: first, we know very little about Bulgaria. The Bulgarian data set does not have either the 'group' or the 'strata' variable; it indicates only which respondents belong to the *nomenklatura*, to the new political and cultural elite and to the new economic elite. At this point, it is difficult to assess how rigorously the Bulgarians followed sampling instructions. Second, we would observe that the Hungarian, Polish and Russian data are the most comparable (with some problems, especially in the deviant definition of new economic elites in Poland). Third, in the light of the comparability problems outlined above, we suggest that one should proceed with special care when comparing the Czech and the Bulgarian data with the other countries (see Table A overleaf for data comparing the structure of elite samples across countries).

*Table A Comparative Data on the Structure of Elite Samples in 5 Countries,
Interviews Actually Completed*

	Bulgaria	Czech Rep.	Hungary	Poland	Russia
NOMENKLATURA					
All	899	734	812	860	850
	(48.5%)	(37.3%)	(46.6%)	(48.7%)	(47%)
High Party		55	24	45	61
		(2.8%)	(1.4%)	(2.5%)	(3.4%)
Low Party		37	132	111	94
		(1.9%)	(7.6%)	(6.3%)	(5.2%)
State		47	206	171	238
		(2.4%)	(11.8%)	(9.7%)	(13.1%)
Local		36	39	72	16
		(1.8%)	(2.2%)	(4.1%)	(0.9%)
Mass organization		15	99	64	61
		(0.8%)	(5.7%)	(3.6%)	(3.4%)
Economy		384	102	236	61
		(19.5%)	(5.9%)	(13.4%)	(3.4%)
Culture		154	187	118	214
		(7.8%)	(10.7%)	(6.7%)	(11.8%)
Foreign		6	23	43	105
		(0.3%)	(1.3%)	(2.4%)	(5.8%)
NEW POLITICAL & CULTURAL ELITE					
All	561	439	353	371	366
	(30.2%)	(22.3%)	(20.2%)	(21.0%)	(20.2%)
State		159	161	190	148
		(8.1%)	(9.2%)	(10.8%)	(8.2%)
Local		18	33	90	79
		(0.9%)	(1.9%)	(5.1%)	(4.3%)
Culture		262	159	91	139
		(13.3%)	(9.1%)	(5.1%)	(7.7%)
NEW ECONOMIC ELITE					
All	394	800	578	534	596
	(21.3%)	(40.5%)	(33.2%)	(30.3%)	(32.9)
TOTAL					
combined elite samples	1854	1973	1743	1765	1812
	(100%)	(100.1%)	(100%)	(100%)	(100.1%)

Note: Numbers may not add up to 100 percent due to rounding.

Appendix II

The 'Master List' of Elite Populations

Compiled by László Hubai in cooperation with Iván Szelényi and János Timár

November 1992

NOMENKLATURA

HUNGARY
AS OF 1 JANUARY, 1988

I. Hungarian Socialist Workers' Party

1. Central Committee (including Politbureau)   107

2. Central Committee's apparatus   79[2]

    2.1 Secretaries
    (1 Secretary-General; 1 Deputy Secretary-General; 7 secretaries)

    2.2 Department of Propaganda
    (1 department head; 4 deputies; 7 departmental division heads)

    2.3 Department of Economic Policy
    (1 department head; 4 deputies; 6 departmental division heads)

209

2.4 Department of Administration
(1 department head; 3 deputies; 3 departmental division heads)

2.5 The Secretariat of the Central Committee
(1 department head; 1 deputy; 1 departmental division head)

2.6 Department of Foreign Affairs
(1 department head; 4 deputies; 1 departmental division head)

2.7 Department of Economic Affairs and Internal Administration of the Party
(1 department head; 2 deputies; 6 departmental division heads)

2.8 Department of Political and Mass Organizations
(1 department head; 3 deputies; 4 departmental division heads)

2.9 Department of Science, Culture and Education
(1 department head; 2 deputies; 4 departmental division heads)

2.10 The apparatus of the Central Control Committee
(1 department head; 1 deputy)

2.11 The journal *Social Studies*
(1 department head; 1 deputy; 1 departmental division head)

2.12 The journal *Party Life*
(1 department head; 1 deputy)

3.   Party organizations of counties and of other organizations which had county administrative status   227

3.1 County party committees
(19 first secretaries; 57 secretaries; 114 heads of departments, including the directors of party schools, i.e. schools of Marxism–Leninism)

3.2 Party Committee of Budapest
(1 first secretary; 4 secretaries; 7 heads of departments, including the directors of party schools, i.e. schools of Marxism–Leninism; 15 deputy department heads)

3.3 Organizations with 'county status'
(Party Committee of the Ministry of Interior: 1 first secretary,
2 secretaries; Party committee of Border Defense Force: 1 first
secretary, 1 secretary; Party Committee of the Ministry of
Foreign Affairs: 1 first secretary, 2 secretaries; Party
Committee of the Army: 1 first secretary, 1 secretary)

4. Directors of Party Enterprises   5
    (Publishing Company of Newspapers and Periodicals;
    'Kossuth' Publishing House, i.e. publishing house of Party;
    Transportation Company, i.e. the firm which managed the
    car-pool of the Party; 'Reflektor' Publishing House, i.e.
    subsidiary company of 'Kossuth' for commercial purposes;
    'Szikra' Printing Company, i.e. the firm which printed party
    materials and publications)

5. Central Party School   28
    (1 rector; 2 deputy rectors; 12 heads of departments;
    13 professors who were not department heads)

6. Leaders of the Research Institutes of the Party   6

    6.1 Institute of Party History
    (1 director; 2 deputy directors)

    6.2 Institute of Social Sciences
    (1 director; 2 deputy directors)

7. Secretaries of Party Committees of Ministries   14

8. Secretaries of Party Committees of large firms   130
    (The 50 largest firms and all other firms included in the
    'Special phone line directory')

9. Secretaries of Party Committees of Universities and Colleges   72

TOTAL (Hungarian Socialist Workers' Party): 668 POSITIONS

II. Mass Organizations

1.   Trade Unions   147

1.1 Union of Miners
(1 president; 1 secretary-general; 2 vice presidents; 3
secretaries)

1.2 Union of Leather Workers
(1 president; 1 secretary-general; 3 vice presidents; 2
secretaries)

1.3 Union of Health Workers
(1 president; 1 secretary-general; 2 vice presidents; 3
secretaries)

1.4 Union of Workers in Food-Processing Industries
(1 president; 1 secretary-general; 1 vice president; 2
secretaries)

1.5 Union of Workers in Construction, Construction Material
Producing and Wood-Processing Industries
(1 president; 1 secretary-general; 3 secretaries)

1.6 Union of Workers in Local Industries and Urban
Management
(1 president; 1 secretary-general; 1 vice president; 3
secretaries)

1.7 Union of Workers in Commerce, Finances and Hotel,
Restaurants, Entertainments
(1 president; 1 secretary-general; 3 vice presidents; 3
secretaries)

1.8 Union of Civil Servants
(1 president; 1 secretary-general; 2 vice presidents; 3
secretaries)

1.9 Union of Transportation Workers
(1 president; 1 secretary-general; 2 vice presidents; 3
secretaries)

1.10 Union of Workers in Agriculture, Forestry and Water-
Management
(1 president; 1 secretary-general; 3 vice presidents; 3
secretaries)

1.11 Union of Artists, Writers and Actors
(1 president; 1 secretary-general; 7 vice presidents; 2
secretaries)

1.12 Union of Workers in Printing, Paper Industry and
Publishing Businesses
(1 president; 1 secretary-general; 2 vice presidents; 3
secretaries)

1.13 Union of Teachers
(1 president; 1 secretary-general; 2 vice presidents; 2
secretaries)

1.14 Union of Postal Workers
(1 president; 1 secretary-general; 1 vice president; 2
secretaries)

1.15 Union of Workers in Clothing Industries
(1 president; 1 secretary-general; 2 vice presidents; 2
secretaries)

1.16 Union of Textile Workers
(1 president; 1 secretary-general; 1 vice president; 2
secretaries)

1.17 Union of Workers in Steel, Metal and Electrical Energy
Industries
(1 president; 1 secretary-general; 2 vice presidents; 4
secretaries)

1.18 Union of Railway Workers
(1 president; 1 secretary-general; 2 vice presidents; 2
secretaries)

1.19 Union of Chemical Workers
(1 president; 1 secretary-general; 1 vice president; 2
secretaries)

1.20 National Council of Trade Unions (SZOT)
(1 president; 5 vice presidents; 1 secretary-general; 4
secretaries; 10 SZOT heads of departments)

2.   Hungarian Youth Organization ('KISZ')   127

2.1 Central Committee of 'KISZ'
(105 members)

2.2 Secretaries of 'KISZ' Central Committee apparatus
(1 first secretary; 6 secretaries)

2.3 Heads of Departments of 'KISZ' Central Committee
apparatus
(6 secretaries of 'social strata committees'; 9 heads of
'functional' departments)

3.   Leaders of the Hungarian National Front   13
(1 president; 8 vice presidents; 1 secretary-general; 3
secretaries)

4.   National Council of Hungarian Women   7
(1 president; 6 vice presidents)

5.   National Peace Council   7
(1 president; 1 secretary-general; 3 vice presidents, 2
secretaries)

6.   Society of Soviet–Hungarian Friendship   10
(1 president; 1 secretary-general; 7 vice presidents;
1 secretary)

7.   Red Cross   7
(1 president; 1 secretary-general; 5 secretaries)

8.   Society for the Advancements of Science and Learning
('MTESZ')   5
(1 president; 1 secretary-general; 3 deputies of the secretary-
general)

9. World Organization of Hungarians   3
    (1 president; 1 secretary-general; 1 deputy secretary-general)

10. Organizations of Ethnic Minorities   12
    (Slovaks; Southern Slavs; Romanians; Germans: 1 president; 1
    secretary-general, 1 secretary each)

11. Scientific and professional associations   10
    (Lawyers; Historians; Economists; Political Scientists; Medical
    Doctors; 1 president and 1 secretary-general each)

12. Association of Hungarian Journalists   5
    (1 president; 1 secretary-general; 1 vice president; 2 secretaries)

13. Writers' Union   8
    (1 president; 1 secretary-general; 2 vice presidents;
    4 secretaries)

14. The Alliance of Hungarian Anti-Fascists and Resistance Fighters   7
    (1 president; 1 secretary-general; 4 vice presidents; 1 secretary)

15. Union of Hungarian Pioneers   4
    (1 secretary-general; 3 secretaries)

TOTAL (Mass Organizations): 372 POSITIONS

III. State administration

1. Parliament   391

    1.1 MPs
    (35 on 'national lists'; 352 from individual electoral districts

    1.2 Parliamentary administration
    (4 leaders)

2. The Presidential Council   21
    (1 president; 2 vice presidents; 1 secretary; 17 members)

3. Members of the Council of Ministers   17
    (1 Prime Minister; 2 deputies; 12 ministers; 1 president of the
    Central Planning Office; 1 president of the Central Control
    Office)

4.   Ministries   268

4.1 The secretariat of the Council of Ministers
(1 head secretary of state; 1 deputy head)

4.2 Ministry of Interior
(1 secretary of state; 5 deputy ministers;[3] several divisional
heads[4])

4.3 Ministry of Construction and Urban Development
(1 secretary of state; 3 deputy ministers; several divisional
heads)

4.4 Ministry of Defense
(1 secretary of state; 6 deputy ministers; several division heads)

4.5 Ministry of Justice
(1 secretary of state; 2 deputy ministers; several division heads)

4.6 Ministry for Industry
(2 secretaries of state; 6 deputy ministers; several division
heads)

4.7 Ministry of Commerce
(3 secretaries of state; 2 deputy ministers; several division
heads)

4.8 Ministry of Environment and Water Management
(1 secretary of state; several division heads)

4.9 Ministry of Transportation
(1 secretary of state; 3 deputy ministers; several division heads)

4.10 Ministry of Foreign Affairs
(1 secretary of state; 5 deputy ministers; several division heads)

4.11 Ministry of Agriculture and Food-processing
(1 secretary of state; 3 deputy ministers; several division heads)

4.12 Ministry of Culture
(1 secretary of state; 5 deputy ministers; several division heads)

4.13 Ministry of Finance
(1 secretary of state; 3 deputy ministers; several division heads)

4.14 Ministry of Health and Social Welfare
(1 secretary of state; 1 deputy minister; several division heads)

4.15 Central Planning Office
(1 secretary of state; 5 deputy ministers; several division heads)

5.   State organizations with 'national authority'   73

5.1 Office of Taxation and Financial Control
(1 leader; 2 deputies)

5.2 State Office for Wage and Labor Affairs
(1 leader; 2 deputies)

5.3 State Office for Religious Affairs
(1 leader; 2 deputies)

5.4 State Office for Youth and Sport Affairs
(1 leader; 4 deputies)

5.5 Central Geographic Office
(1 leader; 1 deputy)

5.6 Central Control Office
(1 leader; 2 deputies)

5.7 Central Statistical Office
(1 leader; 3 deputies)

5.8 Hungarian National Bank
(1 leader; 3 deputies)

5.9 Hungarian Post
(1 leader; 4 deputies)

5.10 Hungarian Radio
(1 leader; 2 deputies)

5.11 Hungarian Office of Licencing
(1 leader; 2 deputies)

5.12 Hungarian News Agency
(1 leader; 2 deputies)

5.13 Hungarian Television
(1 leader; 3 deputies)

5.14 National Command of Civil Guards
(1 leader; 3 deputies)

5.15 National Office of Prices
(1 leader; 2 deputies)

5.16 National Office of Mines
(1 leader; 1 deputy)

5.17 National Meteorological Service
(1 leader; 2 deputies)

5.18 National Office of Measurements
(1 leader; 2 deputies)

5.19 National Council of Work Safety
(1 leader; 1 deputy)

5.20 National Council of Technological Development
(1 leader; 4 deputies)

5.21 National Office of Innovation
(1 leader; 1 deputy)

5.22 National Office for Social Security
(1 leader; 3 deputies)

6.   Leaders of local governments   98

6.1 Budapest
(1 president; 5 vice presidents; 1 executive secretary)

6.2 19 counties
(in each county: 1 president; 3 vice presidents and 1 executive
secretary = 91)

7.   Prosecutor's Office   24

      7.1 Chief Prosecutor and his 3 deputies

      7.2 19 county prosecutors and 1 Budapest prosecutor

8.   Offices of Judges   25

      8.1 The Chief Justice and his 4 deputies

      8.2 19 county Presidents of Court and 1 Budapest President of Court

TOTAL (State Administration): 917 POSITIONS

IV. Economy

1.   CEOs and their deputies of the 50 largest firms   200

2.   CEOs of firms from the 'Special Phone Line' directory   250

3.   CEOs of large banks   7

TOTAL (Economy): 457 POSITIONS

V. Culture, science and mass communications

1.   National dailies   50
      (chief editors and their deputies; about 25 foreign
      correspondents)

2.   Chief editors of county dailies   21

3.   Hungarian Radio   23
      (1 president; 2 vice presidents; 12 chief editors, heads of
      departments; 8 foreign correspondents)

4.   Hungarian Television   35
      (1 president and 3 vice presidents; 1 chief director and 2 CEOs
      for commerce and production; 20 chief editors, i.e. leaders of
      editorial offices and department heads; 8 foreign
      correspondents)

5.   Hungarian News Agency (MTI)   35
      (1 executive director and 2 deputy directors; 12 chief editors
      and division heads; 20 foreign correspondents)

6.   Chief editors of weekly magazines   15

7.   Editors of monthly magazines   10

8.   CEOs of newspaper publishing companies   24
      (4 national firms; 20 county firms)

9.   Directors of publishing houses   20

10.   Hungarian Academy of Sciences   285
      (166 Members of the HAS; 76 Corresponding Members of
      HAS; 20 heads and deputy heads of HAS departments;
      leaders of the National Council for Scientific Degrees (TMB) –
      1 president; 1 secretary; 1 executive secretary; directors of the
      12 most important social science and 8 natural science
      institutes of the HAS)[5]

11.   Executive Officers of universities and colleges   147
      (100 rectors and their deputies; 47 college presidents)

12.   Directors of national cultural institutions   40
      (Such as the National Archive; National Museum; National
      Library; National Gallery, National Theater, National Opera,
      etc.).

**TOTAL (Culture, Science and Mass Communications):
705 POSITIONS**

VI. Foreign Affairs

1.   Ambassadors   96

2.   Leaders of commercial offices   84

3.   Leaders of cultural offices   54

4.   Leaders of Hungarian delegations at international agencies
      (UN, COMECON, etc.)   6

TOTAL (Foreign Affairs): 240 POSITIONS

**ALL ELITE (*NOMENKLATURA*) POSITIONS
AS AT 1 JANUARY, 1988: 3,359**

CURRENT POLITICAL AND CULTURAL ELITE

HUNGARY
AS OF 30 SEPTEMBER, 1992

I. Political elite

1. Parliament   390
   (384 MPs, 2 deceased; 6 Leaders of parliamentary
   administration)

2. State organizations elected by parliament   33

   2.1 President of the Republic
   (1 president; 1 office manager)

   2.2 Constitutional Court
   (1 president; 8 members; 1 executive secretary)

   2.3 Central Financial Control Agency
   (1 president; 2 vice presidents)

   2.4 State Property Agency
   (1 president; 1 executive director; 8 members)

   2.5 Office of the Chief Justice
   (1 president; 2 vice presidents)

   2.6 Office of the Chief Prosecutor
   (1 chief prosecutor; 4 deputies)

3. Members of the government   20
   (1 Prime Minister; 13 ministers with and 6 without portfolio)

4. Ministries   295

   4.1 Office of the Prime Minister
   (4 political secretaries of state; 1 administrative secretary of

state; 3 honorary secretaries of state; 4 deputy secretaries of state; 2 spokesmen; 1 office manager; several division heads)

4.2 Ministry of Interior
(1 political secretary of state; 1 administrative secretary of state; 3 deputy secretaries of state; several division heads)

4.3 Ministry of Agriculture
(1 political secretary of state; 1 administrative secretary of state; 4 deputy secretaries of state; several division heads)

4.4 Ministry of Defense
(1 political secretary of state; 1 administrative secretary of state; 3 deputy secretaries of state; several division heads)

4.5 Ministry of Justice
(1 political secretary of state; 1 administrative secretary of state; 3 deputy secretaries of state; several division heads)

4.6 Ministry of Industry and Commerce
(1 political secretary of state; 1 administrative secretary of state; 4 deputy secretaries of state; several division heads)

4.7 Ministry of Environment and Regional Development
(1 political secretary of state; 1 administrative secretary of state; 4 deputy secretaries of state; several division heads)

4.8 Ministry of Transportation, Communication and Water Management
(1 political secretary of state; 1 administrative secretary of state; 4 deputy secretaries of state; several division heads)

4.9 Ministry of Foreign Affairs
(1 political secretary of state; 1 administrative secretary of state; 4 deputy secretaries of state; several division heads)

4.10 Ministry of Labor
(1 political secretary of state; 1 administrative secretary of state; 2 deputy secretaries of state; several division heads)

4.11 Ministry of Culture and Education
(1 political secretary of state; 1 administrative secretary of state; 3 deputy secretaries of state; several division heads)

4.12 Ministry of Foreign Economic Relations
(1 political secretary of state; 1 administrative secretary of state; 4 deputy secretaries of state; several division heads)

4.13 Ministry of Social Welfare
(1 political secretary of state; 1 administrative secretary of state; 3 deputy secretaries of state; several division heads)

4.14 Ministry of Finance
(1 political secretary of state; 1 administrative secretary of state; 4 deputy secretaries of state; several division heads)

5.   State organizations with 'national authority'   79

5.1 Office of Taxation and Financial Control
(1 president; 2 vice presidents)

5.2 National Health Service
(1 national doctor; 1 national pharmacist)

5.3 National Population Register
(1 leader)

5.4 National Agency for the Protection of Consumers
(1 leader)

5.5 Institute for Frequency Control
(1 general director)

5.6 Office of Economic Competition
(1 president; 2 vice presidents)

5.7 Office for Military Industry
(1 president)

5.8 Office of Hungarians Abroad
(1 president)

5.9 National Command of Border Control
(1 national commander)

5.10 Environmental Protection Agency
(1 leader; 2 deputies)

5.11 Central Geographic Office
(1 president)

5.12 Central Statistical Office
(1 president; 3 deputies)

5.13 Central Military Command
(1 national commander; 1 chief of staff)

5.14 Information Agency of the Hungarian Republic
(1 director-general)

5.15 Office of National Security
(1 director-general)

5.16 Hungarian National Bank
(1 president; 4 deputies)

5.17 Hungarian Radio
(1 president; 1 vice president; 1 executive director)

5.18 Hungarian Office of Licencing
(1 acting president; 1 deputy)

5.19 Hungarian News Agency
(1 director-general; 2 deputies)

5.20 Hungarian Television
(1 president; 1 deputy; 2 executive directors)

5.21 Office for Space Research
(1 president)

5.22 Office of Refugees
(1 leader)

5.23 Office of National Minorities
(1 president; 1 vice president)

5.24 National Commission of Nuclear Energy
(1 leader; 1 deputy)

5.25 National Office of Mines
(1 president; 1 deputy)

5.26 National Office of Tourism
(1 president)

5.27 National Office of Compensation
(1 president; 1 vice president)

5.28 National Meteorological Service
(1 president; 1 vice president)

5.29 National Office of Measurements
(1 president)

5.30 National Council of Work Safety
(1 president; 1 deputy)

5.31 National Council of Technological Development
(1 president; 4 deputies)

5.32 National Police Command
(1 leader; 2 deputies)

5.33 National Office of Innovation
(1 president; 1 deputy)

5.34 National Office for Social Security
(1 leader; 3 deputies)

5.35 National Council for Sports
(1 president; 1 vice president)

5.36 National Office for Water Management
(1 director-general)

5.37 National Council for Civil Defense
(1 national commander)

5.38 Supervisory Agency of Gambling
(1 leader)

5.39 National Fire Command
(1 national commander)

6.   Local government   97

6.1 County councils
(19 presidents of county councils; 26 vice presidents of county
councils[6]; 19 county office managers)

6.2 Budapest
(1 mayor; 3 deputies and one office manager)

6.3 20 Mayors of cities with 'county status'

6.4 8 regional Representatives of the President of the Republic
(the 8 regional Representatives supervise the 19 counties; they
form 8 'regions' from the 19 counties. At county level only self-
government operates; the regional Representatives supervise
the legality of self-governing bodies)

7.   System of Justice   40
(20 Presidents of county courts; 20 County Chief Prosecutors)

TOTAL (Current Political Elite): 954 POSITIONS

II. Culture, science and mass communications

1.   National daily newspapers   60
(35 chief editors and their deputies; 25 foreign
correspondents)[7]

2.   Non-national daily newspapers   23[8]

3.   Hungarian Radio   25
(1 president; 1 vice president; 1 office manager;
12 chief editors and department heads; 10 foreign
correspondents)

4.   Hungarian Television   30
(1 president; 1 vice president; 2 office managers; 16 chief
editors; 10 foreign correspondents)

5.   Hungarian News Agency   29

(1 director-general; 2 deputies; 8 chief editors; 18 foreign
correspondents)

6. Chief editors of 20 major weekly magazines   20

7. Chief editors of 15 major monthly magazines   15

8. CEOs of the 25 major newspaper publishing firms   25

9. CEOs of the 20 major book publishing companies   20

10. Hungarian Academy of Sciences   285
    (166 Members; 76 Corresponding Members; presidents and
    vice-presidents of 10 departments; Officers of the Committee
    of Scientific Degrees – 1 president; 1 secretary, 1 executive
    secretary; directors of the 20 main research institutes – 12 in
    the social sciences, 8 in the natural sciences)

11. Universities and colleges   133
    (23 universities – 1 rector and 3 vice rectors at each; presidents
    of 41 colleges)

12. Leaders of national cultural institutions   40

13. Major cultural foundations   3

TOTAL (Culture, Science, and Mass Communications):
708 POSITIONS

ALL POLITICAL & CULTURAL ELITES AS AT
30 SEPTEMBER, 1992: 1,662

=Appendix III=

Data Sets Created by TARKI

In Chapter 4, we use two firm-level data sets from Hungary. Both were generated by TARKI and made available to us by Matilda Sági.

The first TARKI survey was conducted during autumn 1993. This was a random sample of all firms included in the Hoppenstadt business register. There were 1,001 successfully completed interviews. Interviews were conducted with the CEOs based on a questionnaire similar to the one developed for the Szelényi–Treiman survey, 'Social Stratification in Eastern Europe after 1989'. However, as outlined in Chapter 4, there were some important improvements in measures of firm-level property relations.

In autumn 1996, TARKI surveyed another random sample of firms drawn from the Hoppenstadt business register, but this time they focused exclusively on firms with 50 or more employees. Two hundred and ninety interviews were successfully completed. The questionnaire was similar, though not identical, to the one used in the 1993 TARKI survey. In contrast to the 1993 survey, in the 1996 survey some member of top management (not necessarily the CEO) was interviewed. The questionnaire contained questions on the activities and property relations of the firms, but did not contain questions about the social background or the current social structural position of the respondents.

Notes

Introduction

1. Karl Marx (1919) *Das Kapital: Kritik der politischen Ökonomie*. Hamburg: Meissner; Adam Smith ([1779]1976). *An Enquiry into the Nature and Causes of the Wealth of Nations*. Oxford: Oxford University Press.

2. For the classic statements on the growth of the large corporation and its consequences, see Adolf Berle and Gardiner Means ([1931] 1968) *The Modern Corporation and Private Property*. New York: Harcourt Brace Jovanovich; and Ralf Dahrendorf (1959) *Class and Class Conflict in Industrial Society*. Stanford, CA: Stanford University Press. For a discussion of the increasingly important role of financial institutions, see Neil Fligstein (1990) *The Transformation of Corporate Control*. Cambridge, MA: Harvard University Press; and for arguments which suggest that the role of capital is ending as the primary motor of economic growth in modern capitalism, see, for example, Daniel Bell ([1973] 1976) *The Coming of Post-industrial Society*. New York: Basic Books.

3. See, for example, Maurice Zeitlin (1974) 'Corporate Ownership and Control: The Large Corporation and the Capitalist Class'. *American Journal of Sociology* 79(5): 1073–1119; G. William Domhoff (1967) *Who Rules America?* Englewood Cliffs, NJ: Prentice Hall; G. William Domhoff (1970) *The Higher Circles: The Governing Class in America*. New York: Random House; and G. William Domhoff (1986) *Who Rules America Now? A View from the 1980s*. New York: Simon & Schuster.

4. Neil Fligstein (1995) 'Networks of Power or the Finance Conception of Control?' *American Sociological Review* 60(4): 500–03.

5. Perry Anderson. ([1976] 1992) 'The Notion of Bourgeois Revolution'. pp. 105–18 in *English Questions* by Perry Anderson. London: Verso.

6. Iván Szelényi (1988b) *Socialist Entrepreneurs*. Madison: University of Wisconsin Press; Iván Szelényi and Szonja Szelényi (1995) 'Circulation and Reproduction of Elites in Post-Communist Transformation'. *Theory and Society* 24(5): 615–38; Ákos Rona-Tas (1997) *The Great Surprise of the Small Transformation: The Demise of Communism and the Rise of the Private Sector in Hungary*. Ann Arbor: University of Michigan Press.

7. Eric Hanley and Iván Szelényi (1996). 'Changing Social Structure During Market Transition: The Case of Central Europe'. Paper presented to the workshop on *Economic Transformation and the Reform of the State*. Washington, DC: National Academy of Sciences.

8. Jadwiga Staniszkis (1991a) *The Dynamics of Breakthrough*. Berkeley: University of California Press; Elemér Hankiss (1990) *East European Alternatives*. Oxford: Clarendon Press.

229

9. See, for example, Roman Frydman, Kenneth Murphy and Andrzej Rapaczynski (1996) 'Capitalism with a Comrade's Face'. *Transition* 2 (2): 5–11.

10. Ákos Rona-Tas (1994) 'The First Shall Be The Last? Entrepreneurship and Communist Cadres in the Transition from Socialism'. *American Journal of Sociology* 100(1): 40–69.

11. For the description of the data used in this book, see Iván Szelényi and Donald Treiman (1993–94) 'Social Stratification in Eastern Europe after 1989', Appendix I below.

12. Pierre Bourdieu. ([1983]1986) 'The Forms of Capital'. pp. 241–58 in *Handbook of Theory and Research for the Sociology of Education*, ed. John G. Richardson. New York: Greenwood Press; Pierre Bourdieu (1984) *Distinction: A Sociological Critique of the Judgement of Taste*. Cambridge,. MA: Harvard University Press; Max Weber ([1915–21] 1978) *Economy and Society*. Berkeley: University of California Press, pp. 926–38.

13. For this kind of argument, see Jeffrey Sachs (1995) 'Postcommunist Parties and the Politics of Entitlements'. *Transitions* 6(3):, and Anders Aslund (1985) *Private Enterprise in Eastern Europe – The Non-Agricultural Private Sector in Poland and the G.D.R., 1945–1983*. New York: St. Martin's Press.

14. David Stark (1992) 'Path Dependence and Privatization Strategies in East Central Europe'. *East European Politics and Societies* 6(1): 17–51.

15. In German the term is *Bürgerliche Gesellschaft*. See Jürgen Kocka (1987b) 'Einleitung'. pp. 7–20 in *Bürger und Bürgerlichkeit im 19. Jahrhundert*. Göttingen: Vandenhoeck & Ruprecht; and Lutz Niethammer (1990) 'Einführung–bürgerliche Gesellschaft als Projekt'. pp. 17–41 in *Bürgerliche Gesellschaft in Deutschland*, ed. Lutz Niethammer. Munich: Fischer Taschenbuch Verlag.

16. For a good description of this process in the field of cultural production, see Ivan Berend (1998) *Decades of Crisis: Central and Eastern Europe before World War II*. Berkeley and Los Angeles: University of California Press.

17. See Ulrich Engelhardt (1986) *'Bildungsbürgertum'. Begriffs – und Dogmengeschichte eines Etiketts*. Stuttgart: Klett–Cotta, p. 191.

18. Erzsébet Szalai (1989a) *Gazdasági mechanizmus, reformtörekvések és nagyvállalati érdekek* (Economic mechanism, reform scenarios and the interests of large firms). Budapest: Közgazdasági és Jogi Könyvkiadó.

19. David Stark (1996) 'Recombinant Property in East European Capitalism'. *American Journal of Sociology* 101(4): 993–1027; Larry King (1997). *Pathways from Socialism: The Transformation of Firms in Hungary, the Czech Republic and Slovakia*. Ph.D dissertation, Department of Sociology, UCLA.

20. Erzsébet Szalai (1994a) 'The Power Structure in Hungary after the Political Transition'. pp. 120–43 in *The New Great Transformation*, ed. Christopher G.A. Bryant and Edmund Mokrzycki. London and New York: Routledge; Erzsébet Szalai (1994b) *Utelagazás. Hatalom és értelmiség az államszocializmus után* (At the crossroads: power and intellectuals after state socialism). Budapest: Pesti Szalon Kiadó.

Chapter 1

1. Pierre Bourdieu (1984) *Distinction: A Sociological Critique of the Judgement of Taste*. Cambridge, MA: Harvard University Press, p. 114.

2. Max Weber ([1915–21] 1978) *Economy and Society*. Berkeley: University of California Press, pp. 936–7.

3. In Chapter 2 we present an extended reconstruction of Weber's historical distinction between rank and class. Here, we simply observe that if we historicize the theory of forms of capital, the similarities to Weber's historical sociology become apparent. Weber makes a critical distinction between two systems of social stratification: one by class and the other by rank. Class stratification is obviously based on economic capital, while rank order can be perceived as based either on social capital broadly speaking – thus 'status honor' – or on social capital more narrowly defined, thus on political capital.

4. There are two aspects of Weber's theory of rank and class. The first aspect is his well-known multidimensional view of social structure. The second offers a specific hypothesis

about historical development. The concept of dual stratification was developed in the context of an analysis of Prussian society in the late nineteenth century, with a view to the issue of underdevelopment. Weber's central concern in this connection was that the continued domination of the Junkers would distort or obstruct the development of class relations in Prussia. It is in this sense that Weber saw Prussian society as a dual-stratification system: the dominant form of stratification – rank – prevented the evolution of modern class relations. When we refer to the dual system of stratification, we are using Weber's theory of rank and class in this second sense of the term.

5. On a first reading, the term 'modern rank order' may appear to be a contradiction in terms. However, by rank order we simply mean a stratification system in which social capital is dominant; it can therefore be modern. In other words, we want to detach Weber's distinction between rank and class from its historical framework so that we can combine it with Bourdieu's understanding of the forms of capital.

6. We develop this idea of the *Bildungsbürgertum* further in Chapter 2. At this point, note that it refers to a project to modernize Central European societies, usually formulated and undertaken by members of the Westernized, educated middle classes.

7. For this reason, state socialism – even in the Stalinist period – must be viewed as a major step towards modernization, since it was communists who initiated the dramatic break with feudal rank order in Central Europe.

8. Milovan Djilas (1957) *The New Class: An Analysis of the Communist System.* New York: Holt, Rinehart & Winston.

9. For further analysis of the degree of class closure at the top of Central European societies, see Gil Eyal and Eleanor Townsley (1995) 'The Social Composition of the Communist Nomenklatura: A Comparison of Russia, Poland, and Hungary'. *Theory and Society* 24 (5): 723–50.

10. Alvin Gouldner (1979) *The Future of the Intellectuals and the Rise of the New Class.* New York: The Continuum Publishing Corporation.

11. George Konrád and Iván Szelényi (1979) *The Intellectuals on the Road to Class Power.* New York and London: Harcourt Brace Jovanovich.

12. Victor Zaslavsky (1982) *The Neo-Stalinist State: Class, Ethnicity and Consensus in Soviet Society.* Armonk, NY: M.E. Sharpe.

13. Victor Nee (1989) 'A Theory of Market Transition: From Redistribution to Markets in State Socialism'. *American Sociological Review* 54(5): 663–81.

14. Iván Szelényi (1988b) *Socialist Entrepreneurs.* Madison: University of Wisconsin Press.

15. Ákos Rona-Tas (1994) 'The First Shall Be The Last? Entrepreneurship and Communist Cadres in the Transition from Socialism'. *American Journal of Sociology* 100(1): 40–69.

16. For data on changing patterns of employment, different patterns of recruitment into self-employment and changes in the structure of social inequality, see Eric Hanley and Iván Szelényi (1996) 'Changing Social Structure During Market Transition: The Case of Central Europe'. Paper presented to the workshop on *Economic Transformation and the Reform of the State.* Washington, DC: National Academy of Sciences.

17. For women, the story is more complex, as gender intersects with post-communist opportunities in different ways from under mature capitalism. In general, women received a better education under state socialism than under market capitalism, and on average women were better educated than men. Women were also less likely to be members of the Communist Party. Now, with market transition, human capital has been revalued and political capital has lost much of its clout. In this context, women seem to have been hurt less by the pain of transition than they might have been otherwise. See Éva Fodor (1997a) 'Gender in Transition: Unemployment in Hungary, Poland and Slovakia'. *East European Politics and Societies* 11(3): 470–500; Éva Fodor (1997b) *Power, Patriarchy and Paternalism: An Examination of the Gendered Nature of State Socialist Authority.* Ph.D dissertation. Department of Sociology, UCLA. In Hungary, for instance, women were less likely than men to be unemployed in 1993, or to have opted for early retirement. Moreover, gender does not appear to have affected women's chances of continuing employment in the Czech Republic or Slovakia. Poland is the only country

where being a woman has had a negative effect on remaining in the labor force during the transition. This is probably due to the conservative family values promoted by the Catholic Church, resulting in women being squeezed out of the workforce. Despite the realities of continued male advantage, however, women in the post-communist period have not given up easily. Almost by accident, they have found themselves with resources which are highly valued – education and the lack of a history of party membership – and this appears to have helped women survive the transition to post-communism comparatively well, but note that other material supports for women's paid work activity are under threat all over the region. These include state-provided child-care services and access to reliable contraception, fertility and abortion services.

18. David Stark (1990) 'Privatization in Hungary: From Plan to Market or from Plan to Clan?' *East European Politics and Societies* 4(3): 351–92.

19. Elemér Hankiss (1990) *East European Alternatives*. Oxford: Clarendon Press; Jadwiga Staniszkis (1991a). *The Dynamics of Breakthrough*. Berkeley: University of California Press; Iván Szelényi and Szonja Szelényi (1990) 'Az elite cirkulációja?' (Circulation of elites?) *Kritika* 10 (October): 8–10.

20. Nee, 'A Theory of Market Transition'; Szelényi, *Socialist Entrepreneurs*.

21. David Stark (1992) 'Path Dependence and Privatization Strategies in East Central Europe'. *East European Politics and Societies* 6(1): 17–51.

22. For the idea of involution, see Clifford Geertz (1963). *Agricultural Involution: The Process of Ecological Change in Indonesia*. Los Angeles: University of California Press; Philip Huang (1990) *The Peasant Family and Rural Development in the Yangzi Delta, 1350–1988*. Stanford, CA: Stanford University Press.

23. For this reason, the central question about privatization in the Central European transformation may not be who *owns* what? but who *controls* what? This question is especially important if it is true that economic capital is not the defining capital of post-communist social relations. Rather, in the absence of a *grande bourgeoisie* and with the discrediting of communists and politics, cultural capital – in the form of specific skills or human capital as well as the mastery of the new discourses of civil society and monetarism – may become the dominant capital of post-communism. In earlier work we presented evidence that this is indeed the case: that a managerial class wielding cultural capital rather than a capitalist class wielding economic capital currently controls the economic, political, and cultural institutions of post-communism. See Gil Eyal, Iván Szelényi and Eleanor Townsley (1997) 'Capitalism Without Capitalists: The Theory of Post-Communist Managerialism'. *New Left Review* 222 (March/April): 60–92.

24. Rational choice theorists may reply that if a rational choice is made on the basis of historical experience about the optimality of making entrepreneurial decisions or pursuing profit-maximizing behavior, then this, too, is rational. What we wish to emphasize is that the effects of a state-socialist biography may leave deep imprints that are non-rational and not necessarily immediately available to the maximizing actor. In other words, there may be a deep cultural imprint that defies simple processes of calculation.

25. Roman Frydman, Kenneth Murphy and Andrzej Rapaczynski (1996) 'Capitalism with a Comrade's Face'. *Transition* 2 (2): 5–11.

26. Bourdieu, *Distinction*, pp. 169, 244.

27. Ibid., pp. 169–70, 244–5.

28. Ibid., p. 170.

29. Ibid., p. 172.

30. Anders Aslund (1985) *Private Enterprise in Eastern Europe: The Non-Agricultural Private Sector in Poland and the G.D.R., 1945–1983*. New York: St Martin's Press.

31. Currently, theory requires successful Central Europeans to attain 'entrepreneurial skills', by which Western economists mean what is taught in Western business schools. But the dispositions inculcated by the objective experiences of 'market socialism' spell out a different sort of 'enterprising personality' in Central Europe. While they are probably no less dynamic and calculating than their Western counterparts, Central European entrepreneurs follow a different calculus and endow 'enterprise' with a characteristic meaning.

Chapter 2

1. These debates are summarized in two volumes: R. J. Holton (1976) *The Transition from Feudalism to Capitalism*. New York: St Martin's Press; T. H. Aston and C. H. E. Philips (1985) *The Brenner Debate*. Cambridge: Cambridge University Press.

2. For a summary of the debate, see the excellent volume ed. Ralph W. Greenlaw (1975) *The Social Origins of the French Revolution: The Debate on the Role of the Middle Classes*. Lexington, MA: D.C. Heath, especially the polemics by François Furet (pp. 61–98) and Alfred Cobban (pp. 101–29, 140–49), and the Marxist response by Claude Mazauric (pp. 30–58, 137–9).

3. This point is made by François Furet, 'The Catechism of the French Revolution'; and by George V. Taylor, 'Capitalism and the Origins of the French Revolution'. pp. 61–97, 150–59 in Greenlaw (ed.), *The Social Origins of the French Revolution*.

4. Perry Anderson (1992) 'The Notion of Bourgeois Revolution'. pp. 105–18 in *English Questions* by P. Anderson. London: Verso.

5. Robert Brenner (private communication) argues that a more precise formulation is that individual property (rather than private property) is common to the two systems.

6. Anderson, 'The Notion of Bourgeois Revolution', p. 111.

7. Ibid., pp. 116–17.

8. Herbert Passin (1965) *Society and Education in Japan*. New York: Columbia University Press; Bernard S. Silberman and H. D. Harootunian (eds) (1966) *Modern Japanese Leadership: Transition and Change*. Tucson: University of Arizona Press.

9. Alexander Gerschenkron (1966) *Economic Backwardness in Historical Perspective*. Cambridge, MA: Harvard University Press.

10. By 'Central Europe' we mean the geographical area which includes the economically less developed Eastern German states, some of the Central German states, and the 'sphere of German influence' further East, such as Bohemia, and the Western regions of Poland and Hungary.

11. Jürgen Kocka (1987b) 'Einleitung' pp. 7–20 in *Bürger und Bürgerlichkeit im 19. Jahrhundert*, ed. J. Kocka. Göttingen: Vandenhoeck & Ruprecht. See especially p.10, where he notes that the German 'Sonderweg' is due to the relative unevenness of bourgeois development. See also Jürgen Kocka (1987c) 'Bürgertum und Bürgerlichkeit als Probleme der deutschen Geschichte von spaeten 18. zum früher 20. Jahrhundert'. pp. 21–63 in *Bürger und Bürgerlichkeit im 19. Jahrhundert*, where he attributes the important position of the educated middle classes to the economic backwardness of Germany.

12. Jürgen Kocka (1988b) 'Bürgertum und bürgerliche Gesellschaft in 19. Jahrhundert. Europäische Entwicklung und Deutsche Eigenarten'. pp. 11–78 in *Bürgertum im 19. Jahrhundert*, Vol.1, ed. J. Kocka. Munich: Deutsche Taschenbuch Verlag; Hans-Jürgen Puhle (1991) 'Einleitung'. pp. 7–13 in *Bürger in der Gesellschaft der Neuzeit: Wirtschaft, Politik, Kultur*, ed. H.J. Puhle. Göttingen: Vandenhoeck & Ruprecht.

13. Hence 'professionalism' is the collective mobility project of the West European- and American-educated middle classes. It is a claim to special status within the confines of a hegemonic market rationality (one which accepts the hegemony of the economic bourgeoisie). See Iván Szelényi and Bill Martin (1989) 'The Legal Profession and the Rise and Fall of the New Class', pp. 256–88 in *Lawyers in Society*, ed. Richard L. Abel and Philip S.C. Lewis. Berkeley: University of California Press. Incidentally, we can engage in a little self-criticism here, since in that article 'professionalism' was understood to be the ideal-typical strategy of the educated middle classes under capitalism (understood generally as market integrated society). It is Kocka who has taught us to practice comparative capitalism, and to understand 'professionalism' in its full historical specificity and contingency.

14. Of course, Kocka's claims are not accepted by all scholars. It is important to note that he is but one (albeit an important) voice in a rather old debate about Central European or German 'exceptionalism' [*Sonderweg*]. The comparison with England and France, where capitalism, liberalism and democracy developed hand in hand, has haunted German historiography since the late eighteenth-century. Originally, Central European exceptionalism was emphasized by conservative ideologues. As Brüggermeier points out, German 'Culture'

was perceived as superior to Western 'Civilization', with its liberal, shameless materialism. See Franz-Joseph Brüggermeier (1990) 'Der deutschen Sonderweg'. pp. 244–9 in *Bürgerliche Gesellschaft in Deutschland*, ed. Lutz Niethammer. Munich: Fischer Taschenbuch Verlag, especially pp. 246–7. After World War II, however, the German liberal intelligentsia shifted focus and emphasized how the delayed development of the Central European propertied bourgeoisie, and of embourgeoisement in general, was the cause of the region's historical dead-end and its fatal attraction to fascism. See Jürgen Kocka (1985) 'Einleitung'. pp. 9–26 in *Bildungsbürgertum im 19. Jahrhundert*. vol.1, ed. Werner Conze and Jürgen Kocka. Stuttgart: Klett–Cotta, especially p. 11. This position was foreshadowed in Max Weber's claim that the backwardness of German development was due to the fact that the propertied bourgeoisie was 'feudalized', rather than the Junker class 'bourgeoisified': Kocka, 'Bürgertum und Bürgerlichkeit', p. 52. This idea was later developed into an ambitious comparative theory by Barrington Moore (1966) *Social Origins of Dictatorship and Democracy*. Boston, MA: Beacon Press. Finally, neo-Marxists have questioned whether the cause of fascism was the weakness of the bourgeoisie – or rather, as they argue, the unlimited power of a rather strong bourgeoisie which culminated in right-wing authoritarianism. See Geoff Eley (1992) *From Unification to Nazism: Reinterpreting the German Past*. Boston, MA: Allen & Unwin.

15. Hence the typical anxiety of the educated class, especially in its German 'mandarin' incarnation, and of its tendency to 'apply the brakes' every now and then in the process of transformation. For an account of the more conservative side of the *Bildungsbürgertum*, see Fritz Ringer (1969) *The Decline of the German Mandarins*. Cambridge, MA: Harvard University Press.

16. The classical statements are, of course, Adolf Berle and Gardiner Means ([1931] 1968) *The Modern Corporation and Private Property*. New York: Harcourt Brace Jovanovich; James Burnham ([1941] 1962) *The Managerial Revolution*. Bloomington: Indiana University Press.

17. Maurice Zeitlin (1974) 'Corporate Ownership and Control: The Large Corporation and the Capitalist Class'. *American Journal of Sociology* 79(5): 1073–1119.

18. Davita Silfen Glasberg and Michael Schwartz (1983) 'Ownership and Control of Corporations'. *Annual Review of Sociology* 9: 311–32.

19. Neil Fligstein (1990) *The Transformation of Corporate Control*. Cambridge, MA: Harvard University Press; Neil Fligstein (1995) 'Networks of Power or the Finance Conception of Control?' *American Sociological Review* 60(4): 500–03; Neil Fligstein and Peter Brantley (1992) 'Bank Control, Owner Control, or Organizational Dynamics: Who Controls the Large Modern Corporation', *American Journal of Sociology* 98(2): 280–307; Michael Useem (1980) 'Corporations and the Corporate Elite'. *Annual Review of Sociology* 6: 41–77; Michael Useem (1984) *The Inner Circle: Large Corporations and the Rise of Business Political Activity in the U.S. and the UK*. Oxford: Oxford University Press.

20. This observation complements the one made in Note 13 above. Where the economic bourgeoisie preceded the cultural bourgeoisie, the figure of the professional becomes the ideal-typical representative of the educated classes; where the cultural bourgeoisie preceded the economic, however, 'men of ideas' are the ideal-typical representatives of the claim of the educated middle classes to lead the 'modernization offensive'.

21. The point we make here may be truer for the French than for the English case. It is telling that the English term 'bourgeoisie' is simply borrowed from the French, and it never completely enters popular language.

22. Whatever is said about the German word *Bürger* also applies to the Hungarian word *polgár* and the Czech word *Mešták*. Indeed, *polgár* was one of the very first German words imported into the Hungarian language during the Middle Ages, indicating the importance of German urban dwellers, artisans, and merchant immigrants in early Hungarian 'embourgeoisement'.

23. Kocka cites a German author from 1792 who notes that the German word *Bürger* is associated more with the idea of 'honor' [*Würde*], than the French term 'bourgeoisie'. ('Bürgertum und Bürgerliche Gesellschaft', p. 33). For a semantic comparison of German, English and French terms, which emphasizes the 'plurivalence' of German, see Reinhardt

Koselleck, Ulrike Spree and Willibald Steinmetz (1991) 'Drei bürgerliche Welten? Zur ver-gleichenden Semantik der bürgerlichen Gesellschaft im Deutschland, England und Frankreich'. pp. 14–58 in *Bürger in der Gesellschaft der Neuzeit*, ed. Puhle.

24. See, for example, Karl Marx (1970) *Critique of Hegel's 'Philosophy of Right'*. Cambridge: Cambridge University Press.

25. Karl Marx (1919) *Das Kapital: Kritik der politischen Ökonomie*. Hamburg: O. Meissner.

26. Karl Marx (1974) *Grundrisse der Kritik der politischen Ökonomie*. Berlin: Dietz.

27. See *Meyers Enzyklopaedisches Lexikon* (1979), vol. 24. Mannheim: Lexikon Verlag, p. 435.

28. This is, of course, true for the word 'bourgeois' as well, but in both French and English the meaning of the word changed eventually to denote property owners, and another word was created to capture the political rights associated with urban residence: citizen, or *citoyen*.

29. Kocka, 'Einleitung' (1985), pp. 16–18.

30. Max Weber (1978) 'The City (A Form of Non-Legitimate Domination)'. pp. 1212–1374 in *Economy and Society* by M. Weber. New York: The Bedminster Press.

31. Kocka, 'Einleitung' (1985), p. 10; Puhle, 'Einleitung', p. 9.

32. The term *Bildungsbürgertum* was coined rather late. It first appeared in print in 1920, and became fashionable only during the late 1970s and 1980s. German social historians agree, however, that while the concept as such did not exist in the eighteenth and nineteenth cen-turies, other words were used which carried the same meaning. In the late eighteenth and early nineteenth centuries it was *'gebildete Stände'*, and from the mid nineteenth century *'gebildeter Mittelstand'*. Both terms connote a social group composed of educated individuals who, together with the propertied middle class, constitute the *Bürgertum*. Moreover, both concepts seem to identify a group which, unlike the citydwellers *per se* (or, as Kocka refers to them, the 'old *Bürgers*'), is a 'stranger' in the feudal rank order. See Kocka, 'Einleitung' (1985); Ulrich Engelhardt (1986) *'Bildungsbürgertum'. Begriffs – und Dogmengeschichte eines Etiketts*. Stuttgart: Klett–Cotta.

33. We are grateful to Balazs Szelényi for these ideas. See also Reinhart Koselleck (1990) 'Einleitung – Zur Anthropologischen und Semantischen Structur der Bildung'. pp. 11–46 in *Bildungsbürgertum im 19. Jahrhundert*, vol. 2, ed. Werner Conze and Jürgen Kocka. Stuttgart: Klett–Cotta; Georg Mosse (1990) 'Das deutsche–juedische *Bildungsbürgertum'*. pp. 168–80 in ibid.

34. In this respect, we rescue Marx's original problematic against Marx himself, instead of becoming bogged down in the various answers he gave to it. In the *Critique of Hegel's Philosophy of Law*, Marx's question (taken from Hegel) is 'who is the universal historical agent which will abolish civil society?' We take this to mean, ironically and with Weber, who is the historical agent who will abolish rank order and transform society into a universal, modern, class strat-ified system? This historical agent is defined within this problematic by its task, the project of modernization. Marx's later formulation, his underdeveloped structural theory of classes, is geared towards justifying his answer to the original problematic – that this historical agent is first the bourgeoisie and then the proletariat – but it was taken instead to stand for the whole original problematic. Some German social historians came close to recapturing this prob-lematic when they characterized the concept of 'bourgeois society' as a nineteenth-century *utopian* project. See Lutz Niethammer (1990) 'Einführung – bürgerliche Gesellschaft als Projekt'. pp.17–40 in *Bürgerliche Gesellschaft in Deutschland*, ed. L. Niethammer. Munich: Fischer Taschenbuch Verlag.

35. This idea has been forcefully expounded by Fichte: 'Now, for the first time, therefore, it happens that the fundamental reconstruction of the nation is offered to the educated classes. . . . We shall find that these classes cannot calculate how long it will still remain in their power to place themselves at the head of this movement . . . the people will soon be able to help themselves without any assistance from us'. Johann Gottlieb Fichte ([1807–1808] 1944) *Reden an die deutsche Nation*. Leipzig: F. Meiner.

36. Our task is complicated by the fact that Alvin Gouldner used the term 'cultural bour-geoisie' to describe the 'New Class' of intellectuals and professionals which, he suggested, was in conflict and competition with the economic bourgeoisie. See Alvin Gouldner (1979) *The*

Future of Intellectuals and the Rise of the New Class. New York: The Continuum Publishing Corporation. Our usage of the term is similar, but with an important qualification. Gouldner called the intellectuals a 'cultural bourgeoisie' because he believed they possessed 'cultural capital', which could generate a stream of income much like the means of production at the hands of the economic bourgeoisie (p. 19). No similar claim is implied by our concept of *Bildungsbürgertum*, which is defined by its historical project. Additionally, we see the essence of 'cultural capital' not as the appropriation of 'surplus-value' but as the exercise of symbolic domination. See Bill Martin and Iván Szelényi (1987) 'Beyond Cultural Capital: Towards a Theory of Symbolic Domination'. pp. 16–49 in *Intellectuals, Universities and the State in Western Societies*, ed. Ron Eyerman, Lennart G. Svensson and Thomas Söderqvist. Berkeley, Los Angeles and London: University of California Press.

37. See Pierre Bourdieu and Jean-Claude Passeron (1977) *Reproduction in Education, Culture and Society*. London and Newbury Park, CA: Sage; Pierre Bourdieu (1984) *Distinction: A Sociological Critique of the Judgement of Taste*. Cambridge, MA: Harvard University Press.

38. See Pierre Bourdieu (1977) *Outline of a Theory of Practice*. Cambridge: Cambridge University Press; and Pierre Bourdieu (1990) *The Logic of Practice*. Cambridge: Polity Press.

39. Martin and Szelényi, 'Beyond Cultural Capital'

40. And of course, this is true of a variety of other institutions: hospitals, clinics, laboratories, courts, etc. The function of all these institutions is to mobilize nature and humans in such a way that they can become the objects of symbolic mastery.

41. Ringer, *Decline of the German Mandarins*.

42. Pierre Bourdieu ([1983] 1986) 'The Forms of Capital'. pp. 241–58 in *Handbook of Theory and Research for the Sociology of Education*, ed. John G. Richardson. New York: Greenwood Press. This is, of course, a gross simplification because, as both Marx and Bourdieu emphasize, nothing is capital unless it is inserted into a determinate system of relations which renders it as such. Thus money is not capital if there is no 'free labor' or if there are no capital and labor markets; and credentials are not capital if there are no professional associations or universities. In Bourdieu's terms, credentials are the 'institutionalized' form of cultural capital, as compared with its 'embodied' (as 'habitus') or 'objective' (as works of art, science, etc.) states, and they cannot be understood separately from this institutionalization. The benefit of institutionalization is that it renders a resource transcontextual, and hence easily convertible.

43. Bourdieu and Passeron, *Reproduction . . .*, pp. 11–12, 195. 'Relative autonomy' has to do with the convertibility of capital. As long as money cannot buy everything, and specifically not credentials, and as long as credentials can be converted into political power and influence (as well as incomes), cultural capital can be considered somewhat autonomous even in the most commercially minded capitalist society.

44. But social capital such as membership in ethnic and racial groups, gendered 'old boys' networks', etc., plays a crucial role in the actual constitution of social classes, as the 'secondary criteria' which determine the actual composition of these groups. See Bourdieu, pp. 101–9.

45. See Pierre Bourdieu ([1984] 1988) *Homo Academicus*. Cambridge: Polity Press, especially Appendix 1; Pierre Bourdieu ([1989] 1996) *The State Nobility*. Cambridge: Polity Press.

46. James R. Lincoln, Michael L. Gerlach and Peggy Takahashi (1992) 'Keiretsu Networks in the Japanese Economy: A Dyad Analysis of Intercorporate Ties'. *American Sociological Review* 57(5): 561–85.

47. Richard Zweigenhaft (1992) 'The Application of Cultural and Social Capital: A Study of the 25th Year Reunion Entries of Prep School and Public School Graduates of Yale College'. *Higher Education* 23(3): 311–20.

48. Ferenc Fehér, Agnes Heller and Gyorgy Markus (1983) *Dictatorship Over Needs*. Oxford: Basil Blackwell; Kenneth Jowitt (1983) 'Soviet Neo-traditionalism: The Political Corruption of a Leninist Regime'. *Soviet Studies* 35(3): 275–97; Andrew Walder (1986) *Communist Neo-Traditionalism: Work and Authority in Chinese Society*. Berkeley: University of California Press.

49. Mark Bloch (1961) *Feudal Society*. London: Routledge.

50. Zuzana Kusa (1994) 'To Be of Bourgeois Origins: An Insurmountable Stigma? (On the

Erosive Power of Social Networks in the Period of Communism)'. Institute for Sociology of the Slovak Academy of Sciences. Paper presented in the XIII World Congress of Sociology, Bielefeld, Germany. 18–23 July.

51. In the first period of socialism in Central Europe, roughly between 1948 and 1968, members of the *nomenklatura* were recruited overwhelmingly from peasant and working-class families. See Gil Eyal and Eleanor Townsley (1995) 'The Social Composition of the Communist Nomenklatura: A Comparison of Russia, Poland, and Hungary'. *Theory and Society* 24 (5): 723–50.

52. Walter G. Runciman (1983) *A Treatise on Social Theory*. Cambridge: Cambridge University Press.

53. Frank Parkin (1979) *Marxism and Class Theory: A Bourgeois Critique*. New York: Columbia University Press; Mark Granovetter (1985) 'Economic Action and Social Structure: The Problem of Embeddedness'. *American Journal of Sociology* 91(3): 481–510; Peter Evans, Dietrich Rueschemeyer and Theda Skocpol (eds) (1985) *Bringing the State Back In*. Cambridge: Cambridge University Press.

54. Bourdieu, *Homo Academicus,* p.102. The point of terming these 'secondary characteristics' is not to minimize their importance. In fact, as Bourdieu argues: 'Social class is not defined by a property . . . nor by a collection of properties . . . nor even by a chain of properties strung out from a fundamental property but . . . by the structure of relations between all the pertinent properties which gives its specific value to each of them and to the effect they exert on practices' (p. 106). Thus, the specific value of interpersonal relations, ethnicity, etc., *within the structure of relations characteristic of class stratification* is 'secondary'. They serve as additional criteria of selection and exclusion in the constitution of social classes.

55. Weber, *Economy and Society*, pp. 241–5. The tension between the modes of understanding charisma becomes even clearer on the next page: 'It is recognition on the part of those subject to authority which is decisive for the validity of charisma. This recognition is freely given and guaranteed by what is held to be a proof . . . But where charisma is genuine, it is not this which constitutes the basis of the claim to legitimacy. This basis lies rather in the conception that it is the duty of those subject to charismatic authority to recognize its genuineness and to act accordingly.' Note how the fact that charisma is no longer a matter of individual quality but of social recognition immediately creates a tension between two alternative modes of recognition: 'proof' and 'duty': one rationalistic, the other – dare we say – traditional.

56. On the role of 'recognition' in the production of cultural capital, see Bourdieu, *Distinction*, pp. 318–61.

57. Indeed, Rainer Lepsius argues that the *Bildungsbürgertum* is an 'estate' type of social structuration. See Rainer Lepsius (1992) 'Das Bildungsbürgertum als standische Vergesellschaftung'. pp. 8–18 in *Bildungsbürgertum im 19. Jahrhundert*, vol. 3, ed. Werner Conze and Jürgen Kocka. Stuttgart: Klett–Cotta. Kocka, on the other hand, argues persuasively that neither rank nor class is an appropriate term to describe the social character of the *Bildungsbürgertum*. See Kocka, 'Einleitung' (1987b) and Jürgen Kocka (1990) *Weder Stand noch Klasse: Unterschichten um 1800*. Bonn: Dietz.

58. Randall Collins (1979) *The Credentialling Society*. New York: Academic Press. See especially his discussion of 'credential inflation'.

59. Perry Anderson (1974a) *Passages from Antiquity to Feudalism*. London: Verso; Perry Anderson (1974b) *Lineages of the Absolutist State*. London: Verso.

60. Max Weber ([1906] 1958) 'Capitalism and Rural Society in Germany'. pp. 363–85 in *From Max Weber*, ed. H.H. Gerth and C. W. Mills. New York: Oxford University Press.

61. Karl Mannheim (1985) *Ideology and Utopia: An Introduction to the Sociology of Knowledge*. San Diego, CA: Harcourt Brace Jovanovich.

62. *Meyers Enzyklopaedisches Lexikon* (1972) vol. 4. Mannheim: Lexicon Verlag, p. 195.

63. 'Durch Bildung wird der Mensch zum Bürger'. (It is through *Bildung* that a man becomes a *Bürger*.) See Mosse, 'Das deutsche–jüdische Bildungsbürgertum', pp. 169–80. Kocka is, in a sense, a direct descendant of this mid-nineteenth-century liberal intelligentsia.

While most postwar German liberals see in German exceptionalism the roots of fascism, Kocka does not quite accept this negative interpretation. He argues, for example, that the underdevelopment of the cultural bourgeoisie in the 'classical', English model may not have been an advantage. (Lecture delivered at UCLA, spring 1995)

64. Weber, *Economy and Society*, p. 220. See also p. 226, where he seems to contradict himself by noting the deep-rooted affinity between substantive rationality and bureaucratic mentality, whereas he postulates the essence of legal–rational authority to be formal rather than substantive rationality.

65. Engelhardt, *'Bildungsbürgertum'*, p. 14. This author argues that what he calls 'verbeamten Intelligenz' (the office-holding educated middle class) played a prominent role in the transition to capitalism. He also calls it 'intelligenz Bürgertum', though we believe *'Beamtenbürgertum'* is a more precise term.

66. The term *Bildungsbürger* was coined by Kuno Brombacher, who was one of the early advocates of National Socialism, though his criticism of bourgeois intellectuals could have appealed to the left-wing intelligentsia as well. Engelhardt, *'Bildungsbürgertum'*, pp. 188–91.

67. Pressed on whether the *Bildungsbürgertum* concept reflects historical reality or merely exists in the mind of historians, Kocka argues that it makes sense to use it for the late eighteenth and mid-nineteenth centuries. During this period, he argues convincingly, a fairly homogeneous group existed which could be called a 'cultural bourgeoisie'. In the same article, however, he points out that the term becomes less useful as the nineteenth century progresses, because the unity of this group gradually disappears. Jürgen Kocka (1989) 'Bildungsbürgertum: gesellschaftliche Formation oder Historikerkonstrukt?'. pp. 9–20 in *Bildungsbürgertum im 19. Jahrhundert*, vol. 4, ed. Werner Conze and Jürgen Kocka. Stuttgart: Klett–Cotta.

68. See Ringer, *Decline of the German Mandarins*, pp. 128–99 for the social underpinnings of the struggle between the 'modernist' and 'orthodox' fractions of the mandarin class. His periodization for the disintegration of the mandarin class is close to Kocka's: roughly 1890.

69. Kocka and other social historians argue that Weber greatly overstated the extent to which the bourgeoisie was re-feudalized during the late nineteenth century in Central Europe; thus the 'dual-stratification order' thesis underestimated the development of capitalist class relations. Kocka, 'Einleitung', (1987b), p.10.

70. See Brüggermeier, 'Der deutschen Sonderweg'; D. Blackbourn and G. Eley (1980) *Mythen deutscher Geschichtschreibung. Die gescheiterte bürgerliche Revolution von 1848*. Frankfurt and Berlin: Ullstein.

71. The debate about whether or not Nazism was supported by a powerful capitalist class or whether or not it reflected the relative weakness of the bourgeoisie harks back to the debate about Central European exceptionalism, or the German *Sonderweg*. There are three episodes in the intellectual history of this debate. During the first episode, in the early twentieth century, intellectuals who turned anti-capitalist saw the relative underdevelopment of capitalism in Central Europe as an opportunity to avoid capitalist development altogether. Therefore, they glorified the *Sonderweg*. The second episode, roughly at the end of World War II in Germany, saw liberal intellectuals reinterpreting the *Sonderweg* or the weakness of bourgeois development as the cause of Nazism and an obstacle to be overcome. Hence, they reinvented the role of the cultural bourgeoisie for themselves. In the final episode, central European intellectuals, with the demise of the 'New Left' and state socialism, equate Nazism and Stalinism, and join German liberal intellectuals as part of a new *Bildungsbürgertum*.

72. See George Konrád and Iván Szelényi (1979) *The Intellectuals on the Road to Class Power*. New York: Harcourt Brace Jovanovich.

73. Gouldner, *The Future of the Intellectuals . . .* pp. 28–42.

74. We will develop this point at much greater length in Chapter 3.

75. Jürgen Kocka (ed.) (1987a) *Bürger und Bürgerlichkeit im 19. Jahrhundert*. Göttingen: Vandehoeck & Ruprecht, p. 34.

Chapter 3

1. Milton Friedman (1962) *Capitalism and Freedom*. Chicago: University of Chicago Press; see especially, pp. 38–39; Milton Friedman (1959) *A Program for Monetary Stability*. New York: Fordham University Press; Gregory N. Mankiw (1990) 'A Quick Refresher Course in Macroeconomics'. *Journal of Economic Literature* 28(4): 1645–60; see especially p. 1650; Niels Thygesen (1984) 'Milton Friedman'. pp. 217–50 in *Contemporary Economists in Perspective*, ed. Henry W. Spiegel and Warren J. Samuels. Grenage, CT: JAI Press; see especially pp. 229– 43.

2. This point is made the most forcefully in Friedman, *Capitalism and Freedom*.

3. Michel Foucault (1991) 'Governmentality'. pp. 87–104 in *The Foucault Effect*, ed. Graham Burchell, Colin Gordon and Peter Miller. Chicago: University of Chicago Press.

4. Ibid., pp. 92–3.

5. Peter Miller and Nikolas Rose (1990) 'Governing Economic Life'. *Economy and Society* 19(1): 1–31. The concepts of 'action from a distance', 'mobilization' and 'centers of calculation' are taken from the work of Bruno Latour (1987) *Science in Action*. Cambridge, MA: Harvard University Press.

6. François Ewald (1991) 'Insurance and Risk'. pp. 197–210 in *The Foucault Effect*; Daniel Defert (1991) '"Popular Life" and Insurance Technology'. pp. 211–34 in ibid.

7. Neil Fligstein (1990) *The Transformation of Corporate Control*. Cambridge, MA: Harvard University Press.

8. Friedman, *Capitalism and Freedom*, p. 33.

9. In this connection, note the affinities of monetarism with the core problematics of social conservatism.

10. Note the following words of a prominent Czech dissident, later the first non-communist Prime Minister of the Czech Federal Republic:

> Had money managed to retain its role of universal currency, the situation would not have become so alarming. Under such circumstances some people would have just ended up owning much more than others . . . as it is, however, many people came to be able to wield power which they officially do not have, and which they are not supposed to have. Unfortunately, this kind of power is not mediated through the vehicle of money. It is direct, hidden and uncontrollable. As the result of the power concentrated in the hands of these influential individuals, it becomes almost impossible to ascertain what is actually going on in society. (Petr Pithart [1989–90] 'Social and Economic Developments in Czechoslovakia in the 1980s (part I)'. *East European Reporter* 4(1): 42–5; Petr Pithart [1990] 'Social and Economic Developments in Czechoslovakia in the 1980s (part II)'. *East European Reporter* 4(2): 4–7)

11. Václav Klaus (1989) 'Socialist Economies, Economic Reforms and Economists: Reflections of a Czechoslovak Economist'. *Communist Economies* 1(1): 89–96.

12. Ibid., p. 95.

13. A good example is Havel's polemic against Article 202 of the Czech criminal code: he recounts an episode in which he got into a scuffle with the head waiter of a certain pub, and ponders the possibility that he would have been charged with 'disturbing the peace' in accordance with this article. Article 202, says Havel, reflects a 'certain way of governing' inherited from Tsarist Russia, which seeks to keep citizens under permanent control. It does so by creating malleable laws, such as Article 202, which can easily be extended to include all behaviors, and used according to the whim of the authorities for political repression or settling personal accounts. Alongside the critique of the immorality and repressive nature of the regime, one can sense Havel's disdain for the irrationality of this mode of rule, which thus dispenses with individual self-regulation. Instead of facilitating the exercise of individual responsibility, it requires 'the surrender of one's own dignity and honor and the acceptance of what amounts to an official moral commandment: "don't try to put out a fire that is not burning you".' This centralist power 'sees society as an obedient herd whose duty is to be permanently grateful that it has what it has'. See Václav Havel (1994) 'Article 202'. pp. 1–16 in *Chronicles from Prague*, ed. John Miller and Kirsten Miller. San Francisco: Chronicle Books.

14. The major statements of the ideology of 'anti-politics' can be found in Václav Havel (1985) 'The Power of the Powerless'. pp. 23–96 in *The Power of the Powerless*, ed. John Keane.

London: Hutchinson; György Konrád (1984) *Antipolitics*. London: Quartet Books; David Ost (1990) *Solidarity and the Politics of Anti-Politics*. Philadelphia: Temple University Press. There is relatively little critical discussion of the ideological claims made by these authors, mostly by foreign authors. See, for example, Knud Erik Jorgensen (1992) 'The End of Anti-Politics in Central Europe'. pp. 32–60 in *Democracy and Civil Society in Eastern Europe*, ed. Paul G. Lewis. London: Macmillan; Aviezer Tucker (1993–94) 'Waiting for Meciar', *Telos* 94 (Winter): 167–82.

15. Havel, 'The Power of the Powerless', pp. 31–5; Václav Havel (1986) 'Politics and Conscience'. pp. 136–57 in *Václav Havel or Living in Truth*, ed. Jan Vladislav. London: Faber & Faber.

16. Apart from 'civil society', dissidents had a variety of other names for this community. Havel usually calls it 'the independent life of society'. See Havel, 'The Power of the Powerless', p. 65. One of the most influential formulations was Václav Benda's notion of 'the parallel polis'. See Václav Benda (1991) 'The Parallel Polis'. pp. 35–41 in *Civic Freedom in Central Europe*, ed. H. Gordon Skilling and Paul Wilson. London: Macmillan, and the variety of responses from Czech authors which follow. See also Václav Benda, Milan Simecka, Ivan M. Jirous, Jiri Dienstbier, Václav Havel, Ladislav Hejdanek and Jan Simsa (1988) 'Parallel Polis, or An Independent Society in Central and Eastern Europe: An Inquiry'. *Social Research* 55(1–2): 211–60; and Martin Palous (1989) 'The Parallel Polis after 12 Years'. *Uncaptive Minds* 2(5): 36–40. The philosophical wing of the dissident group has developed an influential notion of community out of the phenomenological concept of 'the natural world'. See Zdzislaw Krasnodebski (1993) 'Longing for Community: Phenomenological Philosophy of Politics and the Dilemmas of European Culture'. *International Sociology* 8(3): 339–53; Roger Scruton (1988) 'The New Right in Central Europe (I): Czechoslovakia'. *Political Studies* 36(September): 449–62.

17. The notion of 'sacrifice' was introduced to dissident discourse by Jan Patocka (1993–94) 'Wars in the 20th Century and the 20th Century as War'. *Telos* 94(Winter): 116–26. See also Ivan Chvatik (1992–93) 'The Solidarity of the Shaken', *Telos* 94(Winter): 163–6; and Ladislav Hejdanek (1985) 'Prospects for Democracy and Socialism in Eastern Europe'. pp. 141–51 in *The Power of the Powerless*, ed. Keane.

18. Michel Foucault (1983) 'The Subject and Power'. pp. 208–26 in *Michel Foucault: Beyond Structuralism and Hermeneutics*, ed. Hubert L. Dreyfus and Paul Rabinow. Chicago: University of Chicago Press.

19. Incidentally, this community, though it was seen as a community of ideas, was also sometimes a 'community of women'. See Karl Marx. ([1848] 1978) 'The Communist Manifesto'. pp. 469–500 in *The Marx–Engels Reader*, 2nd edn., ed. Robert C. Tucker. New York and London: W.W. Norton, especially p. 488. This is not mere gossip, nor was it an incidental feature of the dissident 'form of life'. On the contrary, it was a constitutive feature of this community of intellectuals and their civic ideas, which, we have to acknowledge, were essentially patriarchal, a fact amply documented in the writings of Ivan Klima (1994) *Judge on Trial*. New York: Vintage. In this book, the protagonist's final break with reform communism, and with his job as a judge, neatly corresponds to his first taste of an extramarital love affair with his friend's wife.

20. Ladislav Hejdanek (1985) 'Prospect for Democracy and Socialism in Eastern Europe'. pp. 141–51 in *Power of the Powerless*, ed. Keane, p. 147.

21. Havel, 'The Power of the Powerless', pp. 31–5.

22. Mankiw, 'A Quick Refresher Course in Macroeconomics', pp. 1650–51.

23. Hejdanek, 'Prospect for Democracy . . .', p. 147.

24. Václav Klaus (1991) 'Radical, Realistic Economics: An Interview with Václav Klaus'. pp. 157–65 in *After the Velvet Revolution: Václav Havel and the New Leaders of Czechoslovakia Speak Out*, ed. Tim D. Whipple. New York: Freedom House. See also the quote from Petr Pithart in Note 10 above.

25. Kare Dahl Martinsen (1995) 'From Impotence to Omnipotence: The State and Economic Transition, 1989–1994'. *Bohemia* 36: 330–61.

26. 'Anyone who has been in the west can testify that willingness, regard for others, and respect for their needs are quite common there. This is not in spite of but because of the fact that the market has reigned there for more than two hundred years and its 'invisible hand' has educated citizens in this way . . . readiness to serve, a friendly attitude, and interest in the needs of the customer are basic conditions of survival in the competition of the market'. (Anna Cervenkova in *Lidove Noviny*, 3 September 1990, cited in Ladislav Holy [1996] *The Little Czech and the Great Czech Nation*. Cambridge: Cambridge University Press, p. 155).

27. Russian reformers promised to finish the restructuring of the economy in five hundred days, and though it became clear very quickly that the journey would be longer, not even the most pessimistic Russians expect it to last for five hundred years!

28. Ralf Dahrendorf (1990) *Reflections on the Revolutions in Europe*. London: Times Books.

29. Michel Foucault (1993) 'On the Beginnings of the Hermeneutics of the Self'. *Political Theory* 21(2): 198–227.

30. This is similar to the first years of Bolshevik rule in Russia, when the obstacle on the road to emancipating the workers turned out to be the workers themselves.

31. Martinsen, 'From Impotence to Omnipotence', p. 336.

32. Ibid., p. 337; Sona Szomolanyi (1994) 'Old Elites in the New Slovak State and their Current Transformations'. pp. 63–82 in *The Slovak Path of Transition to Democracy*, ed. Grigorij Meseznikov and Sona Szomolany. Bratislava: Interlingua.

33. Tamás Bauer (1981) *Tervgazdaság, beruházás, ciklusok* (Planned economy, investments and cycles). Budapest: Közgazdasági és Jogi Kiadó, p. 14.

34. In the Czech Republic, there is substantial controversy about the extent of NPF involve-ment in the firms under its control. Some analysts argue that it has recently become very active, especially in appointing members to the boards of directors to these firms. See Karel Brom and Michael Orenstein (1994) 'The Private Sector in the Czech Republic: Government and Bank Control in a Transitional Economy'. *Europe–Asia Studies* 46(6): 893–928. Others argue that the NPF has been a passive owner. See Peter Kenway and Eva Klvacova (1996) 'The Web of Cross-Ownership among Czech Financial Intermediaries'. *Europe–Asia Studies* 48(5): 797–809. None the less, both sides agree that 'the privatized sector . . . exists in a heav-ily managed financial and administrative environment unlike that facing new private companies'. Brom and Orenstein, 'The Private Sector in the Czech Republic', p. 894.

35. Martinsen, 'From Impotence to Omnipotence', p. 330.

36. Ibid., p. 358.

37. Max Weber ([1904–5]1958) *The Protestant Ethic and the Spirit of Capitalism*. New York: Charles Scribner's Sons.

38. 'We live at the expense of the future. Now the bill for all this is being presented to us, in the form of sacrifices. They are considerable, and greater ones await us. They are and will be as great as the loan we all took out of the bank account of our future. The size of this debt is directly proportional to the silence with which we accepted the communist exploitation of the future' (Václav Havel [1993] 'What I Believe'. pp. 60–79 in *Summer Meditations* by Václav Havel. New York: Vintage).

39. Antonio Carlo (1974) 'The Socio-Economic Nature of the USSR'. *Telos* 21(Fall): 2–86; János Kornai (1992) *The Socialist System: The Political Economy of Communism*. Princeton, NJ: Princeton University Press; Ferenc Fehér, Agnes Heller and Gyorgy Markus (1983) *Dictatorship Over Needs*. Oxford: Basil Blackwell.

40. Havel, 'Politics and Conscience', p. 156; Patocka, 'Wars in the 20th Century', p. 121.

41. István Mészáros (1970) *Marx's Theory of Alienation*. New York: Harper Torchbooks.

42. 'What has happened in the past twenty years in Czechoslovakia is that a broad social framework (which used to hold the nation together) has either disintegrated or lost all its meaning. As a result all social norms of behavior have disappeared. . . . Czechoslovaks are increasingly less and less inhibited from using the existing pathological social and economic relations to their advantage . . . only a very small minority is willing to risk their well-being for the sake of change' (Pithart, 'Social and Economic Development in Czechoslovakia in the 1980s [I]', p. 5).

43. No pun intended; as the reader will probably notice, the post-communist ideology bears strong affinities to the neo-conservative critique in the West: the attack on redistribution closely parallels the critique of the welfare state, and the condemnation of socialist egalitarianism and 'counter-selection' echoes the debate on affirmative action and multiculturalism.

44. See Petr Fidelius (pseudonym for Petr Pithart) (1992) 'The Mirror of Communist Discourse'. pp. 193–204 in *Good-bye, Samizdat: Twenty Years of Czechoslovak Underground Writing*, ed. Marketa Goetz-Stankiewicz. Evanston, IL: Northwestern University Press.

45. Havel, 'The Power of the Powerless', pp. 31–5; Miroslav Kusy (1985) 'Chartism and Real Socialism'. pp. 152–77 in *Power of the Powerless*, ed. Keane.

46. Pithart, 'Social and Economic Development in Czechoslovakia in the 1980s [II]', pp. 4–5.

47. Ivan Klima describes the second economy as a conspiracy between the authorities and a portion of the public, the 'conspiracy of real materialists'. See Ivan Klima (1985) *My Merry Mornings*. London: Readers International.

48. 'The public probably would not like it very much to be told that they had certain duties: human, civic, professional duties. Today's nationwide decline may very well be described as a consequence of people's loss of their sense of duty towards themselves, their fellow human beings, their community, their nation, their customers and partners, and (if you will) towards God' (Pithart, 'Social and Economic Development . . . [II]', p. 6.

49. 'It is now high time to stop painting a black picture of the current state of Czechoslovak society. . . . For instance, it would seem that a section of the younger generation has decided to repudiate the way of life of their precursors, who grew up in 1970s and who are now either totally indifferent and passive or who display the conspicuous cynicism of the social climber. These young people get involved in ecological activities, they pursue music, they find their way towards religious faith' (ibid., p. 5).

50. Thus, Czech reformers complained endlessly about the Slovak 'instinct' for collective self-preservation, the age-old strategy of 'survival' devised in the face of Magyarization, but now used to avoid post-communist purification. See Jiri Musil (ed.) (1995) *The End of Czechoslovakia*. Budapest: CEU Press. See in particular the contribution by Petr Pithart in this volume, 'Towards a Shared Freedom' (pp. 201–22).

51. Havel, 'The Power of the Powerless', pp. 31–5.

52. Or the head waiter who denied Havel entrance to a well-known Prague pub, and thus implicated him in a moral dilemma – to disturb or not to disturb the false socialist 'peace'. Havel, 'Article 202', p. 4.

53. Jirina Siklova (1996) 'Lustration, or the Czech Way of Screening'. *East European Constitutional Review* 5(1): 57–62.

54. István Csurka (1993) 'Önátvilágitáss' (Self-lustration). *Magyar Forum*, 30 June.

55. Similarly, the undisputably most popular politician in the Czech Republic readily confessed to joining the Communist Party in the 1980s, acknowledged his guilt, and is admired by most ordinary Czechs. See 'Interview with Vladimir Dlouhy', pp. 27–35 in Martin Komarek and Jana Kasalova (1994–95) *GEN: 100 Cechu Dneska*. Prague: Fischer.

56. Siklova, 'Lustration', pp. 60–61.

57. Bradley F. Abrams (1995) 'Morality, Wisdom and Revision: The Czech Opposition in the 1970s and the Expulsion of the Sudeten Germans'. *East European Politics and Societies* 9(2): 234–55. The following quote is from the historian Jan Mlynarik, whose essay began the debate:

> The transfer with its consequences taught the nation not to respect material values, not to respect the principle of property, a value created over generations. It . . . taught [the nation] to steal. . . . The alienation of property in socialist ownership, which has reached unseen proportions, does not have its source and spring in the origin of socialism, but here in the immense stealing and robbing of German property.

Chapter 4

1. Jadwiga Staniszkis (1991a) *The Dynamics of Breakthrough*. Berkeley: University of California Press; Elemér Hankiss (1990) *East European Alternatives*. Oxford: Clarendon Press. Note that these theories of political capitalism should be distinguished from Weber's theory of political capitalism, which concerns the logic of the economic system rather than the personnel and emergence of a capitalist class. For Weber, political capitalism is capitalism in so far as it is oriented towards the rational acquisition of profits, but it is political because this happens under the tutelage of the state and/or under conditions of systematic political interference in the economic system. This issue is discussed again in Chapter 5.

2. For technical details of this survey and, in particular, for the definition of '*nomenklatura*' and 'elites', see Appendices I and II.

3. Erzsébet Szalai (1989b) 'The New Elite'. *Across Frontiers* 5(Fall–Winter): 25–31. [In Hungarian: Beszélö 26, 1989].

4. To see an earlier version of our theory see Gil Eyal, Iván Szelényi and Eleanor Townsley (1997) 'Capitalism Without Capitalists: The Theory of Post-Communist Managerialism'. *New Left Review* 222(March/April): 60–92.

5. The population of *nomenklatura* members was defined as those individuals occupying the top 3,000–5,000 positions in these countries in 1988, positions for which appointment usually required the approval of some organ or official of the Central Committee of the Communist Party. See Appendices I and II.

6. Our Czech colleagues did not follow our sampling instructions closely enough and this may be responsible, in part, for the surprisingly high level of elite reproduction observed in the Czech Republic. At least part of the Czech 'economic *nomenklatura*' sample appears to have been drawn from among CEOs who were CEOs in 1993. Thus for the Czech economic *nomenklatura*, survivors had a better chance of entering the sample than those who had lost their position since 1989. Since the economic *nomenklatura* was a rather small fraction of the entire *nomenklatura*, however, we do not believe this overrepresentation of former *nomenklatura* members fully explains the high level of reproduction we are observing in the Czech Republic, although it is probably exaggerating observed rates of reproduction.

7. For a detailed discussion of the reasons for 'Hungarian exceptionalism', see Szonja Szelényi, Iván Szelényi and Imre Kovach (1995) 'The Making of the Hungarian Post-Communist Elites: Circulation in Politics and Reproduction in the Economy'. *Theory and Society* 24(5): 697–722.

8. Furthermore, some people occupied *nomenklatura* positions in the communist system without occupying 'positions of authority' in their everyday work. For example, a Member of Parliament could have been an ordinary worker, and a Member of the Academy of Sciences might have been an ordinary university professor without subordinates. Being an MP or an Academician would have qualified both individuals as members of the *nomenklatura* in 1988, but not by virtue of their jobs. Rather, these sorts of *nomenklatura* positions reflected position in the Communist Party hierarchy. In the case of the MP who was and is a worker, but who, in the post-communist transition, is no longer an MP, the 'downward' mobility we are identifying is entirely structural. These individuals have not changed jobs, but they have lost their political positions as a result of regime collapse. The number of such people is reasonably small, however, so we do not think this is a major threat to our findings of massive downward mobility among the *nomenklatura*.

9. Szalai, 'The New Elite'.

10. In both Hungary and Poland during 1988, the regimes launched programs which were referred to as 'spontaneous privatization'. Communist elites acknowledged the necessity of changing property rights, and privatizing publicly held assets, but they initiated this process in a rather unregulated way. Under spontaneous privatization, firms could initiate their own privatization and negotiate their own terms with state organizations (in 1988, this still meant the Communist Party). Indeed, the initial hypotheses about political capitalism put forward by Staniszkis and Hankiss were formulated in reaction to these spontaneous privatization plans.

11. Caution is needed in interpreting the data in Table 4.4. The proportion of CEOs is much larger in the new economic elite than in the old *nomenklatura* and, as we know, managers are more likely to be owners than members of other fractions of the old or new elites. If we compare the old and new political elites, the old political elite is more likely to own businesses than the new political elite. This is probably the result of two factors: (a) the new political elite is under even greater scrutiny not to take advantage of privatization than members of the old political elite; (b) the new political elite needs business ownership less than its communist-era peers, since they all have well-paid jobs with substantial power.

12. Note, too, that our data on the nature and extent of business ownership among former *nomenklatura* members are of poor quality owing to very low response rates on this question. Unanswered questions about the level, extent, and type of business ownership is crucial for making the argument that former *nomenklatura* members are becoming a propertied bour-geoisie. So although we are troubled by missing data problems, given the paucity of good data on ownership, and because, therefore, our data remain the best source of information about the nature of property ownership among former *nomenklatura* members, we rely on them. Note that in the Hungarian case we have much better data on property ownership, which will be presented later in this chapter.

13. Note, in this context, that the distribution of income in Central European societies is quite skewed, and very few respondents in the TARKI survey reported ownership in very large firms. Moreover, among those who did report ownership in a big business, the owner-ship stake was often extremely small. This means that there are very few owners of big businesses. There may be six to a dozen former senior cadre families with more than 10 per-cent ownership shares in a corporation with 300 or more employees in each of these countries. If this property was acquired illegally – and we have no information on this point – then we are observing a non-trivial incidence of corruption, but hardly enough corruption to substantiate the hypothesis that former communist rulers now rule Central Europe as pri-vate proprietors.

14. See Eric Hanley (1996) 'Self-Employment in Post-Communist Eastern Europe: The Emergence of a New Petty Bourgeoisie'. Unpublished manuscript, Department of Sociology, UCLA; Eric Hanley and Iván Szelényi (1996) 'Changing Social Structure During Market Transition: The Case of Central Europe'. Paper presented to the workshop on *Economic Transformation and the Reform of the State*. Washington, DC: National Academy of Sciences.

15. Note, too, that many communist political cadres came from upwardly mobile working-class or peasant families, and it is conceivable that if communism had not occurred in these countries, these people may have become petty-bourgeois anyway. Indeed, one interpretation of this finding about former cadres becoming small business employers in post-communism is that they are simply returning to the trajectory they would have been traveling if communism had never occurred. In other words, it is not only their training as managers and officials in state-socialist redistributive economies which makes these former cadres unlikely to become the Rockefellers or Du Ponts of Central Europe, but also that these former cadres from work-ing-class and peasant origins may not possess the cultural capital or habitus which would produce the dynamic entrepreneurialism we might expect to find among large owners in a new *grande bourgeoisie*.

16. They are older, of course, and less likely to have children living with them, which may partly explain the smaller size of their house/flat. However, the difference is far too large to be attributable only to demographic factors, especially since people in Central Europe are much less likely than those in the United States to move house just because the demographic situation of the household has changed.

17. Indeed, Hankiss was subjected to vitriolic attack when his book *East European Alternatives* was first published in Hungarian during the summer of 1989. Gábor Vági construed Hankiss's argument as advocating such a 'grand coalition'. As far as our reading of Hankiss's work is concerned, this was a false accusation – Hankiss offered a diagnosis rather than a policy rec-ommendation.

18. Note that while Hankiss's prediction about the formation of a 'grand coalition' between

red and expert may have failed in Central Europe, it may be working in China today. China's success in implementing market reforms might be attributed to the fact that stakes in capitalism have been created for at least some communist cadres – in particular in rural industrialization. One driving force of Chinese economic growth is municipally owned firms in villages which, according to many China specialists, may be owned by local cadres *de facto*.

19. Erzsébet Szalai (1981) *Kiemelt vállalat – beruházas – érdek* (Privileged firms, investments, interests). Budapest: Akadémiai Kiadó; Erzsébet Szalai (1989a) *Gazdasági mechanizmus, reformtörekvések és nagyvállalati érdekek* (Economic mechanism, reform scenarios and the interest of large firms). Budapest: Közgazdasági és Jogi Könyvkiadó; Szalai, 'The New Elite'.

20. Szalai, *Gazdasági mechanizmus*, pp. 169–176.

21. There is, of course, a substantial body of literature concerning the differences between 'red' and 'expert', 'bureaucrats' and 'technocrats'. Szalai's main contribution was to locate the major driving force of social change in the conflict between these two fractions of the ruling estate. She was among the first to see that the technocracy was determined to defeat the bureaucracy, and that the technocracy would use the transformation of property rights in the direction of capitalism to try to achieve this aim. By contrast, others anticipated a *rapprochement* or merger between these two fractions (see George Konrád and Iván Szelényi [1979] *The Intellectuals on the Road to Class Power*. New York: Harcourt Brace Jovanovich; Alvin Gouldner [1979] *The Future of Intellectuals and the Rise of the New Class*. New York: The Continuum Publishing Corporation).

22. Szalai, *Gazdasági mechanizmus*, pp. 181–6.

23. Erzsébet Szalai (1996) *Az elitek átváltozása* (Transformation of elites). Budapest: Cserépfalvi Kiadó.

24. Indeed, this phenomenon was so evident that in December 1996, in an 'open letter' to his party, Békesi – a leading personality of the Hungarian Socialist Party who was briefly Minister of Finance in 1994, a position he had held in the last communist government – accused his own party of clientelism, condemning the Socialist Party for promoting party faithfuls into positions of authority too quickly. Békesi argued that party loyalty, especially loyalty to the person of the Prime Minister and Socialist Party Chief (Horn), was beginning to matter more than competence – a situation which recalled the counterselection of the communist period.

25. David Stark (1996) 'Recombinant Property in East European Capitalism'. *American Journal of Sociology* 101(4): 993–1027.

26. Larry King (1997) *Pathways from Socialism: The Transformation of Firms in Hungary, the Czech Republic and Slovakia*. Ph.D dissertation, Department of Sociology, UCLA.

27. See Erich Hoorn (1996) 'Tschechische Banken haben zu viel Macht'. (The Czech Banks Have Too Much Power). *Die Presse*, 20 June, p. 17; Roman Frydman, Cheryl W. Gray and Andrzej Rapaczynski (1996) *Corporate Governance in Central Europe and Russia*. Budapest: Central European University Press.

28. King, *Pathways from Socialism*. See also Éva Voszka (1994) *Centralization, Renationalization, Redistribution* (The Role of Government in Changing Ownership Structure in Hungary, 1989–1993). Budapest: Center for Economic Policy Research, Discussion Papers, Series No. 916.

29. Stark, 'Recombinant Property . . .'.

30. Ibid. We are grateful to David Stark for informally providing information on the bank consolidation process.

31. This happened shortly after the President of the Budapest Bank, Bokros, was appointed Minister of Finance. Leaving his post at the bank, Bokros received a substantial severance payment from an institution that was still publicly owned at the time of his departure.

32. This kind of problem is not a unique feature of the privatization of the Budapest Bank. In Hungary, the costs of privatization are very high, and they represent a high proportion of privatization revenues. Those who advocate the policy of privatization justify this by suggesting that the primary purpose of privatization is not to generate revenues for the government budget, but to relieve government of the burden of future redistribution and to create a

healthy tax base in the long run. Thus you may sell a company for less than it costs you to buy it, and, according to this logic, this is good business – in the long run. Critics of fast privatization policies would object, of course. In the long run, we are all dead.

33. See László Hajnal (1996) 'Visszaállamosították a Polgári Bankot' (The Civic Bank was renationalized), *Magyar Hírlap*, 31 December.

34. These findings should be taken with a grain of salt, however, because, as noted above, there were high refusal rates when we asked our respondents to report the size of the firm in which they possessed ownership. Moreover, we failed to ask respondents whether or not their business ownership was in the firm they managed or in some other firm. Fortunately, three or four months after we completed our survey, TARKI carried out a survey of 1,001 Hungarian managers which followed our sampling procedures closely. TARKI drew their sample from the same population as we did, and they asked a better battery of questions about ownership, achieving a better response rate on firm characteristics, including firm size. The TARKI data also provide information about whether or not managers owned shares in the firms they managed or in other firms. The only limitation of the TARKI data is that they were collected for Hungary only; thus we lose the power of comparative analysis. In Table 4.11 we analyze data from the TARKI survey and, in this way, offer a double check on the reliability of our own data.

35. Note that our data probably overestimate this difference. Our Polish colleagues did not follow our instructions about sampling CEOs closely. They selected fewer firms than our Hungarian colleagues did, focusing on large firms and interviewing more than one person in the management team at each firm. The Hungarian sample, by contrast, is a sample of CEOs only. Notwithstanding this discrepancy, however, the difference between the Polish and Hungarian data is too large to be only an artifact of sampling, although the difference is difficult to interpret without further data collection.

36. These data are available in Matilda Sági (1994) 'Menedzserek. Az uj gazdasagi elit rekrutációja' (Managers. Recruitment into the new economic elite). pp. 334–50 in *Társadalmi Riport, 1994* (Social Indicators), ed. Rudolf Andorka, Tamás Kolosi and György Vukovics. Budapest: TARKI, p. 348.

37. Note that the vast majority of these managers are indeed male.

38. Paul Windolf (1996) 'The Transformation of the East German Economy'. Paper presented at the conference on 'Territoriality and Modern Society', UNC, Chapel Hill, 29–30 March.

39. Here an interesting exception is ownership of stocks and bonds by the Czech economic elite – they own less than members of the political and cultural elite. The only explanation for this we can think of is that there was reprivatization in the Czech Republic; thus ownership of capital assets may be influenced by the pre-communist wealth of respondents. Since the members of the new economic elite are more likely to be former cadres than members of other elite fractions – and therefore to come from worker and peasant backgrounds – they may have received less compensation for the property their family lost as a result of communist nationalization.

40. More complex statistical methods may yield a better sense of the lifestyle similarities among elite fractions, and the cleavages between elite members and the general population. It is also conceivable that life histories, occupational careers, and detailed educational histories of members of the power bloc may show that the social trajectories of members of the post-communist elite are homologous and distinct from the general population, and from those professionals who did not make it into the elite. In this context, note that an important implication of our theory of post-communist managerialism is that the intellectual and professional strata were divided among themselves during the post-communist transition. The intelligentsia as a whole was not upwardly mobile following 1989. Rather, different strata of professionals were differently affected. For example, populous groups of professionals like teachers and medical professionals – two groups which together constitute the largest segment of the professional category – are likely to have been among the losers of post-communist transformation. Members of both of these occupations depended heavily upon public

employment before 1989, and in the context of the post-communist budget crisis their real incomes have deteriorated rapidly. So let us emphasize at this point that our theory of post-communist managerialism in no way implies that 'intellectuals are on the road to class power' – far from it. Instead, we believe that as a result of the post-communist transformation, the category of intellectuals has been greatly diversified. Only certain groups of intellectuals benefited economically in the post-communist transformation, and very few managed to retain their power or appropriate power when the bureaucratic fraction of the communist ruling estate was defeated in 1989.

41. See Gouldner, *The Future of Intellectuals*.

42. Konrád and Szelényi, *The Intellectuals on the Road to Class Power*.

43. Stark, 'Recombinant Property in East European Capitalism', offers important insights about the crucial role of the financial sector in his analysis of the bank consolidation process in Hungary during the early 1990s.

44. David Stark (1992) 'Path Dependence and Privatization Strategies in East Central Europe'. *East European Politics and Societies* 6(1): 17–51.

45. We are grateful to Elemér Hankiss, who reminded us how dependent management is on the politocracy in post-communist formations.

46. See Appendix III below.

47. Only about a third of the firms from our initial 1993 survey reported their property relations to the Hoppenstadt in 1995. Thus we have 1995 data for only 213 enterprises. The small number of cases worried us, and we were also concerned about their representativeness, since it is not unreasonable to suspect that missing data were highly correlated with property form. If one of our suspects 'did it' – i.e., if they ripped off public firms to enrich themselves – it was also quite likely that they declined to inform the Hoppenstadt. We checked to see if the size of the firm (measured by number of employees) was correlated with reporting to the Hoppenstadt, but we found no such correlation. As we documented above, property relations in 1993 varied mainly according to firm size – managerial ownership and individual private ownership were more frequent among smaller firms, while larger firms were more likely to be owned by the government or foreign investors. On this basis, we reasoned that if there were differential rates of reporting by firm size, this would indicate selection bias. Since we found no such correlation, we concluded that these 213 firms were probably a reasonably representative sub-sample of the 600 firms we originally sampled.

48. Before rushing to interpret these new data, however, note that our 1993 survey and the 1996 TARKI survey are not completely comparable. Importantly, for 1993 we cannot distinguish between local and central government ownership of firms. For 1996, we know the extent of business ownership among domestic individuals, but we do not know the size of the ownership stake, or whether or not owners are also managers of the firms they own. Despite these comparability problems, the data still suggest a strikingly different story from the one we have told so far.

49. Iván Szelényi, Éva Fodor and Eric Hanley (1997) 'The Left-turn in Post-Communist Politics: The Hungarian and Polish Elections, 1990–1994'. *East European Politics and Societies* II(I) 190–224.

Chapter 5

1. Iván Szelényi and Bill Martin (1988) 'The Three Waves of New Class Theories'. *Theory and Society* 17(4): 645–67.

2. See, for example, Thornstein Veblen ([1919] 1963) *The Engineers and the Price System*. New York: Harcourt & Brace; Adolf Berle and Gardiner Means ([1931] 1968) *The Modern Corporation and Private Property*. New York: Harcourt Brace Jovanovich; James Burnham ([1941] 1962) *The Managerial Revolution*. Bloomington: Indiana University Press; Ralf Dahrendorf (1972) *Class and Class Conflict in Industrial Society*. Stanford, CA: Stanford University Press; John K. Galbraith (1967) *The New Industrial State*. New York: Houghton Mifflin.

3. Maurice Zeitlin (1974) 'Corporate Ownership and Control: The Large Corporation and

the Capitalist Class'. *American Journal of Sociology* 79(5):1073–1119; G. William Domhoff (1967) *Who Rules America?* Englewood Cliffs, NJ: Prentice Hall; G. William Domhoff (1970) *The Higher Circles: The Governing Class in America*. New York: Random House.

4. Galbraith, in *The New Industrial State*, took this position, and to some extent, so did Daniel Bell ([1973]1976)*The Coming of Post-Industrial Society*. New York: Basic Books. See also Alvin Gouldner (1979) *The Future of Intellectuals and the Rise of the New Class*. New York: The Continuum Publishing Corporation.

5. Roman Frydman, Kenneth Murphy and Andrzej Rapaczynski (1996) 'Capitalism with a Comrade's Face'. *Transition* 2(2): 5–11.

6. Eric Hanley, Natasha Yershova and Richard Anderson (1995) 'Russia: Old Wine in New Bottle? The Circulation and Reproduction of Russian Elites, 1983–1993'. *Theory and Society* 24(5): 639–68.

7. Gil Eyal and Eleanor Townsley (1995) 'The Social Composition of the Communist Nomenklatura: A Comparison of Russia, Poland, and Hungary'. *Theory and Society* 24(5): 723–50.

8. Hanley, Yershova and Anderson, 'Russia: Old Wine in New Bottle?'.

9. Michael Voslensky (1984). *Nomenklatura: The Soviet Ruling Class. An Insider's Report*. New York: Doubleday.

10. David Stark (1996) 'Recombinant Property in East European Capitalism'. *American Journal of Sociology* 101(4): 993–1027; Larry King (1997) *Pathways from Socialism: The Transformation of Firms in Hungary, the Czech Republic and Slovakia*. Ph.D dissertation, Department of Sociology, UCLA.

11. Few Western corporations would allow their CEOs to subcontract lucrative businesses to firms privately owned by their CEOs. Any CEO caught doing this would be fired immediately.

12. Eric Hanley (1996) 'Self-Employment in Post-Communist Eastern Europe: The Emergence of a New Petty Bourgeoisie'. Unpublished manuscript, Department of Sociology, UCLA.

13. Ibid.

14. Sachs and Woo point out that the Chinese model could not be repeated in Central Europe. China could follow a 'dual-track' approach since it had no excessive social expenditures and little foreign debt; therefore it could channel labor from agriculture into newly created private business. Jeffrey Sachs and Wing Thye Woo (1996) 'China's Transition Experience, Reexamined'. *Transitions* 7(3–4): 1–5. Csaba agrees with Sachs by and large, but thinks Central European economic politicians have something to learn from Chinese organizational diversity. László Csaba (1995) *The Political Economy of the Reform Strategy: China and Eastern Europe Compared*. Budapest: Koping Datorg, Discussion Papers No. 34.

15. During the 1980s, some political theorists entertained the notion that in economically backward countries democratic political structures are not suitable for fostering development, arguing that bureaucratic–authoritarian systems are better suited to this task. For example, Latin Americanists made this point with reference to Chile under Pinochet. Note, however, that Barbara Geddes's recent comparative analysis of political institutions and economic development in Latin America challenges this received wisdom. Geddes presents data which show that transitions to democracy are beneficial to economic development. (See Barbara Geddes [1994] *Politician's Dilemma: Building State Capacity in Latin America*. Berkeley: University of California Press.) In this connection, it remains unclear what the relationship between politics and economic development in China is. Our point, however, is that it should not be assumed that Chinese economic success is the result of political authoritarianism.

16. Szelényi and Martin, 'The Three Waves of New Class Theories'.

17. For our non-American readers who may not have followed American electoral campaigns closely, note that during the 1984 presidential campaign, Walter Mondale invoked a McDonald's commercial. In the original commercial an old lady goes to a hamburger stand which is not part of the McDonald's chain, looks at the hamburger of the McDonald's competitor and asks: 'And where is the beef?' Mondale's use of this sentence cast doubt on his challenger: you don't really have a program. You just ask, 'where is the beef?'

18. We try to stay away from the terminology of world system theory as well. The idea of core, semi-periphery, and periphery presupposes *one* capitalist system, composed of different parts. In such a system one part 'exploits' the other; the growth of one part presumes the stagnation of the other. Our aim is very different – we want to think about capitalism as a diversity of forms, or types, which are both vertically and horizontally linked to each other, but each one of which has its – at least relatively – autonomous existence.

19. In writing about classes and states we use the distinction between large/small and strong/weak. The first refers to the share size of the phenomenon; the second to its capacity to achieve its aims, to implement its policies. So a state can be small, or slim, but still very effective in implementing its policies. It can also be big, may operate a huge bureaucracy, but this does not guarantee that it can collect taxes, keep order, deliver public goods; thus it can be weak and large at the same time.

Appendices

1. These Appendices were compiled with the help of Larry King.

2. On rare occasions departmental division heads acted as deputy department heads also. In these instances they are classified in their higher position.

3. Secretaries of state are also deputies to the Minister, but they have more authority than regular deputies.

4. In Hungarian: *'föosztályvezetö'*: a division contains several departments; these are 'heads of department heads'.

5. Note: double counting occurs. Heads and deputy heads of departments are almost always Members of HAS; directors may also be members.

6. There is only one vice president in most counties, but there are 4 in Bekes, 3 in Szolnok, 2 in Pest, and 2 in Veszprem counties.

7. Eleven national daily newspapers are listed.

8. There are 24 such newspapers; but two have the same editor.

Bibliography

Abrams, Bradley F. (1995) 'Morality, Wisdom and Revision: the Czech Opposition in the 1970s and the Expulsion of the Sudeten Germans'. *East European Politics and Societies* 9(2): 234–55.

Alexander, G. and G. Skapska (eds) (1994) *A Fourth Way? Privatization, Property and the Emergence of New Market Economies*. London: Routledge.

Andorka, Rudolf (1994) 'Magyarország a társadalmi jelzöszámok tükrében' (Hungary in the light of social indicators). In *Társadalmi Riport 1994*, ed. Rudolf Andorka, Tamás Kolosi and György Vukovics. Budapest: TARKI.

Andorka, Rudolf and Hedvig Lehman (1996) 'Az átmenet politikai következményei' (Political consequences of the transition). pp. 500–27 in *Társadalmi Riport 1996* (Social Report 1996), ed. Rudolf Andorka, Tamás Kolosi and György Vukovics. Budapest: TARKI.

Anderson, Perry (1974a) *Passages from Antiquity to Feudalism*. London: Verso.

Anderson, Perry (1974b) *Lineages of the Absolutist State*. London: Verso.

Anderson, Perry (1992) *English Questions*. London: Verso.

Anderson, Perry ([1976] 1992) 'The Notion of Bourgeois Revolution'. pp. 105–18 in *English Questions* by Perry Anderson. London: Verso

Arató, Andrew (1981) 'Civil Society Against the State: Poland 1980–81'. *Telos* 47(Spring): 23–47

Arató, Andrew (1994) 'Revolution and Restoration: On the Origins of Right-Wing Radical Ideology in Hungary'. pp. 99–119 in *The New Great Transformation, Change and Continuity in East–Central Europe*, ed. C. Bryant and E. Mokrzycki. London: Routledge.

Aslund, Anders (1985) *Private Enterprise in Eastern Europe: The Non-Agricultural Private Sector in Poland and the G.D.R., 1945–1983*. New York: St Martin's Press.

Aston, T.H. and C. H. E. Philips (1985) *The Brenner Debate*. Cambridge: Cambridge University Press.

Atkinson, A.B. and John Mickleright (1992) *Economic Transformation in Eastern Europe and the Distribution of Income*. Cambridge: Cambridge University Press.

Bakunin, N. (1966) 'Marx, the Bismarck of Socialism'. pp. 80–97 in *Patterns of Anarchy*, ed. L. Krimmerman and L. Perry. New York: Anchor Books.

Balzer, H. (ed.) (1996) *Russia's Missing Middle Class: The Professions in Russian History.* Armonk, NY: M.E. Sharpe.

Bauer, Tamás (1981) *Tervgazdaság, beruházás, ciklusok* (Planned economy, investments and cycles). Budapest: Közgazdasági és Jogi Kiadó.

Bauman, Zygmunt (1974) 'Officialdom and Class: Bases of Inequality in Socialist Society'. pp. 129–48 in *The Social Analysis of Class Structure*, ed. Frank Parkin. London: Tavistock.

Bayard, C. (1992–93) 'The Changing Character of the Prague Intelligentsia'. *Telos* 94(Winter): 131–44.

Bell, Daniel ([1973] 1976) *The Coming of Post-Industrial Society.* New York: Basic Books.

Benda, Václav (1991) 'The Parallel Polis'. pp. 35–41 in *Civic Freedom in Central Europe*, ed. Gordon Skilling and Paul Wilson. London: Macmillan.

Benda, Václav, Milan Simecka, Ivan M. Jirous, Jiri Dienstbier, Václav Havel, Ladislav Hejdanek, and Jan Simsa (1988) 'Parallel Polis, or An Independent Society in Central and Eastern Europe: An Inquiry'. *Social Research* 55 (1–2): 211–60.

Berend, Ivan (1998) *Decades of Crisis: Central and Eastern Europe before World War II.* Berkeley and Los Angeles: University of California Press.

Berle, Adolf and Gardiner Means ([1931]1968) *The Modern Corporation and Private Property.* New York: Harcourt Brace Jovanovich.

Bian, Yanjie and John Logan (1996) 'Market Transition and the Persistence of Power: the Changing Stratification System in Urban China". *American Sociological Review* 61(5): 739–58.

Blackbourn, David and Geoff Eley (1980) *Mythen deutscher Geschichtsschreibung. Die gescheiterte bürgerliche Revolution von 1848.* Frankfurt and Berlin: Ullstein.

Blackbourn, David and Geoff Eley (1984) *The Peculiarities of German History: Bourgeois Society and Politics in Nineteenth-Century Germany.* Oxford: Oxford University Press.

Bloch, Mark (1961) *Feudal Society.* London: Routledge.

Bloomstein, Hans and Michael Marrese (eds) (1991) *Transformation of Planned Economies: Property Rights Reform and Macroeconomic Stability.* Paris: OECD.

Böröcz, Jozsef (1992) 'Dual Dependency and Property Vacuum: Social Change on the State Socialist Semiperiphery'. *Politics and Society* 21(1): 77–104.

Böröcz, Jozsef (1993) 'Simulating the Great Transformation: Property Change under Prolonged Informality in Hungary'. *Archives Européenne de Sociologie* 34(1): 81–107.

Böröcz, Jozsef and Ákos Rona-Tas (1995) 'Small Leap Forward: Emergence of New Economic Elites'. *Theory and Society* 24(5): 751–81

Bourdieu, Pierre (1977) *Outline of a Theory of Practice.* Cambridge: Cambridge University Press.

Bourdieu, Pierre ([1983]1986) 'The Forms of Capital'. pp. 241–58 in *Handbook of Theory and Research for the Sociology of Education*, ed. John G. Richardson. New York: Greenwood Press.

Bourdieu, Pierre (1984) *Distinction: A Sociological Critique of the Judgement of Taste.* Cambridge, MA: Harvard University Press.

Bourdieu, Pierre (1987) 'What Makes a Social Class? On the Theoretical and Practical Existence of Social Groups'. *Berkeley Journal of Sociology* 32: 1–18.

Bourdieu, Pierre ([1984] 1988) *Homo Academicus.* Cambridge: Polity Press.

Bourdieu, Pierre (1990) *The Logic of Practice.* Cambridge: Polity Press.

Bourdieu, Pierre ([1987] 1990) *In Other Words: Essays Toward a Reflexive Sociology.* Cambridge: Polity Press.

Bourdieu, Pierre ([1989] 1996) *The State Nobility.* Cambridge: Polity Press.

Bourdieu, Pierre and Jean-Claude Passeron (1977) *Reproduction in Education, Society and Culture.* London and Newbury Park, CA: Sage.

Bourdieu, Pierre and Loïc Wacquant (1992) *An Invitation to Reflexive Sociology.* Chicago: University of Chicago Press.

van Brabant, Jozef M. (1992) *Privatizing Eastern Europe: The Role of Markets and Ownership in the Transition.* London: Kluwer Academic Publishers.

Brom, Karel and Michael Orenstein (1994) 'The Private Sector in the Czech Republic: Government and Bank Control in a Transitional Economy'. *Europe–Asia Studies* 46(6): 893–928.

Brüggermeier, Franz-Joseph (1990) 'Der deutschen Sonderweg'. pp. 244–9 in *Bürgerliche Gesellschaft in Deutschland*, ed. Lutz Niethammer. Munich: Fischer Taschenbuch Verlag.

Bryant, C. and E. Mokrzycki (eds) (1994) *The New Great Transformation: Change and Continuity in East–Central Europe.* London: Routledge.

Bunce, Valerie (1995a) 'Comparing East and South'. *Journal of Democracy* 6(July): 87–100.

Bunce, Valerie (1995b) 'Should Transitiologists Be Grounded'? *Slavic Review* 55(Spring): 111–27.

Burawoy, Michael (1994) 'Why Coupon Socialism Never Stood a Chance in Russia: The Political Conditions of Economic Transition'. *Politics and Society* 22(4): 585–94.

Burawoy, Michael (1995) 'From Sovietology to Comparative Political Economy'. pp. 72–102 in *Beyond Soviet Studies*, ed. Daniel Orlovsky. Baltimore, MD: Johns Hopkins University Press.

Burawoy, Michael (1997) 'What is Russia and Where is it Going? Towards a Theory of Economic Involution'. Paper presented at the Comparative Social Analysis Workshop, UCLA, January.

Burawoy, Michael and Pavel Krotov (1992) 'The Soviet Transition from Socialism to Capitalism: Worker Control and Economic Bargaining in the Wood Industry'. *American Sociological Review* 57(1): 16–38.

Burawoy, Michael and Pavel Krotov (1993) 'The Economic Basis of Russia's Political Crisis'. *New Left Review* 198(March–April): 49–69.

Burawoy, Michael and János Lukács (1992) *The Radiant Past: Ideology and Reality in Hungary's Road to Capitalism.* Chicago: University of Chicago Press.

Burchell, Graham, Colin Gordon and Peter Miller (eds) (1991) *The Foucault Effect.* Chicago: University of Chicago Press.

Burnham, James ([1941]1962) *The Managerial Revolution.* Bloomington: Indiana University Press.

Campbell. John (1992) 'The Fiscal Crisis of Post-Communist States'. *Telos* 93(Fall): 89–110.

Campbell, Robert W. (ed.) (1994) *The Post-Communist Economic Transformation: Essays in Honor of Gregory Grossman.* Boulder, CO: Westview Press.

Carlo, Antonio (1974) 'The Socio-Economic Nature of the USSR'. *Telos* 21(Fall): 2–86.

Caute, D. (1988) *The Fellow-Travelers: Intellectual Friends of Communism*. London: Yale University Press.

Chiesa, Giulietto and Douglas Taylor Northtrop (1993) *Transition to Democracy: Political Change in the Soviet Union 1987–1991*. Hanover and London: University Press of New England.

Chirot, Daniel (ed.) (1991) *The Crisis of Leninism and the Decline of the Left*. Seattle, WA: Washington University Press.

Chvatik, Ivan (1992–93) 'The Solidarity of the Shaken'. *Telos* 94(Winter): 163–6.

Clarke, S. (1992) 'Privatization and the Development of Capitalism in Russia'. *New Left Review* 196(November–December): 3–27.

Coffee, John C. Jr (1988) 'Shareholders Versus Managers: The Strain in the Corporate Web'. pp. 77–134 in *Knights, Raiders, and Targets: The Impact of Hostile Takeover*, ed. John Coffee Jr, Louis Lowenstein and Susan Rose-Ackerman. New York: Oxford University Press.

Cohen, Jean and Andrew Arató (1992) *Civil Society and Political Theory*. Cambridge, MA: MIT Press.

Collins, Randall (1979) *The Credentialling Society*. New York: Academic Press.

Collins, Randall (1995) 'Predictions in Macrosociology: The Case of Soviet Collapse'. *American Journal of Sociology* 100(6): 1552–93.

Connor, Walter and Piotr Ploszajski (1992) *The Polish Road From Socialism*. New York: Sharpe.

Conze, Werner and Jürgen Kocka (eds) (1985–92) *Bildungsbürgertum im 19. Jahrhundert*, vols. 1–4. Stuttgart: Klett–Cotta.

Crawford, B. (ed.) (1995) *Markets, States, Democracy: The Political Economy of Post-Communist Transformation*. Boulder, CO: Westview Press.

Csaba, László (1994) *Privatization, Liberalization and Destruction: Recreating the Market in Central and Eastern Europe*. Sydney: Dartmouth.

Csaba, László (1995) *The Political Economy of the Reform Strategy: China and Eastern Europe Compared*. Budapest: Koping Datorg, Discussion Papers No. 34.

Csurka, István (1993) 'Önátvilágítás' (Self-lustration) *Magyar Forum* 30 June.

Dahrendorf, Ralf (1959) *Class and Class Conflict in Industrial Society*. Stanford, CA: Stanford University Press.

Dahrendorf, Ralf (1990) *Reflections on the Revolutions in Europe*. London: Times Books.

Defert, Daniel (1991) '"Popular Life" and Insurance Technology'. pp. 211–34 in *The Foucault Effect*, ed. Graham Burchell, Colin Gordon and Peter Miller. Chicago: University of Chicago Press.

Djilas, Milovan (1957) *The New Class: An Analysis of the Communist System*. New York: Holt, Rinehart & Winston.

Dobosiewicz, Zbigniew (1992) *Foreign Investment in Eastern Europe*. London: Routledge.

Domanski, Henryk (1995) 'Occupational Mobility Careers in Six East European Countries: Basic Continuities'. *Polish Sociological Review* 112(4): 304–24.

Domanski, Henryk (1997) 'Constant Fluidity and Rise in Total Mobility Rates: Social Mobility in Six East European Nations'. *Polish Sociological Review* 2.

Domhoff, G. William (1967) *Who Rules America?* Englewood Cliffs, NJ: Prentice Hall.

Domhoff, G. William (1970) *The Higher Circles: The Governing Class in America*. New York: Random House.

Domhoff, G. William (1986) *Who Rules America Now? A View from the 1980s*. New York: Simon & Schuster.

Earl, John S., Roman Frydman and Andrzej Rapaczynski (eds) (1993) *Privatization in the Transition to a Market Economy: Studies of Preconditions and Policies in Eastern Europe*. New York: St Martin's Press.

Earl, John S., Roman Frydman, Andrzej Rapaczynski and Joel Turkewitz (1994) *Small Privatization: The Transformation of Retail Trade and Consumer Services in the Czech Republic, Hungary and Poland*. Budapest: Central European University Press.

Ehrenreich, Barbara and John Ehrenreich (1977) 'The Professional–Managerial Class'. *Radical America* 11(March–April): 7–31.

Einhorn, Barbara (1993) *Cinderella Goes to Market: Citizenship and Women's Movements in East Central Europe*. London: Verso.

Eisenstadt, S.N. (1992) 'The Breakdown of the Communist Regimes and the Vicissitudes of Modernity'. *Daedelus* 121(2): 21–41.

Eley, Geoff (1980) *Reshaping the German Right: Radical Materialism and Political Change after Bismarck*. Ann Arbor: University of Michigan Press.

Eley, Geoff (1992) *From Unification to Nazism: Reinterpreting the German Past*. Boston, MA: Allen & Unwin.

Ely, J. (1992) 'The Politics of "Civil Society"'. *Telos* 93 (Fall): 173–91.

Engelhardt, Ulrich (1986) *'Bildungsbürgertum'. Begriffs – und Dogmengeschichte eines Etiketts*. Stuttgart: Klett–Cotta.

Erdei, Ferenc ([1976]1988) 'Hungarian Society Between the Two World Wars'. pp. 7–94 in *Selected Writings* by Ferenc Erdei. Budapest: Akadémiai Kiadó.

Estrin, Saul (ed.) (1994) *Privatization in Central and Eastern Europe*. London: Longman.

Estrin, Saul, Josef C. Brada, Alan Gelb and Inderjit Singh (eds) (1995) *Restructuring and Privatization in Central Eastern Europe: Case Studies of Firms in Transition*. Armonk, NY: Sharpe.

Evans, Peter, Dietrich Rueschemeyer and Theda Skocpol (eds) (1985) *Bringing the State Back In*. Cambridge: Cambridge University Press.

Ewald, François (1991) 'Insurance and Risk'. pp. 197–210 in *The Foucault Effect*, ed. Graham Burchell, Colin Gordon and Peter Miller. Chicago: University of Chicago Press.

Eyal, Gil and Eleanor Townsley (1995) 'The Social Composition of the Communist Nomenklatura: A Comparison of Russia, Poland, and Hungary'. *Theory and Society* 24(5): 723–50.

Eyal, Gil, Iván Szelényi and Eleanor Townsley (1997) 'Capitalism Without Capitalists: The Theory of Post-Communist Managerialism'. *New Left Review* 222(March–April): 60–92.

Fehér, Ferenc (1982) 'Paternalism as a Mode of Legitimation in Soviet-Type Societies'. pp. 64–81 in *Political Legitimation in Communist Societies*, ed. T.H. Rigby and Ferenc Fehér. London: Macmillan.

Fehér, Ferenc, Agnes Heller and Gyorgy Markus (1983) *Dictatorship Over Needs*. Oxford: Basil Blackwell.

Ferge, Zsuzsa *et al.* (1995) *Social Costs of Transition. International Report*. Vienna: Institute of Human Studies.

Fichte, Johann Gottlieb ([1807–08]1944) *Reden an die deutsche Nation* (Addresses to the German Nation) Leipzig: F. Meiner.

Fidelius, Petr [Petr Pithart] (1992) 'The Mirror of Communist Discourse'. pp. 193–204 in *Goodbye, Samizdat: Twenty Years of Czechoslovak Underground Writing*, ed. Marketa Goetz-Stankiewicz. Evanston, IL: Northwestern University Press.

Fligstein, Neil (1990) *The Transformation of Corporate Control*. Cambridge, MA: Harvard University Press.

Fligstein, Neil (1995) 'Networks of Power or the Finance Conception of Control?' *American Sociological Review* 60(4): 500–03.

Fligstein, Neil and Peter Brantley (1992) 'Bank Control, Owner Control, or Organizational Dynamics: Who Controls the Large Modern Corporation'. *American Journal of Sociology* 98(2): 280–307.

Fodor, Éva (1997a) 'Gender in Transition: Unemployment in Hungary, Poland and Slovakia'. *East European Politics and Societies* 11(3): 470–500.

Fodor, Éva (1997b) *Power, Patriarchy and Paternalism: An Examination of the Gendered Nature of State Socialist Authority*. Ph.D dissertation. Department of Sociology, UCLA.

Foucault, Michel (1978) *The History of Sexuality*. New York: Vintage Books.

Foucault, Michel (1983) 'The Subject and Power'. pp. 208–26 in *Michel Foucault: Beyond Structuralism and Hermeneutics*, ed. Hubert L. Dreyfus and Paul Rabinow. Chicago: University of Chicago Press.

Foucault, Michel (1984) *The Use of Pleasure*. Harmondsworth: Penguin.

Foucault, Michel (1991) 'Governmentality'. pp. 87–104 in *The Foucault Effect*, ed. Graham Burchell, Colin Gordin and Peter Miller. Chicago: University of Chicago Press.

Foucault, Michel (1993) 'On the Beginnings of the Hermeneutics of the Self'. *Political Theory* 21(2): 198–227.

Fretzel-Zagorska, J. and Zagorski, K. (1989) 'East European Intellectuals on the Road to Dissent'. *Politics and Society* 17(March): 89–113.

Friedman, Milton (1959) *A Program for Monetary Stability*. New York: Fordham University Press.

Friedman, Milton (1962) *Capitalism and Freedom*. Chicago: University of Chicago Press.

Frydman, Roman, Cheryl W. Gray and Andrzej Rapaczynski (1996) *Corporate Governance in Central Europe and Russia*. Budapest: Central European University Press.

Frydman, Roman, Kenneth Murphy and Andrzej Rapaczynski (1996) 'Capitalism with a Comrade's Face'. *Transitions* 2(2): 5–11/'Az elvtársi arcú kapitalizmus'. *Magyar Hirlap*, 8 March, p. 9.

Frydman, Roman, Andrzej Rapaczynski and John S. Earle (1993) *The Privatization Process in Central Europe*. Budapest: Central European University Press.

Fukuyama, Francis (1992) *The End of History and the Last Man*. New York: Free Press.

Furet, François (1975) 'The Catechism of the French Revolution'. pp. 61–97 in *The Social Origins of the French Revolution: The Debate on the Role of the Middle Classes*, ed. Ralph W. Greenlaw. Lexington, MA: D.C. Heath.

Galbraith, John K. (1967) *The New Industrial State*. New York: Houghton Mifflin.

Garcelon, Mac (1997) 'The Estate of Change: The Specialist Rebellion and the Democratic Movement in Moscow, 1989–1991'. *Theory and Society*, vol. 26: 38–85.

Geddes, Barbara (1994) *Politician's Dilemma: Building State Capacity in Latin America*. Berkeley: University of California Press.

Geertz, Clifford (1963) *Agricultural Involution: The Process of Ecological Change in Indonesia*. Los Angeles: University of California Press.

Gellner, Ernest (1994) *Conditions of Liberty: Civil Society and its Rivals.* Harmondsworth: Penguin.

Gerschenkron, Alexander (1966) *Economic Backwardness in Historical Perspective.* Cambridge, MA: Harvard University Press.

Glasberg, Davita Silfen and Michael Schwartz (1983) 'Ownership and Control of Corporations'. *Annual Review of Sociology* 9: 311–32.

Glasman, M. (1994) 'The Great Deformation: Polanyi, Poland and the Terrors of Planned Spontaneity'. *New Left Review* 204(March-April): 59–86.

Goetz-Stankiewicz, Marketa (ed.) (1992) *Goodbye, Samizdat: Twenty Years of Czechoslovak Underground Writing.* Evanston, IL: Northwestern University Press.

Gouldner, Alvin (1979) *The Future of Intellectuals and the Rise of the New Class.* New York: The Continuum Publishing Corporation.

Gowan, Peter (1995) 'Neo-Liberal Theory and Practice for Eastern Europe'. *New Left Review* 213(September–October): 3–60.

Gowan, Peter (1996) 'Eastern Europe, Western Power and Neo-Liberalism'. *New Left Review* 216(March-April): 129–40.

Granovetter, Mark (1985) 'Economic Action and Social Structure: The Problem of Embeddedness'. *American Journal of Sociology* 91(3): 481–510.

Greenlaw, Ralph W. (ed.) (1975) *The Social Origins of the French Revolution: The Debate on the Role of the Middle Classes.* Lexington, MA: D.C. Heath.

Hajnal, László (1996) 'Visszaállamositották a Polgári Bankot' (The Civic Bank was renationalized), *Magyar Hirlap*, 31 December.

Hankiss, Elemér (1990) *East European Alternatives.* Oxford: Clarendon Press.

Hanley, Eric (1996) 'Self-Employment in Post-Communist Eastern Europe: The Emergence of a New Petty Bourgeoisie'. Unpublished manuscript, Department of Sociology, UCLA.

Hanley, Eric (1997) *Privatization and Marketization in Eastern Europe.* Ph.D. dissertation. Department of Sociology, UCLA.

Hanley, Eric and Petr Mateju (1998) 'The Making of Post-Communist Elites in Eastern Europe: A Comparison of Political and Economic Elites in the Czech Republic, Hungary and Poland'. Forthcoming in *Eliten im Wandel*, ed. Magarditsch Hatschikjan and Franz-Lothar Altman. Munich: Oldenbourg Verlag.

Hanley, Eric and Iván Szelényi (1996) 'Changing Social Structure During Market Transition: The Case of Central Europe'. Paper presented to the workshop on *Economic Transformation and the Reform of the State.* Washington, DC: National Academy of Sciences.

Hanley, Eric, Natasha Yershova and Richard Anderson (1995) ' Russia: Old Wine in New Bottle? The Circulation and Reproduction of Russian Elites, 1983–1993'. *Theory and Society* 24(5): 639–68.

Hausner, J. (1992) *Populist Threat in Transformation of Socialist Society.* Warsaw: Friedrich–Ebert Foundation.

Hausner, J. and G. Mosur (1993) *Transformation Processes in Eastern Europe: Western Perspectives and the Polish Experience.* Cracow: Institute of Political Studies.

Havel, Václav (1985) 'The Power of the Powerless'. pp. 23–96 in *The Power of the Powerless*, ed. John Keane. London: Hutchinson.

Havel, Václav (1986) 'Politics and Conscience'. pp. 136–57 in *Václav Havel or Living in Truth*, ed. Jan Vladislav. London: Faber & Faber.

Havel, Václav (1988) 'Anti-Political Politics'. pp. 381–98 in *Civil Society*, ed. John Keane. London: Verso.

Havel, Václav (1993) *Summer Meditations*. New York: Vintage.

Havel, Václav (1994) 'Article 202'. pp. 1–16 in *Chronicles from Prague*, ed. John Miller and Kirsten Miller. San Francisco: Chronicle Books.

Hejdanek, Ladislav (1985) 'Prospects for Democracy and Socialism in Eastern Europe'. pp. 141–51 in *The Power of the Powerless*, ed. John Keane. London: Hutchinson.

Holton, R.J. (1976) *The Transition from Feudalism to Capitalism*. New York: St Martin's Press.

Holy, Ladislav (1996) *The Little Czech and the Great Czech Nation*. Cambridge: Cambridge University Press.

Hoorn, Erich (1996) 'Tschechische Banken haben zu viel Macht' (The Czech Banks Have Too Much Power) *Die Presse*, 20 June, p. 17.

Horváth, Ágnes and Árpád Szakolczay (1992) *The Dissolution of Communist Power: The Case of Hungary*. London: Routledge.

Huang, Philip (1990) *The Peasant Family and Rural Development in the Yangzi Delta, 1350–1988*. Stanford, CA: Stanford University Press.

Jorgensen, Knud Erik (1992) 'The End of Anti-Politics in Central Europe'. pp. 32–60 in *Democracy and Civil Society in Eastern Europe*, ed. Paul G. Lewis. London: Macmillan.

Jowitt, Kenneth (1983) 'Soviet Neo-Traditionalism: The Political Corruption of a Leninist Regime'. *Soviet Studies* 35(3): 275–97.

Jowitt, Kenneth (1992) *New World Disorder: The Leninist Extinction*. Berkeley: University of California Press.

Keane, John (ed.) (1985) *The Power of the Powerless*. London: Hutchinson.

Kennedy, Michael D. (1991) *Professionals, Power and Solidarity in Poland: A Critical Sociology of Soviet-Type Society*. Cambridge: Cambridge University Press.

Kenway, Peter and Eva Klvacova (1996) 'The Web of Cross-Ownership among Czech Financial Intermediaries'. *Europe–Asia Studies* 48(5): 797–809.

King, Larry (1997) *Pathways from Socialism: The Transformation of Firms in Hungary, the Czech Republic and Slovakia*. Ph.D dissertation. Department of Sociology, UCLA.

Klaus, Václav (1989) 'Socialist Economies, Economic Reforms and Economists: Reflections of a Czechoslovak Economist'. *Communist Economies* 1(1): 89–96.

Klaus, Václav (1991) 'Radical, Realistic Economics: An Interview with Václav Klaus'. pp. 157–65 in *After the Velvet Revolution: Václav Havel and the New Leaders of Czechoslovakia Speak Out*, ed. Tim. D. Whipple. New York: Freedom House.

Klima, Ivan (1985) *My Merry Mornings*. London: Readers International.

Klima, Ivan (1994) *Judge on Trial*. New York: Vintage.

Kocka, Jürgen (ed.) (1981) *Angestellte in europäischen Vergleich*. Göttingen: Vandenhoeck & Ruprecht.

Kocka, Jürgen (1985) 'Einleitung'. pp. 9–26 in *Bildungsbürgertum im 19. Jahrhundert*, Vol. 1, ed. Werner Conze and Jürgen Kocka. Stuttgart: Klett–Cotta.

Kocka, Jürgen (ed.) (1986a) *Arbeiter und Bürger im 19. Jahrhundert: Varianten ihres Verhaeltnisses im europäischen Vergleich*. Munich: Oldenbourg.

Kocka, Jürgen (1986b) 'Problems of Working-Class Formation in Germany: The Early Years, 1800–1875'. pp. 279–351 in *Working-Class Formation*, ed. Ira Katznelson and Aristide Zolberg. Princeton, NJ: Princeton University Press.

Kocka, Jürgen (ed.) (1987a) *Bürger und Bürgerlichkeit im 19. Jahrhundert*. Göttingen: Vandehoeck & Ruprecht.

Kocka, Jürgen (1987b) 'Einleitung'. pp. 7–20 in *Bürger und Bürgerlichkeit im 19. Jahrhundert*, ed. Jürgen Kocka. Göttingen: Vandenhoeck & Ruprecht.

Kocka, Jürgen (1987c) 'Bürgertum und Bürgerlichkeit als Probleme der deutschen Geschichte von späten 18. zum früher 20. Jahrhundert'. pp. 21–63 in *Bürger und Bürgerlichkeit im 19. Jahrhundert*, ed. Jürgen Kocka. Göttingen: Vandehoeck und Ruprecht.

Kocka, Jürgen (1988a) *Bürgertum im 19 Jahrhundert: Deutschland im europäischen Vergleich*. Munich: Deutsche Taschenbuch Verlag.

Kocka. Jürgen (1988b) 'Bürgertum und bürgerliche Gesellschaft in 19. Jahrhundert. Europäische Entwicklung und deutsche Eigenarten'. pp. 11–78 in *Bürgertum im 19. Jahrhundert*, vol. 1, ed. Jürgen Kocka. Munich: Deutsche Taschenbuch Verlag.

Kocka, Jürgen (1988c) 'Bürgertum und bürgerliche Gesellschaft im 19. Jahrhundert. Europäische Entwicklung und deutsche Eigenarten'. In *Bürgertum im 19. Jahrhundert*. vol. 1, ed. Jürgen Kocka and Ute Frevert. Munich: Deutsche Taschenbuch Verlag.

Kocka, Jürgen (1989) 'Bildungsbürgertum: gesellschaftliche Formation oder Historikerkonstrukt?' pp. 9–20 in *Bildungsbürgertum im 19. Jahrhundert*, vol. 4, ed. Werner Conze and Jürgen Kocka. Stuttgart: Klett–Cotta.

Kocka, Jürgen (1990) *Weder Stand noch Klasse: Unterschichten um 1800*. Bonn: Dietz.

Kocka, Jürgen (ed.) (1993) *Bourgeois Society in Nineteenth-Century Europe*. Oxford: Providence.

Köhler, Ernst (1970) *Bildungsbürgertum und nationale Politik*. Bad Homburg: Atheum.

Komarek, Martin and Jana Kasalova (1994–95) *GEN: 100 Cechu Dneska*. Prague: Fischer.

Konrád, György (1984) *Antipolitics*. London: Quartet.

Konrád, George and Iván Szelényi (1979) *The Intellectuals on the Road to Class Power*. New York and London: Harcourt Brace Jovanovich.

Konrád, George and Iván Szelényi (1991) 'Intellectuals and Domination under Post-Communism'. pp. 337–61 in *Social Theory for a Changing Society*, ed. James Coleman and Pierre Bourdieu. Boulder, CO: Westview Press.

Kornai, János (1980) *Economics of Shortage*. New York: Elsevier North-Holland.

Kornai, János (1990a) *The Road to a Free Economy: Shifting from a Socialist System*. New York: Norton.

Kornai, János (1990b) 'The Affinity Between Ownership Forms and Coordination Mechanisms: The Common Experience'. *Journal of Economic Perspectives* 4(3): 131–47.

Kornai, János (1992) *The Socialist System: The Political Economy of Communism*. Princeton: Princeton University Press.

Kornai, János (1994) 'Transformational Recession: The Main Causes'. *Journal of Comparative Economics* 19(1): 39–63.

Koselleck, Reinhart (1990) 'Einleitung – Zur Anthropologischen und Semantischen Structur der Bildung'. pp. 11–46 in *Bildungsbürgertum im 19. Jahrhundert*, vol. 2, ed. Werner Conze and Jürgen Kocka. Stuttgart: Klett–Cotta.

Koselleck, Reinhardt, Ulrike Spree and Willibald Steinmetz (1991) 'Drei bürgerliche Welten? Zur vergleichenden Semantik der bürgerlichen Gesellschaft in

Deutschland, England und Frankreich'. pp. 14–58 in *Bürger in der Gesellschaft der Neuzeit*, ed. Hans-Jürgen Puhle. Göttingen: Vandenhoeck & Ruprecht.

Krasnodebski, Zdzislaw (1993) 'Longing for Community: Phenomenological Philosophy of Politics and the Dilemmas of European Culture'. *International Sociology* 8(3): 339–53.

Kuczynska, Teresa (1992) 'The Capitalists Among Us'. *Telos* 92(Summer): 159–63.

Kusa, Zuzana (1994) 'To Be of Bourgeois Origins: An Insurmountable Stigma?' (On the Erosive Power of Social Networks in the Period of Communism)'. Paper presented at the XIII World Congress of Sociology, Bielefeld, Germany.

Kusy, Miroslav (1985) 'Chartism and Real Socialism'. pp. 152–77 in *The Power of the Powerless*, ed. John Keane. London: Hutchinson.

Laki, Mihály (1993) 'The Chances for the Acceleration of Transition: The Case of Hungarian Privatization'. *East European Politics and Societies* 7(3): 440–51.

Laki, Mihály (1994–95) 'Opportunities for Workers' Participation in Privatization in Hungary: The Case of the Eger Flour Mill'. pp. 15–39 in *Participation and Changes in Property Relations in Post-Communist Societies*, ed. Mihály Laki, Julia Szalai and Ágnes Vajda. Budapest: Active Society Foundation.

Laki, Mihály, Julia Szalai and Ágnes Vajda (eds) (1994–95) *Participation and Changes in Property Relations in Post-Communist Societies*. Budapest: Active Society Foundation.

Lampe, John (ed.) (1992) *Creating Capital Markets in Eastern Europe*. Washington, DC: The Woodrow Wilson Center Press.

Lane, David (ed.) (1995) *Russia in Transition: Politics, Privatization and Inequality*. London: Longman.

Langewische, Dieter (1989) 'Bildungsbürgertum und Liberalismus im 19. Jahrhundert'. In *Politischer Einfluss und Gesellschaftliche Formation*, ed. Jürgen Kocka. Stuttgart: Klett–Cotta.

Latour, Bruno (1987) *Science in Action: How to Follow Scientists and Engineers Through Society*. Cambridge, MA: Harvard University Press.

Lepsius, M. Rainer (1992) 'Das Bildungsbürgertum als standische Vergesellschaftung'. pp. 8–18 in *Lebensführung und standische Vergesellschaftung*, ed. M. R. Lepsius. Stuttgart: Klett–Cotta.

Levitas, A. and P. Strzalkowski (1990) 'What Does "Uwlaszczenie Nomenklatury" (Propertization of the *Nomenklatura*) Really Mean?' *Communist Economies* 2(3): 413–16.

Lincoln, James R., Michael L. Gerlach, and Peggy Takahashi (1992) 'Kereitsu Networks in the Japanese Economy: A Dyad Analysis of Intercorporate Ties'. *American Sociological Review* 57(5): 561–85.

Machonin, Pavel (1996a) 'Modernization and Social Transformation in the Czech Republic'. *Czech Sociological Review* 4(2): 171–86.

Machonin, Pavel (1996b) 'Social Metamorphoses'. pp. 111–226 in *Czechoslovakia 1918–1992: A Laboratory for Social Change*, ed. J. Krejci and Pavel Machonin. New York: St Martin's Press.

Machonin, Pavel and Milan Tucek (1994) 'A Historical Comparison of Social Structures in the Czech Republic in 1984 and 1993'. *Czech Sociological Review* 2(2): 149–72.

Major, Ivan (1993) *Privatization in Eastern Europe: A Critical Approach*. Brookfield, VT: Edward Elgar.

Manchin, Robert and Iván Szelényi (1987) 'Social Policy under State Socialism'. pp. 102–39 in *Stagnation and Renewal in Social Policy*, ed. Gosta Esping-Anderson, Lee Rainwater and Mary Rein. White Plains, NY: Sharpe.

Mankiw, Gregory N. (1990) 'A Quick Refresher Course in Macroeconomics'. *Journal of Economic Literature* 28(4): 1645–60.

Mannheim, Karl (1985) *Ideology and Utopia: An Introduction to the Sociology of Knowledge*. San Diego, CA: Harcourt Brace Jovanovich.

Marer, Paul (1993) 'Economic Transformation in Central and Eastern Europe'. pp. 173–88 in *Making Markets: Economic Transformation in Eastern Europe and the Post-Soviet States*, ed. Shafiqul Islam and Michael Mandelbaum. New York: Council on Foreign Relations.

Martin, Bill and Iván Szelényi (1987) 'Beyond Cultural Capital: Towards a Theory of Symbolic Domination'. pp. 16–49 in *Intellectuals, Universities and the State in Western Societies*, ed. Ron Eyerman, Lennart G. Svensson and Thomas Söderqvist. Berkeley, Los Angeles and London: University of California Press.

Martinsen, Kare Dahl (1995) 'From Impotence to Omnipotence: The State and Economic Transition; 1989–1994'. *Bohemia* 36: 330–61.

Marx, Karl ([1848]1978) 'The Communist Manifesto'. pp. 469–500 in *The Marx–Engels Reader*, 2nd edn., ed. Robert C. Tucker. New York and London: W.W. Norton.

Marx, Karl (1919) *Das Kapital: Kritik der politischen Ökonomie*. Hamburg: Meissner.

Marx, Karl (1970) *Critique of Hegel's 'Philosophy of Right'*. Cambridge: Cambridge University Press.

Marx, Karl (1974) *Grundrisse der Kritik der politischen Ökonomie*. Berlin: Dietz.

Mateju, Petr (1997a) 'In Search of Explanations for Recent Left-Turns in Post-Communist Countries'. *International Journal of Comparative Public Policy* 7: 43–82.

Mateju, Petr (1997b) 'Who Votes Left After the Fall of Communism?' *International Journal of Comparative Sociology* 32.

Mateju, Petr and Nelson Lim (1995) 'Who Has Gotten Ahead After the Fall of Communism? The Case of the Czech Republic'. *Czech Sociological Review* 3(2): 117–136.

Meseznikov, Grigorij and Sona Szomolanyi (eds) (1994) *The Slovak Path of Transition to Democracy*. Bratislava: Interlingua.

Mészáros, István (1970) *Marx's Theory of Alienation*. New York: Harper Torchbooks.

Meyers Enzyklopaedisches Lexikon (1972–7) vols 4, 5, 24. Mannheim: Lexikon Verlag.

Miller, John and Kirsten Miller (1994) *Chronicles from Prague*. San Francisco: Chronicle Books.

Miller, Peter and Nikolas Rose (1990) 'Governing Economic Life'. *Economy and Society* 19(1): 1–31.

Mizsei, Kálmán (1992) 'Privatization in Eastern Europe: A Comparative Study of Poland and Hungary'. *Soviet Studies* 44(2): 283–96.

Mladek, Jan (1993) 'The Different Path of Privatization: Czechoslovakia'. pp. 121–46 in *Making Markets: Economic Transformation in Eastern Europe and the Post-Soviet States*, ed. Shafiqul Islam and Michael Mandelbaum. New York: Council on Foreign Relations.

Moore, Barrington (1966) *Social Origins of Dictatorship and Democracy*. Boston, MA: Beacon Press.

Musil, Jiri (ed.) (1995) *The End of Czechoslovakia*. Budapest: Central European University Press.

Mizruchi, Mark (1982) *The American Corporate Networks, 1904–1974*. Beverly Hills, CA: Sage.

Mizruchi, Mark and Michael Schwartz (1987) *Intercorporate Relations: The Structural Analysis of Business*. Cambridge: Cambridge University Press.

Mosse, Georg (1990) 'Das deutsche–jüdische Bildungsbürgertum'. pp. 168–80 in *Bildungsbürgertum im 19. Jahrhundert*, vol. 2, ed. Werner Conze and Jürgen Kocka. Stuttgart: Klett–Cotta.

Nee, Victor (1989) 'A Theory of Market Transition: From Redistribution to Markets in State Socialism'. *American Sociological Review* 54(5): 663–81.

Nee, Victor (1991) 'Social Inequalities in Reforming State Socialism: Between Redistribution and Markets in China'. *American Sociological Review* 56(3): 267–82.

Nee, Victor (1996) 'The Emergence of Market Society: Changing Mechanisms of Stratification in China'. *American Journal of Sociology* 101(4): 908–49.

Nee, Victor and P. Lian (1994) 'Sleeping with the Enemy: A Dynamic Model of Declining Political Commitment in State Socialism'. *Theory and Society* 23(2): 253–96.

Nee, Victor and Rebecca Matthews (1996) 'Market Transition and Societal Transformation in Reforming Socialism'. *Annual Review of Sociology* 22: 401–36.

Niethammer, Lutz (1990) 'Einführung – bürgerliche Gesellschaft als Projekt'. pp. 17–40 in *Bürgerliche Gesellschaft in Deutschland*, ed. Lutz Niethammer. Munich: Fischer Taschenbuch Verlag.

Offe, Claus (1991) 'Capitalism by Design? Democratic Theory Facing the Triple Transition in East Central Europe'. *Social Research* 58(4): 865–92.

Offe, Claus (1994) *Der Tunnel am Ende des Lichts*. Frankfurt: Campus Verlag.

Ost, David (1990) *Solidarity and the Politics of Anti-Politics*. Philadelphia, PA: Temple University Press.

Ost, David (1993) 'The Politics of Interest in Post-Communist East Europe'. *Theory and Society* 22(4): 453–86.

Palous, Martin (1989) 'The Parallel Polis after 12 Years'. *Uncaptive Minds* 2(5): 36–40.

Parkin, Frank (1979) *Marxism and Class Theory: A Bourgeois Critique*. New York: Columbia University Press.

Passin, Herbert (1965) *Society and Education in Japan*. New York: Columbia University Press.

Patocka, Jan (1993–94) 'Wars in the 20th Century and the 20th Century as War'. *Telos* 94(Winter): 116–26.

Patterson, Perry L. (ed.) (1993) *Capitalist Goals, Socialist Past: The Rise of the Private Sector in Command Economies*. Boulder, CO: Westview Press.

Paul, C. Edward (1997) 'Toward an Explanation of Variation in the Reproduction and Circulation of Elites Both Within and Between Countries, in the Transition from Socialism in Eastern Europe'. *Journal of Political and Military Sociology*, June.

Pithart, Petr (1989–90) 'Social and Economic Development in Czechoslovakia in the 1980s (part I)'. *East European Reporter* 4(1): 42–5.

Pithart, Petr (1990) 'Social and Economic Development in Czechoslovakia in the 1980s (part II)'. *East European Reporter* 4(2): 4–7.

Pithart, Petr (1995) 'Towards a Shared Freedom'. pp. 201–22 in *The End of Czechoslovakia*, ed. Jiri Musil. Budapest: Central European University Press.

Przeworski, Adam (1991) *Democracy and the Market: Political and Economic Reforms in Eastern Europe and Latin America*. New York: Cambridge University Press.

Przeworski, Adam (1992) 'The Neoliberal Fallacy'. *Journal of Democracy* 3(3): 45–59.

Puhle, Hans-Jürgen (ed.) (1991) *Bürger in der Gesellschaft der Neuzeit*. Göttingen: Vandenhoeck & Ruprecht.

Puhle, Hans-Jürgen (1991) 'Einleitung'. pp. 7–13 in *Bürger in der Gesellschaft der Neuzeit*, ed. H.-J. Puhle. Göttingen: Vandenhoeck & Ruprecht.

Ray, Larry J. (1996) *Social Theory and the Crisis of State Socialism*. Cheltenham: Edward Elgar.

Rigby, T.H. and Ferenc Fehér (eds) (1992) *Political Legitimation in Communist Societies*. London: Macmillan.

Ringer, Fritz (1969) *The Decline of the German Mandarins*. Cambridge, MA: Harvard University Press.

Robert, Péter (1996) 'Vállalkozók és vállalkozások' (Entrepreneurs and firms) *Társadalmi Riport 1996* (Social Report 1996), ed. Rudolf Andorka, Tamás Kolosi and György Vukovics. Budapest: TARKI.

Rona-Tas, Ákos (1994) 'The First Shall Be the Last? Entrepreneurship and Communist Cadres in the Transition from Socialism'. *American Journal of Sociology* 100(1): 40–69.

Rona-Tas, Ákos (1997) *The Great Surprise of the Small Transformation: The Demise of Communism and the Rise of the Private Sector in Hungary*. Ann Arbor: University of Michigan Press.

Rona-Tas, Ákos and József Böröcz (1995) 'Small Leap Forward: Emergence of the New Economic Elites'. *Theory and Society* 24(5): 751–81.

Rondinelli, Denis A. (ed.) (1994) *Privatization and Economic Reform in Central Europe. The Changing Business Climate*. London: Quorum.

Runciman, Walter G. (1983) *A Treatise on Social Theory*. Cambridge: Cambridge University Press.

Rutland, P. (1992–93) 'Thatcherism Czech-Style: Transition to Capitalism in the Czech Republic'. *Telos* 94(Winter): 103–30.

Sachs, Jeffrey (1995) 'Postcommunist Parties and the Politics of Entitlements'. *Transitions* 6 (3).

Sachs, Jeffrey and Wing Thye Woo (1996) 'China's Transition Experience, Reexamined'. *Transitions* 7(3–4): 1–5.

Sági, Matilda (1994) 'Menedzserek. Az uj gazdasagi elit rekrutációja' (Managers. Recruitment into the new economic elite) pp. 334–50 in *Társadalmi Riport, 1994* (Social Indicators), ed. Rudolf Andorka, Tamás Kolosi and György Vukovics. Budapest: TARKI.

Scruton, Roger (1988) 'The New Right in Central Europe (I): Czechoslovakia'. *Political Studies* 36(September): 449–62.

Siegrist, Hannes (ed.) (1988) *Bürgerliche Berufe – zur Sozialgeschichte der freien und akademischen Berufe in internationalen Vergleich* (Vorwort von Jürgen Kocka) Göttingen: Vandenhoeck & Ruprecht.

Siklova, Jirina (1996) 'Lustration, or the Czech Way of Screening'. *East European Constitutional Review* 5(1): 57–62.

Silberman, Bernard S. and H. D. Harootunian (eds) (1966) *Modern Japanese Leadership: Transition and Change*. Tucson: University of Arizona Press.

Skilling, Gordon and Paul Wilson (eds) (1991) *Civic Freedom in Central Europe*. London: Macmillan.

Slomczynski, Kazimierz M. and Goldie Shabad (1997) 'Systemic Transformation and the Salience of Class Structure in East Central Europe'. *East European Politics and Societies* 11(1): 1–26.

Smith, Adam ([1779]1976) *An Enquiry into the Nature and Causes of the Wealth of Nations*. Oxford: Oxford University Press.

Staniszkis, Jadwiga (1991a) *The Dynamics of Breakthrough*. Berkeley: University of California Press.

Staniszkis, Jadwiga (1991b) 'Political Capitalism in Poland'. *East European Politics and Societies* 5(1): 127–41.

Staniszkis, Jadwiga (1992) *The Ontology of Socialism*. New York: Oxford University Press.

Stark, David (1986) 'Rethinking Internal Labor Markets: New Insights from a Comparative Perspective'. *American Sociological Review* 51(4): 492–504.

Stark, David (1989) 'Coexisting Organizational Forms in Hungary's Emerging Mixed Economy'. pp. 137–68 in *Remaking the Economic Institutions of Socialism: China and Eastern Europe*, ed. David Stark and Victor Nee. Stanford, CA: Stanford University Press.

Stark, David (1990) 'Privatization in Hungary: From Plan to Market or from Plan to Clan?' *East European Politics and Societies* 4(3): 351–92.

Stark, David (1992) 'Path Dependence and Privatization Strategies in East Central Europe'. *East European Politics and Societies* 6(1): 17–51.

Stark, David (1996) 'Recombinant Property in East European Capitalism'. *American Journal of Sociology* 101(4): 993–1027.

Szalai, Erzsébet (1981) *Kiemelt vállalat – beruházas – érdek* (Privileged firms, investments, interests). Budapest: Akadémiai Kiadó.

Szalai, Erzsébet (1989a) *Gazdasági mechanizmus, reformtörekvések és nagyvállalati érdekek* (Economic mechanism, reform scenarios and the interests of large firms). Budapest: Közgazdasági és Jogi Könyvkiadó.

Szalai, Erzsébet (1989b) 'The New Elite'. *Across Frontiers* 5(Fall–Winter):25–31. [In Hungarian: Beszélö, No. 26, 1989.]

Szalai. Erzsébet (1991) 'Integration of Special Interests in the Hungarian Economy: the Struggle Between Large Companies, the Party and State Bureaucracy'. *Journal of Comparative Economics* 15(June): 304–24.

Szalai, Erzsébet (1992) *Gazdaság és hatalom* (Economy and power). Budapest: Aula.

Szalai, Erzsébet (1994a) 'The Power Structure in Hungary after the Political Transition'. pp. 120–43 in *The New Great Transformation*, ed. Christopher G.A. Bryant and Edmund Mokrzycki. London and New York: Routledge.

Szalai, Erzsébet (1994b) *Utelagazás. Hatalom és értelmiség az államszocializmus után* (At the cross-roads: power and intellectuals after state socialism). Budapest: Pesti Szalon Kiadó.

Szalai, Erzsébet (1996) *Az elitek átváltozása* (Transformation of elites). Budapest: Cserépfalvi Kiadó.

Szelényi, Iván (1978) 'Social Inequalities in State Socialist Redistributive Economies'. *International Journal of Comparative Sociology* 19: 63–87.

Szelényi, Iván (1986–87) 'Prospects and Limits of the East European New Class Project'. *Politics and Society* 15(2): 103–44.

Szelényi, Iván (1988a) 'Socialism in an Epoch of Crisis'. pp. 208–32 in *Remaking the*

Economic Institutions of Socialism, ed. David Stark and Victor Nee. Stanford, CA: Stanford University Press.

Szelényi, Iván (1988b) *Socialist Entrepreneurs*. Madison: University of Wisconsin Press.

Szelényi, Iván, Eva Fodor and Eric Hanley (1997) 'The Left-turn in Post-Communist Politics: The Hungarian and Polish Elections, 1990–1994'. *East European Politics and Societies* 11(1): 190–224.

Szelényi, Iván and Eric Kostello (1996) 'The Market Transition Debate: Toward a Synthesis?' *American Journal of Sociology* 101(4): 1082–96.

Szelényi, Iván and Bill Martin (1988) 'The Three Waves of New Class Theories'. *Theory and Society* 17(4): 645–67.

Szelényi, Iván and Bill Martin (1989) 'The Legal Profession and the Rise and Fall of the New Class'. pp. 256–88 in *Lawyers in Society*, vol. 3, ed. Richard L. Abel and Philip S.C. Lewis. Berkeley: University of California Press.

Szelényi, Iván and Szonja Szelényi (1990) 'Az elite cirkulációja?' (Circulation of elites?) *Kritika* 10(October): 8–10.

Szelényi, Iván and Szonja Szelényi (1995) 'Circulation and Reproduction of Elites in Post-Communist Transformation'. *Theory and Society* 24(5): 615–38

Szelényi, Szonja (1987) 'Social Inequality and Party Membership'. *American Sociological Review* 52(5): 559–73.

Szelényi, Szonja (1997) *Equality by Design: The Grand Experiment in Destratification in Socialist Hungary*. Stanford, CA: Stanford University Press.

Szelényi, Szonja, Iván Szelényi and Imre Kovach (1995) 'The Making of the Hungarian Post-Communist Elites: Circulation in Politics and Reproduction in the Economy'. *Theory and Society* 24(5): 697–722.

Szelényi, Szonja, Iván Szelényi and Winifred R. Poster (1996) 'Interests and Symbols in Post-Communist Political Culture: The Case of Hungary'. *American Sociological Review* 61(3): 466–77.

Szomolanyi. Sona (1994) 'Old Elites in the New Slovak State and their Current Transformation'. pp. 63–82 in *The Slovak Path of Transition to Democracy*, ed. Grigorij Meseznikov and Sona Szomolanyi. Bratislava: Interlingua.

Tardos, Márton (1989) 'Economic Organizations and Ownership'. *Acta Oeconomica* 40(1–2): 17–37.

Taylor, George V. (1975) 'Capitalism and the Origins of the French Revolution'. pp. 150–9 in *The Social Origins of the French Revolution: The Debate on the Role of the Middle Classes*, ed. Ralph W. Greenlaw. Lexington, MA: D.C. Heath.

Thygesen, Niels (1984) 'Milton Friedman'. pp. 217–50 in *Contemporary Economists in Perspective*, ed. Henry W. Spiegel and Warren J. Samuels. Grenage, CT: JAI Press.

Tucker, Aviezer (1993–4) 'Waiting for Meciar'. *Telos* 94(Winter): 167–82.

Useem, Michael (1980) 'Corporations and the Corporate Elite'. *Annual Review of Sociology* 6: 41–77.

Useem, Michael (1984) *The Inner Circle: Large Corporations and the Rise of Business Political Activity in the U.S. and UK*. Oxford: Oxford University Press.

Veblen, Thornstein ([1919]1963) *The Engineers and the Price System*. New York: Harcourt & Brace.

Vladislav, Jan (1986) *Václav Havel or Living in Truth*. London: Faber & Faber.

Vondung, Klaus (ed.) (1976) *Das Wielhelmische Bildungsbürgertum*. Göttingen: Vandenhoeck & Ruprecht.

Voslensky, Michael (1984) *Nomenklatura: The Soviet Ruling Class. An Insider's Report.*
New York: Doubleday.

Voszka, Éva (1993) 'Spontaneous Privatization in Hungary'. pp. 89–107 in
*Privatization in the Transition to a Market Economy: Studies of Preconditions and Policies in
Eastern Europe*, ed. John S. Earle, Roman Frydman, and Andrzej Rapaczynski.
New York: St Martin's Press.

Voszka, Éva (1994) *Centralization, Renationalization, Redistribution* (The Role of Government
in Changing Ownership Structure in Hungary, 1989–1993) Budapest: Center for
Economic Policy Research, Discussion Papers, Series No. 916.

Walder, Andrew (1986) *Communist Neo-Traditionalism: Work and Authority in Chinese
Society.* Berkeley: University of California Press.

Walder, Andrew (1995) 'Career Mobility and the Communist Political Order'.
American Sociological Review 60(3): 309–28.

Walder, Andrew (1996) 'Market and Inequality in Transitional Economies: Toward
Testable Theories'. *American Journal of Sociology* 101(4): 1060–73.

Wasilewski, Jacek (1995a) 'The Crystallization of the Post-Communist and Post-
Solidarity Political Elite'. pp. 117–33 in *After Communism: A Multidisciplinary
Approach to Radical Social Change*, ed. Edmund Wnuk-Lipinski. Warsaw: Institute of
Political Studies.

Wasilewski, Jacek (1995b) 'The Forming of the New Elite: How Much
Nomenklatura is Left?' *Polish Sociological Review* 110(2): 113–23.

Wasilewski, Jacek and Edmund Wnuk-Lipinski (1995) 'Poland: Winding Road from
the Communist to the Post-Solidarity Elite'. *Theory and Society* 24(5): 69–96.

Weber, Max ([1904–05]1958) *The Protestant Ethic and the Spirit of Capitalism.* New
York: Charles Scribner's Sons.

Weber, Max ([1906]1958) 'Capitalism and Rural Society in Germany'. pp. 363–85
in *From Max Weber*, ed. H. H. Gerth and C. Wright Mills. New York: Oxford
University Press.

Weber, Max ([1915–21]1978) *Economy and Society.* New York: The Bedminster Press.

Whipple, Tim D. (ed.) (1991) *After the Velvet Revolution: Václav Havel and the New Leaders
of Czechoslovakia Speak Out.* New York: Freedom House.

Windolf, Paul (1996) 'The Transformation of the East German Economy'. Paper
presented at the conference on 'Territoriality and Modern Society', UNC,
Chapel Hill, March 29–30.

Xie, Yu and Emily Hannum (1996) 'Regional Variation of Earning Inequality in
Reform-Era Urban China'. *American Journal of Sociology* 101(4): 950–92.

Zaslavsky, Victor (1982) *The Neo-Stalinist State: Class, Ethnicity and Consensus in Soviet
Society.* Armonk, NY: M.E. Sharpe.

Zeitlin, Maurice (1974) 'Corporate Ownership and Control: The Large
Corporation and the Capitalist Class'. *American Journal of Sociology* 79(5):
1073–1119.

Zubek, Voytek (1991) 'The Polish Communist Elite and the Petty Entrepreneurs'.
East European Quarterly 25(3): 339–62.

Zweigelhaft, Richard (1992) 'The Application of Cultural and Social Capital: A
Study of the 25th Year Reunion Entries of Prep School and Public School
Graduates of Yale College'. *Higher Education* 23(3): 311–20.

Index

266